Film
Review
1993

F. Maurice Speed began his working life as an apprentice on the *Harrow Observer*. From early on, his work reflected an interest in the cinema, and he calculates that he has now spent well over seven years watching films. He has contributed to many newspapers, journals and magazines in both Britain and America, and his books include the pre-war *Movie Cavalcade* and the later *Western Film and TV Annual*. His position as the grand old man of British film criticism was confirmed when the London Film Critics' Circle presented him in 1991 with a special award in recognition of his lifetime achievement and the 48 years over which he has now edited *Film Review*.

James Cameron-Wilson became a committed film buff when he moved to London at the age of seventeen. After a stint at the Webber Douglas Academy of Dramatic Art, he joined *What's On in London* and took over from F. Maurice Speed as cinema editor. He was also editor of *Showbiz* and commissioning editor of *Film Review* and *What's On*, and works as a consultant for several film reference books. He was a TV presenter and movie quizmaster for BSkyB, and is the author of *The Cinema of Robert De Niro*.

Film Review 1993

INCLUDING VIDEO RELEASES

F. Maurice Speed

AND

James Cameron-Wilson

ST. MARTIN'S PRESS
NEW YORK

0–312–092–85–7 HB
0–312–092–86–5 PB

Library of Congress Cataloging in Publication Data
(available on request)

First published in Great Britain by Virgin Books, an imprint of
Virgin Publishing Ltd

First US Edition May 1993

10 9 8 7 6 5 4 3 2 1

Designed by Fred Price

Phototypeset by Intype, London

Printed in Great Britain
by Scotprint Ltd, Musselburgh

Contents

Introduction

F. MAURICE SPEED surveys the cinematic year

So, what's been new in 1992?

The continuing recession appears to have made little impact on the average moviegoer. More or less the same number of films has been shown, and indeed made, with still too many of the latter for them all to get a cinema release. (In some cases they don't even make it on to video, but simply stay on the shelf, unseen.) And the numbers of good, bad and indifferent movies seem to be much the same as well, with the familiar megabuck blockbusters, some of them smash hits and some embarrassing failures. Not much change there.

It's still possible to get financial backing for a production in Hollywood, and though it's getting harder, and the lenders are more cautious, the money can still be found. But there's growing talk of 'value for money', and it's rare now to hear producers boasting of spending $3 million on a script – and then having it rewritten for another $1 million. The accountants, with their awkward questions about useless expenditure, are making their presence felt. Oh, yes, it's a tough life in Hollywood.

Just how tough was revealed by Peter Bart in one of his contributions to *Variety*. As Bart said: 'Welcome to the new Hollywood, folks: it's fear and loathing time! Meet a friend for a drink and he'll tell you he is scared of losing his job. Grips and art directors are trying to figure out why they seem to be making less money on each successive gig – if they're working at all. Talk to production chiefs and they're all painfully reconfiguring their strategies – trying to fit the business back into Show Business . . . And, as usual, Hollywood is a microcosm of the community as a whole – a community that seems to be coming apart at the seams . . . In once bountiful Los Angeles county one person in seven is on welfare.' Even if not all those one-in-seven used to work in the movies, you can see what he means.

Of course, Los Angeles hasn't been a happy place recently in other ways. The terrifying riots in the spring of 1992 swept as far as Sunset Boulevard; the shutters went up, and shivers ran down those rich and famous spines when it looked as though the mayhem might actually reach their privileged enclaves. All round, not a comfortable time for the moguls.

It hasn't been a year of wine and roses in Britain, either. If anything, British moviemakers have found it even harder than before to get financial backing, and the unfortunate producer who spent three years raising enough funding to get his small-scale project into production was not all that unusual.

Britain is still the only member of the European Community not to provide state support for the film industry. Other European countries subsidise production directly, but even indirect funding doesn't seem to be on the British Government's agenda. Without Channel 4, the BBC and occasional US finance, it is doubtful that any British films would get made at all. And although the BBC makes about twenty films a year – only two or three of these having any hope of a cinema release – in 1992 its Film Unit announced plans to shed some thirty employees . . .

If one puts beside this scenario the simple facts that, by the end of 1992, the other members of the European Community will have invested in the region of $70 million in film production, and that co-productions between France, Germany, Italy and Spain are on the increase, one has to admire the tenacity and determination of filmmakers who go on working in the unpromising climate of the UK.

Whatever the trials of the filmmakers, however, all the indications are that movie audiences in Britain haven't fallen back from last year's record levels, so the demand for the end-product still seems to be there. In the US, perhaps more surprisingly, audiences have remained stationary for the last 30 years, in spite of the fact that during that time the US population has grown by approximately 30 million. (The basic cinema audience figure remains at around the 1 billion mark.)

The current fashion seems to be for animation features, which is understandable: Disney's *Beauty and the Beast* is expected to earn more than $100 million on initial release, with the longer term anticipation that it could make the company a profit of $200 million. Similar results are expected from Disney's *The Little Mermaid*. Figures like these make Disney Studios' success the envy of the other major Hollywood companies. Envy leads to emulation, so it's no surprise to find that there are between ten and fifteen animated features planned for release in 1993, including *Tom and Jerry: The Movie*, already released in the US and now sold to 40 countries, where it should be seen by early 1993.

Lavish musicals are back in fashion, too, with all the major Hollywood studios laying plans for imminent extravaganzas. Projects include *The Phantom of the Opera* and *Les Miserables*, and we can expect to hear the music of Kurt Weill, Danny (*Batman*) Elfman, Stephen Sondheim, Andrew Lloyd Webber and others. As *Variety* put it, 'The Hollywood hills are alive with the sound of music.'

Last year's threatened takeover of the Hollywood film industry by the Japanese appears no longer to be imminent. The sudden flood of cash, enquiries and negotiations seems to have subsided, and the sacks of yen have quietly been withdrawn. Evidently Sunset Boulevard is not about to give way to the Rising Sun just yet.

All in all, then, no dramatic changes or developments to speak of, and perhaps less visible shrinkage in the film industry than some might have expected during the year. Certainly, with more than 1000 annual film festivals in Europe alone, and at least 300 more throughout the rest of the world, there is clearly no lack of commitment or interest – though there are apparently too few 'festival' films available to satisfy this enormous demand. So the great moviemaking machine is just as much alive and kicking as it was when I brought out the very first edition of *Film Review* 48 years ago. The world was very different then, as was *Film Review*, but the purpose remains the same: to present the richness and variety of the year's cinema, its facts, films, fun and folly – everything, in fact, that makes moviegoing so endlessly enjoyable.

Another two years will see *Film Review* reach its first half century of publication. I look forward to sharing that achievement with you all – and I would be particularly pleased to hear from anyone who has collected all the annuals up to now – but above all I look forward to the artistry, the excitement and the sheer entertainment of what this book has always been about: the movies themselves.

THE TOP TWENTY BOX-OFFICE HITS IN THE UK

1. *Robin Hood: Prince of Thieves*
2. *Terminator 2: Judgment Day*
3. *The Silence of the Lambs*
4. *Basic Instinct*
5. *Hook*
6. *The Addams Family*
7. *Cape Fear*
8. *The Naked Gun 2½ – The Smell of Fear*
9. *My Girl*
10. *Wayne's World*
11. *The Commitments*
12. *JFK*
13. *The Hand That Rocks the Cradle*
14. *Hot Shots!*
15. *Father of the Bride*
16. *Bill & Ted's Bogus Journey*
17. *Backdraft*
18. *Star Trek VI: The Undiscovered Country*
19. *Misery*
20. *Point Break*

Top Ten Box-Office Stars

2. Arnold Schwarzenegger   1. Kevin Costner   3. Robin Williams

4. Michael Douglas   5. Julia Roberts   6. Robert De Niro   7. Nick Nolte

8. Patrick Swayze   9. Keanu Reeves   10. Winona Ryder

The UK list of top-ten stars is calculated on the box-office performance of films released in the July 1991–June 1992 period – and on the stars' track record at the wickets. Last year Julia Roberts was No. 1 thanks to a trio of smash-hits, namely *Pretty Woman*, *Flatliners* and *Sleeping with the Enemy*. This year she is still riding high in video sales and has aided the popularity of Steven Spielberg's phenomenally successful *Hook* – which, in spite of malicious reviews, won a huge and dedicated audience. Kevin Costner, who was rated No. 3 last year, is now King after starring in *Robin Hood:* *Prince of Thieves*, the year's highest-grossing movie (that's £20,201,390 in ticket sales), and *JFK*, the latter lassoing £6,936,136.

For your further erudition we now include a top-twenty chart of the most successful films released in Britain (opposite), and here, for the record, are last year's top ten stars: 1, Julia Roberts; 2, Arnold Schwarzenegger; 3, Kevin Costner; 4, Harrison Ford; 5, Mel Gibson; 6, Michael J. Fox; 7, Bruce Willis; 8, Warren Beatty; 9, Patrick Swayze; 10, Gerard Depardieu.

Releases of the Year

In this section you will find details of all the films released in Great Britain from 1 July 1991 to the end of June 1992 – the period covered by all the reference features in the book. The precise dating of some of these releases is a little tricky, but the date given generally refers to the film's London release, unless otherwise stated.

The normal abbreviations operate as follows: Dir – for Director; Pro – for Producer; Assoc Pro – for Associate Producer; Ex Pro – for Executive Producer; Pro Ex – for Production Executive; Pro Sup – for Production Supervisor; Co-Pro – for Co-Producer; Pro Co-Ord – for Production Co-ordinator; Ph – for Photographer; Ed – for Editor; Art – for Art Director; Pro Des – for Production Designer; M – for Music; and a few others which will be obvious.

Abbreviations for the names of film companies are also pretty obvious when used, such as Fox for 20th Century-Fox, Rank for Rank Film Distributors, and UIP for Universal International Pictures. Where known, the actual production company is given first, the releasing company last.

When it comes to nationality of the film, you will find that this is noted wherever possible – those films without any mention of country of origin can usually be taken as being American – but in these days of increasing international co-productions between two, three or even four countries it is sometimes difficult to sort out where the premier credit is due.

Unless otherwise specified (i.e. black-and-white), it can be taken that the film is made in Technicolor or a similar process.

Censorship certificates: *U* represents films suitable for persons of any age; *PG* (Parental Guidance) represents films which some parents might consider unsuitable for their children; *12* or *15* means no persons under that age will be admitted; and films certified with an *18* (approximately the old 'X' certificate) means that nobody under that age will be admitted to the cinema while that film is showing. 'No cert' means that no certificate has been issued by the *initial showing of the film* but this does not mean that one will not subsequently be issued.

Films are reviewed by F. Maurice Speed and James Cameron-Wilson, with Frederick Deeps Malone, Charles Bacon, Karen Krizanovich and Barbie Wilde. Each review is followed by its writer's initials.

The Addams Family. Witty, stylish, big-screen adaptation of the cult 1964–6 ABC sitcom about a family of ghoulish weirdos. Sitcoms seldom improve under the cinematic magnifying glass, but this is not a bad try. Cinematographer Barry Sonnenfeld (*Misery, Raising Arizona*) makes his directorial debut with enormous gusto, but lets the visual gags do the joking. Anjelica Huston (Morticia), Raul Julia (Gomez) and particularly Christina Ricci (Wednesday), all underplay their parts to hilarious effect, never pushing the pun-laden script over the top (Morticia: 'Don't

Sword dancing: Raul Julia as Gomez and Christopher Lloyd as Fester indulge in a traditional, macabre jig in Barry Sonnenfeld's The Addams Family (*from Columbia Tri-Star*).

torture yourself, Gomez. That's my job'). Only Christopher 'I've Never Heard of Underacting in My Life' Lloyd (as Fester/Gordon) charges through the movie in a state of panto-mimic possession. [JC-W]

Also with: Jimmy Workman (Pugsley), Christopher Hart (Thing), Carel Struycken (Lurch), Judith Malina (Granny), Dan Hedaya (Tully), Elizabeth Wilson (Abigail), Dana Ivey (Margaret), Paul Benedict (Judge Womack), John Franklin (Cousin It), Lauren Walker, Valerie Walker, Maureen Sue Levin, Darlene Levin, Barry Sonnenfeld (passenger on toy train).
   Dir: Barry Sonnenfeld. Pro: Scott Rudin. Ex Pro: Graham Place. Co-Pro: Jack Cummins. Screenplay: Caroline Thompson and Larry Wilson; based on the cartoon characters created by Charles Addams. Ph: Owen Roizman. Ed: Dede Allen. Pro Des: Richard MacDonald. M: Marc Shaiman; *Addams Groove* performed by Hammer. Costumes: Ruth Myers. (Orion/Paramount–Columbia Tri-Star.) Rel: 13 December 1991. 99 mins. Cert PG.

The Adjuster. Deeply depressing, alienating and sporadically startling Canadian drama about an insurance adjuster who evaluates the material loss of fire victims. Hailed as an angel of mercy by his clientele, Noah Render (Elias Koteas) takes sexual liberties with a number of them, while ignoring his wife, a withdrawn film censor. The film's strength is its surprising revelations and bleak, ephemeral touches of humour, but is definitely an acquired taste. From the Armenian, Cairo-born director of *Family Viewing* and *Speaking Parts*. [JC-W]

Also with: Arsinee Khanjian (Hera Render), Maury Chaykin (Bubba), Gabrielle Rose (Mimi), Jennifer Dale (Arianne), David Hemblen (Bert), Rose Sarkisyan (Seta), Don McKellar (Tyler), Armen Kokorian, Jacqueline Samuda, Gerard Parkes, Patrica Collins, John Gilbert, Stephen Ouimette, Tony Nardi, Paul Bettis.
   Dir and Screenplay: Atom Egoyan. Co-Pro: Camelia Frieberg. Ph: Paul Sarossy. Ed: Susan Shipton. Pro Des: Linda Del Rosario and Richard Paris. M: Mychael Danna. Costumes: Maya Mani. Sound: Steven Munro. (Ego Film Arts–Metro.) Rel: 29 May 1992. 102 mins. Cert 18.

The Adventures of Milo and Otis. This one has been kicking around for quite a while; it was originally shown, with its original Japanese title of *Koneko Monogatari*, at the original length of 90 minutes (now cut to 76),

Film censor Arsinee Khanjian secretly records the steamy bits in husband Atom Egoyan's very strange and strangely memorable The Adjuster *(from Metro).*

at the Cannes Film Festival of 1986. The film now has a new soundtrack (spoken by Dudley Moore) and a new musical score. It's certainly original; about a male cat, the film hasn't a single human being in the cast. All the animals are treated with respect, although they act like humans! Hailed as a 'stunning achievement' at Cannes, it remains worth seeing if only for its novelty value. [FDM]

Dir and Screenplay: Masanori Hata. Assoc Dir: Kon Ichikawa. (Virgin Vision.) Rel: 26 July 1991. 76 mins. Cert U.

Afraid of the Dark. If it isn't an insult to the prospective viewer it would be unsporting to reveal too much about the 'plot' of this psychological 'thriller'. Suffice it to say that the main character is an unsympathetic 11-year-old boy with a vacuous stare, and that blindness is a second character. There are also lots of knitting needles, razors, a beautiful dog and an enigmatic white stetson. Only for those who enjoy being led up the garden path – and then tripped up at the end of it. Filmed in West London. [JC-W]

Cast includes: James Fox (Frank), Fanny Ardant (Miriam), Paul McGann (Tony

Playing cheat: Ben Keyworth grapples with his sinister blind spot in Mark Peploe's fraudulent thriller Afraid of the Dark *(from Rank).*

Dalton), Clare Holman (Rose), Susan Wooldridge (Lucy Trent), Ben Keyworth (Lucas), Robert Stephens, David Thewlis, Struan Rodger, Rosalind Knight, Jeremy Flynn, Star Acri, Niven Boyd, Sheila Burrell, Frances Cuka, Hilary Mason, Catriona McColl, Lola Peploe, Gwynneth Strong, Cassie Stuart, Frederick Treves.

Dir and Screenplay: Mark Peploe. Pro: Simon Bosanquet. Ex Pro: Jean Nachbaur and Sylvaine Sainderichin. Ph: Bruno De Keyzer. Ed: Scott Thomas. Pro Des: Caroline Amies. M: Richard Hartley. Costumes: Louise Stjernsward. Sound: Mark Auguste. (Sovereign/Telescope Films/Les Films Ariane/Cine Cinq–Rank.) Rel: 21 February 1992. 91 mins. Cert 18.

After Dark, My Sweet. A dishevelled, slovenly drifter with beautiful clear blue eyes wafts into a sleepy desert town. With nowhere to go, he hooks up with the beautiful Mrs Fay Anderson, a widow and alcoholic. But what is her relationship with the menacing Uncle Bud, a shady smooth operator who claims he's an ex-detective? Pass the tequila and tell us a story. Nobody is who they seem in this over-plotted, virtually stationary *film noir*, which director James Foley tries to spice up with meaningful close-ups and smart camera moves. Dreadfully dull. Filmed on location in Indio, California, *After Dark, My Sweet* marks the sixth screen adaptation of a Jim Thompson novel, shortly preceding *The Grifters*. [JC-W]

Cast includes: Jason Patric (Collie – Kevin 'Kid' Collins), Rachel Ward (Mrs Fay Anderson), Bruce Dern (Uncle Bud), George Dickerson (Doc Goldman), James Cotton

Femme fatale or victim? Rachel Ward adds sex appeal to James Foley's otherwise tortured After Dark, My Sweet *(from Virgin Vision).*

Alice's adventures in Manhattan: Mia Farrow samples a magic potion from the late Keye Luke in Woody Allen's mannered and disappointing Alice *(from Rank).*

(Charlie), Corey Carrier, Rocky Giordani, Jeanie Moore, Tom Wagner, Michael G. Hagerty, James E. Bowen Jr.

Dir: James Foley. Pro: Ric Kidney and Bob Redlin. Ex Pro: Cary Brokaw. Screenplay: Redlin; from the novel by Jim Thompson. Ph: Mark Plummer. Ed: Howard Smith. Art: Kenneth A. Hardy. M: Maurice Jarre. Sound: David Brownlow. (Avenue Pictures–MCEG/Virgin Vision.) Rel: 2 August 1991. 111 mins. Cert 18.

Alice. Mia Farrow stars as Alice Tate, a mousy Manhattan housewife, in Woody Allen's twentieth film as writer and director. Alice has given her life to her home, her children and affluent husband, Doug (William Hurt), but has now decided to start a career as a TV writer. However, those around her – her so-called friends – are distracted by their own heavy schedules of gossip, cultural sightseeing and social climbing, and Alice is left to fend for herself. Help comes in the shape of a gruff, mysterious Dr Yang (the late Keye Luke in the film's plum part, his last role), who prescribes some magical herbs. More urban paranoia from Woody, this time wrapped in an adult fairy tale. Magical realism in Manhattan sounds fun, but the old jokes about religious and sexual guilt are wearing thin and a fabulous cast is largely wasted. [JC-W]

Also with: Alec Baldwin (Ed), Blythe Danner (Dorothy), Judy Davis (Vicki), Joe Mantegna (Joe), Bernadette Peters (muse), Cybill Shepherd (Nancy Brill), Gwen Verdon (Alice's mother), David Spielberg (Ken), June Squibb, Marceline Hugot, Julie Kavner, Holland Taylor, Robin Bartlett, Linda Wallem, Diane Cheng, Patrick O'Neal, Caroline Aaron, James Toback, Elle MacPherson, Diane Salinger, Bob Balaban, Jodi Long, Judith Ivey.

Dir and Screenplay: Woody Allen. Pro: Robert Greenhut. Ex Pro: Jack Rollins and Charles H. Joffe. Co-Pro: Helen Robin and Joseph Hartwick. Ph: Carlo Di Palma. Ed: Susan E. Morse. Pro Des: Santo Loquasto. M: numbers performed by Jackie Gleason, Artie Shaw & His Orchestra, Erroll Garner, Thelonius Monk, Count Basie, Liberace etc. Costumes: Jeffrey Kurland. Sound: James Sabat. (Orion–Rank.) Rel: 19 July 1991. 105 mins. Cert 12.

All I Want for Christmas. Two kids fervently wish that their divorced parents will come together again so they can all have a family Christmas. Aimed at the festive yuletide audience – and evidently rushed through to meet the deadline. [FDM]

Playing God: John Lithgow and Aidan Quinn find their faith tested in Hector Babenco's bloated At Play in the Fields of the Lord *(from Entertainment).*

Cast: Ethan Randall (Ethan), Thora Birch (Hallie), Harley Jane Kozak (Catherine), Jamey Sheridan (Michael), Lauren Bacall (Lillian Brooks, Leslie Nielsen (Santa Claus)

Dir: Robert Lieberman. Pro: Marykay Powell. Ex Pro: Stan Rogow. Screenplay: Thom Eberhardt and Richard Kramer. Ph: Robbie Greenberg. Ed: Peter Berger and Dean Goodhill. Pro Des: Herbert Zimmerman. Art: Randall McIlvain. M: Bruce Broughton. Sound: Henry W. Garfield. (Paramount–UIP.) Rel: 29 November 1991. 90 mins. Cert U.

Ama. Intriguing Anglo-African film about a Ghanaian family living in London. Ama is the 12-year-old daughter of the Ababio family, who discovers that she has powers of spiritual prophecy when an enigmatic floppy disk predicts death and affliction for her kin. Unfortunately, this set-up is undermined by some of the worst acting seen in a British feature for some time. The potential for an original and striking film is all here, but the filmmaking is of the home movie variety. Experience and a larger budget would have helped. [JC-W]

Cast includes: Georgina Ackerman (Ama), Anima Misa (Corni), Thomas Baptiste (Babs), Roger Griffiths (Joe), Joy Elias-Rilwan (Araba), Evans Nii Oma Hunter (UK), Alexandra Duah, Gary Marius, Verona Marshall, Okon Jones.

Dir and Pro: Kwate Nee-Owoo and Kwesi Owusu. Screenplay: Owusu. Ph: Jonathan Collinson and Roy Cornwall. Ed: Justin Krish. Art: Ruhi Chaudry, Nigel Ashby and Keith Khan. M: Owusu and Vico Mensah; tracks performed by Pauline Oduro, Ken Boothe, Pan African Orchestra etc. Sound: Jacky Gaston. (Efiri Tete Films/Channel Four–Artificial Eye). Rel: 22 November 1991. 100 mins. Cert 15.

An American Tail: Fievel Goes West. Vibrant, frequently violent and (sadly) charmless sequel to Steven Spielberg's first, and highly successful, foray into animation. This time little Fievel, the Russian mouse and New York immigrant, pursues his dream to ride shotgun in the Wild West. There are some genuinely inspired moments (a rollercoaster ride in a sewer sticks in the mind) and the dialogue is above average for this sort of thing, but the film benefits particularly from the voices of James Stewart (as a decrepit bloodhound), John Cleese (as a slick, no-good English cat) and Amy Irving (as a brassy Mae West feline with a heart of gold). Not a box-office success, however. [JC-W]

Voices include: Phillip Glaser (Fievel), Dom DeLuise (Tiger), James Stewart (Wylie Burp), John Cleese (Cat R. Waul), Amy Irving (Miss Kitty), Cathy Cavadini (Tanya Mousekewitz), Jon Lovitz (T. R. Chula), Nehemiah Persoff (Poppa Mousekewitz), Erica Yohn (Mama Mousekewitz).

Dir: Simon Wells and Phil Nibbelink. Pro: Steven Spielberg and Robert Watts. Ex Pro: Kathleen Kennedy, Frank Marshall and David Kirschner. Screenplay: Flint Dille; based on Charles Swenson's story from characters created by Kirschner. Ed: Nick Fletcher. Art: Neil Ross. M: James Horner; songs by Horner and Will Jennings. (Amblin/Universal–UIP.) Rel: 13 December 1991. 74 mins. Cert U.

At Play in the Fields of the Lord. The populace of the backwater Amazonian town Mae de Deus are facing economic ruin. They need more room to expand, but are surrounded by endless jungle populated by barbaric Indians. It would be easy to suppress the natives,

Hot to trot: Kurt Russell plays hero in Ron Howard's rousing Backdraft *(from UIP).*

but four American missionaries stand in the way – though even they are not sure whose side God is on. Producer Saul Zaentz (*One Flew Over the Cuckoo's Nest, Amadeus*) first read Peter Matthiessen's novel in the month of its publication in 1965. When he turned producer, he sought to buy the rights from MGM. Twenty-four years after reading the book, Zaentz finally acquired the rights for $1.4 million. The resultant film, at a cost of $36 million, is simply not good enough. An excellent cast tries valiantly to inject credibility into their roles, the Amazon scenery struggles to dwarf them and the tragic events surrounding the fate of the Niaruna Indians hang in the air like a miasma. The film's ultimate downfall is its pedestrian direction, slow pacing and excessive length. Nevertheless, the politics of the book still, occasionally, hit their mark. [JC-W]

Cast includes: Tom Berenger (Lewis Moon), John Lithgow (Leslie Huben), Daryl Hannah (Andy Huben), Aidan Quinn (Martin Quarrier), Tom Waits (Wolf), Kathy Bates (Hazel Quarrier), Stenio Garcia (Boronai), Nelson Xavier (Father Xantes), Jose Dumont (Commandante Guzman), Niilo Kivirinta, S. Yriwana Karaja, Jose Renato Lana, Rui Polanah.
  Dir: Hector Babenco. Pro: Saul Zaentz. Ex Pro: Francisco Ramalho Jr and David Nichols. Screenplay: Babenco and Jean-Claude Carriere; from the novel by Peter Matthiessen. Ph: Lauro Escorel. Ed: William Anderson. Pro Des: Clovis Bueno. M: Zbigniew Preisner. Costumes: Rita Murtinho. Sound: Alan Splet. (Saul Zaentz Co.–Entertainment.) Rel: 10 April 1992. 186 mins. Cert 15.

Aunt Julia and the Scriptwriter (US: *Tune in Tomorrow*). Stylish, funny satire of 1950s radio soap opera, with Peter Falk as Pedro Carmichael, an audacious concoctor of melodrama both on the air waves and in the lives of his comrades. While idealistic, would-be writer Martin Loader (Keanu Reeves) romances his goofy Aunt Julia (Barbara Hershey), Carmichael's popular radio melodrama intermingles with their reality, feeding it and stealing from it. 'Art', Carmichael says, 'is two cannibals on a desert island dying of starvation. Eat or be eaten!' Scenarist William Boyd has brewed a lively screenplay from the celebrated novel by Mario Vargas Llosa – into which British director Jon Amiel (*The Singing Detective, Queen of Hearts*) breathes wonderful life. And Peter Falk has a heyday. [JC-W]

Also with: Patricia Clarkson (Aunt Olga), Jerome Dempsey (Sam & Sid), Richard B. Shull (Leonard Pando), Henry Gibson (Big John Coot), Bill McCutcheon, Richard Portnow, Paul Austin, Joel Fabiani, Crystal Field, Jayne Haynes, Mary Joy, Rob Kramer, Irving Metzman, Dedee Pfeiffer, Danny Aiello III. Soap Opera Players: Peter Gallagher, Dan Hedaya, Buck Henry, Hope Lange, John Larroquette, Elizabeth McGovern, Robert Sedgwick.
  Dir: Jon Amiel. Pro: John Fielder and Mark Tarlov. Ex Pro: Joe Caracciolo Jr. Screenplay: William Boyd; from Mario Vargas Llosa's novel. Ph: Robert Stevens. Ed: Peter Boyle. Pro Des: Jim Clay. M: Wynton Marsalis. Costumes: Betsy Heimann. (Polar Films–HoBo.) Rel: 11 October 1991. 107 mins. Cert 12.

Autobus – Aux Yeux du Monde. Mildly diverting French black comedy/

Hell in Hollywood: John Turturro as the tortured, self-righteous Barton Fink *(from Rank).*

moral fable about a bored youth who hijacks a schoolbus to impress his girlfriend. Dorset-born Kristin Scott-Thomas is very good in the thankless role of a sympathetic hostage, while abductor Yvan Attal behaves like a hoodlum straight out of a David Mamet play. A very dry, quirky second feature from the director of *A World Without Pity*. [JC-W]

Cast includes: Yvan Attal (Bruno), Kristin Scott-Thomas (schoolteacher), Charlotte Gainsbourg (Juliette), Marc Berman (driver).

Dir and Screenplay: Eric Rochant. Pro: Alain Rocca. Ph: Pierre Novion. Ed: Catherine Quesemand. Art: Pascale Fenouillet. M: Gerard Torikian. Sound: Jean-Jacques Ferran. (Les Productions Lazennec/Canal Plus, etc–Artificial Eye.) Rel: 19 June 1992. 95 mins. Cert 15.

Backdraft. Chicago, today. Kurt Russell and William Baldwin top-bill as the feuding McCaffrey brothers, both firemen, the former a heroic veteran,

the latter a timid graduate. You can work out what happens. There's also a sub-plot (painfully slow in developing) in which Robert De Niro attempts to discover the culprit of a series of dramatic arson attacks. The special effects steal the show from an impressive cast, while the seat-shaking soundtrack sends shivers up our spines and obscures the dialogue. Unfortunately the screenplay, scripted by former firefighter Gregory Widen, is almost as impenetrable as the fires that rage through this predictable spectacular. Many real firemen make up the supporting cast. [JC-W]

Cast includes: Kurt Russell (Stephen McCaffrey), William Baldwin (Brian McCaffrey), Scott Glenn (John Adcox), Jennifer Jason Leigh (Jennifer Vaitkus), Rebecca DeMornay (Helen McCaffrey), Donald Sutherland (Ronald Bartel), Robert De Niro (Donald Rimgale), Jason Gedrick (Tim Krizminski), J. T. Walsh (Martin Swayzak), Tony Mockus Sr, Cedric Young, Jack McGee, Richar Lexsee, Kevin M. Casey, Juan Ramirez, Mark Wheeler, Clint Howard, David Crosby.

Dir: Ron Howard. Pro: Richard B. Lewis, Pen Densham and John Watson. Ex

Pro: Brian Grazer and Raffaella DeLaurentiis. Screenplay: Gregory Widen. Ph: Mikael Salomon. Ed: Daniel Hanley and Michael Hill. Pro Des: Albert Brenner. M: Hans Zimmer; numbers performed by Los Lobos, Cream, Martha & The Vandellas, Bruce Hornsby & The Range etc. Costumes: Jodie Tillen. Pyrotechnics: Allen Hall. Sound: Glenn Williams. (Imagine/Trilogy Entertainment/Universal–UIP.) Rel: 2 August 1991. 136 mins. Cert 15.

Barton Fink. 1941, Los Angeles. An idealistic New York playwright is tempted to Hollywood to write a wrestling movie for Wallace Beery. Once there, he is plagued by writer's block – and an enigmatic, overweight neighbour. From the brothers Coen – who brought us *Blood Simple, Raising Arizona* and *Miller's Crossing* – this stark, surreal comedy moves at a studied, occasionally stodgy pace, but is a witty, assured original. Winner of the Palme d'Or, best director award and, for John Turturro, the best actor nod at the 1991 Cannes festival. [JC-W]

Cast includes: John Turturro (Barton Fink), John Goodman (Charlie Meadows), Judy Davis (Audrey Taylor), Michael Lerner

(Lt Walker), Leilani Sarelle (Roxy), Dorothy Malone (Hazel Dobkins), Wayne Knight (John Correli), Bruce A. Young, Chelcie Ross, Daniel von Bargen, Stephen Tobolowsky, Benjamin Mouton, Jack McGee, Bill Cable.
   Dir: Paul Verhoeven. Pro: Alan Marshall. Ex Pro: Mario Kassar. Screenplay: Joe Eszterhas. Ph: Jan de Bont. Ed: Frank J. Urioste. Pro Des: Terence Marsh. M: Jerry Goldsmith; numbers performed by Chanel X, The Doo Wah Riders, LaTour, Chris Rea. Costumes: Ellen Mirojnick. Sound: Nelson Stoll. (Carolco/Le Studio Canal Plus–Guild.) Rel: 8 May 1992. 128 mins. Cert 18.

Bathroom Intimacies – Intimidades en un Cuarto de Bano. This one has to be seen to be avoided. The entire film takes place in the bathroom of a loopy middle-class Mexican family, the stationary camera concealed behind the loo mirror. No action here, unless you consider domestic flatulence the stuff of high drama. The director, Jaime Humberto Hermosillo, went on to make the equally boring *Homework* (qv). [CB]

Cast includes: Gabriela Roel, Alvaro Guerrero, Marta Navarro, Maria Rojo, Emilio Echeverria.
   Dir, Screenplay and Ed: Jaime Humberto Hermosillo. Pro: Lourdes Rivera. Ph: Guillermo Navarro. Art: Leticia Venzor. (Sociedad Cooperativa de Produccion Cinematografica Jose Revueltas–Metro.) Rel: 6 September 1991. 78 mins. No cert.

Lust or bust: Michael Douglas and Jeanne Tripplehorn steam up the screen in Paul Verhoeven's slick, vacuous Basic Instinct *(from Guild).*

(Jack Lipnick), John Mahoney (W. P. Mayhew), Tony Shalhoub (Ben Geisler), Jon Polito (Lou Breeze), Steve Buscemi (Chet), David Warrilow, Richard Portnow, Christopher Murney, I. M. Hobson, Megan Faye, Lance Davis, Harry Bugin.
   Dir: Joel Coen. Pro: Ethan Coen. Ex Pro: Ben Barenholts, Ted Pedas, Jim Pedas and Bill Durkin. Co-Pro: Graham Place. Screenplay: Coen and Coen. Ph: Roger Deakins. Ed: Roderick Jaynes. Pro Des: Dennis Gassner. M: Carter Burwell. Costumes: Richard Hornung. Sound: Skip Lievsay. (Manifesto Film Sales/Circle Films–Rank.) Rel: 14 February 1992. 116 mins. Cert 15.

Basic Instinct. Carolco paid Joe Eszterhas $3 million for his script and they were duped. Treading the same ground as *Sea of Love* and the writer's own *Jagged Edge*, *Basic Instinct* is formulaic and tricksy, devoid of suspense *and* credibility. Michael Douglas, slimmed down by 25 pounds, is Nick Curran, a San Francisco cop obsessed by prime suspect Catherine Tramell (Sharon Stone), an Arctic blonde with a hot bedside manner. A writer of erotic murder stories, Ms Tramell finds that her nearest and dearest are dying of ice-pick wounds – just like in her novels. Of course, she's too smart to re-enact her own fiction, and it's up to Curran to weed out the real killer. Meanwhile, Ms Tramell is writing a new book about the murder of a cop – modelled on Curran. Much controversy and outrage surrounded the film's depiction of psychotic bisexual behaviour, which naturally helped it to become one of the most popular pictures of the year. [JC-W]

Also with: George Dzundza (Gus), Jeanne Tripplehorn (Dr Beth Garner), Denis Arndt

Batman Returns Messy, bloated, undisciplined sequel to the 1989 phenomenon that made Jack Nicholson a very, very rich man. This time there's no Joker, Robin has been left on the cutting room floor and it's up to the Caped Crusader, Penguin and Catwoman to save the movie. Sadly, Danny DeVito's grotesque birdman lacks the sheer evil charisma of Nicholson, although Michelle Pfeiffer is a sharper romantic foil to Bruce Wayne than was Kim Basinger's Vicky Vale. The problem is, it is never satisfactorily explained why Michelle's bumbling Selina Kyle becomes Catwoman in the first place. And what has she got against Batman? A lack of logic dogs the film from the word go and the plot – when you can follow it – is virtually non-existent. The effects, too, are surprisingly humdrum (considering the film cost $80 million), while Michael

Animal attraction: Danny DeVito as the grotesque Penguin plotting with Michelle Pfeiffer's Catwoman to destroy the Caped Crusader – in Tim Burton's Batman Returns *(from Warner).*

Keaton does nothing to make his part more interesting (if anything, he transforms Bruce Wayne into an absolute dweeb). The film has also lost its sense of time, place and fantasy – witness Wayne's contemplation that he could become compared to Norman Bates and (wait for it) Ted Bundy. *They know about Bundy in Gotham City?* The biggest disappointment of the year. [JC-W]

Cast: Michael Keaton (Batman/Bruce Wayne), Danny DeVito (Penguin/Oswald Cobblepott), Michelle Pfeiffer (Catwoman/Selina Kyle), Christopher Walken (Max Schreck), Michael Gough (Alfred), Michael Murphy (Mayor), Cristi Conaway, Andrew Bryniarski, Pat Hingle, Vincent Schiavelli, Steve Witting, Jan Hooks, John Strong, Rick Zumwalt, Paul Reubens, Diane Salinger.

Dir: Tim Burton. Pro: Burton and Denise Di Novi. Ex Pro: Jon Peters, Peter Guber, Benjamin Melniker and Michael Uslan. Screenplay: Daniel Waters; from a story by Waters and Sam Hamm, based upon characters created by Bob Kane. Ph: Stefan Czapsky. Ed: Chris Lebenzon. Pro Des: Bo Welch. M: Danny Elfman; *Face to Face*

sung by Siouxsie & The Banshees. Costumes: Bob Ringwood and Mary Vogt. Penguin make-up and SFX: Stan Winston. Sound: Richard L. Anderson and David Stone. (Warner.) Rel: 10 July 1992. 127 mins. Cert 12.

But is it art? Emmanuelle Beart poses for Michel Piccoli in Jacques Rivette's self-indulgent, provocative and over-long La Belle Noiseuse *(from Artificial Eye).*

La Belle Noiseuse. No film about a painting should be four hours long. Although Jacques Rivette manages to capture the emotional pain and anxiety that goes into creating art, and has coaxed two extraordinary performances from his leads – Michel Piccoli and Emmanuelle Beart – his film can only be recommended to those with cast-iron derrieres. Piccoli is predictably commanding as the reclusive painter

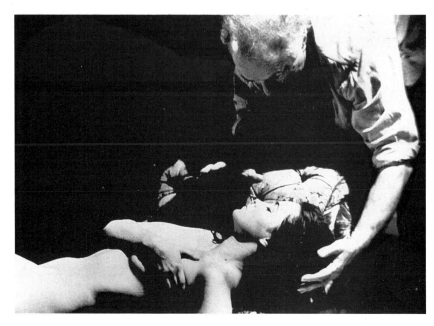

Hell is an air guitar: Keanu Reeves and Alex Winter enjoy themselves – awesomely, dudes – in the surprisingly infectious insanity of Columbia Tri-Star's Bill & Ted's Bogus Journey.

Dutch courage: Drew Preston (Nicole Kidman) faces up to Dutch Schultz (Dustin Hoffman) in Robert Benton's elegant story of violence, Billy Bathgate *(from Warner).*

slumming it in the South of France with his *magnum opus* half-finished. Then along comes Mlle Beart who finally inspires him to raise a pencil – if little else. Fascinating and infuriating by turns, *La Belle Noiseuse* must be the most boring masterpiece of the year. Winner of the Grand Prix at Cannes and voted Best Foreign Film by the LA Critics. (A shorter version, *La Belle Noiseuse – Divertimento*, which ran for two hours, six minutes, was released on 8 April.) [JC-W]

Cast includes: Michel Piccoli (Edouard Frenhofer), Jane Birkin (Liz Frenhofer), Emmanuelle Beart (Marianne), Marianne Denicourt (Julienne), David Bursztein (Nicolas), Gilles Arbona (Porbus), Bernard Dufour (the hand of the painter).
  Dir: Jacques Rivette. Pro: Martine Marignac. Screenplay: Rivette, Pascal Bonitzer and Christine Laurent; from Honoré de Balzac's novel *Le Chef-d'Oeuvre Inconnu*. Ph: William Lubtchansky. Ed: Nicole Lubtchansky. Pro Des: Emmanuel de Chauvigny. M: Igor Stravinsky. Costumes: Laurence Struz. Sound: Florian Eidenbenz. (Pierre Grise/FR3 Films/George Reinhart/Centre National de la Cinematographie/Canal Plus/Sofica Investimage 2 and 3–Artificial Eye.) Rel: 20 March 1992. 240 mins. Cert 15.

Bill & Ted's Bogus Journey. Those most excellent dudes, the retarded, time-travelling William S. Preston (Alex Winter) and Theodore Logan (Keanu Reeves), find themselves in real trouble in their second film comedy. A totally heinous time lord, De Nomolos (Joss Ackland as your textbook villain), sends two robotic replicas of Bill & Ted to the present (1991) to exterminate our whacky heroes. Along the way, B & T encounter The Grim Reaper, 'The Dude Downstairs', God, Benjamin Franklin and the Easter Bunny. *Bogus Journey* violates logic, often looks thrown together and misses many wonderful opportunities (did God *have* to be a commanding, sonorous and Anglo-Saxon male voice?). But ultimately, a film this audacious defies criticism. [JC-W]

Also with: William Sadler (Grim Reaper), George Carlin (Rufus), Sarah Trigger (Joanna), Annette Azcuy (Elizabeth), Hal Landon Jr, Amy Stock-Poynton, Chelcie Ross, Hal Landon Sr, Pam Grier, Roy Brocksmith, Taj Mahal, William Shatner.
  Dir: Pete Hewitt. Pro: Scott Kroopf. Ex Pro: Ted Field and Robert W. Cort. Screenplay: Ed Solomon and Chris Matheson. Ph: Oliver Wood. Ed: David Finfer and Spencer

Gross. Pro Des: David L. Snyder. M: David Newman. Costumes: Marie France. Creature/SFX make-up: Kevin Yagher. (Nelson/Interscope Communications/Orion–Columbia Tri-Star.) Rel: 3 January 1992. 93 mins. Cert PG.

Billy Bathgate. Atmospheric, slow-moving homage to the gangster era, a sort of arty *GoodFellas*. Billy (like Henry Hill in the earlier film) is a young outsider in awe of the gangster way of life, in particular the power that Arthur 'Dutch' Schultz holds over the rest of the establishment. With open-mouthed innocence, Billy becomes a member of Dutch's gang, only to fall in love with the mobster's moll, Drew Preston. Dustin Hoffman is a little mannered as Dutch and Bruce Willis is incongruous casting in the small role of playboy Bo Weinberg, but the little-known players deliver the goods, particularly Steven Hill as Dutch's adviser, Otto Berman. An exquisitely made, costly ($40 million-plus) period piece, which could've used more suspense. A box-office bomb. [JC-W]

Also with: Nicole Kidman (Drew Preston), Loren Dean (Billy Bathgate), Steve Buscemi (Irving), Billy Jaye (Mickey), Stanley Tucci (Lucky Luciano), Mike Starr (Julie Martin), Moira Kelly (Becky), John Costelloe, Tim Jerome, Robert F. Colesberry, Stephen Joyce, Frances Conroy, Kevin Corrigan, Paul Herman, Xander Berkeley, Barry McGovern, Katharine Houghton, Rick Washburn.
  Dir: Robert Benton. Pro: Arlene Donovan and Robert F. Colesberry. Screenplay: Tom Stoppard; from the book by E. L. Doctorow. Ph: Nestor Almendros. Ed: Alan Heim and Robert Reitano. Pro Des: Patrizia Von Brandenstein. M: Mark Isham; numbers performed by Eddy Duchin and His Orchestra, Helen Donath, James P. Johnson. Costumes: Joseph G. Aulisi. Choreography: Pat Birch. (Touchstone/Touchwood Pacific Partners–Warner.) Rel: 10 January 1992. 107 mins. Cert 15.

Black Robe. After a somewhat uninspired opening, Bruce Beresford's adaptation of Brian Moore's 1985 novel settles into a powerful and authentic portrayal of the Canadian Indians in the seventeenth century. Lothaire Blutheau (*Jesus of Montreal*) stars as 'Black Robe', a devout French Jesuit priest who undertakes a perilous journey in the harsh winter of 1634. He is accompanied by a troupe of Algonquin Indians, who escort him through the forests and across the St Lawrence in

Striking cinema: Lothaire Bluteau, as Father Laforgue, punishes himself for naughty thoughts in Bruce Beresford's potent, challenging Black Robe *(from Entertainment).*

search of a Huron mission. Black Robe, who believes his companions are a savage, godless people, finds his own spirituality challenged by the great wasteland of God's forgotten country and by the suffering he encounters. What the film lacks in great acting, it more than makes up for in the force of its message and the bleak, scenic locations. Thought-provoking, if grim (and occasionally very brutal) viewing. The first official Canadian-Australian co-production, and winner of six Canadian 'Genies'. [JC-W]

Cast includes: Lothaire Blutheau (Father

19

Laforgue), Aden Young (Daniel), Sandrine Holt (Annuka), August Schellenberg (Chomina), Billy Two Rivers (Ougebmat), Jean Brousseau (Champlain), Tantoo Cardinal, Lawrence Bayne, Harrison Liu, Frank Wilson, Francois Tasse, Yvan Labelle, George Pachanos.

Dir: Bruce Beresford. Pro: Robert Lantos, Stephanie Reichel and Sue Milliken. Ex Pro: Jake Eberts, Brian Moore and Denis Heroux. Screenplay: Moore; based on his novel. Ph: Peter James. Ed: Tim Wellburn. Pro Des: Herbert Pinter. M: Georges Delerue. Costumes: Renee April and John Hay. (Alliance Communications/ Samson Prods–Entertainment.) Rel: 31 January 1992. 100 mins. Cert 15.

Blame It on the Bellboy. In the tradition of the cross-cultural success of *A Fish Called Wanda*, Hollywood Pictures attempt to repeat the formula with this sporadically amusing farce of mistaken identity. A mild-mannered clerk (Dudley Moore), a lecherous adulterer on a 'Medi-Date' (Richard Griffiths) and an Australian hit-man (Bryan Brown) all check into the same Venice hotel at the same time. The bellboy (Bronson Pinchot) mixes up their names (Melvyn Orton, Maurice Horton and Mike Lawton respectively) and creates a scenario for bedlam. The acting varies from the absurd to the po-faced, with varying results. Still, it's a joy to see the rugged Bryan Brown hit it off with our very own mousey Penelope Wilton. [JC-W]

The old mistaken briefcase routine: Bryan Brown, Patsy Kensit, Alison Steadman and Richard Griffiths struggle for laughs in Warner's Blame It on the Bellboy.

Local hood Ice Cube leans on the hood of his motor in the bad neighbourhood of South Central Los Angeles – in John Singleton's commanding Boyz N The Hood *(from Columbia Tri-Star).*

Also with: Andreas Katsulas (Scarpa), Patsy Kensit (Caroline Wright), Alison Steadman (Rosemary Horton), Penelope Wilton (Patricia Fulford), Jim Carter, Alex Norton, John Grillo, Ronnie Stevens, Enzo Turrin, Andy Bradford, Lindsay Anderson (the voice of Mr Marshall).

Dir and Screenplay: Mark Herman. Pro: Jennifer Howarth. Ex Pro: Steve Abbott. Ph: Andrew Dunn. Ed: Mike Ellis. Pro

Des: Gemma Jackson. M: Trevor Jones; solo guitar: John Williams. Costumes: Lindy Hemming. (Hollywood Pictures–Warner.) Rel: 24 January 1992. 79 mins. Cert 12.

Blonde Fist. A tough, gritty British film about female boxing, set in Liverpool and New York. Margi Clarke wins her bouts in and out of the ring with splendid reality. [FDM]

Rest of cast: Carroll Baker (Lovelle), Ken Hutchison, Sharon Power, Angela Clarke, Lewis Bester.

Dir and Screenplay: Frank Clarke. Pro: Joseph D'Marais and Christopher Figg. Ph: Bruce McGowan. Ed: Brian Peachey. Pro Des: Colin Pocock. M: Alan Gill. Sound: Ed Leatham. (Blue Dolphin in assoc with Film Four Int.) Rel: 1 November 1991. 99 mins. Cert 15.

Book of Love. Retrospective look at the romantic innocence of 1956 – when middle-aged advertising writer Jack Twiller (Michael McKean) was just a gooey-eyed, would-be Romeo (Chris Young). Nostalgic teen fodder just aching with banality. Interestingly, the title hit was actually recorded in 1958 – by The Monotones (and *that* should be a warning). Set in Pennsylvania, but actually filmed in Los Angeles (in 1989). [CB]

Also with: Keith Coogan (Crutch Kane), Aeryk Egan (Peanut), Josie Bissett (Lily), Tricia Leigh Fisher (Gina Gabooch), Danny

Tainted innocence: Emma Heatherington (Tabitha Allen, centre), with her sisters (Karina and Dominique Rossi), enjoys the calm before the storm in Syd Macartney's arresting story of a painting – The Bridge (from Electric).

Nucci, John Cameron Mitchell, Beau Dremann, Jill Jaress, John Achorn, Lewis Arquette, Elizabeth Rainey, Anna Berger, Jack McGee.

Dir: Robert Shaye. Pro: Rachel Talalay. Ex Pro: Sara Risher. Screenplay: William Kotzwinkle; based on his short story *Jack in the Box*. Ph: Peter Deming. Ed: Terry Stokes. Pro Des: C. J. Strawn. M: Stanley Clarke; numbers performed by Ben E. King and Bo Diddley, The Monotones, John Lee Hooker, Chuck Berry, The Diamonds, Little Richard, Frankie Lymon and The Teenagers, Gene Vincent, The Platters, Big Daddy, The Drifters etc. Costumes: Susie Desanto. (Entertainment.) Rel: 8 May 1992. 87 mins. Cert 15.

Boyz N The Hood. The story (inspired by real events in the director's life) of three teenagers on the streets of South Central Los Angeles, *Boyz N The Hood* told us to 'Increase the Peace' but became the catalyst for riots, gang warfare, the shooting of at least thirty cinemagoers and the murder of one 23-year-old man. Such is the force of this film, a gritty, colourful and muscular picture that tackles authentic, black issues head-on. However, its concerns deal equally with divorce, fatherhood, virginity and family harmony, although the feeling of violence (from the police and neighbourhood gangs) is always present. Powerful entertainment, all the more extraordinary from a 23-year-old first-time director. [JC-W]

Cast includes: Ice Cube (Doughboy), Cuba Gooding Jr (Tre Styles), Morris Chestnut (Ricky Baker), Larry Fishburne (Furious Styles), Angela Bassett (Reva Styles), Tyra Ferrell (Mrs Baker), Redge Green (Chris), Desi Arnez Hines II (Tre aged 10), Nia Long (Brandi), Hudhail Al-Amir, Lexie Bigham, Kenneth A. Brown, Ceal, Darneicea Corley, John Cothran Jr, Jesse Ferguson, Baha Jackson, Kirk Kinder, Whitman Mayo, Donovan McCrary, Leonette Scott, John Singleton, Vonte Sweet.

Dir and Screenplay: John Singleton. Pro: Steve Nicolaides. Ph: Charles Mills. Ed: Bruce Cannon. Art: Bruce Bellamy. M: Stanley Clarke; numbers performed by Newcleus, Zapp, Run-DMC, Yo-Yo, 2 Live Crew, Quincy Jones, Ice Cube etc. (Columbia Tri-Star.) Rel: 25 October 1991. 111 mins. Cert 15.

The Bridge. The summer of 1887, Walberswick, Suffolk. Period romance based on the 1986 novel by Maggie Hemingway, itself inspired by Philip Wilson Steer's impressionist painting. An imaginary story of Steer's liaison with a Victorian woman trapped in a stifling marriage, *The Bridge* is full of knowing looks and deep stares, accompanied by a sweeping Mahleresque score. A little directorially self-conscious, the film also suffers from clumsy editing and a performance of some uncertainty from David O'Hara (in his first film lead) as Steer. But the familiar irony of Hemingway's original story hits its mark. [JC-W]

Also with: Saskia Reeves (Isobel Heatherington), Joss Ackland (Smithson), Rosemary Harris (Aunt Jude), Anthony Higgins (Reginald Heatherington), Geraldine James (Mrs Todd), Tabitha Allen (Emma), Dominique Rossi, Peter Blythe, Tim Baker.

Dir: Syd Macartney. Pro: Lyn Goleby. Screenplay: Adrian Hodges. Ph: David Tat-

Home movie: Corey Parker and Anne Bancroft talk of the past and future, in Neil Simon's endearing Broadway Bound *(from Blue Dolphin).*

Bugsy *Siegel and his dream, a gambling casino in the middle of the Nevada desert. Warren Beatty stars, Warner distributes.*

tersall. Ed: Michael Ellis. Pro Des: Terry Pritchard. M: Richard G. Mitchell. Costumes: Jenny Beavan. (British Screen/Film Four Int/Moonlight Films–Electric.) Rel: 10 January 1992. 102 mins. Cert 12.

Broadway Bound, filmed for American TV, completes Neil Simon's autobiographical trilogy which began with *Brighton Beach Memoirs* and *Biloxi Blues*. Now that childhood, sex and the army are out of the way, Simon concentrates on the strife of growing old (Grandpa is soiling his sheets), marital tension (Pop is seeing another woman) and finding work in post-war Brooklyn. Eugene Morris Jerome (Corey Parker, who played an army recruit in *Biloxi*) is now an aspiring comedy writer, wrestling for ideas with his older brother Stan (Jonathan Silverman, Eugene in *Brighton Beach*). Strapped for subject matter, the brothers turn to their own family battlefield and discover a goldmine of material. Director Paul Bogart (*Torch Song Trilogy*) makes no attempt to open up out the play, focusing instead on Simon's superb dialogue, illuminated by an exemplary cast. Well observed, poignant, sentimental and very funny. [JC-W]

Also with: Anne Bancroft (Kate), Hume Cronyn (superb, as Ben), Jerry Orbach (Jack), Michele Lee (Blanche), with the voices of Marilyn Cooper, Pat McCormick, Jack Carter.

Dir: Paul Bogart. Pro: Terry Nelson. Ex Pro: Michael Brandman and Emanuel Azenberg. Screenplay: Neil Simon; based on his play. Ph: Isidore Mankofsky. Ed: Andy Zall. Pro Des: Ben Edwards. M: David Shire. Costumes: Rita Riggs. Sound: Jill Bowers. (Vision International/ABC Productions–Blue Dolphin.) Rel: 24 April 1992. 87 mins. Cert PG.

Bugsy has all the ingredients for an exceptionally entertaining saga. There's romance, glamour, money, corruption, unexpected violence and hopes and dreams. It's also true – the story of the prince of gangsters, a man willing to sacrifice all for his mistress. Benjamin 'Bugsy' Siegel himself – as portrayed here – is an intriguing combination of charm, danger and naivety. Co-producer Warren Beatty, who waited six years for James Toback's script, is particularly energetic in the title role, and is matched tooth-and-nail by Annette Bening as the mercurial Virginia Hill. But the story's violence, passion, suspense and irony failed to seize this

Back projection: Robert De Niro scares the chic out of a wealthy Southern family in Martin Scorsese's horrific Cape Fear *(from UIP).*

critic. A handsome, studied production, based on a tremendous script, *Bugsy* is too slow-moving for its own good and ultimately an empty experience. [JC-W]

Also with: Harvey Keitel (Mickey Cohen), Ben Kingsley (Meyer Lansky), Joe Mantegna (George Raft), Elliott Gould (Harry Greenberg), Richard Sarafian (Jack Dragna), Wendy Phillips (Esta Siegel), Bill Graham (Charlie Luciano), Lewis Van Bergen (Joey Adonis), James Toback (Gus Greenbaum), Bebe Neuwirth, Gian-Carlo Scandiuzzi, Stefanie Mason, Kimberly McCullough, Andy Romano, Robert Beltran, Joseph Roman, Eric Christmas, Debrah Farentino, Paul Roache, Traci Lind.

Dir: Barry Levinson. Pro: Levinson, Mark Johnson and Warren Beatty. Screenplay: James Toback. Ph: Allen Daviau. Ed: Stu Linder. Pro Des: Dennis Gassner. M: Ennio Morricone; numbers performed by Johnny Mercer, Tommy Dorsey, Joe Stafford, Margaret Whiting, Kay Kyser, Glenn Miller, Peggy Lee etc. Costumes: Albert Wolsky. Sound: Richard Beggs. (Mulholland Prods/Baltimore Pics–Columbia Tri-Star.) Rel: 20 March 1992. 135 mins. Cert 18.

Cabeza de Vaca. Reminiscent of the classic *Aguirre, Wrath of God*, though less harrowing and slightly less violent. This remarkable Mexican production is based on the memoirs of Alva Nunez Cabeza de Vaca, and set in Florida during the Spanish conquest of 1528–36, where de Vaca is shipwrecked, captured by Indians, and taught their magic. Director Nicolas Echevarria painstakingly re-creates the life of the Indians in a documentary style, using very little dialogue but with great visual flair. A magical and fascinating film. [FDM]

Cast: Juan Diego (de Vaca), Daniel Giminez Cacho (Dorantes), Roberto Sosa (Cascabel/Araino), Carlos Castanon (Castillo), Gerardo Villareal, Roberto Cobo, Jose Flores, Eli Machuca, Josefina Echanove, Oscar Yoldi.

Dir: Nicolas Echevarria. Pro: Rafael Cruz, Jorge Sanchez and Julio Solorzano Foppa. Ex Pro: Bertha Navarro. Screenplay: Echevarria and Guillermo Sheridan; based on the book *Shipwrecks* by Alvar Nunez Cabeza de Vaca. Ph: Guillermo Navarro. Ed: Rafael Castandeo. Pro Des: Jose Luis Aguilar. Costumes: Totita Figueroa. M: Mario Lavista. (Producciones Iguana-Television Espanol in assoc with Channel 4 TV, American Playhouse Theatrical Films–Metro.) Rel: 13 September 1991. 112 mins. No cert.

Cape Fear. Martin Scorsese's Hitchcockian remake of the 1962 thriller – about a Southern family terrorised by an ex-con – stars Nick Nolte as Sam Bowden (the character originated by Gregory Peck), the defence lawyer who puts the brutal Max Cady behind bars for a vicious rape. Fourteen years later Cady (Robert De Niro) is loose and determined to exact his revenge on Bowden and his family. But Cady is no fool, and he acts within the law, turning Bowden against his wife, Leigh (Jessica Lange), and daughter Danielle (the excellent Juliette Lewis). Again, De Niro is stunning in a Scorsese-directed performance (his seventh), and his scenes dominate the film. Here, the director attempts to darken the psychological simplicity of the original by presenting Cady as an embodiment of Catholic sexual guilt. However, by doing this Scorsese robs the thriller of its emotional impact, as Bowden comes off as a two-faced wimp and Cady as an intelligent, charming seducer. The film has its share of chills – and cinematic bravura – but lacks a human core. Still, *Cape Fear* (on a budget of $34 million) was a much-needed commercial boost for a director trapped in the role of critics' darling. Gregory Peck, Robert Mitchum and Martin Balsam, all of whom starred in the original, are given supporting roles here, while Bernard Herrmann's 1962 score is remodelled by Elmer Bernstein. [JC-W]

Also with: Joe Don Baker (Claude Kersek), Robert Mitchum (Lt Elgart), Gregory Peck (Lee Heller), Martin Balsam (Judge), Illeana Douglas (Lori Davis), Fred Dalton Thompson (Tom Broadbent), Zully Montero, Edgar Allan Poe IV, Domenica Scorsese, Billy Lucas, Catherine Scorsese, Charles Scorsese.
    Dir: Martin Scorsese. Pro: Barbara DeFina. Ex Pro: Kathleen Kennedy and Frank Marshall. Screenplay: Wesley Strick. Ph: Freddie Francis. Ed: Thelma Schoonmaker. Pro Des: Henry Bumstead. M: Bernard Herrmann, adapted by Elmer Bernstein; numbers performed by Guns N' Roses, Aretha Franklin, Jane's Addiction, The Cramps, etc. Costumes: Rita Ryack.

Life in the slow lane: Philippe Caubere, Nathalie Roussel, Therese Liotard and Didier Pain enjoy the good things in life – in Yves Robert's sublime Le Château de Ma Mère *(from Palace).*

Urban mosaic: Vincent Spano and Barbara Williams find each other in John Sayles's outstanding City of Hope *(from Mainline).*

Sound: Tod Maitland. Titles: Elaine and Saul Bass. (Amblin/Cappa Films/Tribeca/Universal–UIP.) Rel: 6 March 1992. 127 mins. Cert 18.

Le Château de Ma Mère (My Mother's Castle). Following on from *My Father's Glory*, this reliably charming sequel (filmed back-to-back with the first film) returns us to the hills of Provence where the young Marcel Pagnol engages in more adventures. The Pagnols' house in the mountains has now become a regular weekend retreat where the young Marcel encounters the precocious Isabelle, a hospitable count and a friendly lock-keeper. Told with an inimitable, leisurely style, this is a treat for all Francophiles that beguiles the eye, seduces the ear and opens the mind. [JC-W]

Cast includes: Philippe Caubère (Joseph), Nathalie Roussel (Augustine), Didier Pain (Uncle Jules), Thérèse Liotard (Aunt Rose), Jean Carmet (drunk keeper), Jean Rochefort (Lois de Montmajour), Georges Wilson (the Count Colonel), Philippe Uchan (Bouzigue), Julien Ciamaca (Marcel), Victorien Delamare (Paul), Joris Molinas (Lili des Bellons), Julie Timmerman (Isabelle), Jean-Pierre Darras (Marcel's voice), Paul Crauchet, Patrick Prejean, Jean-Marie Juan.
    Dir: Yves Robert. Pro: Alain Poiré. Screenplay: Robert and Jerome Tonnerre; from the book by Marcel Pagnol. Ph: Robert Alazraki. Ed: Pierre Gillette. M: Vladimir Cosma. Costumes: Agnès Nègre. Sound: Claude Villand and Bernard Leroux. (Gaumont/Productions De La Gueville/TFI Films/Centre National de la Cinematographie–Palace.) Rel: 26 July 1991. 98 mins. Cert U.

Chattahoochee. Gloomy story, based on truth, of a victimised patient in a Deep South hospital for the criminally

insane. Even a bravura performance by Gary Oldman can't begin to salvage the wreck. [FDM]

Rest of cast: Dennis Hopper (Walker), Frances McDormand, Pamela Reed, Ned Beatty, M. Emmett Walsh.

Dir: Mick Jackson. Pro: Faye Schwab. Ex Pro: Aaron Schwab. Co-Pro: Sue Baden Powell. Screenplay: James Hicks. Ph: Andrew Dunn. Ed: Don Fairservice. Art: Patrick Tagliaferro. M: John Keane. (Hemdale.) Rel: 18 October 1991. 97 mins. Cert 15.

City of Hope. Thirty-eight characters squabble, double-cross and make love to each other in the crumbling urban nightmare of Hudson City, New Jersey. John Sayles, with his most ambitious film to date, has created a colourful world of dubious people fighting for their lives in a neighbourhood gone wild. His extraordinarily complex, vibrant script sets new standards in film writing, and is given life by a wonderful cast of Sayles regulars. If the subject matter itself was not so familiar, this could've been The Great American Film of the year. [JC-W]

Cast includes: Vincent Spano (Nick), Tony Lo Bianco (Joe), Joe Morton (Wynn), Todd Graff (Zip), Jace Alexander (Bobby), John Sayles (Carl), Gloria Foster (Jeanette), Angela Bassett (Reesha), David Strathairn (Asteroid), Anthony John Denison (Rizzo), Barbara Williams (Angela), Josh Mostel (Mad Anthony), Joho Smollett (Desmond), Edward Jay Townsend Jr (Tito), Louis Zorich (Mayor Baci), Gina Gershon (Laurie), Bill Raymond (Les), Stephen Mendillo, Chris Cooper, Charlie Yanko, Scott Tiler, Frankie Faison, Tom Wright, Maggie Renzi, Marianne Leone, S. J. Lang, Kevin Tighe, Michael Mantell, Joe Grifasi, Miriam Colon, Rose Gregorio, Daryl Edwards, Mason Daring, Lawrence Tierney, Ray Aranha.

Dir, Screenplay and Ed: John Sayles. Pro: Sarah Green and Maggie Renzi. Ex Pro: John Sloss and Harold Welb. Ph: Robert Richardson. Pro Des: Dan Bishop and Dianna Freas. M: Mason Daring; numbers performed by Louis Prima, Jace Alexander, The Band That Time Forgot, The Nelson Brothers etc. Costumes: John Dunn. (Samuel Goldwyn–Mainline.) Rel: 15 November 1991. 129 mins. Cert 15.

City Slickers. Three New York guys, struggling in the grip of mid-life crisis, discover themselves on a wild 'cattle drive' holiday out West. Exceptionally well-written comedy by the reliable

Norman, is that you? Billy Crystal replaces his urban nightmare with a calf called Norman in Ron Underwood's pleasantly diverting City Slickers *(from First Independent).*

team of Lowell Ganz and Babaloo Mandel (*Splash, Parenthood* etc) comes together neatly under the direction of Ron Underwood (*Tremors*). Billy Crystal is on top form as the 39-year-old radio adman who has lost his smile and a reason to get up in the mornings, and who inevitably lands into trouble because of his smart-ass comments. He's in real schtuck when he comes up against trail boss Jack Palance ('a saddle-bag with eyes'), who makes the Marlboro Man look like a fairy. Very funny, well-told saga, which neatly balances a roll of sharp one-liners with some well-drawn characters. You even forgive the film for its home-grown homilies. [JC-W]

Cast includes: Billy Crystal (Mitch Robbins), Daniel Stern (replacing Rick Moranis as Phil Berquist), Bruno Kirby (Ed Furillo), Patricia Wettig (Barbara Robbins), Helen Slater (Bonnie Rayburn), Jack Palance (Curly), Josh Mostel (Barry Shalowitz), David Paymer (Ira Shalowitz), Noble Willingham (Clay Stone), Bill Henderson (Ben Jessup), Tracey Walter (Cookie), Phill Lewis (Steve Jessup), Karla Tamburelli (Arlene Berquist), Jeffrey Tambor, Kyle Secor, Dean Hallo, Yeardley Smith, Robert Costanzo, Walker Brandt, Molly McClure, Lindsay Crystal, Danielle Harris, Eddie Palmer.

Dir: Ron Underwood. Pro: Irby Smith. Ex Pro: Billy Crystal. Screenplay: Lowell Ganz and Babaloo Mandel. Ph: Dean Semler. Pro Des: Lawrence G. Paull. M: Marc Shaiman; *Young at Heart* performed by Jimmy Durante; *Where Did My Heart Go?* by James Ingram. Costumes: Judy Ruskin. (Castle Rock/Nelson Entertainment–First Independent.) Rel: 18 October 1991. 114 mins. Cert 12.

Close My Eyes. Richard Gillespie (Clive Owen) is a young, idealistic and successful architect. Natalie (Saskia Reeves), his sister, is older, bored and unhappy. One night in despair and loneliness she kisses her brother on the mouth. Five years later Natalie is married to a fantastically rich financial advisor, Sinclair Bryant (Alan Rickman), lives in a large house on the Thames and has lifted herself up a class, complete with new accent. Richard, meanwhile, has jettisoned his former flash lifestyle and has turned into an 'architectural reactionary', an all-Green urban reformer. No longer the cocksure high-achiever, Richard falls under his sister's spell when she decides to spice up her sexual ennui . . . Although filmed in London and in the home counties, *Close My Eyes* shimmers like a story from

25

Family matters: Clive Owen and Saskia Reeves explore forbidden territory in Stephen Poliakoff's intriguing Close My Eyes *(from Artificial Eye).*

another country, another time. Writer-director Stephen Poliakoff has placed his film in a context of yesterday set in tomorrow, utilising futuristic buildings in London's docklands and then cutting to dreamy, Renoiresque picnics in the country. The look is the thing, while the dialogue occasionally sticks in the actors' mouths. Only Alan Rickman, as Natalie's Bohemian husband, can transform the tricksy script into gilt-edged prose. [JC-W]

Also with: Karl Johnson (Colin), Lesley Sharp (Jessica), Kate Gartside (Paula), Karen Knight, Niall Buggy, Campbell Morrison, Marie Passarelli, Jan Winters.
    Dir and Screenplay: Stephen Poliakoff. Pro: Therese Pickard. Ph: Witold Stok. Ed: Michael Parkinson. Pro Des: Luciana Arrighi. M: Michael Gibbs. Costumes: Amy Roberts. Sound: Hugh Strain. (Film Four International/Beambright–Artificial Eye.) Rel: 6 September 1991. 107 mins. Cert 18.

The Commitments. After directing the likes of Dennis Quaid, Gene Hackman, Mickey Rourke and Robert De Niro, Islington's Alan Parker returns to the ensemble, unknown-cast formula of *Bugsy Malone* and *Fame* that estab-lished him. Here, he follows the progress of a group of Dublin youths as they attempt to create a band that puts the sex back into soul. The humour of the script, by Dick Clement, Ian La Frenais and Roddy Doyle, is a little obvious, and the story somewhat contrived, but Parker has managed to milk a freshness from the genre without resorting to gimmickry. If occasionally self-conscious as a filmmaker, Parker knows how to thrash a performance out of an actor, whether star or unknown. *The Commitments* is fun, but it's no more enlightening than an episode of *Bread* set to music. [JC-W]

Cast includes: Robert Arkins (Jimmy Rabbitte), Michael Aherne (Steve Clifford), Angeline Ball (Imelda Quirke), Maria Doyle (Natalie Murphy), Dave Finnegan (Mickah Wallace), Bronagh Gallagher (Bernie McGloughlin), Felim Gormley (Dean Fay), Glen Hansard (Outspan Foster), Dick Massey (Billy Mooney), Johnny Murphy (Joey 'The Lips' Fagan), Kenneth McCluskey (Derek Scully), Andrew Strong (Deco Cuffe), Colm Meaney (Mr Rabbitte), Anne Kent (Mrs Rabbitte), Andrea Corr, Gerard Cassoni, Ruth and Lindsay Fairclough, Michael O'Reilly, Liam Carney, Mark O'Regan, Phelim Drew, Tricia Smith, Alan Parker.
    Dir: Alan Parker. Pro: Roger Randall-Cutler and Lynda Myles. Ex Pro: Armyan Bernstein, Tom Rosenberg and Souter Harris. Co-Pro: Dick Clement, Ian La Frenais and Marc Abraham. Screenplay: Clement, La Frenais and Roddy Doyle; from Doyle's novel. Ph: Gale Tattersall. Ed: Gerry Hambling. Pro Des: Brian Morris. M: The Commitments. Costumes: Penny Rose. Sound: Clive Winter. (Beacon/First Film/Dirty Hands–Fox.) Rel: 4 October 1991. 117 mins. Cert 15.

Coupe de Ville. 1963, the USA. The brothers Marvin, Buddy and Bobby Libner (Daniel Stern, Arye Gross, Patrick Dempsey) have never seen eye to eye. Even now that they are young adults, the old hostilities still bubble under. So when the Libner Bros. are tricked by their father into driving a '54 Cadillac from Michigan to Florida, a lot of ghosts are unleashed. Apparently based on fact, this is a warm, funny tale of sibling rivalry that is never quite as predictable as it might have been. The performances are strong, and so is the tide of sentimentality. Great soundtrack of sixties songs. [JC-W]

Also with: Annabeth Gish (Tammy), Rita Taggart (Betty Libner), Joseph Bologna (Uncle Phil), Alan Arkin (Fred Libner, the father), James Gammon, Ray Lykins, Chris Lombardi, Josh Segal, John Considine, Edan Gross, Michael Weiner, Dean Jacobson.
    Dir: Joe Roth. Pro: Larry Brezner and Paul Schiff. Ex Pro: James G. Robinson. Co-Pro and Screenplay: Mike Binder. Ph: Reynaldo Villalobos. Ed: Paul Hirsch. Pro Des: Angelo Graham. M: James Newton Howard; numbers performed by Dion, The Everly Brothers, The Crystals, The Temptations, The Cadillacs, The Flamingos, Smokey Robinson & The Miracles, The Del-Vikings, Rita Taggart, The Kingsmen etc. Costumes: Deborah Scott. (Morgan Creek–Warner.) Rel: 17 January 1992. 98 mins. Cert 12.

Cross My Heart – La Fracture du Myocarde. The French cinema continues to rummage through its childhood with this affecting comedy-drama. Set in a generic provincial French town, the film follows the conspiracy of secrecy that surrounds the sudden death of the mother of a 12-year-old boy. Ganging together to prolong the lie, a group of eighth-graders discover a new resourcefulness, *esprit de corps* and responsibility that sets them apart from the unthinking adult fraternity. Director-screenwriter Jacques Fansten solicits strikingly naturalistic performances from his young cast, and writes with the unwavering accuracy of a former child who hasn't forgotten what it was like. Formerly a TV movie, and now the blueprint for a Steven Spielberg tearjerker. [JC-W]

Cast includes: Sylvain Copans (Martin), Nicolas Parodi (Jérome), Cecilia Rouaud (Marianne), Olivier Montiege (Antoine), Lucie Blossier (Claire), Francois Dyrek (Titanic), Delphine Gouttman, Kaldi El Hadj, Mathieu Poussin, Wilfried Flandrin, Romuald Jarny, Benoit Gautier, Wilfrid Blin, Dominique Lavanant, Jacques Brunet, Maurice Benichou, Gerard Croce.
Dir and Screenplay: Jacques Fansten. Pro: Fansten and Ludi Boeken. Ph: Jean-Claude Saillier. Ed: Colette Farruggia. Pro Des: Gilbert Gagneux. M: Jean-Marie Sénia. Sound: Jules Dantan. (Belbo Films/Antenne 2/Canal Plus–Palace.) Rel: 28 February 1992. 100 mins. Cert PG.

Curly Sue. Chicago – today. An itinerant con man and his cute kid, Curly Sue, trick a heartless, wealthy lawyer into a free lunch. The lawyer, Grey Ellison (Kelly Lynch), obviously has a few lessons to learn about being human, but how will Curly Sue transform the bitch? You know what's going to happen after the first five minutes, but the film strolls along in an affable sort of way and was a mild hit at the box-office. Glucose-machine John Hughes wrote, directed and produced with his usual flair for the unsurprising, but is helped here by a decent performance from Ms Lynch as the ice queen with a heart of marzipan. [JC-W]

Also with: James Belushi (Bill Dancer), Alisan Porter (Curly Sue), John Getz (Walker McCormick), Fred Dalton Thompson, Cameron Thor, Branscombe Richmond, Steven Carell, Gail Boggs, Burke Byrnes, Viveka Davis, Barbara Tarbuck, Edie McClurg, John Ashton.
Dir, Pro and Screenplay: John Hughes. Ex Pro: Tarquin Gotch. Ph: Jeffrey L. Kimball. Ed: Peck Prior and Harvey Rosenstock. Pro Des: Doug Kraner. M: Georges Delerue; numbers performed by Ringo Starr, 2YZ. Costumes: Michael Kaplan. (Warner.) Rel: 26 December 1991. 102 mins. Cert PG.

The Dark Wind. A young, inexperienced Indian cop seems to be making a lot of mistakes in his new post in the heart of Navajo country. Assigned to guard a vandalised windmill, Jim Chee (Lou Diamond Phillips, eighth-Cherokee) smells corruption, witchcraft and death, but nobody will take him seriously. Not, that is, until some corrupt feds show up . . . The first in a

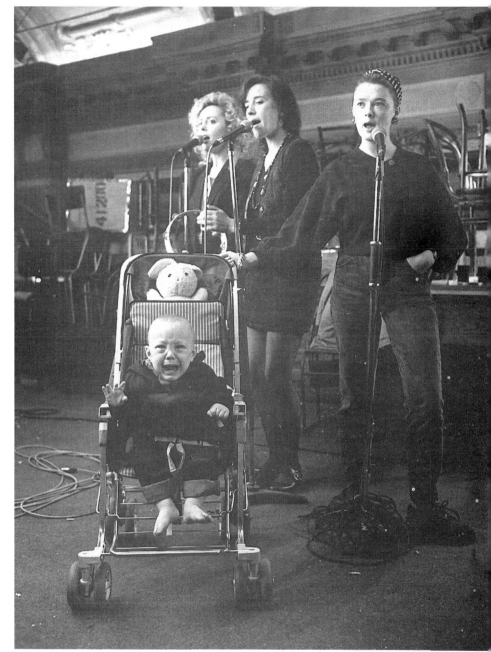

Black music comes to Dublin in Alan Parker's lively The Commitments *(from Fox). Seen here: Angeline Ball, Maria Doyle and Bronagh Gallagher.*

planned series of Indian mysteries based on the popular novels of Tony Hillerman, *The Dark Wind* could do with a breath of fresh air. 'Artily' photographed, the film falls foul of deadly pacing and a somnambulant turn from Phillips. Yet when the plot *does* get going, it's too jumbled to follow. [JC-W]

Also with: Gary Farmer (Cowboy Albert Dashee), Fred Ward (Lt Joe Leaphorn), Guy Boyd (Agent Johnson), John Karlen (Jake West), Jane Loranger (Gail Pauling), Blake Clark (Ben Gaines), Gary Basaraba, Faye B. Tso, Michelle Thrush.
Dir: Errol Morris. Pro: Patrick Markey. Ex Pro: Robert Redford and Bonni Lee. Screenplay: Neal Jimenez, Eric Bergren and Mark Horowitz; based on the novel by Tony Hillerman. Ph: Stefan Czapsky. Ed: Susan Crutcher and Freeman Davies. Pro Des: Ted Bafaloukos. M: Michel Colombier. Costumes: Eugenie Bafaloukos. Sound: David Brownlow. (Carolco–Guild.) Rel: 15 May 1992. 112 mins. Cert 15.

Mild-mannered Sam Neill trapped in terrible circumstances in John Ruane's stuttering Death in Brunswick *(from Electric).*

Dial-a-thriller: Goldie Hawn drops the giggles in favour of Damian Harris's implausible Deceived *(from Warner).*

Dead Again. Los Angeles, the present/ 1948. Kenneth Branagh's first Hollywood film as director and star, an unashamedly melodramatic Gothic-supernatural romantic thriller. Citizen Ken is an irritatingly flip LA private eye, Mike Church, who's asked to look after an attractive amnesiac (Emma Thompson, aka Mrs Branagh). When, under hypnosis, she recalls a traumatic time in 1948, Mike Church himself would appear to be involved. Mere coincidence? A recklessly implausible tale, that could have transcended its genre if it hadn't borrowed so many obvious B-movie clichés. [JC-W]

Cast includes: Kenneth Branagh (Roman Strauss/Mike Church), Andy Garcia (Gray Baker), Derek Jacobi (Franklyn Madson), Hanna Schygulla (Inga), Emma Thompson (Margaret Strauss/Grace), Robin Williams (Dr Cozy Carlisle), Wayne Knight ('Piccolo' Pete), Gregor Hesse (Frankie), Campbell Scott (Doug), Lois Hall, Richard Easton, Jo Anderson, Patrick Doyle, Obba Babatunde, Christine Ebersole.

Dir: Kenneth Branagh. Pro: Lindsay Doran and Charles H. Maguire. Ex Pro: Sydney Pollack. Screenplay: Scott Frank. Ph: Matthew F. Leonetti. Ed: Peter E. Berger. Pro Des: Tim Harvey. M: Patrick Doyle. Costumes: Phyllis Dalton. (Mirage/ Paramount–UIP.) Rel: 25 October 1991. 101 mins. Cert 15.

Death in Brunswick. Melbourne, 1990. Carl Fitzgerald is an out-of-work cook, separated from his wife and burdened by his mother. However, he is determined to improve his lot. Life looks up when he gets a job as chef at the Bombay Club and hooks up with its pretty barmaid, Sophie Papafagas. But Carl's troubles have only just begun . . . An eccentric black comedy that is always surprising, occasionally shocking and sporadically amusing, *Death in Brunswick* is never the laugh-riot it could've been, due to the central presence of Sam Neill. No mean actor, Neill has clocked up first-class performances in such movies as *My Brilliant Career*, *A Cry In the Dark* and *Dead Calm*, but he's no comic performer. A brave piece of casting against type, this, but a perilous one. [JC-W]

Also with: Zoe Carides (Sophie), John Clarke (Dave), Yvonne Lawley (Mrs Fitzgerald), Nico Lathouris (Mustafa), Boris Brkic (Laurie), Nicholas Papademetriou, Doris Younane, Deborah Kennedy.

Dir and Screenplay: John Ruane. Pro:

Miss Blacula: Cynthia Bond (right) *doles out the lovebites in James Bond III's fresh and funny* Def by Temptation *(from BFI).*

Timothy White. Ex Pro: Bryce Menzies. Assoc Pro: Lynda House. Ph: Ellery Ryan. Ed: Neil Thumpston. Pro Des: Chris Kennedy. M: Philip Judd. Sound: Lloyd Carrick. (Meridian Films–Electric.) Rel: 7 February 1992. 109 mins. Cert 15.

Deceived. How well do you *really* know your friends? For that matter, how well do you know your wife or husband? Goldie Hawn stars as a forty-ish New York success story, a happy wife, mother and sought-after art-restorer. Then, overnight, she begins to have doubts about her husband . . . A flaccid psychological thriller that begins well but grinds to a halt just as the tension should start mounting. Cheap shots, too, with the traditional 'startled pigeons' and 'screeching cat' shock shots. Ultimately, it's the audience that's deceived. [JC-W]

Cast includes: Goldie Hawn (Adrienne Saunders), John Heard (Jack Saunders), Ashley Peldon (Mary Saunders), Tom Irwin (Harvey Schwartz), Jan Rubes (Tomasz Kestler), Francesca Buller (Lillian), Amy Wright (Evelyn), Kate Reid (Rosalie), Robin Bartlett, Beatrice Straight, George R. Robertson, Laura Hawn.

Dir: Damian Harris. Pro: Michael Finnell, Wendy Dozoretz and Ellen Collett. Ex Pro: Teri Schwartz and Anthea Sylbert. Screenplay: Mary Agnes Donoghue and Derek Saunders. Co-Pro: Donoghue. Ph: Jack N. Green. Ed: Neil Travis. Pro Des: Andrew McAlpine. M: Thomas Newman; numbers performed by The Denny Zeitlin Trio, The Penguins, Andy Summers etc. Costumes: Linda Matheson. Sound: David Bartlett. (Touchstone/Silver Screen–Warner.) Rel: 3 April 1992. 108 mins. Cert 15.

Def by Temptation is a fresh angle on the vampire thriller, with colourful dialogue and engaging performances compensating for the film's microscopic budget (under $300,000). The diminutive director-producer-writer James Bond III (*sic*) saves *some* cash by step-

ping into the lead role himself – as Joel, the country boy who comes to New York for one final fling before taking up the cloth. There he encounters one 'hot-natured freakazoid', a satanic beast disguised as a sexually rampant seductress. Using 'sexuality to hold morality hostage', the vampiress (Cynthia Bond) needs a total innocent to consummate her evil. This is familiar terrain injected with a fresh enthusiasm, souped up by a full-blooded performance from Ms Bond as the physical manifestation of AIDS. [JC-W]

Also with: Kadeem Hardison ('K'), Bill Nunn (Dougy), Samuel L. Jackson (Minister Garth), Minnie Gentry (Grandma), Melba Moore (Madam Sonya), Rony Clanton, Stephen Van Cleef, John Canada Terrell, Guy Davis, Freddie Jackson, Najee.

Dir, Pro and Screenplay: James Bond III. Ex Pro: Charles Huggins, Kevin Harewood and Nelson George. Co-Pro: Kervin Simms and Hajna O. Moss. Ph: Ernest Dickerson. Pro Des: David Carrington. M: Paul Laurence; numbers performed by Freddie Jackson, Melba Moore, Ashford & Simpson, Najee, Paul Laurence, Slick Love, Eric Gable, Paid 'N' Full, Z' Looke etc. Sound: Charles R. Hunt. (Troma–BFI.) Rel: 22 May 1992. 95 mins. Cert 18.

In the worst possible taste: Dominique Pinon as Louison, in Jean-Pierre Jeunet and Marc Caro's anarchic Delicatessen *(from Electric).*

Delicatessen. An innovative and fast-paced debut from former animators Jeunet and Caro, *Delicatessen* sports a sense of humour of the blackest kind. Louison, a former clown, lands up in a dilapidated tenement in a post-Armageddon near-future, run by a crazed butcher with a taste for human flesh. He is hired to be the building's handyman, not suspecting that he's scheduled to end up as dinner for all the slavering tenants. Luckily, Louison falls for the butcher's cello-playing daughter, who tries to save him from being turned into cassoulet by contacting the local militant vegetarians – the Troglodists – who live in the sewers and make it their business to interfere in the vile plans of the meat-eaters above ground. A totally mad, cartoon-like style and a novel point of view make this film one of the most original debuts of '91. [BW]

Cast includes: Dominique Pinon (Louison), Marie-Laure Dougnac (Julie), Jean-Claude Dreyfus (butcher), Rufus (Robert), Ticky Holgado (husband), Anne-Marie Pisani (wife), Silvie Laguna, Jean-Francois Perrier, Dominique Zardi, Karin Viard, Chick Ortega.

Dir: Jean-Pierre Jeunet and Marc Caro. Pro: Claudie Ossard. Screenplay: Jeunet, Caro and Gilles Adrien. Ph: Darius Khondji. Ed: Herve Schneid. Pro Des: Jean-Philippe Carp. M: Carlos D'Alessio. Sound: Jerome Thiault. (Constellation/UGC/Hachette Premiere–Electric.) Rel: 3 January 1992. 97 mins. Cert 15.

Doc Hollywood. Sweet, innocuous romantic comedy about a Hollywood-bound would-be plastic surgeon stuck in 'Hee-Haw hell'. Having run over the judge's white picket fence on the outskirts of a South Carolina town, Dr Ben Stone (Michael J. Fox) is sentenced to 32 hours of community service, during which time he falls in love with ambulance driver Lou. Newcomer Julie Warner is a real find as Lou, while Fox settles pleasantly into the role of light leading man. Some delightful characters and neat touches of comic invention make this an agreeable diversion. Dare one say that this is as close as we're likely to get to a modern, home-grown Capraesque fable? [JC-W]

Also with: Barnard Hughes (Dr Hogue), Woody Harrelson (Hank), David Ogden Stiers (Nick Nicholson), Frances Sternhagen (Lillian), Bridget Fonda (Nancy Lee), George Hamilton (Dr Halberstrom), Roberts Blossom (Judge Evans), Eyde Byrde (Nurse Packer), Mel Winkler, Helen Martin, Tom Lacy, Macon McCalman, Raye Birk, William Cowart, Amzie Strickland, Time Winters, Kelly Jo Minter, Michael Caton-Jones, Michael Chapman.

Dir: Michael Caton-Jones. Pro: Susan Solt and Deborah D. Johnson. Ex Pro: Marc Merson. Screenplay: Jeffrey Price, Peter S. Seaman and Daniel Pyne; from Neil B. Shulman's book *'What? . . . Dead Again?'* Ph: Michael Chapman. Ed: Priscilla Nedd-Friendly. Pro Des: Lawrence Miller. M: Carter Burwell; numbers performed by Chesney Hawkes, Patsy Cline, Buckwheat Zydeco etc. Costumes: Richard Hornung. Sound: Richard King. (Warner.) Rel: 18 October 1991. 104 mins. Cert 12.

Docteur Petiot is a tireless MD, a devoted husband and father and a great lover of small children. He is also helping Jews to escape Nazi-occupied Paris. A surreal, stylised film, drained of primary colours, *Docteur Petiot* holds the attention thanks to Michel Serrault's bizarre, manic central performance. Dashing around Paris at the rate of knots, roughhousing patients with a

Family man, antiques collector and serial killer: the superb Michel Serrault as Docteur Petiot *(from Electric).*

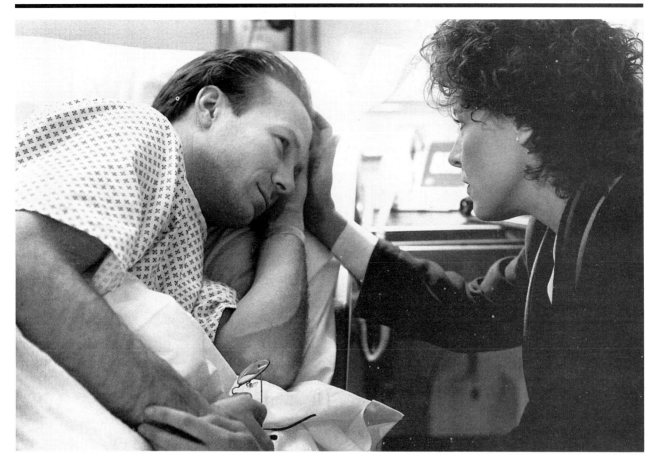

Doctor's orders: William Hurt as the surgeon-turned-patient, with wife Christine Lahti, in Randa Haines's compassionate, trenchant comedy-drama The Doctor *(from Warner).*

good-natured *bonhomie*, Marcel Petiot is an enigma. Then, absentmindedly, he chucks aside a severed head he has been carrying in his bag. A former mayor of Villeneuve, Petiot is in fact France's most notorious serial killer (convicted of 27 murders, admitting to 63), a fiendishly clever man with boundless energy. Petiot's victims were all Jews, whose life savings he pocketed while he 'protected' them from the Nazis – permanently. A fascinating, unsettling, sinister film from a master filmmaker. [JC-W]

Also with: Pierre Romans (Drezner), Zbigniew Horoks (Nathan Guzik), Berangère Bonvoisin (Georgette Petiot), Maxime Collion (Gerard Petiot), Aurore Prieto, Andre Chaumeau, Axel Bogousslavski, André Julien, Nini Crepon, Nita Klein, Martine Mongermont.

Dir: Christian de Chalonge. Pro: Alain Sarde and Philippe Chapelier-Dehesdin. Screenplay: de Chalonge and Dominique Garnier. Ph: Patrick Blossier. Ed: Anita Fernandez. Pro Des: Yves Brover. M: Michel Portal. Sound: Marie-Jeanne Wyckmans. (MS Pro/Sara Films/Canal +/Sofica Investimage/Investimage 2–Electric.) Rel: 25 October 1991. 102 mins. Cert 12.

The Doctor. Jack Mackee (William Hurt) is a top San Francisco heart surgeon with a good life. Blessed with a wacky sense of graveside humour, he believes the fastest route to a cure is a straight line – followed by a suture. He is a 'get in, fix it, get out' kinda guy. When he's told – bluntly – that he has a tumour on his throat, he sees, for the first time, the real pain of being a patient. Yet there is still something else he has to learn – the trauma of being a patient's spouse. Director Randa Haines (*Children of a Lesser God*) fought Disney to retain the hard edge of her film, and the effort pays off. Some scenes in the operating theatre may put off the squeamish, but even these are loaded with humour. Hurt is at the top of his form as an impatient, intelligent man encountering new emotions, while the two women in his life, played by Christine Lahti and Elizabeth Perkins, give him a run for his money. A harrowing, funny, touching film, served by a superb, literate script. [JC-W]

Also with: Christine Lahti (Anne MacKee), Elizabeth Perkins (June Ellis), Mandy Patinkin (Murray Caplan), Adam Arkin (Eli Blumfield), Charlie Korsmo (Nicky), Wendy Crewson (Leslie Abbott), Bill Macy, J. E. Freeman, William Marquez, Kyle Secor, Nicole Orth-Pallavicini, Richard McKenzie, Nancy Parsons.

Dir: Randa Haines. Pro: Laura Ziskin. Ex Pro: Edward S. Feldman. Screenplay: Robert Caswell; based on the book *A Taste of My Own Medicine* by Ed Rosenbaum, MD. Ph: John Seale. Ed: Bruce Green and Lisa Fruchtman. Pro Des: Ken Adam. M: Michael Convertino; numbers performed by Frankie Valli and The Four Seasons, Jimmy Buffett, Laurie Anderson etc. Costumes: Joe I. Tompkins. Sound: Jerry Ross. (Touchstone/Silver Screen-Warner.) Rel: 10 April 1992. 123 mins. Cert 12.

Don't Tell Her It's Me. Charleston, South Carolina, 1990. Bizarre romantic comedy starring Steve Guttenberg as Gus Kubiak, a cartoonist recovering from Hodgkin's disease. Bald and bloated, Gus is unable to win the heart of beautiful journalist Emily Pear, whom he describes as 'the Playmate of the Millennium'. Enter Lizzie, Gus's sister, romance novelist and part-time matchmaker who transforms her brother (with the help of nature and bodybuilding) into a handsome New Zealand biker. A really dumb film that is so offbeat that it is almost charming. Previously known as *The Boyfriend School*. [JC-W]

Also with: Jami Gertz (Emily Pear), Shelley Long (Lizzie Potts), Kyle MacLachlan (Trout), Kevin Scannell (Mitchell), Mark Hudson, Madchen Amick, Perry Anzilotti, Nada Despotovich, Beth Grant, Don Hood, Sally Elizabeth Lund, Caroline Paige Lund.

Dir: Malcolm Mowbray. Pro: George G. Braunstein and Ron Hamady. Ex Pro: John Daly and Derek Gibson. Screenplay: Sarah Bird; based on her novel *The Boyfriend School*. Ph: Reed Smoot. Ed: Marshall Harvey. Pro Des: Linda Pearl. M: Michael Gore. Costumes: Carol Wood. (Sovereign Pictures–Rank.) Rel: 17 January 1992. 102 mins. Cert 12.

Don't Tell Mom the Babysitter's Dead. Los Angeles, 1991. Five undisciplined, rebellious kids are left at home alone when their ancient babysitter ('a deranged Mary Poppins') drops dead of natural causes. Faced with 'a negative

Mary Poppins meets heavy metal: Eda Reiss Merin as the nanny from hell, in Stephen Herek's quite amusing Don't Tell Mom the Baby-sitter's Dead *(from First Independent).*

cash-flow' problem, the brood have to fend for themselves until the return of Mom – in two months' time. A lively, funny and well-plotted mix of *Risky Business* and *The Secret of My Success* that knows its audience. Sentimental and predictable, but efficient. [JC-W]

Cast includes: Christina Applegate (Sue Ellen 'Swell' Crandell), Joanna Cassidy (Rose Lindsey), John Getz (Gus Brandon), Josh Charles (Bryan), Keith Coogan (Kenny Crandell), Concetta Tomei (Mom), Kimmy Robertson (Cathy), Jayne Brook (Carolyn), Eda Reiss Merin (Mrs Sturak), Robert Hy Gorman (Walter Crandell), Danielle Harris (Melissa Crandell), Christopher Pettiet (Zach Crandell), Sydney Lassick (Franklin), David Duchovny, Chris Claridge, Jeff Bollow, Michael Kopelow, Alejandro Quezada, Wendy Brainard, Sarah Buxton, Kawena Charlot, Laurie Morrison, Deborah Tucker, Michelle Mais, Frank Dent, Bryan Clark, Christopher Plummer.

Dir: Stephen Herek. Pro: Robert Newmyer, Brian Reilly and Jeffrey Silver. Ex Pro: Michael Phillips. Assoc Pro: Caroline Baron. Screenplay: Neil Landau and Tara Ison. Ph: Tim Suhrstedt. Ed: Larry Bock. Pro Des: Stephen Marsh. M: David Newman; numbers performed by Beat Goes Bang, Flame, Timothy B. Schmit, Boom Crash Opera, Army of Lovers, Modern English, Valentine, Spinal Tap etc. Costumes: Carol Ramsey. Sound: Leslie Hatz. (HBO/ Cinema Plus LP/Mercury/Douglas/Outlaw –First Independent.) Rel: 22 May 1992. 105 mins. Cert 12.

Double Impact. Jean-Claude Van Damme, the muscles from Brussels,

returns to Hong Kong to play twin brothers avenging their father's death. It's endearing to watch Van Damme try so hard to act (the one brother bright-eyed and bushy-tailed, the other snarling a lot), and the locations are well filmed by veteran cinematographer Richard Kline. Six-times Ms Olympia Cory Everson makes a stimulating villainess, but the acting is of the robotic variety, the stunts unimaginative and the mix of violence and sentimentality very unwholesome. [JC-W]

Cast includes: Jean-Claude Van Damme (Chad/Alex), Geoffrey Lewis (Frank Avery), Alan Scarfe (Nigel Griffith), Philip Chan Yan Kin (Raymond Zhang), Alonna Shaw (Danielle Wilde), Cory Everson (Kara), Sarah-Jane Varley, Andy Armstrong, Bolo Yeung, Kamel Krifa, Peter Malota.

Dir: Sheldon Lettich. Pro: Ashok Amritraj and Jean-Claude Van Damme. Ex Pro: Moshe Diamant and Charles Layton. Co-Pro: Lettich and Terry Martin Carr. Screenplay: Lettich and Van Damme. Ph: Richard Kline. Ed: Mark Conte. Pro Des: John Jay Moore. M: Arthur Kempel. Costumes: Joseph Porro. Stunt coordinator: Vic Armstrong. Fight choreography: Van Damme. (Stone Group–Columbia.) Rel: 31 January 1992. 100 mins. Cert 18.

The Double Life of Veronique – La Double Vie de Veronique. Sensual, enigmatic story of two 20-year-old women, both singers, one Polish, the other French. Although of different nationalities, the women – Weronika and Veronique – feel a closeness with one another. They have never met, but share the same pain . . . From the director of *A Short Film About Killing* and *A Short Film About Love*, this Polish-French co-production demands one's full concentration, but rewards us with its emotional and aesthetic power. Irene Jacob, in the dual role, is simply sensational. Winner of the International Film Critics' prize and Best Actress award at the 1991 Cannes festival. [JC-W]

Also with: Philippe Volter (Alexandre Fabbri), Aleksander Bardini (the conductor), Louis Ducreux (the professor), Sandrine Dumas (Catherine), Claude Duneton (Veronique's father), Halina Gryglaszewska (the aunt), Kalina Jedrusik (the gaudy woman), Wladyslaw Kowalski, Jerzy Gudejko, Lorraine Evanoff.

Dir: Krzysztof Kieslowski. Pro: Leonardo De La Fuente. Ex Pro: Bernard-P. Guiremand. Screenplay: Kieslowski and Krzysztof Piesiewicz. Ph: Slawomir Idziak. Ed: Jacques Witta. Art: Patrice Mercier. M:

Twin piques: the sensational Irene Jacob contemplates her doppelganger in Kryzysztof Kieslowski's probing The Double Life of Veronique *(from Gala).*

Zbigniew Preisner. (Sideral/Tor/Le Studio Canal Plus–Gala.) Rel: 28 February 1992. 98 mins. Cert 15.

Double X. Hopelessly inept thriller that joyfully breaks all the ground rules of filmmaking. Norman Wisdom – in his first large screen role for 23 years – plays Arthur Clutten, an old safecracker who decides to retire from The Organisation. However, his boss (Bernard Hill doing Dr Strangelove) believes Rigby's commitment should be 'till death do us part'. Literally . . . But old Rigby 'has a plan'. Yes, Norman Wisdom can still make us laugh – albeit unintentionally this time round. (Previously known as *Double X – The Name of the Game*.) [JC-W]

Also with: William Katt (Michael Cooper), Gemma Craven (Jenny), Simon Ward (Edward Ross), Bernard Hill (Iggy), Chloe Annett (Sarah Clutten), Leon Herbert, Vladek Sheybal, Derren Nesbitt.
　Dir, Pro and Screenplay: Shani S. Grewal. Ex Pro: Noel Cronin. Ph: Dominique Grosz. Ed: Alfie Cox. Pro Des: Colin Pocock. M: Raf Ravenscroft. Costumes:

Andrew Edwards and John Cowell. (String of Pearls–Feature Film Co.) Rel: 5 June 1992. 97 mins. Cert 15.

Driving Me Crazy (US: *Dutch*). Intermittently funny, drippingly sentimental, production-line road comedy from writer-producer John Hughes, employing plot segments from Hughes' *Planes, Trains and Automobiles*, *Uncle Buck* and *Curly Sue*. TV's Ed O'Neill (*Married . . . With Children*) stars as the well-meaning, working-class Dutch Dooley who volunteers to drive his new girlfriend's 13-year-old son from Atlanta to Chicago. Trouble is, Doyle Standish (Ethan Randall) is a spoilt, selfish and generally insufferable snob, who looks down on Dutch and is determined to make his life hell. You've seen it all before, but the trip is reasonably diverting. [JC-W]

Also with: JoBeth Williams (Natalie), Christopher McDonald (Reed), Ari Meyers (Brock), E(lizabeth) G. Daily (Halley), L. Scott Caldwell (homeless woman).
　Dir: Peter Faiman. Pro: John Hughes and Richard Vane. Ex Pro: Tarquin Gotch. Screenplay: Hughes. Ph: Charles Minsky. Ed: Paul Hirsch and Adam Bernardi. Pro Des: Stan Jolley. M: Alan Silvestri; numbers performed by Little Caesar, The Ventures, 2YZ, Yello, Dwight Yoakim, Johnny Cash etc. Costumes: Jennifer Parsons. Sound: Stephan Von Hase. (Hughes Enter-

tainment–Fox.) Rel: 24 January 1992. 107 mins. Cert 12.

Drop Dead Fred. When she was young, Elizabeth Cronin (Phoebe Cates) had an imaginary friend to help her in moments of extreme unhappiness. Twenty-one years later, she loses

With friends like him, who needs nightmares? Phoebe Cates and Rik Mayall in the utterly infantile Drop Dead Fred *(from Rank).*

Designer fatality: Julia Roberts and Campbell Scott love and weep in Joel Schumacher's Dying Young *(from Fox).*

all her money, her car, job and husband in one lunch hour and soon 'Drop Dead Fred' is back in her life. As portrayed by Rik Mayall, Fred is no friendly white rabbit, but a destructive demon who elicits laughs from Elizabeth by smearing snot on her face and rubbing dog shit in her mother's expensive carpet. Marsha Mason as Mom is the villainess of the piece, relegated to third-billing for once banishing Elizabeth's friend after a particularly horrendous prank. Count me in with Marsha. Somewhere there's an interesting movie here, but this manic, infantile and scatalogical version isn't it. Besides, I like expensive carpets. [JC-W]

Also with: Tim Matheson (Charles), Carrie Fisher (Janie), Keith Charles (Murray), Daniel Gerroll (Nigel), Ashley Peldon (Young Elizabeth), Ron Eldard (Mickey Bunce), Bridget Fonda (Annabella), Eleanor Mondale, Bob Reid, Peter Thoemke, Steve Cochran.

Dir: Ate de Jong. Pro: Paul Webster. Ex Pro: Tim Bevan, Carlos Davis and Anthony Fingleton. Screenplay: Davis and Fingleton; from a story by Elizabeth Livingston. Ph: Peter Deming. Ed: Marshall Harvey. Pro Des: Joseph T. Garrity. M: Randy Edelman. Costumes: Carol Wood. (Polygram/ Working Title–Rank.) Rel: 11 October 1991. 99 mins. Cert 12.

Dying Young. The healthy character is called O'Neal, the other is slowly dying and they're from opposite ends of the market. Oh yeah, and they're desperately in love. Yep, you guessed it, this is *Love Story* updated for the '90s – with Julia Roberts not so much making love to Campbell Scott as to the camera. That's the good news (at least, for us guys). Campbell Scott (son of George C.) smiles enigmatically a lot and throws up when he's not being charming. The music is suitably tender, the photography suitably lush and the dialogue unbelievable ('I have only one thing to give you – my heart'). Unfortunately, these are not characters we can believe in or even care about, but Julia Roberts looks great in a mini-skirt. [JC-W]

Cast includes: Julia Roberts (Hilary O'Neal), Campbell Scott (Victor Geddes), Vincent D'Onofrio (Gordon), Colleen Dewhurst (Estelle Whittier), David Selby (Richard Geddes), Ellen Burstyn (Mrs O'Neal), Dion Anderson (Cappy), George Martin (Malachi), A. J. Johnson (Shauna), Daniel Beer, Behrooz Afrakhan, Michael Halton.

Dir: Joel Schumacher. Pro: Sally Field and Kevin McCormick. Screenplay: Richard Friedenberg; from the novel by Marti Leimbach. Ph: Juan Ruiz Anchia. Ed: Robert Brown. Art: Guy J. Comtois. M: James Newton Howard. Costumes: Susan Becker. Sound: David MacMillan. (Fogwood Films–Fox.) Rel: 30 August 1991. 112 mins. Cert 12.

Edward Scissorhands. Following the commercial success of *Batman*, Twentieth Century-Fox were keen to let Tim Burton realise his own personal project. The result is this quirky, funny, modern fairy tale, both a sweet, touching allegory and a satirical stab at suburban America. Edward (Johnny Depp) is a gentle abomination, a man-boy-machine with 12-inch scissors instead of hands. But Edward's creator

(Vincent Price) dies before he can repair the damage. Up pops Avon lady Peg Boggs (Dianne Wiest), who discovers the frightened, lonely Edward in his deserted castle. Without thinking of the consequences, she adopts the boy and tries to infiltrate him into modern suburban society. Here, Burton has the most fun, pitting the barbecue set against the unknown and coming up with some magical ideas. The tragedy of Edward is that, though he is different, he is not a monster, and although he can touch our heart he cannot *physically* touch his loved ones. Instead, he indulges in a bit of topiary and hairdressing which turns him into a local celebrity. Both children and adults should love this weird, delightful abnormality. [JC-W]

Also with: Winona Ryder (Kim Boggs), Anthony Michael Hall (Jim), Kathy Baker (Joyce Monroe), Alan Arkin (Bill Boggs), Robert Oliveri (Kevin Boggs), Conchata Ferrell, Caroline Aaron, Dick Anthony Williams, O-Lan Jones, John Davidson, Biff Yeager, John McMahon, Victoria Price, Aaron Lustig, Alan Fudge, Peter Palmer, Red Fox.
 Dir: Tim Burton. Pro: Burton and Denise Di Novi. Ex Pro: Richard Hashimoto. Screenplay: Caroline Thompson; from a story by Burton and Thompson. Ph: Stefan Czapsky. Ed: Richard Halsey. Pro Des: Bo Welch. M: Danny Elfman; numbers performed by Tom Jones. Costumes: Colleen Atwood. Sound: Petur Hliddal. Make-up effects: Stan Winston. (Fox.) Rel: 26 July 1991. 105 mins. Cert PG.

Edward II. Derek Jarman's bold – some might say brazen – gay film about the homosexual English king. A stripped-to-the-bone adaptation of Christopher Marlowe's play about the monarch whose sexual preferences eventually brought about a civil war. Jarman, using modern dress and settings, uses this as a pretext for a diatribe about the way homosexuals are treated in Britain today. [FMS]

Cast: Steven Waddington (Edward II), Kevin Collins (Lightborn), Andrew Tiernan (Gaveston), John Lynch (Spencer), Dudley Sutton (Bishop of Winchester), Tilda Swinton (Isabella), Jerome Flynn (Kent), Jody Graber (Prince Edward), Nigel Terry (Mortimer), Jill Balcon, Barbara New, Andrea Miller, Brian Mitchell, David Glover, John Quentin, Andrew Charleson, Roger Hammond, Allan Corduner, Annie Lennox, Tony Forsyth, Lloyd Newson, Nigel Charnock etc.

Shear delight: Johnny Depp as Edward Scissorhands, part-man, part-machine, part-scissors.

Historical licence: Steven Waddington in the title role of Edward II (from Palace), Derek Jarman's return-to-form.

Eccentrics abroad: Michael Kitchen and Polly Walker take the moonlight in Miramax's charming Enchanted April.

Dir: Derek Jarman. Pro: Steve Clark-Hall and Antony Root. Screenplay: Jarman, Stephen McBride and Ken Butler. Ex Pro: Sara Radclyffe and Simon Curtis. Ph: Ian Wilson. Ed: George Akers. Pro Des: Christopher Hobbs. Art: Rick Eyres. M: Simon Fisher Turner. (British Films and BBC Working Title Pro/Jarman–Palace Pictures.) Rel: 18 October 1991. 88 mins. Cert 18.

1871. Lavish, sprawling, technically first-class and well acted if somewhat static music drama about the uprising of the left-wing French Commune against Napoleon III, which left more than 25,000 dead. Action-packed historical spectacular. [FDM]

Cast: Roshan Seth (Lord Grafton), Ana Padrao (Severine), John Lynch (O'Brien), Jack Claff (Cluseret), Timothy Spall (Ramborde), Maria de Medeiros (Maria), Jacqueline Dankworth, Ian McNeice, Dominique Pinon, Mel Hondo (Karl Marx), Cedric Michaels, Jack Rieff, Carlos Cesar, Jose Pedro Ruivo, Bill Shaw etc.

Dir: Ken McMullen. Pro: Stewart Richards. Ex Pro: McMullen, Anders Palm, Lars Johannson, Antonio da Cunha and Telles. Assoc Pro: Oliver Stewart. Screenplay: Terry James, James Leahy and Ken McMullen. Ph: Elso Roque. Ed: William Diver. Pro Des: Paul Cheetham. Art: Joao Martins. M: Barrie Guard. (Film Four International in assoc with La Sept (France) – ICA.) Rel: 19 July 1991. 100 mins. Cert 15.

Enchanted April. To escape the April showers of a depressed, post-war London, oppressed housewife Lottie Wilkins (Josie Lawrence in her film debut) answers a personal ad in *The Times* and hires an Italian castle for a month. With no friends of her own, she is forced to share the rent with a trio of female strangers. Released from her wifely position, Lottie is transformed, and in turn transforms the lives of her three new friends. Adapted by Peter Barnes from the novel by Elizabeth Von Arnim, *Enchanted April* captures the flavour and dialogue of the original with an authoritative sixth sense. A delicious piece of British filmmaking, superbly acted and sensitively directed. [JC-W]

Also with: Miranda Richardson (Rose), Polly Walker (Lady Caroline), Joan Plowright (Mrs Fisher), Alfred Molina (Mellersh Wilkins), Michael Kitchen (Mr Briggs), Jim Broadbent (Frederick Arbuthnot), Neville Phillips, Stephen Beckett, Vittorio Duse.

Dir: Mike Newell. Pro: Ann Scott. Ex Pro: Mark Shivas and Simon Relph. Screenplay: Peter Barnes. Ph: Rex Maidment. Ed: Dick Allen. Pro Des: Malcolm Thornton. M: Richard Rodney Bennett. Costumes: Sheena Napier. Sound: John Pritchard. (BBC/Greenpoint–Miramax.) Rel: 29 November 1991. 95 mins. Cert U.

Europa (US: *Zentropa*). You could either view this as an imaginative, boldly original masterpiece or as a gimmicky, pretentious pile of celluloid. Actually, *Europa* is a brave piece of cinema that doesn't always work. Exploring the political dichotomy of Germany at the end of World War II, the film features Jean-Marc Barr as a young American who visits the Fatherland to show compassion to his forebears' country. Far from being welcomed by his family, he is plunged into a Kafkaesque nightmare, taking a job

French actor and British resident Jean-Marc Barr plays an American of German ancestry in Lars Von Trier's fractured, surreal Europa *(from Electric).*

Joakim Holbek. Costumes: Manon Rasmussen. Sound: Per Streit Jensen. (Nordisk Film & TV–Electric.) Rel: 17 April 1992. 117 mins. Cert 15.

as a sleeping car conductor and manipulated by all around him. Shot in black-and-white, but periodically highlighting salient objects and characters in colour, the film lurches from one dream-like sequence to another, while Max Von Sydow's hypnotic voice-over drones away on the soundtrack. A Danish-French-German-Swedish co-production. [JC-W]

Cast includes: Jean-Marc Barr (Leopold Kessler), Barbara Sukowa (Katharina Hartmann), Udo Kier (Lawrence Hartmann), Ernst-Hugo Jaregard (Uncle Kessler), Eddie Constantine (Colonel Harris), Erik Mork, Jorgen Reenberg, Henning Jensen, Lars Von Trier, Max Von Sydow (narrator).
    Dir: Lars Von Trier. Pro: Peter Aalbaek Jensen and Bo Christensen. Ex Pro: Gerard Mital, Gunnar Obel, Patrick Godeau and Francois Duplat. Screenplay: Von Trier and Niels Vorsel. Ph: Henning Bendtsen, Jean-Paul Meurisse and Edward Klosinsky. Ed: Herve Schneid. Pro Des: Henning Bahs. M:

Europa, Europa. Multi-award-winning Franco-German epic about a handsome, 14-year-old Jewish boy who enlists with the Nazis to save his skin.

An extraordinary true story, *Europa, Europa* grabs the attention from the opening scene in which Solly (Marco Hofschneider) recalls his circumcision. It is this sacred act that plagues Solly

Incredible, but true: Marco Hofschneider as the Jewish Nazi in Agnieszka Holland's award-laden Europa, Europa *(from Arrow Films).*

Marcello Mastroianni unknowingly babysits for his own grandchild in Giuseppe Tornatore's moving Everybody's Fine *(from Rank).*

in the war years as he resists the advances of a homosexual Nazi and the beautiful, anti-Semitic Leni (Julie Delpy), and attempts to force-grow a foreskin (in a painfully explicit sequence). The film flows with a cinematic flourish from scene to scene, artfully displaying Solly's political and emotional confusion. Voted best foreign film by the New York and Boston Film Critics' Circles, the US National Board of Review and the Hollywood Foreign Press Association. [JC-W]

Cast includes: Marco Hofschneider (Solomon Perel – aka Solly/Josef Peters/'Jupp'), Ashley Wanninger (Gerd), Solomon Perel (himself as an old man), Rene Hofschneider (Isaak Perel), Klaus Abramowsky, Nathalie Schmidt, Delphine Forest, Andrzej Mastalerz, Martin Maria Blau, Klaus Kowatsch, Holger Hunkel, Andre Wilms, Hanns Zichler, Jorg Schnass, Halina Labonarska.

Dir and Screenplay: Agnieszka Holland; from Solomon Perel's autobiography. Pro: Margaret Menegoz and Artur Brauner. Ph: Jacek Petrycki. Ed: Ewa Small and Isabelle Lorente. Pro Des: Allan Starski. M: Zbigniew Preisner. Costumes: Wieslawa Starska and Malgorzata Stefaniak. Sound: Elisabeth Mondi. (Les Films Du Losange [Paris]/CCC Filmkunst [Berlin]–Arrow Films.) Rel: 15 May 1992. 115 mins. Cert 15.

Everybody's Fine – Stanno Tutti Bene. Matteo Scuro, 74, Sicilian civil servant, just loves his five children, who are scattered across the mainland of Italy. On a whim he decides to visit each and every one – in Naples, Rome, Milan and Turin – without telling them. An unpractised tourist, he chats away to his fellow passengers, telling them about his five offspring – who, in his eyes, are all successful in their chosen fields. But Matteo has six harsh lessons to learn, the last about himself. *Everybody's Fine* is another masterful slice of cinema from Giuseppe Tornatore, who previously directed the Oscar-winning *Cinema Paradiso*. Tornatore's new film is equally saturated in sentimentality, but is so visually arresting, so well told, that it is all part and parcel of the same experience. Marcello Mastroianni is terribly affecting as the pathetic old man and Ennio Morricone's score is a classic. Probably the saddest film of the year. [JC-W]

Also with: Michele Morgan (lady in the train), Marino Cenna (Canio), Roberto Nobile (Guglielmo), Valeria Cavali (Tosca), Norma Martelli (Norma), Salvatore Cascio ('Little Alvaro'), Antonella Attili, Giorgio Libassi, Giocchino Civiletti, Nicola De Pinto, Sylvie Fennec, Christopher Thompson.

Dir: Giuseppe Tornatore. Pro: Angelo Rizzoli. Ex Pro: Mario Cotone. Screenplay: Tornatore, Tonino Guerra and Massimo De Rita. Ph: Blasco Giurato. Ed: Mario Morra. Art: Andrea Crisanti. M: Ennio Morricone. (Sovereign–Rank.) Rel: 2 August 1991. 126 mins. Cert 12.

Father of the Bride. An LA tennis shoe manufacturer attempts to come to terms with his only daughter getting married. However, losing his daughter is one thing, the wedding is another – especially when each guest is going to cost him $250! A sentimental, slapstick re-make of the 1950 classic, with Steve Martin an unlikely (and uncomfortable) choice in the old Spencer Tracy role. Still, the movie pushes all the right buttons, although its message of paying dearly for love leaves a lot to be desired. Phoebe Cates was due to play the daughter (essayed by Elizabeth Taylor in the original), but pulled out when she got pregnant. Newcomer Kimberly Williams is a suitable replacement in her first professional role. Scripted by husband-and-wife team Charles Shyer and Nancy Meyers (*Baby Boom, Irreconcilable Differences*). [JC-W]

Cast includes: Steve Martin (George Stanley Banks), Diane Keaton (Nina Banks), Kimberly Williams (Annie Banks), Martin Short (Franck), George Newbern (Bryan MacKenzie), Kieran Culkin (Matty Banks), B. D. Wong (Howard Weinstein), Peter Michael Goetz (John MacKenzie), Kate McGregor Stewart (Joanna MacKenzie), Carmen Hayward, Richard Portnow, Martha Gehman, Hallie Meyers-Shyer, Annie Meyers-Shyer, Patricia Meyers, Irving Meyers, Steve Tyrell, Eugene Levy, Tom Irish.

Dir: Charles Shyer. Pro: Nancy Meyers, Carol Baum and Howard Rosenman. Ex Pro: Sandy Gallin, James Orr and Jim Cruickshank. Co-Pro: Cindy Williams. Screenplay: Meyers, Shyer, Frances Goodrich and Albert Hackett; based on the novel by Edward Streeter. Ph: John Lindley. Ed:

The man in the middle: Steve Martin, flanked by Diane Keaton and Kimberly Williams, grapples with nuptial tradition in Warner's diverting remake Father of the Bride.

Richard Marks. Pro Des: Sandy Veneziano. M: Alan Silvestri; numbers performed by The Temptations, The Dixie Cups, Darlene Love, Steve Tyrell etc. Costumes: Susan Becker. Sound: C. Darin Knight. (Touchstone/Touchwood Pacific Partners/Sandollar Prods–Warner.) Rel: 21 February 1992. 105 mins. Cert PG.

The Favour, the Watch and the Very Big Fish. The strange story of a virginal devotional photographer, a psychotic pianist and a mysterious woman. Based on a 10-page story by Marcel Ayme (*Uranus*), and filmed in Paris, this stylised, quirky comedy is oddly endearing in its own eccentric way, as it glides from one coincidental event to another. Bob Hoskins is unusually

A very tall tale: ex-con Jeff Goldblum lets religion go to his halo – in Ben Lewin's unusual The Favour, the Watch and the Very Big Fish *(from Rank)*.

A double life: Colin Firth and Lisa Zane in Andre Guttfreund's Femme Fatale *(from Republic).*

affecting as the gullible cameraman in search of a photogenic Christ, Jeff Goldblum unpredictably amusing as the man for the job and Natasha Richardson delightful as the woman who unites and divides them. The fish is a red herring. [JC-W]

Cast includes: Bob Hoskins (Louis Aubinard), Jeff Goldblum (pianist), Natasha Richardson (Sybil), Michel Blanc (Norbert), Jean-Pierre Cassel (Zalman), Sacha Vikouloff (violinist), Jacques Villeret, Angela Pleasence, Samuel Chaimovitch, Carlos Kloster, Gerard Zalcberg, Pamela Goldblum, Caroline Jacquin.

Dir and Screenplay: Ben Lewin; from the short story *Rue Saint-Sulpice* by Marcel Ayme. Pro: Michelle De Broca. Ex Pro: Antoine de Clermont-Tonnerre. Co-Pro: Simon Perry. Ph: Bernard Zitzermann. Ed: John Grover. Pro Des: Carlos Conti. M: Vladimir Cosma. Costumes: Elisabeth Tavernier. Sound: Edward Tise. (Sovereign/A Films Ariane/Fildebroc/Umbrella Film–Rank.) Rel: 14 February 1992. 89 mins. Cert 15.

Femme Fatale. Another variation on the old schizophrenic theme (remember Joanne Woodward in the classic *Three Faces of Eve*?). A nice young man meets, woos and wins a lovely young girl . . . but wakes up on the first morning of their honeymoon to find that she has vanished. Doggedly pursuing clues, he finds his wife in a wheelchair and entangled with a drugs ring. Flawed by an ambiguous ending, it's nevertheless quite watchable, with nice performances. Oddly, this film failed to get any cinema bookings in the US and went straight to video, though it did win a limited release in the UK. [FMS]

Cast: Colin Firth (Joe Prince), Lisa Zane (Elizabeth/Cynthia/Maura), Billy Zane (Elijah), Scott Wilson (Dr Beaumont), Lisa Blount, Suzanne Snyder, Pat Skipper, John Laviachielli, Carmine Caridi.

Dir: Andre Guttfreund. Pro: Andrew Lane and Nancy Rae Stone. Ex Pro: Joel Levine. Screenplay: Michael Ferris and John D. Brancato. Ph: Joey Forsyte. Ed: Richard Candib. Pro Des: Pam Warner. Sound: Giovanni di Simone. (Gibraltar Entertainment–Republic Pictures.) Rel: 18 October 1991. 96 mins. Cert 15.

Final Analysis. San Francisco, 1991. Terrific corkscrew thriller with Richard Gere as an altruistic psychiatrist caught up in the dangerous lives of two seductive sisters. Modifying the rules of his profession, Gere finds himself trapped in an impossible scenario which he rides with the cunning of a man at the top of his field. But who really has the upper hand – doctor, patient or police detective? Spielberg protégé Phil Joanou (*State of Grace*) frames his film in telling close-ups, but then slowly opens up the narrative into a Hitchcockian rollercoaster ride. Flavour-of-the-month screenwriter Wesley Strick (*Arachnophobia*, *Cape Fear*, *Batman Returns*) revels in the pocketbook psychobabble, but twists his plot once too often for credibility. [JC-W]

Cast includes: Richard Gere (Isaac Barr), Kim Basinger (Heather Evans), Uma Thurman (Diana Baylor), Eric Roberts (Jimmy Evans/Dimitri Vandalous), Paul Guilfoyle (Mike O'Brien), Keith David (Det. Huggins), Robert Harper (Alan Lowenthal), Augustin Rodriguez (Pepe Carrero), Rita Zohar (Dr Grusin), Tony Genaro (Hector), Harris Yulin (DA Brakhage), George Murdock, Shirley Prestia, Katherine Cortez, Wood Moy, Derick Alexander.

Dir: Phil Joanou. Pro: Charles Roven, Paul Junger Witt and Tony Thomas. Ex Pro: Richard Gere and Maggie Wilde. Screenplay: Wesley Strick; from a story by Strick and Robert Berger. Ph: Jordan Cronenweth. Ed: Thom Noble. Pro Des: Dean Tavoularis. M: George Fenton. Costumes: Aude Bronson-Howard; Giorgio Armani. Sound: Blake Leyh. (Warner.) Rel: 10 April 1992. 125 mins. Cert 15.

The Fisher King. Beware, you are in Terry Gilliam country. Transporting the Arthurian Percival legend to contemporary New York, Gilliam excels in magnificent fantasy sequences and illusions, while turning New York into a Kafkaesque nightmare. Jeff Bridges plays a successful, anarchic disc jockey who becomes inadvertently responsible for a mass-killing. Turning in his career and his life, he is spiritually saved by an encounter with the husband of one of his 'victims', a life-loving loony played by Robin Williams. There's plenty to admire in this overlong, $24 million piece of self-indulgence and plenty to bore you silly, so you'll either go with it or hate it. For me, there was too much ranting and raving by half. [JC-W]

Cast includes: Robin Williams (Parry), Jeff Bridges (Jack Lucas), Amanda Plummer (Lydia), Mercedes Ruehl (Anne Napolitano), Michael Jeter, Ted Ross, Lara Harris, Kathy Najimy, Harry Shearer, Richard LaGravenese, Christian Clemenson.

Dir: Terry Gilliam. Pro: Debra Hill and Lynda Obst. Screenplay: Richard LaGravenese. Ph: Roger Pratt. Ed: Lesley Walker. Pro Des: Mel Bourne. M: George Fenton. Costumes: Beatrix Pasztor. (Columbia Tri-Star.) Rel: 8 November 1991. 137 mins. Cert 15.

Prisoner of his dreams: Kim Basinger begs Richard Gere for help in Phil Joanou's cuticle-chewing thriller Final Analysis *(from Warner).*

The Five Heartbeats. North America, 1965 to the present day. Vibrant rags-to-riches musical-drama following the shaky spiral to success of a rhythm 'n' blues quintet. Written, produced, directed, co-starring and exhaustively researched by the multi-talented Robert Townsend (*Hollywood Shuffle*), the film is packed with cliché, sentimentality, melodrama and tremendous vocals – and is never less than entertaining. Loosely inspired by the vintage Chicago group The Dells. [JC-W]

Cast includes: Robert Townsend (Donald 'Duck' Matthews), Michael Wright (Eddie King Jr), Leon (James Thomas 'J.T.'

Cod royal: Robin Williams and Amanda Plummer in a rare moment of tenderness in Terry Gilliam's boisterous, aggressive romantic fantasy, The Fisher King *(from Columbia Tri-Star).*

School manners: Kym Wilson, Thandie Newton, Noah Taylor, Naomi Watts and the killing Bartholomew Rose in John Duigan's unforgettable, poetic Flirting *(from Warner).*

Matthews), Harry J. Lennix (Terrence 'Dresser' Williams), Tico Wells (Anthony 'Choirboy' Stone), Harold Nicholas (Ernest 'Sarge' Johnson), John Canada Terrell (Michael 'Flash' Turner), Chuck Patterson (Jimmy Potter), Hawthorne James (Big Red), Troy Beyer (Baby Doll), Carla Brothers (Tanya Sawyer), Diahann Carroll, Tressa Thomas, Roy Fegan, Deborah Lacey, Theresa Randle, John Witherspoon, Anne-Marie Johnson, Bobby McGee, Lamont Johnson, David McKnight, Phyllis Applegate, Paul Benjamin, Norma Donaldson, Freddie Asparagus, Christopher Bradley, Donnie Simpson.

Dir and Ex Pro: Robert Townsend. Pro: Loretha C. Jones. Screenplay: Townsend and Keenen Ivory Wayans. Co-Pro: Nancy Israel. Ph: Bill Dill. Ed: John Carter. Pro Des: Wynn Thomas. M: Stanley Clarke; numbers performed by Babydoll & The Crystals, Flash & The Ebony Sparks, The Dells, The Four Tops, The Delfonics, Jennifer Holiday, Patti Labelle, Billy Valentine etc. Costumes: Ruthe Carter. Choreography: Michael Peters. Sound: Richard

Hymns. (Fox.) Rel: 5 June 1992. 121 mins. Cert 15.

Flirting. 'Rural Australia', 1965. An intelligent, biting satire of boarding-school life that is never obvious, but terrifyingly real and often extremely funny. Memories of Quink Ink, *National Geographic* and obsessions with Ursula Andress are recalled, as well as all the embarrassments of growing up, girls and constipation. A sequel to the award-laden *The Year My Voice Broke*, and the second film in a proposed trilogy, *Flirting* is a cornucopia of wonderful moments, some tender, some horrific, some hilarious, all unexpected. Noah Taylor repeats his role as the pensive, shy Danny Embling, who is this time involved with an intelligent, beautiful student from Uganda, Thandiwe Adjewa (English newcomer Thandie Newton). Winner of four 1990 Australian Oscars, including one for Best Film. [JC-W]

Also with: Nicole Kidman (Nicola Radcliffe), Bartholomew Rose ('Gilby' Fryer), Felix Nobis (Jock Blair), Kym Wilson (Melissa Miles), Naomi Watts (Janet Odgers),

Malcolm Robertson (Bruce Embling), Judi Farr (Sheila Embling), Freddie Paris (Solomon Adjewa), Femi Taylor (Letitia Adjewa), Josh Picker, Kiri Paramore, Marc Gray, Greg Palmer, Jeff Truman, Marshall Napier, John Dicks, Lisa Spinadel, Francesca Raft, Gillian Hyde.

Dir and Screenplay: John Duigan. Pro: George Miller, Doug Mitchell and Terry Hayes. Assoc Pro: Barbara Gibbs. Ph: Geoff Burton. Ed: Robert Gibson. Pro Des: Roger Ford. M: Duigan, Vaughan Williams, Duke Ellington, The Troggs etc. (Kennedy Miller–Warner.) Rel: 25 October 1991. 100 mins. Cert PG.

For the Boys. The most expensive musical ever made (at $45 million), this is a flag-waving American history lesson of the twentieth century set to music. Spanning 50 years (1942–91), the story focuses on the love-hate relationship of a song-and-comedy duet, the sassy, toilet-mouthed Dixie Leonard (Bette Midler on all cylinders) and the predatory, ladies' man Eddie Sparks (James Caan). This is old-fashioned Hollywood manipulation – with brass bands on – that never misses a melodramatic moment. But it's done with such professional know-how (if not the style it begs for), that the film's 140 minutes pass entertainingly enough until the final, gushingly sentimental showdown. [JC-W]

Also with: George Segal (Art Silver), Patrick O'Neal (Shepard), Christopher Rydell (Danny), Arye Gross (Jeff Brooks), Normal Fell (Sam Schiff), Shannon Wilcox (Margaret Sparks), Rosemary Murphy, Bud York, Dori Brenner, Jack Sheldon, Karen Martin, Michael Green, Melissa Manchester, Richard Portnow, Brandon Call, Matthew Faison, Xander Berkeley, David Bowe.

Dir and Ex Pro: Mark Rydell. Pro: Bette Midler, Bonnie Bruckheimer and Margaret South. Co-Pro: Ray Hartwick. Screenplay: Marshall Brickman, Neal Jimenez and Lindy Laub. Ph: Stephen Goldblatt. Ed: Jerry Greenberg and Jere Huggins. Pro Des: Assheton Gorton. M: Dave Grusin. Costumes: Wayne Finkelman. (All Girl Prods–Fox.) Rel: 7 February 1992. 140 mins. Cert 15.

Frankie & Johnny. Slick, well-written romantic comedy about two losers trying to connect. Kathy Bates and F. Murray Abraham originated the roles of the shy waitress and short-order cook in the original New York play, and are glossed up here by Michelle Pfeiffer and Al Pacino in funny, charismatic versions. Pfeiffer is sensational, if ultimately unbelievable, as Frankie, a thirty-something woman permanently damaged by love, while Pacino piles on the charm and mannerisms as the cute ex-con in search of commitment. The script wins through in spite of the Hollywood treatment (and an overblown $29m budget), and the supporting cast is superb (with Kate Nelligan unrecognisable as a tough-talking floozy). [JC-W]

Also with: Hector Elizondo (Nick), Kate Nelligan (Cora), Nathan Lane (Frankie's neighbour Tim), Jane Morris (Nedda), Al Fann (Luther), Greg Lewis (Tino), Fernando Lopez (Jorge), Glenn Plummer (Peter), Ele Keats, Tim Hopper, Harvey Miller, Sean O'Bryan.

Dir and Pro: Garry Marshall. Ex Pro: Alexandra Rose and Charles Mulvehill. Co-Pro: Nick Abdo. Screenplay: Terrence McNally; based on his play *Frankie and Johnny in the Clair de Lune*. Ph: Dante Spinotti. Ed: Battle Davis and Jacqueline Cambas. Pro Des: Albert Brenner. M: Marvin Hamlisch. Costumes: Rosanna Norton. Sound: Keith A. Wester. (Paramount–UIP.) Rel: 17 January 1992. 117 mins. Cert 15.

Fifty years on: James Caan and Bette Midler entertain the troops in World War II, Korea and Vietnam – in Mark Rydell's epic musical melodrama For the Boys *(from Fox).*

Love at first bite: Michelle Pfeiffer and Al Pacino struggle for happiness in Garry Marshall's entertaining Frankie & Johnny *(from UIP).*

Dream on: A young Freddy Kreuger (Tobe Sexton, right) threatens his alcoholic father (Alice Cooper) in the obsolete Freddy's Dead: The Final Nightmare *(from Guild).*

Body language: Emilio Estevez (right) confronts Mick Jagger in a fight for the right to his own anatomy, in Geoff Murphy's Freejack *(from Warner).*

Freddy's Dead – The Final Nightmare. Sixth in the *A Nightmare on Elm Street* series created by Wes Craven, this one purports to be the last – however, be warned, it also had the biggest box-office opening of the entire series. This time Freddy Kreuger (Robert Englund) attempts to escape from the confines of Springwood, Ohio, through the dreams of his own daughter, Maggie (Lisa Zane). By smudging the line between reality and dream, this edition is a real cop-out, further hampered by amateur acting, poor special effects and Z-grade direction. The final sequence was filmed in 3-D. Pass the smelling salts. [JC-W]

Also with: Shon Greenblatt (John), Lezlie Deane (Tracy), Ricky Dean Logan (Carlos), Breckin Meyer (Spencer), Yaphet Kotto (Doc), Roseanne Arnold, Tom Arnold, Elinor Donahue, Matthew Faison, Mel Scott-Thomas, Alice Cooper, Johnny Depp.
  Dir: Rachel Talalay. Pro: Robert Shaye and Aron Warner. Ex Pro: Michael DeLuca. Screenplay: DeLuca; based on a concept created by Wes Craven. Ph: Declan Quinn. Ed: Janice Hampton. Pro Des: C. J. Strawn. M: Brian May. (New Line Cinema–Guild.) Rel: 17 January 1992. 90 mins. Cert 18.

Freejack. 1991–2009. Alex Furlong died today and in eighteen years' time they're going to want his body. After all, he's toxin-free, nuclear-clean and good-looking – in an Emilio Estevez sort of way. But whose mind will take him over? Action-packed, forgettable

Over-baked: Oscar-winning actresses Kathy Bates and Jessica Tandy become friends in Jon Avnet's flavourful Fried Green Tomatoes at the Whistle Stop Cafe *(from Rank).*

time-travel adventure with plenty of gags, running, shoot-ups and not a shred of plausibility. Ropey special effects, too. [JC-W]

Cast includes: Emilio Estevez (Alex Furlong), Mick Jagger (Vacendak), Anthony Hopkins (McCandless), Rene Russo (Julie Redlund), Jonathan Banks (Michelette), David Johansen (Brad), Amanda Plummer, Grand L. Bush, Frankie Faison, John Shea, Esai Morales, Wilbur Fitzgerald, Jerry Hall, Danny De La Paz, Mike Starr.

Dir: Geoff Murphy. Pro: Ronald Shusett and Stuart Oken. Ex Pro: James G. Robinson, David Nicksay and Gary Barber. Screenplay: Shusett, Steven Pressfield and Dan Gilroy; based on the novel *Immortality Inc.* by Robert Sheckley. Ph: Amir Mokri; Matthew Leonetti. Ed: Dennis Virkler. Pro Des and Assoc Pro: Joe Alves. M: Trevor Jones; numbers performed by Scorpions, Jesus Jones, Eleven, 2 Die 4, Little Feat, Ministry, Jesus and Mary Chain and Jane Child. Costumes: Lisa Jensen. Sound: Louis L. Edemann and Donald J. Malouf. Visual

FX: Richard Hoover. (Morgan Creek–Warner.) Rel: 27 March 1992. 110 mins. Cert 15.

Fried Green Tomatoes at the Whistle Stop Cafe. Evelyn Couch (Kathy Bates) is an overweight, timid Alabama housewife addicted to chocolate bars. However, her world is opened up when she encounters 82-year-old Ninny Threadgoode (82-year-old Jessica Tandy) who tells her of the adventures of Idgie Threadgoode (Mary Stuart Masterson), the plucky cafe owner in Whistle Stop, Alabama, fifty years earlier. This film, adapted from the novel by Fannie Flagg, jumps uneasily between past and present, Ninny's stories eventually consuming centre stage. Whereas the present is conceived in broad caricature, the story of the Whistle Stop Cafe is of a more sombre tone, bringing in themes of racism, wife-battering and poverty. Plenty to enjoy here, though, if one is willing to swallow the film's awkward format. The performances of the four leading actresses are particularly to be savoured. [JC-W]

Also with: Mary-Louise Parker (Ruth), Cicely Tyson (Sipsey), Stan Shaw (Big George), Gailard Sartain (Ed Couch), Gary Basaraba (Grady Kilgore), Nick Searcy (Frank Bennett), Chris O'Donnell (Buddy), Tim Scott (Smokey Lonesome), Richard Riehle, Grace Zabriskie, Grayson Fricke, Lashondra Phillips, Enjolik Oree, Ginny Parker, Lois Smith, Danny Nelson, Afton Smith, Raynor Scheine, Macon McCalman, Bob Hannah, Tom Even, Fannie Flagg.

Dir: Jon Avnet. Pro: Avnet and Jordan Kerner. Ex Pro: Norman Lear and Andrew Meyer. Screenplay: Avnet and Fannie Flagg. Ph: Geoffrey Simpson. Ed: Debbie Neil. Pro Des: Barbara Ling. M: Thomas Newman. Costumes: Elizabeth McBride. (Act III Prods./Electric Shadow–Rank.) Rel: 13 March 1992. 130 mins. Cert 12.

FX2 – The Deadly Art of Illusion. Special effects (FX) wizard Rollie Tyler (Bryan Brown) is once again forced to use his talents to fight crime. And once again the set-up misfires. Entertaining, slick sequel that barely pauses for breath, mixing humour and violence with gay abandon. Brown and buddy Brian Dennehy have enormous fun as the carefree, macho good guys, while the girls are there to be terrorised.

45

A cyborg from hell, a figment of our imagination or a special effect? James Stacy supplies some chills in Columbia Tri-Star's witty FX2 – The Deadly Art of Illusion.

Good script, and the FX are tremendous. Filmed in Los Angeles, New York, Toronto and Rome. [JC-W]

Also with: Brian Dennehy (Leo McCarthy), Rachel Ticotin (Kim Brandon), Joanna Gleason (Liz Kennedy), Philip Bosco (Ray Silak), Kevin J. O'Connor (Matt Neely), Tom Mason (Mike Brandon), Dominic Zamprogna (Chris Brandon), Josie DeGuzman (Velez), John Walsh (Rado), Lisa Fallon (Kylie), Peter Boretski, Lee Broker, Philip Akin, Tony de Santis, James Stacy, Biff Yeager, Caroline Yeager.

Dir: Richard Franklin. Pro: Jack Wiener and Dodi Fayed. Ex Pro: Lee R. Mayes. Screenplay: Bill Condon; based on characters created by Robert T. Megginson and Gregory Fleeman. Ph: Victor J. Kemper. Ed: Andrew London. Pro Des: John Jay Moore. M: Lalo Schifrin. Costumes: Linda Matheson. SFX: Eric Allard. (Orion–Columbia Tri-Star.) Rel: 20 September 1991. 108 mins. Cert 15.

Get Back. What do Yasser Arafat, George Bush, Golda Meir, Mikhail Gorbachev and Yoko Ono have in common? They all appear in newsreel footage used to garnish Richard Lester's record of the 1989/90 Paul McCartney *Get Back* World Tour. Not that a concert featuring McCartney singing old Beatles favourites needs much garnish. Lester's jumbled, retrogressive family album is surprisingly facile and uninspired, but the music more than makes up. [JC-W]

Also with: Linda McCartney and Paul 'Wix' Wickens (keyboards), Hamish Stuart (guitar, bass and vocals), Robbie McIntosh (lead guitar), Chris Whitten (drums).

Dir: Richard Lester. Pro: Philip Knatchbull and Henry Thomas. Ex Pro: Jake Eberts. Ph: Jordan Cronenweth and Robert Paynter. Ed: John Victor Smith. M: McCartney and The Beatles. Sound: Leslie Hodgson. (Allied Filmmakers/MPL/Front Page Films–Entertainment.) Rel: 19 September 1991. 90 mins. Cert PG.

Gladiator. Chicago's South Side, today. Computer-programmed, adrenalin-pumping boxing melodrama about a white kid forced to put up his dukes in illegal matches to pay his father's gambling debts. James Marshall, who looks like Dolph Lundgren injected by Sting, is a young lead with controlled presence and is neatly rivalled by Brian Dennehy as the corrupt manager. Slick, manipulative, efficient and ultimately rather unpleasant exploitation. [JC-W]

Cast includes: Cuba Gooding Jr (Lincoln), James Marshall (Tommy Riley), Robert Loggia (Pappy Jack), Ossie Davis (Noah), Brian Dennehy (Jimmy Horn), Jon Seda (Romano), Cara Buono (Dawn), Francesca P. Roberts (Miss Higgins), John Heard (John Riley), Lance Slaughter, T. E. Russell, Laura Whyte, Jeon-Paul Griffin, Debra Sandlund, Mike Nussbaum.

Dir: Rowdy Herrington. Pro: Frank Price

Macca plays it for the fans in Richard Lester's concert film Get Back *(from Entertainment).*

Domestic blitz: Mary McDonnell and Kevin Kline confront the dreaded 'fortysomethings' in Lawrence Kasdan's powerful, intelligent Grand Canyon *(from Fox).*

and Steve Roth. Screenplay: Lyle Kessler and Robert Mark Kamen; from a story by Kamen and Djordje Milicevic. Ph: Tak Fujimoto. Ed: Peter Zinner and Harry B. Miller III. Pro Des: Gregg Fonseca. M: Brad Fidel; numbers performed by Seal, 3RD Bass, Lisa Lisa & Cult Jam, LL Cool J, PM Dawn, Cheap Trick, Gerardo, Hammer, Warrant etc. Costumes: Donfeld. Sound: Stephen H. Flick and David A. Whittaker. (Price Entertainment–Columbia.) Rel: 26 June 1992. 101 mins. Cert 15.

Grand Canyon. Lawrence Kasdan, who wrote and directed *The Big Chill* and *Silverado*, returns to the ensemble picture with this grim, hard-edged look at life in Los Angeles (*before* the riots). The Grand Canyon itself serves as metaphor, warning and promise as nine people from different directions attempt to sort out their lives. A very personal project for Kasdan (who co-scripted with his wife, Meg), the film is a superbly crafted catharsis for the director, although it is often self-indulgent and far too long. However, the heart-pounding sequence in which Mack (Kevin Kline) gets lost in a violent LA neighbourhood is worth the price of admission alone. [JC-W]

Also with: Danny Glover (Simon), Steve Martin (Davis, modelled on producer Joel Silver), Mary McDonnell (Claire), Mary-Louise Parker (Dee), Alfre Woodard (Jane), Jeremy Sisto (Roberto), Tina Lifford (Deborah), Patrick Malone (Otis), Sarah Trigger (Vanessa), Randle Mell, Destinee DeWalt, Shaun Baker, K. Todd Freeman, Todd Allen, Carole Ita White, Basil Wallace, Georgina Lindsey, Jack Kehler, Marlee Shelton, Mary Ellen Trainor, Gary Cervantes, Brett A. Jones, Antonio Royuela, Roxanne Kasdan.

Dir: Lawrence Kasdan. Pro: Lawrence Kasdan, Charles Okun and Michael Grillo. Assoc Pro: Meg Kasdan. Screenplay: Lawrence Kasdan and Meg Kasdan. Ph: Owen Roizman. Ed: Carol Littleton. Pro Des: Bo Welch. M: James Newton Howard; numbers performed by Warren Zevon, NWA, Gardner Cole and Souled Out. Costumes: Aggie Guerard Rodgers. Sound: Robert Grieve. (Fox.) Rel: 1 May 1992. 134 mins. Cert 15.

The Hand That Rocks the Cradle. Seattle, 1992. Skilful thriller in the *Fatal Attraction* mould which does for babysitters what *Jaws* did for sharks. Rebecca De Mornay is the sweet, sexy

Would you let this woman look after your child? Rebecca De Mornay (with Madeline Zima) steals the notices in Curtis Hanson's slick hit, The Hand That Rocks the Cradle (from Warner).

and, yes, *maternal* Peyton Flanders – who seems a godsend to the happy home-makers Michael and Claire Bartel (Matt McCoy, Annabella Sciorra). However, Peyton bears a terrible grudge and is unhinged by recent tragic events – and *boy* is she clever. This is a shamelessly manipulative film (and an enormous box-office success), but is so well written that it hits every mark. Call it emotional engineering. [JC-W]

Also with: Ernie Hudson (Solomon), Julianne Moore (Marlene), Madeline Zima (Emma), John de Lancie (Dr Mott), Kevin Skousen, Mitchell Laurance, Justin Zaremby, Susan Chin, Tom Francis.

Dir: Curtis Hanson. Pro: David Madden. Ex Pro: Ted Field, Rick Jaffa and Robert W. Cort. Screenplay: Amanda Silver. Ph: Robert Elswit. Ed: John F. Link. Pro Des: Edward Pisoni. M: Graeme Revell. Costumes: Jennifer Von Mayrhauser. Sound: Dane A. Davis. (Hollywood Pictures/Interscope Communications/Nomura Babcock & Brown–Warner.) Rel: 24 April 1992. 110 mins. Cert 15.

Hangin' with the Homeboys. A gritty and uncompromisingly realistic look at life in the Bronx, as four young lay-abouts while away the weekend. Neatly written and directed, on a slim ($2 million) budget. [FDM]

Dir and Screenplay: Joseph P. Vasquez. Pro: Richard Brick. Ex Pro: Janet Grillo. Ph: Anghel Decca. Ed: Michael Schweitzer. Art: Isabel Bau Madden. Sound: William Sarokin. M: Joel Sill and David Chackler. (New Line Cinema–Palace.) Rel: 22 November 1992. 90 mins. Cert 15.

Harley Davidson and The Marlboro Man. While we're talking about product placement, if films were graded by drinks this would be a Bud Lite. Mickey Rourke, lightening up his act, is a thick-skulled biker driving around LA in the year 1996. Don Johnson is a creaky, outdated cowboy who accompanies him on drinking bouts and philosophical discussions. When their favourite watering hole, the Rock 'n' Roll Bar and Grill, comes under threat by heavies, they rob a bank to finance a counter-attack. But they steal from the wrong people . . . Pop video entertainment for macho rednecks. [JC-W]

Also with: Chelsea Field (Virginia Slim), Daniel Baldwin (Alexander), Giancarlo Esposito (Jimmy Jiles), Vanessa Williams (Lulu Daniels), Tom Sizemore (Chance Wilder), Julius Harris ('Old Man'), Eloy Casados (Jose), Big John Studd (Jack Daniels), Robert Ginty, Tia Carrere, Branscombe Richmond, Sven-Ole Thorsen, Cody Glenn, Debbie Lynn Ross.

Dir: Simon Wincer. Pro: Jere Henshaw. Co-Pro and Screenplay: Don Michael Paul. Ph: David Eggby. Ed: Corky Ehlers. Pro Des: Paul Peters. M: Basil Poledouris; numbers performed by Bon Jovi, Peter Frampton & Steve Marriott, Copperhead, The Screaming Jets, Vanessa Williams, Waylon Jennings etc. Costumes: Richard Shissler. (Krisjair/Laredo/MGM–UIP.) Rel: 11 October 1991. 98 mins. Cert 12.

Hear My Song. Whimsical romantic fable – inspired by fact – set in the Irish quarter of Liverpool. Micky O'Neill, a young, opportunistic Irish concert promoter, upsets his customers with a series of scam acts (Franc Cinatra, for one), but really steps out of line when he hires 'Mr X', who pretends to be the legendary tenor Josef Locke. To make up – and to win back his fiancée – O'Neill goes in search of the real Locke, who has been in hiding for tax evasion for the last thirty years. Idiosyncratic and full of local character and detail, *Hear My Song* casts a genuine spell of magic as it follows the misadventures of a romantic fool who dares to follow his dreams. [JC-W]

Cast includes: Ned Beatty (Josef Locke), Adrian Dunbar (Micky O'Neill), Shirley Anne Field (Cathleen Doyle), Tara Fitzgerald (Nancy Doyle), William Hootkins (Mr X), Harold Berens (Benny Rose), David McCallum (Chief Constable Jim Abbott), James Nesbitt (Fintan O'Donnell), John Dair, Stephen Marcus, Britta Smith, Gladys Sheehan, Gina Moxley, Norman Vaughan (as himself), Phil Kelly, John Neville Rufus Altman, Joe Cuddy (Franc Cinatra), Mary Mcleod, Bill Maynard, Vernon Midgley (the voice of Josef Locke).

Dir: Peter Chelsom. Pro: Alison Owen-Allen. Ex Pro: Simon Fields, Russ Russell and John Paul Chapple. Screenplay: Chelsom and Adrian Dunbar. Ph: Sue Gibson. Ed: Martin Walsh. Pro Des: Caroline Hanania. M: John Altman. Costumes: Lindy Hemming. Sound: Glenn Freemantle. (Film Four Int./British Screen/Windmill Lane/Limelight–Miramax.) Rel: 13 March 1992. 103 mins. Cert 15.

Hearts of Darkness – A Filmmaker's Apocalypse. A documentary account of the trials and tribulations of the 238 days it took Francis Coppola to make *Apocalypse Now*, and a fascinating behind-the-scenes look at the way a film is made. [FDM]

Ex in charge of Pro: Steven Hewitt. Footage Dir: Eleanor Coppola. Dir: Fax Bahr and George Hickenlooper. (Zaloom Mayfield in assoc with Zoetrope Studios–Blue Dolphin.) Rel: 6 December 1991. 96 mins. Cert 15.

Hello Hemingway. 1956, Cuba. Bordering Ernest Hemingway's opulent estate just outside Havana lives a 16-year-old schoolgirl with dreams of higher education. Her family is poor, but Larita (Laura de la Uz) is working hard for a scholarship to take her to the United States to study art and philosophy. However, poverty and political unrest stand in her way, with only

William Hootkins as Mr X, the real-life impersonator of the legendary Josef Locke – in Adrian Dunbar and Peter Chelsom's delightful mix of fact and fancy, Hear My Song *(from Miramax).*

Hemingway's *The Old Man and the Sea* left to fuel her hopes. A modest work, layered with irony and metaphor, highlighted by a spirited performance from young de la Uz. [JC-W]

Also with: Raul Paz (Victor), Herminia Sanchez (Josefa), Jose Antonio Rodriguez (Tomas), Marta de Rio, Micheline Calvert.

Dir: Fernando Perez. Screenplay: Mayda Royero. Ph: Julio Valdes. Ed: Jorge Abello. Art: Onelio Larralde. M: Edesio Alejandro. (Empressa/ICAIC–Metro.) Rel: 10 January 1992. 90 mins. No cert.

Henry: Portrait of a Serial Killer. Back by popular demand! *Henry*, reviewed here for the record two years ago, has now been given a 'regular'

A reflection of evil: Michael Rooker in John McNaughton's chilling Henry: Portrait of a Serial Killer *(from Electric).*

Low comedy with a stiletto edge: the lovely Victoria Abril in Pedro Almodovar's High Heels *(from Rank).*

release to cash in on the public's interest in serial killers. Inspired by the grandaddy of them all, Henry Lee Lucas (who confessed to 601 murders), and by Thomas Harris's novel *Red Dragon*, this is a bleak, *cinéma vérité* account of a casual killer and his life-style. No questions are answered, or even a plot developed as such, and the film plays like cheap pornography. There's even a dangerous element of black humour to be detected, which makes one wonder at the intentions of the filmmakers, a former director of McDonald's commercials (Jones) and Burger King decorator (McNaughton). Filmed in 1986 on 16mm, one year before Krzystof Kieslowski's similar *A Short Film About Killing*. [JC-W]

Cast includes: Michael Rooker (Henry), Tracy Arnold (Becky), Tom Towles (Otis), Ray Atherton (Fence), David Katz, Kurt Naebig, Lily Monkus, Eric Young, Rick Paul, Lisa Temple, Waleed B. Ali, Donna Dunlap.

Dir: John McNaughton. Pro: McNaughton, Lisa Dedmond and Steven A. Jones. Ex Pro: Waleed B. Ali and Malik B. Ali. Screenplay: McNaughton and Richard Fire. Ph: Charlie Lieberman. Ed: Elena Maganini. Art: Rick Paul. M: Robert McNaughton, Ken Hale and Steven A. Jones. Costumes: Patricia Hart. Sound: Maganini.

(Maljack–Electric.) Rel: 12 July 1991. 90 mins. Cert 18.

High Heels – Tacones Lejanos. Disappointingly heavy-handed comic melodrama from Pedro Almodovar, set in the world of Spanish media. Rebecca (Victoria Abril) is a newscaster based in Madrid who has always had a tumultuous relationship with her mother, the legendary pop star Becky del Paramo (Marisa Paredes). When the latter returns to Spain after an absence of fifteen years, her arrival stirs up old hostilities and rivalry and leads to a web of love, hate, sex and death. Full of the stock Almodovar plot twists, *High Heels* has its delightful moments, but not enough to keep the story moving. A pair of scissors might've helped. [JC-W]

Also with: Miguel Bose (Judge/Letal/Hugo), Feodor Atkin (Manuel), Ana Lizaran (Margarita), Pedro Diez Del Corral, Rocio Munoz, Mairata O'Wisiedo, Miriam Diaz Aroca, Cristina Marcos, Bibi Andersson.

Dir and Screenplay: Pedro Almodovar. Ex Pro: Agustin Almodovar. Assoc Pro: Enrique Posner. Ph: Alfredo Mayo. Ed: Jose Salcedo. Set design: Pierre-Louis Thevenet. M: Ryuichi Sakamoto; songs performed by Luz Casal. Costumes: Jose M. Cossio. Sound: Jean Paul Mugel. (El Deseo SA/Ciby 2000 Prods–Rank.) Rel: 27 March 1992. 115 mins. Cert 18.

Cop or Jew? Joe Mantegna after answers in David Mamet's gritty, witty Homicide *(from First Independent).*

Homework – La Tarea. Described as a Mexican *sex, lies and videotape*, this is clumsy sexual satire at its most embarrassing. An ageing student working on a TV project, Virginia (the buxom Maria Rojo) invites an old flame to her apartment in which she has hidden a video camera. Her aim is to make an honest, tasteful statement on pornography while freeing her own inhibitions as a person. The result is an interminable single take that has less to do with cinema than celluloid masturbation. [JC-W]

Also with: Jose Alonso (Marcelo).

Dir and Screenplay: Jaime Humberto Hermosillo. Pro: Pablo and Francisco Barbachano. Ex Pro: Lourdes Rivera. Ph: Tony Kuhn. Pro Des: Laura Santa Cruz. M: Luis Arcaraz. Sound: Nerio Barberis. (Clasa Films Mundiales–Metro.) Rel: 19 June 1992. 85 mins. Cert 18.

Homicide. Bobby Gold (Joe Mantegna) is a caring cop with a foul mouth. A product of the streets of Chicago, he calls a spade a spade and several other names as well. Thanks to a giant lapse of tact, Bobby drops himself into a quagmire of guilt involving an anti-Semitic conspiracy. Meanwhile, he's the vital cog in another case involving a ruthless drug dealer and cop-killer, whose mother will only talk to Bobby in order to have her son brought in peacefully. The good cop doesn't know whether he's coming or going – all he knows is that he just wants to be a decent officer of the law. A little over-plotted perhaps, and at times rather sluggish, David Mamet's third film as director boasts some marvellous dialogue and a tense, stark atmosphere. [JC-W]

Also with: William H. Macy (Tim Sullivan), Natalija Nigulich (Chava), Ving Rhames (Randolph), Rebecca Pidgeon (Miss Klein), Jack Wallace (Frank), Marge Kotlinsky, Vincent Guasteferro, Lionel Mark Smith, Paul Butler, Colin Stinton, Adolph Mall, Erica Gimpel.

Dir and Screenplay: David Mamet. Pro: Michael Hausman and Edward R. Pressman. Ex Pro: Ron Rotholz. Ph: Roger Deakins. Ed: Barbara Tulliver. Pro Des: Michael Merritt. M: Aleric Jans. Costumes: Nan Cibula. (Cinehaus–First Independent.) Rel: 25 October 1991. 102 mins. Cert 15.

Hook. What if the boy 'who would never grow up' grew up? An overweight, cholesterol-clogged Robin

By Hook *or by crook: Dustin Hoffman in the title role of Steven Spielberg's vastly entertaining epic, a film that the critics hated and audiences loved (especially children) – from Columbia Tri-Star.*

Williams is Peter Banning, a hotshot 40-year-old San Francisco lawyer. British by birth, Banning lost his parents and was adopted by an American couple and brought to the States. Now he is due to fly his family back to England to attend a tribute to his 92-year-old childhood friend 'Granny' Wendy (Maggie Smith in make-up). Then his two children are kidnapped by Captain James Hook. But who's Hook? Banning cannot remember anybody by that name, so it's up to Tinkerbell ('the firefly from hell') to help this fat oaf to remember a few things. But Banning doesn't believe in fairies – yet. If anybody could have brought this $70 million epic fantasy to life it is Steven Spielberg. And he has done it. Savaged by the critics who seemed to miss the whole point, *Hook* went on to be *the* US Christmas box-office hit of '91. Spielberg has managed to revisit a classic children's tale and update it, making it accessible, funny, entertaining and – above all – magical, *without* being cute. Barely a minute goes by that doesn't reveal a uniquely imaginative touch or a display of bravura acting or filmmaking. Special effects, production design, costumes, photography, John Williams's best score for eons and Dustin Hoffman's outrageous

The scars of war: Hippolyte Girardot in Maroun Bagdadi's disturbing, topical Hors la Vie *(from Mainline).*

Captain Hook all set new standards to aspire to. Thank God Steven Spielberg never grew up. [JC-W]

Also with: Julia Roberts (Tinkerbell), Bob Hoskins (Smee), Charlie Korsmo (Jack Banning), Caroline Goodall (Moira Banning), Amber Scott (Maggie Banning), Dante Basco (Rufio), Laurel Cronin, Phil Collins, Arthur Malet, Isaiah Robinson, Jasen Fisher, Raushan Hammond, James Madio, Thomas Tulack, Ryan Francis, Maxwell Hoffman, Kelly Rowan, Rebecca Hoffman, Jacob Hoffman, Geoff Lower, David Crosby, Nick Tate, Tony Burton, Glenn Close.

Dir: Steven Spielberg. Pro: Kathleen Kennedy, Frank Marshall and Gerald R. Molen. Co-Pro: Gary Adelson and Craig Baumgarten. Ex-Pro: Dodi Fayed and Jim V. Hart. Screenplay: Hart and Malia Scotch Marmo; from a story by Hart and Nick Castle. Ph: Dean Cundey. Ed: Michael Kahn. Pro Des: Norman Garwood. M: John Williams; lyrics: Leslie Bricusse. Costumes: Anthony Powell. Visual consultant: John Napier. (Amblin/Tri-Star–Columbia.) Rel: 10 April 1992. 141 mins. Cert U.

Hors la Vie (Out of Life). 1987, Beirut. Relentless, unflinchingly authentic retelling of the captivity of French photojournalist Roger Auque. Risking his life to record the war in Beirut, Auque is kidnapped and held hostage for nine months in order to secure the release of a political prisoner. In that time Auque is kept in solitary confinement, deprived of his dignity and subjected to cruel emotional torture. Filmed in France and Palermo, Sicily, this Franco-Italian-German co-production is remarkably realistic in capturing the documentary feel of a city in ruins. There are no heroes . . . only victims. Directed by the Lebanese filmmaker Maroun Bagdadi. Winner of the Special Jury prize at Cannes. [JC-W]

Cast includes: Hippolyte Girardot (Patrick Perrault – Roger Auque), Rafic Ali Ahmad (Walid), Hussein Sbeity (Omar), Habib Hammoud (Ali/'Philippe'), Magdi Machmouchi (Moustaph), Hassan Farhat Hahmed/'Frankenstein'), Hamzah Nasrullah (De Niro), Hassan Zhib, Nabila Zeitouni, Sami Hawat, Sabrina Leurquin.

Dir and Screenplay: Maroun Bagdadi; based on the book by Roger Auque, with the collaboration of Patrick Forestier. Pro: Jacques Perrin. Ex Pro: Hugues Nonn and Fabienne Tsai. Ph: Arnaud Borrel and Jeanne-Louise Bulliard. Ed: Luc Barnier. Pro Des: Dan Weill. M: Nicola Piovani. Costumes: Magali Guidasci and Frédérique Santerre. Sound: Guillaume Sciama, Chantal Quaglio and Dominique Hennequin. (Galatee Films/Films A2/Filmalpha/Lamy Films/Canal Plus/Raidue–Mainline.) Rel: 31 January 1992. 97 mins. Cert 15.

Hot Shots! Over-the-top and predictably jokey spoof of *Top Gun* and any other film in its path. Charlie Sheen, arching his eyebrows a little too high, stars as Sean 'Topper' Harley, a renegade Navy pilot who's given up the service to live with Indians and a wolf. Persuaded to come out of retirement to spearhead a dangerous mission, Topper falls hard for Ramada Thompson (Valeria Golino), who sings on the tops of pianos. Lampooning everything from *Gone with the Wind* to *Dances with Wolves*, Jim Abrahams' *Hot Shots!* signals its jokes long in advance and thinks *any* film reference must be a hoot. Still, it made lots of money. [JC-W]

Also with Cary Elwes (Kent Gregory), Lloyd Bridges (Admiral Benson), Kevin Dunn (Lt-Cdr Block), Jon Cryer (Jim 'Wash Out' Pfaffenbach), William O'Leary (Pete 'Dead Meat' Thompson), Bill Irwin (Buzz Harley), Kristy Swanson, Efrem Zimbalist Jr, Heidi Swedberg, Bruce A. Young, Ryan Stiles, Rino Thunder, Mark Arnott, Ryan Cutrona, Marc Shaiman, Jimmie Ray Weeks.

Dir: Jim Abrahams. Pro: Bill Badalato. Ex Pro: Pat Proft. Screenplay: Abrahams and Proft. Ph: Bill Butler. Ed: Jane Kurson and Eric Sears. Pro Des: William A. Elliott. M: Sylvester Levay. Costumes: Mary Malin. Sound: Sandy Berman and Randle Akerson. (PAP Inc–Fox.) Rel: 29 November 1991. 85 mins. Cert 12.

Howards End. The artistic team that brought us *A Room with a View* and *Maurice* return to the same territory with this masterful adaptation of E. M. Forster's novel. Emma Thompson is the sweet-natured Miss Margaret Schlegel who befriends the frail Mrs Ruth Wilcox (Vanessa Redgrave), the latter leaving her country estate, Howards End, to Margaret in a hastily scribbled (and non-legally binding) will. Widower Henry Wilcox (Anthony Hopkins) destroys the note and finds himself repeatedly bumping into the unknowing Margaret. A second story, of the poor clerk with a romantic vision, mushrooms into the first with ironic twists and turns. Above all, *Howards End* boasts a great story, embellished with all the polished skill that director James Ivory and scripter Ruth Prawer Jhabvala can bring to a film (although the emotional payoff is disappointingly low-key). Ms Thompson, as usual, is a standout, and is fortified by a first-class cast. [JC-W]

Also with: Helena Bonham Carter (Helen Schlegel), James Wilby (Charles Wilcox), Samuel West (Leonard Bast), Prunella Scales (Aunt Juley), Adrian Ross Magenty (Tibby Schlegel), Nicola Duffett (Jacky Bast), Joseph Bennett, Jo Kendall, Jemma Redgrave, Mary Nash, Siegbert Prawer, Susie Lindeman, Mark Tandy, Barbara Hicks, Peter Cellier, Crispin Bonham Carter, Simon Callow.

Dir: James Ivory. Pro: Ismail Merchant. Ex Pro: Paul Bradley. Co-Pro: Ann Win-

When worlds collide: Anthony Hopkins and Emma Thompson bridge an emotional ravine in James Ivory's deliciously ironic Howards End *(from Mayfair Palace).*

gate. Screenplay: Ruth Prawer Jhabvala. Ph: Tony Pierce-Roberts. Ed: Andrew Marcus. Pro Des: Luciana Arrighi. M: Richard Robbins. Costumes: Jenny Beavan and John Bright. Sound: Campbel Askew. (Merchant Ivory/Film Four–Mayfair Palace.) Rel: 1 May 1992. 140 mins. Cert PG.

Hudson Hawk. Nicknamed *Hudson the Duck*, this $50m turkey was a dream child of Bruce Willis's for almost a decade. He not only stars and co-produces, but receives a co-story and co-scoring credit. Willis is Hawk, a cat burglar determined to go straight (aren't they all?), who is forcibly involved in an elaborate plan to take over the world. Richard E. Grant and Sandra Bernhard ham it up horribly as the villains who need Hawk's finesse to help them operate a machine (invented by Leonardo Da Vinci) to turn lead into gold. Willis's idea was to meld the black humour of *Heathers* with the spectacle of *Die Hard*, but he ended up with a poorly made spoof that trips up on its own budget. Poor sound, murky photography and an intrusive score all help to bury this dog. [JC-W]

Also with: Danny Aiello (Tommy 'Five-Tone' Messina), Andie MacDowell (Anna Baragli), Richard E. Grant (Darwin Mayflower), Sandra Bernhard (Minerva Mayflower), Donald Burton (Alfred, the butler), James Coburn (George Kaplan), Don Harvey (Snickers), David Caruso (Kit Kat), Andrew Bryniarski (Butterfinger), Lorraine Toussaint (Almond Joy), Stephano Molinari

A charmless, goofy Bruce Willis plays cat burglar Hudson Hawk *in Columbia Tri-Star's mammoth flop.*

Madonna and minions bare all in Alek Keshishian's revealing and entertaining documentary, In Bed with Madonna *(from Rank).*

(Leonardo Da Vinci), Giselda Volodi (Mona Lisa), Massimo Ciprari (the Pope), William Conrad (narrator), Burtt Harris, Frank Stallone, Carmine Zozorra, John Savident, Leonardo Cimino.
Dir: Michael Lehmann. Pro: Joel Silver. Ex Pro: Robert Kraft. Co-Pro: Michael Dryhurst. Assoc Pro: David Willis and Suzanne Todd. Screenplay: Steven E. De Souza and Daniel Waters; from a story by Kraft and Bruce Willis. Ph: Dante Spinotti (replacing Jost Vacano). Ed: Chris Lebenzon and Michael Tronick. Pro Des: Jack DeGovia. M: Michael Kamen, Robert Kraft and Bruce Willis; numbers performed by Dr

John, James Brown, SNAP and Bing Crosby. Costumes: Marilyn Vance-Straker. Sound: Jerry Ross. (Silver Pictures/Ace Bone Prods/Tri-Star–Columbia Tri-Star.) Rel: 12 July 1991. 100 mins. Cert 15.

I, the Worst of All – Yo, la Peor de Todas. Impressive Argentine film with a fine central performance by Assumpta Serna as a 17th-century nun who becomes the enemy of a powerful archbishop. [FDM]

Also with: Dominique Sanda (Viceroy's wife), Hector Alterio (Viceroy), Lautaro Murua (archbishop).
Dir: Maria Luisa Bemberg. Pro: Lita Standic. Ex Pro: Gilbert Marouani. Screenplay: Bemberg and Antonio Larreta; based

on the book by Octavio Paz. Ph: Felix Monti. Pro Des: Voytek. (GEA–Electric.) Rel: 4 October 1991. 105 mins. No cert.

In Bed with Madonna (US: *Truth or Dare*). What started out as a routine document of Madonna's Blond Ambition world tour has been transformed into an eye-opening record of the singer herself. Pop video director Alek Keshishian (taking over from *Alien III*'s David Fincher) pokes his camera where no lens has dared to probe before. While the sizzling concert footage is filmed in colour, the backstage sequences are shot in grainy, *cinéma vérité* black-and-white. Madonna talks about sex, loneliness, sex, fame, sex and the pressures of superstardom. Former boyfriend Warren Beatty lurks in the background, looking decidedly uncomfortable; Madonna's father complains about her masturbation sequence on stage; the star herself flashes her breasts at the camera; and so on. This is how rockumentaries ought to be: provocative, insightful, honest and wildly entertaining. But then Madonna is a superb subject. [JC-W]

Also with: Sandra Bernhard, Kevin Costner, Olivia Newton-John, Al Pacino, Mandy Patinkin etc.
Dir: Alek Keshishian. Pro: Tim Clawson and Jay Roewe. Ex Pro: Madonna. Ph: Robert Leacock, Doug Nichol and Toby Phillips. Ed: Barry Alexander Brown. M: Madonna. (Propaganda Films/Boy Toy Inc/ Dino De Laurentiis Communications– Rank.) Rel: 19 July 1991. 119 mins. Cert 18.

The Indian Runner. Nebraska, 1968. Sean Penn's first film as director and writer, a surprisingly mature, well-crafted melodrama that serves both the actor and cinematographer particularly well. The story of two brothers, a heroic cop and a self-destructive ex-con, *The Indian Runner* labours its message about the Plain Indian's rites of passage (out-running a deer and sucking in its final breath), and is frequently self-indulgent to a fault (one too many close-ups of a character smoking thoughtfully). But then again, there is much to admire here, from an actor who has obviously studied the greats – David Lean is an obvious influence. Penn's own life, too, is reflected in the narrative, particularly in the rivalry of the brothers, the prison scenes and the childbirth. A promising debut – inspired by the Bruce Springsteen song *Highway Patrolman*. [JC-W]

Cast includes: David Morse (Sheriff Sergeant Joe Roberts), Viggo Mortensen (Frank Roberts), Valeria Golino (Maria Roberts), Patricia Arquette (Dorothy), Jordan Rhodes (Randall), Dennis Hopper (Caesar), Sandy Dennis (Mother), Charles Bronson (Father), Enzo Rossi, Harry Crews, Eileen Ryan, Annie Pearson, James J. Luxa.
   Dir and Screenplay: Sean Penn. Pro: Don Phillips. Ex Pro: Thom Mount, Stephen K. Bannon and Mark Bisgeier. Co-Pro: Patricia Morrison. Ph: Anthony B. Richmond. Ed: Jay Cassidy. Pro Des: Michael Haller. M: Jack Nitzsche; numbers performed by Traffic, Jefferson Airplane, Creedence Clearwater Revival, Janis Joplin, The Band etc. (Mount Film Group/MICO/NHK Enterprises–Columbia Tri-Star.) Rel: 29 November 1991. 126 mins. Cert 15.

The Inner Circle. Moscow, 1939–53. Earnest, over-acted melodrama based on the real-life experiences of Stalin's projectionist. Ivan Sanshin (Tom Hulce) is a geeky, devoted party man, commandeered to show movies in the Kremlin on his wedding night. From then on he is a sucker for the KGB and even tells his wife that Stalin is his first love (which unsurprisingly leads to tears). The film purports to be an authentic account of Moscow at that time, and was filmed on actual locations, including (for the first time) the interior of the Kremlin. However, such brushes with realism are tripped up by some *theeck* Hollywood-esque Russian accents and a wide-eyed, theatrical performance from Mr Hulce. Nevertheless, Russian actor Alexandre Zbruev is superb as Stalin (replacing Robert Duvall) and the snow looks very real. [JC-W]

Also with: Lolita Davidovich (Anastasia), Bob Hoskins (Lavrenti Beria), Feodor Chaliapin Jr (Professor Bartnev), Bess Meyer (Kathy, aged 16), Marla Baranova (Kathy, aged 10), Irina Kuptchenko, Vladimir Khulishov, Vsevolod Larionov, Aleksandr Filippenko, Evdokia Germanova, Liubov Matiushina, Aleksandr Garin.
   Dir: Andrei Konchalovsky. Pro: Claudio Bonivento. Assoc Pro: Laura Balbi. Screenplay: Konchalovsky and Anatoli Usov. Ph: Ennio Guarnieri. Ed: Henry Richardson. Pro Des: Ezio Frigerio. M: Eduard Artemyev. Costumes: Nelli Fomina. Sound: Eddy Joseph. (Columbia.) Rel: 26 June 1992. 137 mins. Cert 15.

Demons of the government or of the mind? Tim Robbins is pursued by strange spectres in Adrian Lyne's frightening, designer-horror film Jacob's Ladder *(from Guild).*

Iron Maze A young Japanese tycoon, who has bought a rusting steel mill in Pennsylvania (to transform into an amusement park), is almost killed by an unseen assailant. The scenario looks simple enough: resentment, jealousy and lust have converged to create a crime of passion. Not necessarily so. A variety of statements from a quartet of participants clash with the truth. *Rashomon* revisited (updated from the same short story, *In a Grove*) – and very clumsily at that. Missed opportunities abound. [JC-W]

Cast includes: Jeff Fahey (Barry), Bridget Fonda (Chris), Hiroaki Murakami (Sugita), J. T. Walsh (Jack Ruhle), Gabriel Damon (Mikey), John Randolph (Mayor Peluso). Peter Allas, Carmen Filpi, Francis John Thornton.
   Dir: Hiroaki Yoshida. Pro: Ilona Herzberg and Hidenori Ueki. Ex Pro: Edward R. Pressman and Oliver Stone. Screenplay: Tim Metcalfe; from *In a Grove* by Ryunosuke Akutagawa. Ph: Morio Saequsa. Ed: Bonnie Koehler. Pro Des: Toby Corbett. M: Stanley Myers; numbers performed by Earl Grant, Gabriel Damon, Vertical Smile etc. Costumes: Susie DeSanto. (Trans-Tokyo Corp–First Independent.) Rel: 29 November 1991. 102 mins. Cert 15.

Jacob's Ladder. Visually provocative, disturbing mind trip about a Vietnam veteran who starts experiencing horrific hallucinations back in New York. Or does he? People vanish, old wives reappear and demons roam the streets. 'It's just New York,' says his live-in girlfriend – although she's deeply worried. To say much more would be to spoil the game, as this film's success is directly related to the surprises it slips us. A nightmarish crossword puzzle, *Jacob's Ladder* keeps one glued and guessing until the final gruesome frame. From the writer, associate producer and composer of *Ghost*, with which this film shares more than the prevalence of spectral subway trains. *Very* weird, but compulsive (and sometimes repugnant) viewing. [JC-W]

Cast includes: Tim Robbins (Jacob Singer), Elizabeth Pena (Jezzie), Danny Aiello (Louis), Matt Craven (Michael), Pruitt Taylor Vince (Paul), Jason Alexander (Geary), Patricia Kalember (Sarah), Macaulay Culkin (Gabe Singer), Eriq La Salle, Ving Rhames, Brian Tarantina, Anthony Allessandro, Brent Hinkley, S. Epatha

55

Making pictures: Philippe Maron as a young Jacques Demy, already attracted to the moving image – in Agnes Varda's enchanting Jacquot de Nantes *(from Gala).*

Scapegoat or assassin? Gary Oldman makes a convincing Lee Harvey Oswald in Oliver Stone's contentious JFK *(from Warner).*

Merkerson, Suzanne Shepherd, Doug Barron, Sam Coppola, Antonia Rey.

Dir: Adrian Lyne. Pro: Alan Marshall. Ex Pro: Mario Kassar and Andrew Vajna. Screenplay: Bruce Joel Rubin. Ph: Jeffrey L. Kimball. Ed: Tom Rolf. Pro Des: Brian Morris. M: Maurice Jarre. Costumes: Ellen Mirojnick. (Carolco–Guild.) Rel: 27 September 1991. 113 mins. Cert 18.

Jacquot de Nantes. A compassionate, loving reconstruction of the childhood of French filmmaker Jacques Demy, assembled and directed by his wife Agnes Varda. While his childhood is affectionately recreated in black-and-white with actors, the narrative is interspersed with scenes from Demy's films and by Demy himself speaking directly to his wife's 16mm camera. A most unusual and arresting homage. [JC-W]

Cast includes: Philippe Maron (Jacquot No. 1), Edouard Joubeaud (Jacquot No. 2), Laurent Monnier (Jacquot No. 3), Brigitte De Villepoix (Marilou), Daniel Dublet (Raymond), Clement Delaroche, Rody Averty, Helene Pors, Marie-Sidonie Benoist, Julien Mitard, Jeremie Bader, Jeremie Bernard, Cedric Michaud, Guillaume Navaud, Edwige Dalaunay, Henri Janin, Christine Renaudin.

Dir: Agnes Varda. Pro: Varda, Perrine Bauduin and Danielle Vaugon. Screenplay: Varda, Jacques Demy and Josyane Morand. Ed: Marie-Jo Audiard. Art: Robert Nardone and Olivier Radot. M: Joanna Bruzdowicz. Costumes: Francoise Disle. Sound: Aurique Delannoy. (Cine-Tamaris/Canal Plus/La Sept/La Sofiarp/Centre National de la Cinematographie/Ministere de la Culture and de la Communication/Le Conseil Municipal de la Ville de Nantes/Conseil General De Loire Atlantique/Conseil Regional des Pays de la

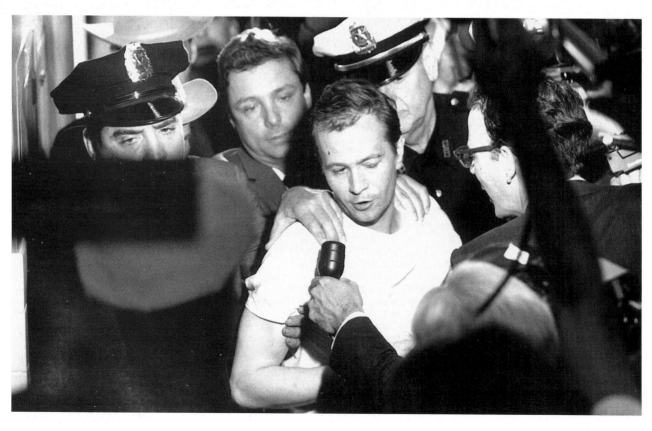

Loire et l'ARPCA–Gala.) Rel: 8 May 1992. 118 mins. Cert PG.

J'Embrasse Pas – I Don't Kiss. Pierre, an ingenuous teenage boy from the mountainous region of Gascony, moves to Paris to escape the boredom of village life. Full of sap and ideals, he is soon taught a number of harsh lessons in the big city, his youthful innocence corrupted beyond repair. This really is a hard, unyieldingly pessimistic look at humanity, unalloyed by humour or compassion. From the director of *Rendez-vous*. [JC-W]

Cast includes: Philippe Noiret (Romain), Emmanuelle Beart (Ingrid), Manuel Blanc (Pierre), Helene Vincent (Evelyne), Ivan Desny (Dimitri), Roschdy Zem (Said), Christophe Bernard, Raphaeline Goupilleau, Michele Moretti.

Dir: Andre Techine. Pro: Maurice Bernart, Jacques-Eric Strauss and Jean Labadie. Ex Pro: Alain Centonze. Screenplay: Techine, Jacques Nolot and Michel Grisolia. Ph: Thierry Arbogast. Ed: Claudine Merlin and Edith Vassard. Pro Des: Vincent Mateu-Ferrer. M: Philippe Sarde. Costumes: Claire Fraisse. Sound: Jean-Louis Ughetto. (President Films/BAC/Salome SA/ Cine Cinq Roger/Andre Larrieu Gruppo Bema/Canal Plus/Centre National de la Cinematographie–Gala.) Rel: 20 March 1992. 115 mins. Cert 18.

Cool fool: Brad Pitt as a Ricky Nelson wannabe in Tom DiCillo's unique celebration of retro-hip, Johnny Suede *(from Artificial Eye).*

JFK. In his continuing exploration of the Sixties, Oliver Stone contributes his own version of the Kennedy conspiracy, casting aspersions on LBJ, the CIA, KGB and Mafia. As always, Stone grabs our attention with both hands, and even restrains his usually fidgety camerawork, for once allowing his actors to hold centre screen. As crusading New Orleans DA Jim Garrison, Kevin Costner is a little tedious at times, and Joe Pesci over-acts as the reptilian David Ferrie – but Tommy Lee Jones, as conspirator Clay Bertrand Shaw, and Gary Oldman, as would-be assassin Lee Harvey Oswald, are superb. Stone's daring, gripping movie may be a fictionalisation of the truth, but it is factual *enough* to be a scary examination of the power of politics and of the inconsistency of history. Besides, 73 per cent of all Americans believe JFK *was* killed by a conspiracy. Garrison himself appears, briefly, as his arch-nemesis Earl Warren. [JC-W]

Also with: Kevin Bacon (Willie O'Keefe), Laurie Metcalf (Susie Cox), Michael Rooker (Bill Broussard), Jay O. Sanders (Lou Ivon), Sissy Spacek (Liz Garrison), Brian Doyle-Murray (Jack Ruby), Wayne Knight (Numa Bertel), Beata Pozniak (Marina Oswald), Tom Howard (LBJ), Walter Matthau (Senator Long), Donald Sutherland (X), Sally Kirkland, Ed Asner, Jack Lemmon, Vincent D'Onofrio, Gary Grubbs, Sean Stone, Amy Long, Scott Krueger, Allison Pratt Davis, Pruitt Taylor Vince, Tony Plana, Tomas Milian, John Candy, Jo Anderson, T. J. Kennedy, Carolina McCullough, J. J. Johnston, Dale Dye, John Seitz, Bob Gunton, Nathan Scott, John Finnegan, Frank Whaley.

Dir: Oliver Stone. Pro: Stone and A. Kitman Ho. Ex Pro: Arnon Milchan. Co-Pro: Clayton Townsend. Screenplay: Stone and Zachary Sklar; based on the books *On the Trail of the Assassins* by Jim Garrison and *Crossfire: The Plot That Killed Kennedy* by Jim Harris. Ph: Robert Richardson. Ed: Joe Hutshing and Pietro Scalia. Pro Des: Victor Kempster. M: John Williams; numbers performed by Sidney Bechet, Brent Lewis, Dinah Washington, Valladares y Su Conjunto, Jim Robinson, Tony Bennett etc. Costumes: Marlene Stewart. Sound: Tod A. Maitland. (Le Studio Canal/Regency Enterprises/Alcor Films/Ixtlan Corp–Warner.) Rel: 24 January 1992. 190 mins. Cert 15.

Johnny Suede is the ultimate solipsistic anti-hero, a beautiful, muscular, baby-faced dope who stares in the mirror and writes his name on the wall. Johnny, an aspiring (untalented) musician, knows little about women, but is always falling in love with picture-postcard bimbos, and then meets his match when he picks up a real-life, human fireball, Yvonne (Catherine Keener). *Johnny Suede*, shot for a parsimonious $1 million around the streets of Brooklyn, wears its pop-cultured postmodernism on its sleeve and then injects a shot of reality when we least expect it. At times genuinely amusing, occasionally hilarious and inevitably slow (the film marks the directorial debut of Jim Jarmusch's former cinematographer), *Johnny*

The affecting Mehmet Ali in Xavier Koller's Oscar-winning Journey of Hope *(from Mainline).*

Suede's greatest surprise comes via the calibre of its acting, with Hot New Thing Brad Pitt the perfect narcissistic moron and Ms Keener a real find as Johnny's introduction to authentic womanhood. A US-Swiss co-production. [JC-W]

Also with: Calvin Levels (Deke), Alison Moir (Darlette Fontaine), Nick Cave (Freak Storm), Peter McRobbie (Flip Doubt), Tom Jarmusch (Conan), Samuel L. Jackson (B-Bop), Michael Luciano, Ron Vawter, Tina Louise, Michael Mulheren, Joseph Barry.

Dir and Screenplay: Tom DiCillo; based on his one-man show. Pro: Yoram Mandel and Ruth Waldburger. Ex Pro: Waldburger and Steven Starr. Ph: Joe Desalvo. Ed: Geraldine Peroni. Pro Des: Patricia Woodbridge. M: Jim Farmer and Link Wray; numbers performed by Ricky Nelson and Nick Cave. Sound: Neil Danziger. (Vega Film AG/Balthazar/Arena/Starr–Artificial Eye.) Rel: 12 June 1992. 95 mins. Cert 15.

In the heat of the jungle: Annabella Sciorra and Wesley Snipes practise miscegenation in Spike Lee's commanding Jungle Fever *(from UIP).*

Journey of Hope – Reise Der Hoffnung. A poor Turkish goatherd, his wife and 7-year-old son embark on a journey that will change their lives forever. Selling his goats and land to finance the trip, Haydar leaves behind his other six children and begins the perilous passage to Switzerland – where, he believes, 'Paradise' awaits them. Told in bold, simple thrusts, this is a moving story of ignorance and hope and a significant lesson to us all. Photography and music are both admirable and paper over the cruder narrative patches. Surprise winner of the 1991 Oscar for Best Foreign Film. [JC-W]

Cast includes: Necmettin Çobanoğlu (Haydar), Nur Sürer (Meryem), Emin Sivas (Mehmet Ali), Mathias Gnädinger (Ramser), Dietmar Schönherr, Yaman Okay, Erdinç Akbaş, Yaşar Kutbay, Liliana Heimberg, Teco Celio.

Dir: Xavier Koller. Pro: Alfi Sinniger and Peter-Christian Fueter. Screenplay: Koller and Feride Çiçekoglu. Ph: Elemer Ragalyi. Ed: Galip Iyitanir. M: Jan Gabarek and Terje Rypdal. Sound: Milan Bor. (Catpics AG/Condorfeatures/Film Four Int-Mainline.) Rel: 26 July 1991. 110 mins. Cert PG.

Julia Has Two Lovers. A dissatisfied woman (Daphna Kastner) dumps her stodgy boyfriend only to fall for a telephone Lothario (David Duchovny). An enjoyably light, verbose romantic comedy that pivots on one long phone call which ultimately makes three people face up to their weaknesses – changing their lives forever. This independent production was so low-budget ($20,000!), that Duchovny (best known as the transvestite in *Twin Peaks*) laughingly admits he was paid only $1 for his troubles. [KK]

Cast includes: Daphna Kastner (Julia), David Duchovny (Daniel), David Charles (Jack), Tim Ray (Leo), Clare Bancroft (Jackie), Martin Donovan (Freddy), Anita Olanick, Al Samuels, Julie Roswal, C. H. Lehenhof, Laureen Fitch.

Dir and Pro: Bashar Shbib. Ex Pro: C. H. Lehenhof and Randall Davis. Screenplay: Shbib and Daphna Kastner. Ph: Stephen Reizes. Ed: Shbib and Dan Foegelle. M: Emilio Kauderer; numbers composed and performed by Tim Ray. Sound: Al Samuels. (Oneira Pictures–Mainline.) Rel: 4 October 1991. 86 mins. Cert 15.

Jungle Fever. Spike Lee's best joint to date, a powerful, colourful Romeo and Juliet story set in the twin hellholes of

Ice men: Michael Biehn and Matt Craven brave the elements in Franc Roddam's exhilarating K2 *(from Entertainment).*

Harlem and Bensonhurst. Flipper Purify (Wesley Snipes) is a successful black architect and a happy family man. Angela Tucci (Annabella Sciorra) is a working-class Italian secretary and slave to her father and brothers. Employed as Flipper's secretary, Angela becomes the catalyst in the architect's downfall as an explosion of racial hatred rocks their respective lives. This is angry stuff, pumped with broad humour and shot through with a muscular, assertive style. Snipes is particularly good as the middle-class black, and is bolstered by a starry supporting cast. Stevie Wonder's background score is OK, but intrudes too often on the dialogue. [JC-W]

Also with: Spike Lee (Cyrus), Anthony Quinn (Lou Carbone), Ossie Davis (The Good Reverend Doctor Purify), Ruby Dee (Lucinda Purify), Samuel L. Jackson (Gator Purify), Lonetta McKee (Drew), John Turturro (Paulie Carbone), Nicholas Turturro (Vinny), Michael Badalucco (Frankie Botz),

Frank Vincent, Halle Berry, Tyra Ferrell, Veronica Webb, Veronica Timbers, David Dundara, Michael Imperioli, Steven Randazzo, Joe D'Onofrio, Anthony Nocerrino, Debi Mazar, Gina Mastrogiacomo, Tim Robbins, Brad Dourif, Rick Aiello.

Dir, Pro and Screenplay: Spike Lee. Co-Pro: Monty Ross. Ph: Ernest Dickerson. Ed: Sam Pollard. Pro Des: Wynn Thomas. M: Stevie Wonder and Terence Blanchard; numbers performed by Mahalia Jackson, Public Enemy, Frank Sinatra, The Boys Choir of Harlem, Stevie Wonder etc. Costumes: Ruth E. Carter. Sound: Skip Lievsay. (40 Acres/Mule Filmworks/Universal–UIP.) Rel: 6 September 1991. 132 mins. Cert 18.

K2 is the world's second highest mountain and the most technically challenging to climb. Twenty-seven people have died trying to conquer what is now nicknamed 'the savage mountain'. Taylor Brooks (Michael Biehn) is a handsome, no-bull attorney from Seattle, a man 'too dumb to let reality stand in the way of success'. His best friend is the more cautious Harold Jamieson (Matt Craven), a physicist with a wife and young child. Together they take on the mountaineering challenge of their lives: the savage mountain. And it could cost them *more* than their lives. *K2* is not only an engineering miracle in that director Franc Roddam and his crew have captured some of the most devastating mountaineering footage on 35mm, but also a hymn to human endeavour. Man versus nature and man versus himself come together in a stirring, superbly photographed epic that cannot fail to enthral. Filmed on location in remotest Kashmir and Pakistan, with British Columbia's treacherous Mount Waddington standing in for K2. [JC-W]

Also with: Raymond J. Barry (Phillip Claiborne), Hiroshi Fujioka (Takane Shimuzu), Luca Bercovici (Dallas Woolf), Patricia Charbonneau (Jacki Metcalfe), Julia Nickson-Soul (Cindy Jamieson), Jamal Shah, Annie Grindlay, Elena Stiteler, Blu Mankuma, Antony Holland.

Dir: Franc Roddam. Pro: Jonathan Taplan, Marilyn Weiner and Tim Van Rellim. Ex Pro: Melvyn J. Estrin and Hal Weiner. Screenplay: Patrick Meyers and Scott Roberts; from Meyers' play. Ph: Gabriel Beristain. Ed: Sean Barton. Pro Des: Andrew Sanders. M: Chaz Jankel. Costumes: Kathryn Morrison. (Trans Pacific/

Dangerous games: angry boyfriend Michael Madsen confronts private eye Val Kilmer in John R. Dahl's corkscrew Kill Me Again *(from Rank).*

Alfie *meets the San Francisco police force in this innocuous, preposterous concoction. Christian Slater and Milla Jovovich co-star in* Kuffs *(from Entertaimment).*

Majestic Films Int–Entertainment.) Rel: 22 November 1991. 110 mins. Cert 15.

Kill Me Again. If your boyfriend's a sadistic killer, then you don't double-cross him and steal his $875,000. Fay Forrester (Joanne Whalley-Kilmer) has done just that, and so she goes to in-debt Reno private eye Jack Andrews to help alter her identity. Needing her ready dough, Jack agrees to fake Fay's death – landing him in no end of trouble with the police, his money lenders, Fay's boyfriend and the Mafia, who want their cash back. A guy could get killed in a movie like this. Val Kilmer (looking more and more like a young Jeff Bridges) exhibits laid-back charisma as Jack, but his real-life partner, Joanne Whalley-Kilmer, acts a little too hard as Faye. However, some unusual locations and trim editing make this an above-average stab at *film noir*. [JC-W]

Also with: Michael Madsen (Vince Miller), Jonathan Gries (Alan Swayzie), Duane Tucker (Brian, collection agent No. 2), Robert Schuch, Bibi Besch, Michael Sharrett, Debby Lynn Ross, Michael Greene, James Henriksen, Darrel Wayne.
Dir: John R. Dahl. Pro: Sigurjon Sighvatsson, Steve Golin and David W. Warfield. Ex Pro: Michael Kuhn and Nigel Sinclair. Screenplay: Dahl and Warfield. Ph: Jacques Steyn. Ed: Frank E. Jimenez, Jonathan Shaw and Eric Beason. Pro Des: Michelle Minch. M: William Olvis; Haydn; numbers performed by Jackson Leap, Dinah Washington, Oscar Peterson etc. (ITC/Propaganda–Rank.) Rel: 12 July 1991. 96 mins. Cert 18.

Kuffs. San Francisco, 1991. Comic book caper about a 21-year-old dropout who inherits a police precinct when his brother is murdered. Brandishing a potpourri of styles – ranging from slapstick to gratuitous violence – *Kuffs* is occasionally entertaining but on the whole pretty painful to watch. (Formerly known as *Hero Wanted*.) [JC-W]

Cast includes: Christian Slater (George Kuffs), Tony Goldwyn (Ted Bukovsky), Milla Jovovich (Maya Carlton), Bruce Boxleitner (Brad Kuffs), George De La Pena (Sam Jones), Leon Rippy (Kane), Mary Ellen Trainor (Nick), Troy Evans (Capt. Morino), Joshua Cadman, Kim Robillard, Scott Williamson, Aki Aleong, Henry G. Sanders, Lu Leonard, Stephen Park.
Dir: Bruce A. Evans. Pro: Raynold Gideon and Mel Dellar. Screenplay: Evans and Gideon. Ph: Thomas Del Ruth. Ed: Stephen Semel. Pro Des: Victoria Paul. M:

Don't mess with these guys: Bruce Willis and Damon Wayans face the opposition in Tony Scott's flash-bang-wallop-cuss The Last Boy Scout *(from Warner).*

Harold Faltermeyer; numbers performed by Timbuk 3, The Regulators, Eddie Money etc. Costumes: Mary E. Vogt. Sound: David Brownlow and Agamemnon Andrianos. (Dino De Laurentiis–Entertainment.) Rel: 3 April 1992. 102 mins. Cert 15.

The Lady from the Shanghai Cinema – Adama Do Cine Shanghai. Real life imitates celluloid as a randy estate agent pursues a glamorous woman he meets at the Shanghai Cinema – whilst a *film noir* programme is showing. Stood up by her at a Chinese bar, the agent is mistaken for a hit man and becomes involved in a murder. But what role in all this does the beautiful and mysterious cinemagoer have? Is she involved at all? Does her husband care? Do we? This is an absurd Brazilian *film noir* comedy that trips up over its own complexities and fails to conjure up the atmosphere of the movies it is imitating. Worse still, Antonio Fagundes is a most unbecoming leading man. [JC-W]

Cast includes: Maite Proenca (Suzana), Antonio Fagundes (Lucas), Jose Lewgoy (Linus), Jorge Doria (Velho), Jose Mayer, Miguel Falabella, Paulo Villaca, Sergio Mamberti, Imara Reis, John Doo, Julio Calasso Jr.

Dir and Screenplay: Guilherme de Almeida Prado. Ex Pro: Assuncao Hernandes. Ph: Claudio Portioli and Jose Roberto Eliezer. Ed: Jair Garcia Duarte. Art: Chico Andrade. (Star Films/Raiz Producoes Cinematograficas–Metro.) Rel: 2 August 1991. 109 mins. Cert 15.

Ladybugs. Truly abysmal vehicle for the fast-talking, eye-bulging Rodney Dangerfield. The star of such hits as *Caddyshack*, *Easy Money* and *Back to School*, Dangerfield this time coaches an all-girl soccer team, including his fiancée's son – in drag. Unbelievably, this witless farce was shot by Sidney J. Furie, who once made *Lady Sings the Blues*. They shoot better clay pigeons. [CB]

Cast includes: Rodney Dangerfield (Chester Lee); Jackee (Julie Benson), Jonathan Brandis (Matthew/Martha), Ilene Graff (Bess), Vinessa Shaw (Kimberly Mullen), Tom Parks (Dave Mullen), Jeanetta Arnett (Glyn-

nis Mullen), Nancy Parsons, Blake Clark, Tommy Lasorda.

Dir: Sidney J. Furie. Pro: Albert S. Ruddy and Andre E. Morgan. Ex Pro: Gray Frederickson. Screenplay: Curtis Burch. Ph: Dan Burstall. Ed: John W. Wheeler and Timothy N. Board. Pro Des: Robb Wilson King. M: Richard Gibbs. Costumes: Isis Mussenden. Sound: Jim Emerson (Ruddy & Morgan–Warner.) Rel: 26 June 1992. 90 mins. Cert PG.

The Last Boy Scout. Hard-hitting, fast-talking and pretty damn entertaining action-comedy from Joel Silver (*Lethal Weapon*, *Die Hard*), Hollywood's outspoken Czar of Schlock. Bruce Willis is your clichéd, seedy ex-cop-cum-private eye, having trouble with his wife, finances and razor. Damon Wayans is an uneducated, bald-headed ex-football pro on cocaine who sees his girlfriend gunned down in cold blood. It turns out she was blackmailing a crooked sports tycoon, and *he* wants to frame Willis for the assassination of an unbribable senator. So what gives? Willis is marginally better than usual – as a real bastard, 'and then some', in his own words. There's also

Tron *meets* Being There: *Pierce Brosnan wired to go in 'The UK's First Virtual Reality Film'* – The Lawnmower Man (*from First Independent*).

plenty of guns, girls and gays in this mish-mash of mirth and mayhem, lifted by a cracking script stuffed with throwaway one-liners. The screenplay should be good – it was auctioned round town by Shane Black and bought by Warners for $1.75 million. [JC-W]

Cast includes: Bruce Willis (Joe Hallenbeck), Damon Wayans (Jimmy Dix), Chelsea Field (Sarah Hallenbeck), Noble Willingham (Sheldon Marcone), Taylor Negron (Milo), Danielle Harris (Darian Hallenbeck), Halle Berry (Cory), Bruce McGill (Mike Matthews), Chelcie Ross (Senator Baynard), Billy Blanks (Billy Cole), Ed Beheler (the President), Badja Djola, Kim Coates, Joe Santos, Clarence Felder, Bill Medley, Vern Lundquist, Dick Butkus, Lynn Swann, Morris Chestnut, Denise Ames, Eddie Griffin, Jack Kehler, Rick Ducommun.

Dir: Tony Scott. Pro: Joel Silver and Michael Levy. Ex Pro: Shane Black and Barry Josephson. Screenplay: Black; from a story by Black and Greg Hicks. Ph: Ward Russell. Ed: Stuart Baird, Mark Goldblatt and Mark Helfrich. Pro Des: Brian Morris. M: Michael Kamen; numbers performed by Bill Medley, Pat Boone, Prince & The New Power Generation and Boys Don't Cry. Costumes: Marilyn Vance-Straker. (Geffen–Warner.) Rel: 28 February 1992. 105 mins. Cert 18.

Late For Dinner. Santa Fe, New Mexico, 1962–91. Two brothers – one on the run from an accidental shooting, the other too dim to care – find their way into a scientist's lab and become frozen for 29 years. When they thaw out, it takes them an entire day to realise they're not in the 1950s any more. A brilliant idea watered down into a hokey, homespun mess. [KK]

Cast includes: Brian Wimmer (Willie Husband), Peter Berg (Frank Lovegren), Marcia Gay Harden (Joy Husband), Colleen Flynn (Jessica Husband), Kyle Secor (Leland Shanks), Michael Beach (Dr David Arrington), Peter Gallagher (Bob Freeman), Cassy Friel, Ross Malinger, Steven Schwartz-Hartley, John Prosky, Bo Brundin, Donald Hotton, Billy Vera, Drew Snyder.

Dir: W. D. Richter. Pro: Richter and Dan Lupovitz. Screenplay: Mark Andrus. Ph: Peter Sova. Ed: Richard Chew and Robert Leighton. Pro Des: Lilly Kilvert. M: David Mansfield; numbers performed by The Dubs, Barbara Lynn, Marty Robbins, Elvis Presley, Doris Day, Linda Ronstadt etc. Costumes: Aggie Guerard Rodgers. (Castle Rock–First Independent.) Rel: 20 March 1992. 93 mins. Cert PG.

The Lawnmower Man. Imagine a machine that can translate your thought processes into physical actions. Imagine that this machine can provide you with an abstract landscape in which you can play computer games. Imagine that this machine can trigger dormant processes in your brain. Imagine that this machine can unleash all the hidden powers of the mind. Imagine what could happen if this machine fell into the wrong hands. A short story by Stephen King is once again given the celluloid treatment, this time backed by mind-blowing special effects. The concept is great, the computer graphics sophisticated and hallucinatory and the moral questions worthy of examination. All the film needed was some real people. [JC-W]

Cast includes: Jeff Fahey (Jobe Smith), Pierce Brosnan (Lawrence Angelo), Jenny Wright (Marnie Burke), Mark Bringleson (Sebastian Timms), Geoffrey Lewis (Terry McKeen), Jeremy Slate (Father McKeen), Dean Norris (director), Rosalee Mayeux (Carla Parkette), Austin O'Brien (Peter Parkette), Colleen Coffey, Troy Evans, Michael Gregory, Joe Hart, John Laughlin, Ray Lykins, Jim Landis.

Dir: Brett Leonard. Pro: Gimel Everett. Co-Pro: Milton Subotsky. Ex Pro: Edwards Simons, Steve Lane, Robert Pringle and Clive Turner. Screenplay: Leonard and

Everett; based on a short story by Stephen King. Ph: Russell Carpenter. Ed: Alan Baumgarten. Pro Des: Alex McDowell. M: Dan Wyman; numbers performed by Sterling, Creative Rite and Carnal Garage. Costumes: Mary Jane Fort. Sound: Russell Fager. Computer Animation and Design: Xaos. (Allied Vision/Fuji Eight Co–First Independent.) Rel: 5 June 1992. 108 mins. Cert 15.

'Let Him Have It'. Croydon, London, 1952. Derek Bentley, 19, an illiterate epileptic with the mental age of an 11-year-old, is persuaded by his friend Christopher Craig, 16, to rob a confectioner's warehouse. Intercepted by police, Bentley is arrested and yells at his friend to 'let him [the arresting officer] have it', pleading to Craig to give up his gun. Instead, Craig wounds one policeman and shoots another between the eyes. After failing to kill himself, Craig mutters to his captors, 'I hope I killed the bloody lot.' Due to his youth, Craig is sentenced to prison, while Bentley is sentenced to death as an accessory to murder. Two hundred Members of Parliament pleaded for Bentley's pardon, but to no avail. The truth is that Bentley was mentally unfit to stand trial, let alone hang for it. An intelligent, compassionate recreation of a genuine *cause célèbre*, which is still

Building suspense: Pamela Gidley and Kevin Anderson are drawn to a mysterious building – and themselves – in Mike Figgis's intriguing thriller, Liebestraum *(from UIP).*

being disputed to this day as Bentley's sister fights to have her brother's name cleared. [JC-W]

Cast includes: Christopher Eccleston (Derek Bentley), Paul Reynolds (Chris Craig), Tom Bell (Detective-Constable Frederick Fairfax), Eileen Atkins (Lilian Bentley), Tom Courtenay (William Bentley), Clare Holman (Iris Bentley), Michael Gough (Lord Goddard), Mark McGann (Niven Craig), Serena Scott-Thomas (Stella), Peter Eyre (Christmas Humphries), James Villiers (F. H. Cassels), Robert Morgan (PC Sydney George Miles), Karl Johnson (E. J. Parris), Ian Deam, Bert Tyler-Moore, Steve Nicholson,

Innocent or innocent? Christopher Eccleston as the notorious scapegoat Derek Bentley in Peter Medak's workmanlike 'Let Him Have It' (from First Independent).

Niven Boyd, Ronald Fraser, Michael Elphick, Murray Melvin, Linda Marlowe, Francis Hope, Peter Jonfield, Rudolph Walker, Glyn Grain, Joe Melia, Vernon Dobtcheff, Jeremy Sinden, Terence Skelton, Norman Rossington, Clive Revill, Iain Cuthbertson, Bill Dean.

Dir: Peter Medak. Pro: Luc Roeg and Robert Warr. Ex Pro: Jeremy Thomas. Screenplay: Neal Purvis and Robert Wade. Ph: Oliver Stapleton. Ed: Ray Lovejoy. Pro Des: Michael Pickwoad. M: Michael Kamen. Costumes: Pam Tait. Sound: Rene Borisewitz. (Le Studio Canal Plus/Film Trustees/British Screen/Vivid–First Independent.) Rel: 4 October 1991. 115 mins. Cert 15.

Liebestraum is a passage of music written by Franz Liszt, which is heard playing as an anonymous man makes love to a beautiful heiress in an empty department store at night. Years later, architecture buff Nick Kaminsky (Kevin Anderson) finds himself mysteriously drawn to the department store, which is about to be demolished. He's in town to meet his natural mother for the first time who, like the building, has one week left to live. Her dying wish is to see her son at last, so that she can exorcise some pretty disturbing

The magic of the thousand strings: Liu Zhong-yuan in Chen Kaige's mystical Life on a String *(from ICA).*

ghosts. These ghosts haunt Nick at night and he's determined to get to the bottom of them. That's just *one* way of looking at this multi-faceted erotic thriller, which constantly disturbs and misleads its captive audience. English director-writer-composer Mike Figgis knows how to lay on the atmosphere, and layers his plot with intriguing metaphor. Slow, to be sure, but a worthwhile journey. [JC-W]

Also with: Pamela Gidley (Jane Kessler), Bill Pullman (Paul Kessler), Kim Novak (Mrs Anderssen), Graham Beckel (Sheriff Ricker), Zach Grenier (Barnett Ralston IV), Thomas Kopache (Dr Parker), Anne Lange, Jack Wallace, Catherine Hicks, Bill Raymond, Waldemar Kalinowski.

Dir, Screenplay and M: Mike Figgis. Pro: Eric Fellner. Co-Pro: Michael Flynn. Ph: Juan Ruiz Anchia. Ed: Martin Hunter. Pro Des: Waldemar Kalinowski. Costumes: Sharon Simonaire. Sound: John Pritchett.

(Initial/MGM–UIP.) Rel: 10 January 1992. 112 mins. Cert 18.

Life On a String – Bian Zhou Bian Chang. Stunningly photographed film from Chen Kaige (director of *Yellow Earth*, *The Big Parade*, *King of the Children*), this outgrowth of China's New Wave cinema is the dislocated story of the conflict between two blind musicians. One is a saintly old man enmeshed in the mythology of his past, the other a rebellious teenager who falls for a village girl against the wishes of his mentor and her family. Financed from a variety of international sources (including Germany and Britain), the film succeeds as a poetic picture of life in Inner Mongolia, but falls foul of its plodding pace. However, Liu Zhongyuan is wonderful as the old saint. [CB]

Also with: Huang Lei (Shitou), Xu Qing (Lanxiu), Ma Ling (noodleshop owner's wife).

Dir and Screenplay: Chen Kaige; from a short story by Shi Tiesheng. Pro: Don Ranvaud. Ex Co-Pro: Cai Rubin and Karl Baumgartner. Ph: Gu Changwei. Ed: Pei Xiaonan. Pro Des: Shao Ruigang. M: Qu Xiaosong. Sound: Tao Jing. (Pandora Film/Beijing Film Studio/China Film/Herald Ace/Channel 4/Berling Filmforderung–ICA.) Rel: 31 January 1992. 109 mins. No cert.

Life Stinks. Relying less on parody, gags and out-of-context jokes than usual, Mel Brooks has come up with a rather sweet, old-fashioned and often amusing parable about the homeless in Los Angeles. He stars as Goddard Bolt, a ruthless businessman who, in order to gain control of a decaying city, takes on a bet to live on the streets for 30 days. Along the way we are introduced to some delightful supporting characters and a classic, climatic battle between giant earth-diggers, resembling prehistoric monsters. This is a gentler side to the *enfant terrible* of scatological cinema, and all the more enjoyable for that. [JC-W]

Also with: Lesley Ann Warren (Molly), Jeffrey Tambor (Vance Crasswell), Stuart Pankin (Pritchard), Howard Morris (Sailor),

That stinking feeling: Lesley Ann Warren, Mel Brooks, Teddy Wilson and Howard Morris share the streets in Brooks's enjoyable Life Stinks *(from Fox).*

Rudy De Luca (J. Paul Getty), Teddy Wilson (Fumes), Michael Ensign, Matthew Faison, Billy Barty, Brian Thompson, Raymond O'Connor, John Welsh, Stanley Brock, Larry Cedar.

Dir and Pro: Mel Brooks. Ex Pro: Ezra Swerdlow. Screenplay: Brooks, Rudy De Luca, Steve Haberman and Ron Clark. Ph: Steven Poster. Ed: David Rawlins. Pro Des: Peter Larkin. M: John Morris. Costumes: Mary Malin. (Brooksfilms–Fox.) Rel: 20 September 1991. 95 mins. Cert 12.

Light Sleeper. Paul Schrader updates the spiritual quest of the underworld loner to the 1990s, with Willem Dafoe as the New York drug dealer attempt-

ing to resurrect himself. Dafoe is surprisingly self-effacing, even gauche, as John LeTour, a delivery boy for upscale dealer Ann, played by Susan Sarandon. But it is LeTour's ex, Marianne (Dana Delaney), who leads him

on the road to spiritual catharsis. Like Schrader's previous celluloid loners – Travis Bickle (Robert De Niro) in *Taxi Driver* (1976) and Julian Kay (Richard Gere) in *American Gigolo* (1980) – the ultimate exorcism must arise through

Sleepwalking: Susan Sarandon as the smart, upscale drug supplier in Paul Schrader's story of nineties alienation, Light Sleeper *(from Guild).*

65

Foster child: Adam Hann-Byrd as the child prodigy in Jodie Foster's eye-opening Little Man Tate *(from Columbia).*

violence. *Light Sleeper* was inspired by a dream Schrader had, and the title comes, he says, from the New Testament. This seems in keeping with the film's sleep-walking feel and with its pretentious theological undertones. Very dull. [JC-W]

Also with: David Clennon (Robert), Mary Beth Hurt (Teresa), Victor Garber (Tis), Jane Adams (Randy), Paul Jabara (Eddie),

Robert Cicchini, Sam Rockwell, Rene Rivera.

Dir and Screenplay: Paul Schrader. Pro: Linda Reisman. Ex Pro: Mario Kassar. Co-Pro: G. Mac Brown. Co-Ex Pro: Ronna B. Wallace. Ph: Ed Lachman. Ed: Kristina Boden. Pro Des: Richard Hornung. M: Michael Been; numbers performed by Wizdom-N-Motion and Kane Roberts. Costumes: Giorgio Armani. Sound: Doug

Memories of ennui: Leigh McCormack (centre) at the picture show, putting the boredom of Liverpool life behind him – in Terence Davies' The Long Day Closes *(from Mayfair Entertainment/Palace).*

Michael. (Grain of Sand Prods.–Guild.) Rel: 13 March 1992. 103 mins. Cert 15.

Listen Up: The Lives of Quincy Jones. Infuriatingly neurotic documentary on musical guru Quincy Jones. Apparently terrified of boring its audience, *Listen Up* bombards us with nearly two hours of fractured conversations, snippets of music and snatches of home movie. No one song or composition is allowed to play its course nor is one full statement savoured. This is pop video rockumentary at its most unbearable, assaulting the eyes with strobe-like images and teasing the ears with overlapping dialogue. Quincy himself, here depicted as some kind of god, is the stuff of a fascinating documentary, if only somebody would make as slick a job of it as the man's music. [JC-W]

Also with: George Benson, Richard Brooks, Ray Charles, Miles Davis, El DeBarge, Sheila E., Billy Eckstine, Ella Fitzgerald, Aretha Franklin, Dizzy Gillespie, Lesley Gore, Alex Haley, Herbie Hancock, Ice-T, James Ingram, Jesse Jackson, Michael Jackson, Al Jarreau, Sidney Lumet, Bobby McFerrin, Melle Mel, Frank Sinatra, Steven Spielberg, Barbra Streisand, Sarah Vaughan, Oprah Winfrey etc.

Dir: Ellen Weissbrod. Pro: Courtney Sale Ross. Line Pro: Melissa Powell. Ph: Stephen Kazmierski. Ed: Milton Moses Ginsberg, Pierre Kahn, Andrew Morreale, Laure Sullivan and Paul Zehrer. M: Quincy Jones. Sound: Anthony (Chic) Ciccolini III. (Warner.) Rel: 2 August 1991. 115 mins. Cert 12.

Little Man Tate. Jodie Foster, former child star, makes her directorial debut aged 28 with this mature, thought-provoking and frequently funny human drama about a 7-year-old child prodigy. The man of the title is Fred Tate who could read at one, write poetry at 4 and play the piano *backwards* at 7. Fred Tate is blessed with an intelligence far beyond the adults around him, and it is no joke. All Fred wants is a normal life. His mother, Dede Tate (Jodie Foster), is single and struggling, and gives Fred all the love that he could need. But Fred requires more than love. Jane Grierson (Dianne Wiest), single and successful, can cater to the boy's intellectual needs, but cannot supply the warmth. Perhaps, together, they can help Fred with his problems. The film's trump card is the casting of

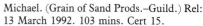

Adam Hann-Byrd, who is totally believable in the title role – and even looks like Jodie Foster. At times the film aims for the obvious buttons to push, but on the whole is an engrossing work on a fascinating subject. [JC-W]

Also with: Harry Connick Jr (Eddie), David Pierce (Garth), P. J. Ochlan (Damon Wells), Nathan Lee, Celia Weston, Danitra Vance, Debi Mazar, George Plimpton, Josh Mostel, Michael Mantell, Bob Balaban.

Dir: Jodie Foster. Pro: Scott Rudin and Peggy Rajski. Ex Pro: Randy Stone. Screenplay: Scott Frank. Ph: Mike Southon. Ed: Lynzee Klingman. Pro Des: Jon Hutman. M: Mark Isham; Mozart, Brahms; *I Get a Kick Out of You* performed by Ella Fitzgerald. Costumes: Susan Lyall. (Orion–Columbia.) Rel: 17 January 1992. 99 mins. Cert PG.

London Kills Me. This slice of seamy London life is the first directorial effort by the scriptwriter of *My Beautiful Laundrette*, Hanif Kureishi. Judging by this, his skills are greater on the page than behind the camera. [FDM]

Cast: Justin Chadwick (Clint), Steven Mackintosh (Muffdiver), Emer McCourt (Sylvie), Rohan Seth (Dr Bubba), Fiona Shaw (Headley), Brad Dourif (Hemingway), Tony Haygarth (Burns), Steven Rimkus, Eleanor David, Alun Armstrong, Nick Dunning, Naveen Andrews, Gary Cooper.

Dir and Screenplay: Hanif Kureishi. Pro: Tim Bevan. Ex Pro: Graham Bradstreet. Co-Pro: Judy Hunt. Ed: Jon Gregory. Pro Des: Stuart Walker. Sound: Albert Bailey and Sue Baker. M: Mark Springer and Sarah Sarhandi. (Polygram/Working Title in assoc with Film Four International.) Rel: 13 December 1991. 105 mins. Cert 18.

The Long Day Closes. Liverpool, 1955–6. Terence Davies, who collected seventeen international awards for his autobiographical first feature *Distant Voices, Still Lives*, here continues the saga as Bud, aged 13, falls in love with 'the pictures'. This is an uncompromisingly personal work, unstinting in its dedication to detail, but so slow and studied and *uneventful* that few could find much to catch their attention. Having said that, some critics went bananas over it. [JC-W]

Cast includes: Marjorie Yates (Mother), Leigh McCormack (Bud), Anthony Watson, Nicholas Lamont, Ayse Owens, Tina Malone, Jimmy Wilde, Robin Polley, Peter Ivatts, Joy Blakeman, Denise Thomas, Marcus Heath, Brenda Peters.

Dir and Screenplay: Terence Davies. Pro:

Hard times: Anthony Andrews (foreground) strives for dignity and hope in a Russian gulag, in Alexander Mitta's harrowing Lost in Siberia *(from Spectator Entertainment).*

Olivia Stewart. Ex Pro: Ben Gibson and Colin MacCabe. Ex in charge of Production: Angela Topping. Ph: Michael Coulter. Ed: William Diver. Pro Des: Christopher Hobbs. M: Bob Last and Robert Lockhart; various radio songs. Costumes: Monica Howe. Sound: Moya Burns. (Film Four International/BFI–Mayfair Entertainment/ Palace.) Rel: 22 May 1992. 83 mins. Cert 12.

Lost in Siberia. Persia/Moscow/Siberia, 1945. Financed by Britain and filmed in Moscow and Yaroslavl by the Russians, this politically significant film falls foul of the pitfalls of international co-production but then rises above them. Anthony Andrews (over twenty pounds lighter and in his best celluloid performance to date) stars as Andrei Miller, an English archaeologist working in Persia who is mistaken for an American spy and taken to Moscow. Realising their mistake, the KGB cover up the blunder by dispatching Miller

Lust story: Tony Leung and Jane March enjoy a bit of slap and tickle in Jean-Jacques Annaud's laborious The Lover *(from Guild).*

to a Siberian gulag. The film, like a young calf learning to walk, is artless, clumsy and naive. There is poor dubbing and appalling sound, phony backdrops and erratic standards of photography. But the power of the subject matter eventually takes over, and the simplicity of the narrative drives this terrible (and true) story straight into the heart. Grim going, maybe, but an important step forward for *glasnost*, Mosfilm and Spectator Entertainment International, whose first film this is. [JC-W]

Also with: Yelena Mayorova (Anna), Vladimir Ilyin (Capt Malakhov), Ira Mikhalyova (Lilka), Yevgeni Mironov (Volodya), Nicolas Chagrin (the Shah), Elena Secota (the Shah's wife), Alexei Zharkov, Valentin Gaft, Alexander Bureyev, Valdimir Prozorov, Hark Bohm.
 Dir: Alexander Mitta. Pro: Anthony Andrews, Gagik Gasparyan and Alexander Moody. Ex Pro: Benjamin Brahms. Screenplay: Mitta, Valery Fried (based on his own experiences), Yuri Korotkov and James Brabazon. Ph: Vladimir Shevtsik. Ed: Anthony Sloman and Nadesdha Veselovskaya. Art: Valery Yurkevitch and Vatali Klimenkov. M: Leonid Desyatnikov. Costumes: T. Lichmanova. Sound: Yekaterina Popova. (Spectator Entertainment International–Winstone Film Distributors.) Rel: 8 May 1992. 108 mins. Cert 15.

The Lover – L'Amant. Saigon, the 1920s. Sexually frank, big-budget ($22 million) love story between a wealthy 32-year-old Chinaman and a 17-year-old French schoolgirl. He loves her with his heart, she just needs to sate her sexual curiosity. Tears will follow. The photography, in the tradition of *Emmanuelle*, is lovely, but the acting is so stilted that the characters never come alive. The French girl, played by Eng-

Fairy tales in the blender: Pinocchio and Cinderella team up in Yoram Gross's dainty The Magic Riddle *(from Rank).*

lish newcomer Jane March (dubbed the 'Sinner from Pinner' by the media), *is* gorgeous, but can't act her way out of a pair of knickers. The film itself is long, slow and bum-numbing. [JC-W]

Also with: Tony Leung (the Chinaman), Frederique Meininger (the mother), Arnaud Giovaninetti (the elder brother), Melvil Poupaud (the little brother), Lisa Faulkner (Helene Lagonelle), Ann Schaufuss, Jeanne Moreau (the Voice).
 Dir: Jean-Jacques Annaud. Pro: Claude Berri. Screenplay: Annaud and Gerard Brach; based on the memoir by Marguerite Duras. Ph: Robert Fraisse. Ed: Noelle Boisson. Art: Thanh At Hoang. M: Gabriel Yared. Costumes: Yvonne Sassinot de Nesle. Sound: Laurent Quaglio. (Renn Prods/Films A2/Burrill Prods–Guild.) Rel: 19 June 1992. 117 mins. Cert 18.

The Lunatic. Unusual, largely engaging satire about a strange Jamaican youth, Aloysius (Paul Campbell), whose only companion in the world is a tree. That is until he is befriended by the large, amorous German tourist Inga (Julie T. Wallace), who takes him as her love slave. Later, she establishes a *ménage à trois* by adding a local butcher to the stew. Directed by ex-musician and music video creator Lol Creme (10CC, Godley & Creme), this is a spirited feature debut, enhanced by a playful screenplay and lively performances – but prone to an occasional attack of the cutes. [CB]

Also with: Reggie Carter (Busha), Carl Bradshaw (Service), Winston Stona (Lindstrom), Linda Gambrill (Sarah), Rosemary Murray (Widow Dawkins), Lloyd Reckord (the judge).

Dir: Lol Creme. Pro: Paul Heller and John Pringle. Ex Pro: Chris Blackwell and Dan Genetti. Screenplay: Anthony C. Winkler; based on his novel. Ph: Richard Greatrex. Ed: Michel Connell. Art: Giorgio Ferrarri. M: Wally Badarou. Costumes: Patricia Griffiths. Sound: Kim Ornitz. (Island–Oasis.) Rel: 14 February 1992. 95 mins. Cert 15.

The Magic Riddle. An enterprising animated musical from Australia, in which an old woman admits to her grandchildren that she can get her stories a little muddled. And so Cinderella encounters the Big Bad Wolf in the forest, and escapes to hide out with the Seven Dwarfs *and* Pinocchio. And so on. The film makes no technical or artistic breakthroughs in animation, but should delight most small children. [CB]

Female voices: Robyn Moore; male voices: Keith Scott.

Dir and Pro: Yoram Gross. Screenplay: Gross, Leonard Lee and John Palmer; based on the stories of Jakob and Wilhelm Grimm, Hans Christian Andersen and others. Background Design: Richard Zaloudek. M: Guy Gross; lyrics: John Palmer; *Ordinary Miracles* sung by Julie Anthony. Sound: Phil Judd. (Yoram Gross Film Studios/Beyond International/AFFC–Rank.) Rel: 10 April 1992. 93 mins. Cert U.

The Mambo Kings. 1952, Havana/New York. Eloquently directed musical-drama about two Cuban brothers – one a singer/pianist, the other a songwriter/trumpeter – who travel to New York to make the big time. There, jealousy, sex and music combine to produce a combustible, enjoyable film that ends all too abruptly, without its story being fully resolved. However, it looks great, Armand Assante gives the performance of his career (as the fiery, life-devouring womaniser Cesar Castillo) and the Latin beat is irresistible. Arne Glimcher, who produced *Gorillas in the Mist* and *The Good Mother*, makes a remarkably assured directorial debut, well serving Cynthia Cidre's polished screenplay. [JC-W]

Also with: Antonio Banderas (Nestor Castillo), Cathy Moriarty (Lanna Lake), Maruschka Detmers (Delores Fuentes), Desi Arnaz Jr (Desi Arnaz Sr), Celia Cruz (Evalina Montoya), Roscoe Lee Browne (Fernando Perez), Tito Puente (himself), Talisa

Feel the music: Antonio Banderas and Armand Assante increase the pulse in Arne Glimcher's stylish The Mambo Kings *(from Warner).*

Soto (Maria Rivera), Jose Alberto (Johnny Casanova), Pablo Calogero, Scott Cohen, Mario Grillo, Vondie Curtis-Hall, Anh Duong, Helena Carroll, Frank Grillo, Anita Banderas, Karen Assante.

Dir: Arne Glimcher. Pro: Glimcher and Arnon Milchan. Ex Pro: Steven Reuther. Co-Pro: Jack B. Bernstein. Screenplay: Cynthia Cidre; based on the novel *The Mambo Kings Play Songs of Love* by Oscar Hijuelos. Ph: Michael Ballhaus. Ed: Claire Simpson. Pro Des: Stuart Wurtzel. M: Robert Kraft and Carlos Franzetti; numbers performed by Celia Cruz, Tito Puente, Duke Ellington,

Linda Ronstadt, Jo Stafford, Beny Moré, Los Lobos etc. Costumes: Ann Roth, Gary Jones and Bridget Kelly. Sound: Michael Kirchberger. (Le Studio Canal Plus/Regency Enterprises/Alcor Films–Warner.) Rel: 29 May 1992. 104 mins. Cert 15.

The Man in the Moon. Louisiana, the 1950s. Heart-warming, tear-jerking melodrama set in the Deep South where two teenage sisters (one 17, the other 14) fall for the same good ol' boy. The substantially autobiographical screenplay at times feels like a filmed play (and at others a TV movie), but Robert Mulligan's assured direction and the forcefulness of the performances make this an A-grade movie to

It started with a kiss: Reese Witherspoon and Jason London break the rules in Robert Mulligan's alluring drama of sexual awakening, The Man in the Moon *(from UIP).*

admire. Fourteen-year-old newcomer Reese Witherspoon is particularly impressive as the life-infatuated tomboy on the threshold of sexuality, but then the 67-year-old Mulligan is one of the best directors of children in Hollywood (witness *To Kill a Mockingbird*, *Summer of '42*, *The Other*, *Clara's Heart* etc). [JC-W]

Cast includes: Sam Waterston (Matthew Trant), Tess Harper (Abigail Trant), Gail Strickland (Marie Foster), Reese Witherspoon (Dani Trant), Jason London (Court Foster), Emily Warfield (Maureen Trant), Bentley Mitchum (Robert's grandson, as Billy Sanders), Ernie Lively, Dennis Letts, Earleen Bergeron.
Dir: Robert Mulligan. Pro: Mark Rydell. Ex Pro: William S. Gilmore and Shari Rhodes. Screenplay: Jenny Wingfield. Ph: Freddie Francis. Ed: Trudy Ship. Pro Des: Gene Callahan. M: James Newton Howard; *Loving You* performed by Elvis Presley. Costumes: Peter Saldutti. Sound: Peter Bentley. (MGM–UIP.) Rel: 28 February 1992. 99 mins. Cert PG.

Mannequin on the Move. Forgettable re-make of the 1987 comedy *Mannequin*, about a shop-window dummy coming to life and causing chaos. Yawn. [FDM]

Cast: Meshack Taylor (Mr Hollywood), William Ragsdale (Jason), Kristy Swanson (Jessie), Terry Kiser (Count Spretzle), Stuart Pankin (Mr James), Cynthia Harris, Andrew Hill Newman, John Edmondson, Phil Latella, Mark Gray, Julie Foreman.
Dir: Stewart Rafill. Pro: Edward Rugoff. Ex Pro: John Foreman. Screenplay: Rugoff, David Isaacs, Ken Levine, Betsy Israel. Ph: Larry Pizer. Ed: John Rosenberg and Joan Chapman. Pro Des: William Creber. Art: Norman B. Dodge Jr. M: David McHugh. (Gladden Entertainment–Fox.) Rel: 18 October 1991. 93 mins. Cert PG.

Mátador. Pedro Almodovar proves yet again what a wonderfully sick puppy he is with this release of one of his earlier films (made in 1986). Two charming psychopaths, a wounded ex-matador and a luscious lady lawyer (who is his ardent fan), are cheerfully murdering people in Madrid unbeknownst to each other. They are brought together to defend a young innocent, Angel (Antonio Banderas), a psychic trainee matador with a guilt complex, who is claiming to have committed their murders. Nothing is sacred in a film which begins with a man vigorously masturbating in front of a TV showing women being sawn in half, and that ends with the most satisfying of denouements for those of us who don't believe in Hollywood-style justice. Almodovar again takes on sex, fashion, bullfighting, religion and love – true love – in this witty, arousing film. [BW]

Also with: Assumpta Serna (Maria Cadinal), Nacho Martinez (Diego), Eva Cobo (Eva), Julietta Serrano (Berta), Chus Lampreave, Carmen Maura, Bibi Andersson, Pedro Almodovar.
Dir: Pedro Almodovar. Ex Pro: Andres Vicente Gomez. Screenplay: Almodovar and Jesus Ferrero. Ph: Angel Luis Fernandez. Ed: Jose Salcedo. Pro Des: Romano Arango, Jose Morales and Josep Rosell. M: Ernard Bonezzi. Costumes: Jose M. Cossio. (Metro.) Rel: 6 December 1991. 96 mins. Cert 18.

Medicine Man. Sean Connery stars as Dr Robert Campbell, an eccentric, charismatic biochemist living with the natives deep in the Venezuelan rain forest. Enter cantankerous Dr Rae 'Bronx' Crane (Lorraine Bracco), his new, over-qualified, under-experienced research assistant sent in to check up on him. Sparks will fly, but if you were the only girl in the jungle and I was the only boy . . . Connery was reportedly paid $10 million for his role, the film's budget escalated to $40m and the look of the film (shot in Mexico) is stupendous. What else do you expect from John McTiernan, director of *Predator*, *Die Hard* and *The Hunt For Red October*? But not even McTiernan can elicit romantic chemistry from two egos who apparently failed to see eye to eye. With the right stars this could've been riveting cinema. Previously known as *The Stand* and *The Last Days of Eden*. [JC-W]

Also with: Jose Wilker (Dr Ornega), Francisco Tsi'Reme (Jahausa), Elias Monteiro (Palala), Edenei Dos Santos, Bekana Caiapo.
Dir: John McTiernan. Pro: Andrew G. Vajna and Donna Dubrow. Ex Pro: Sean Connery. Screenplay: Tom Schulman, Sally Robinson and (uncredited) Tom Stoppard. Ph: Donald McAlpine. Ed: Michael R. Miller. Pro Des: John Krenz Reinhart Jr. M: Jerry Goldsmith. Costumes: Marilyn Vance-Straker. Sound: George H. Anderson. (Cinergi-Guild.) Rel: 29 May 1992. 105 mins. Cert PG.

Meet the Feebles. It is twelve hours before the Feebles' Variety Show is due to go on the air and rehearsals are in a shambles. The lead singer, Heidi, is a bulimic, flatulent hippopotamus on the verge of a nervous breakdown; the MC, Harry, is a horny hare with AIDS; and the knife-thrower, Wynyard, is a frog with the shakes and a phenomenal drug habit. Other characters include the local reporter, a shit-eating fly; Daisy,

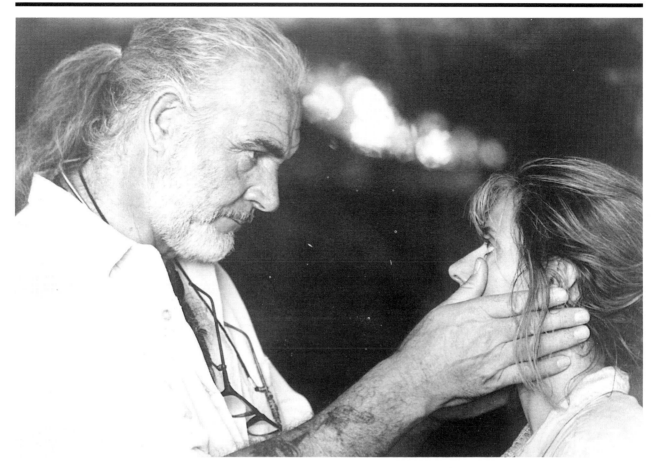

Romantic eco-escapism: Sean Connery and Lorraine Bracco do Bogart and Hepburn in the Amazon, in John McTiernan's Medicine Man *(from Guild).*

a bovine porn star with haemorrhoids; and the vulpine director, Sebastian, who is determined to perform his own song, 'Sodomy'. Peter Jackson, the 30-year-old New Zealand director who gave us *Bad Taste*, again assaults all our most sacred cows (including Daisy) with this outlandish, side-splitting, fiercely original puppet musical, a sort of *Muppet Show* on LSD. And all this on a budget the size of Miss Piggy's chocolate bill. [JC-W]

Characters include: Heidi the Hippo (prima donna), Bletch the Walrus (producer and gangster), Harry the Hare (MC), Wobert the Hedgehog (pennant carrier), Sebastian the Fox (director), Arfur the Worm (stage manager), Denis the Anteater (office boy), Lu-

cille the Poodle (rising star), Barry the Bulldog (opera singer and bodyguard), Sid the Elephant, Sandy the Chicken, Arbee Bargwan the Contortionist, Wynyard the Frog, Trevor the Rat, Daisy the Cow, Wally the Cockroach, Mr Big the Whale, The Fly, The Guppy (auditioning singer and lunch).

Voices: Donna Akersten, Stuart Devenie, Mark Hadlow, Ross Jolly, Brian Sergent, Peter Vere Jones, Mark Wright.

Dir: Peter Jackson. Pro: Jackson and Jim Booth. Screenplay: Jackson, Daniel Mulheron, Frances Walsh and Stephen Sinclair. Ph: Murray Milne. Ed: Jamie Selkirk. Pro

Toilet humour: MC and sex maniac Harry the Hare encounters a muck-raking journalist fly in Peter Jackson's affectionate, perverted homage to the puppet musical – Meet the Feebles *(from Arrow Films).*

Farce and opera sit uneasily together in David Puttnam's first foray into European cinema with Meeting Venus *(from Warner). Seen here: Glenn Close and Niels Arestrup.*

Des: Michael Kane. M: Peter Dasent. Puppet designer: Cameron Chittock. (Wignut Films–Arrow Films.) Rel: 10 April 1992. 96 mins. Cert 18.

Meeting Venus. Drawing from his own experience of directing Wagner's opera *Tannhauser* in Paris, Hungarian filmmaker Istvan Szabo uses the petty jealousies, love affairs and union walk-outs at the Opera Europa as a metaphor for the new Europe. The French actor Niels Arestrup plays an unknown but respected Hungarian conductor who arrives in Paris to oversee a spectacular production of *Tannhauser*. For him, everybody must give their all for the music, for the sheer love of it, and he is appalled to find out that his musicians and singers are more interested in their meal breaks than the opera. Fellini covered similar territory with his 1978 *Orchestra Rehearsal*, and did it far more succinctly. Here, Szabo, opens our eyes

to a revered art form, the participants of which are as human and vulgar as the rest of us. Unfortunately, *Meeting Venus* is neither one thing nor the other. While attempting to examine the stress of the creative process with some gravity, the film at times teeters on the edge of black farce, and then lurches into predictable melodrama at the drop of a baton. Lovely music, though. [JC-W]

Cast includes: Glenn Close (Karin Anderson, the diva), Niels Arestrup (Zoltan Szanto), Erland Josephson (Jorge Picabia), Johanna Ter Steege (Monique Angelo), Maite Nahyr, Victor Poletti, Maria De Medeiros, Jay O. Sanders, Marian Labuda, Dieter Laser, Macha Meril, Etienne Chicot, Moscu Alcalay, Roberto Pollack, Rita Scholl, André Chaumeau, Francois Delaive, Dorottya Udvaros, Ildiko Bansagi.
Dir: Istvan Szabo. Pro: David Puttnam. Screenplay: Szabo and Michael Hirst. Ph: Lajos Koltai. Ed: Jim Clark. Pro Des: Attila Kovacs. M: Richard Wagner; Elizabeth sung by Kiri Te Kanawa, Tannhauser by René Kollo. Costumes: Catherine Leterrier. Sound: Simon Kaye. (Fujisankei Communications Group/BSB/County Natwest Ventures/Enigma–Warner.) Rel: 27 September 1991. 120 mins. Cert 12.

Memoirs of an Invisible Man. Highly inventive, entertaining take on the old Claude Rains classic updated to contemporary San Francisco. A slimmed-down Chevy Chase stars as Nick Halloway, a successful, irresponsible stock market analyst who likes to keep himself to himself, undergoing 'a state of molecular flux' when a clandestine experiment goes terribly wrong. Determined to cover his ass, corporate baddy David Jenkins (Sam Neill) sets out to eliminate his invisible victim at all costs. Artfully combining comedy, suspense and romance (Daryl Hannah is the beauty who sees straight through Nick), *Memoirs* is a jaw-stretching showcase for the special effects of ILM (aided by a $40 million budget), backed up by a hilarious set of one-liners. Chevy Chase has never been better, keeping his mugging to a minimum and – in spite of the transparentness of his role – creating his most fleshed out character to date. [JC-W]

Also with: Daryl Hannah (Alice Monroe), Michael McKean (George Talbot), Stephen Tobolowsky (Warren Singleton), Jim Norton (Dr Bernard Wachs), Gregory Paul

Martin (Richard), Patricia Heaton (Ellen), Pat Skipper, Paul Perri, Richard Epcar, Steven Barr, Rosalind Chao.

Dir: John Carpenter. Pro: Bruce Bodner and Dan Kolsrud. Ex Pro: Arnon Milchan. Screenplay: Robert Collector, Dana Olsen and William Goldman; based on the book by H. F. Saint. Ph: William A. Fraker. Ed: Marion Rothman. Pro Des: Lawrence G. Paull. M: Shirley Walker. Sound: John Leveque and Gordon Ecker. (Regency Enterprises/Alcor Films/Le Studio Canal Plus–Warner.) Rel: 15 May 1992. 99 mins. Cert PG.

Men of Respect. Over-blown, stagey gangster melodrama 'based' on *Macbeth*. A wild-eyed John Turturro is back in The Family (after killing his way through *The Sicilian*, *State of Grace* and *Miller's Crossing*), in a futuresque New York plagued by disturbing headlines (the ozone layer has gone to pot). Katherine Borowitz, alias Mrs Turturro, alias Lady Macbeth, is the *femme fatale* with blood on her hands and madness around the corner, while familiar dons Rod Steiger, Dennis Farina and Peter Boyle go through their paces as, respectively, Duncan, Banquo and Macduff. More bad than Bard. [JC-W]

Cast includes: John Turturro (Mike Battaglia), Katherine Borowitz (Ruthie Battaglia), Dennis Farina (Bankie Como), Peter Boyle (Duffy), Stanley Tucci (Mal D'Amico), Rod Steiger (Charlie D'Amico), David Thornton (Philly Como), Lilia Skala (Signora Lucia), Steven Wright (Sterling), Rick Washburn, Nicholas Turturro.

Dir and Screenplay: William Reilly. Pro: Ephraim Horowitz. Ex Pro: Arthur Goldblatt and Eric Kitain. Ph: Bobby Bukowski. Ed: Elizabeth King. Pro Des: William Barclay. M: Misha Segal. (Central City Film Company–Columbia.) Rel: 28 February 1992. 113 mins. Cert 18.

Merci la Vie (Thank You, Life). A bizarre satire on movies, sexuality and the twentieth century – or what you will. Two girls meet by the sea and find themselves in a film (complete with flashbacks and monochrome) about AIDS and the Nazi occupation. Inspired by Blier's own *Les Valseuses* (1973), prompting the director to see 'whether I was still capable of making such a daring film at the age of fifty'. Self-indulgent to a fault. [JC-W]

Cast includes: Charlotte Gainsbourg (Camille), Anouk Grinberg (Joelle), Gerard Depardieu (Marc Antoine), Michel Blanc, Jean Carmet, Catherine Jacob, Thierry Fre-

Forbidden love: Sarita Choudhury deliberates on the dilemma of interracial romance in Mira Nair's observant Mississippi Masala *(from Palace).*

mont, Francois Perrot, Didier Benureau, Jean-Louis Trintignant, Annie Girardot.

Dir and Screenplay: Bertrand Blier. Pro: Bernard Marescot. Ph: Philippe Rousselot. Ed: Claudine Merlin. Pro Des: Theobold Meurisse. M: Philip Glass, Jacques Brel, David Byrne, Chopin, Beethoven, Dean Martin, Vivaldi, Puccini etc. Costumes: Jacqueline Bouchard. Sound: Pierre Gamet. (Cine Valse/Film par Film/Orly Film/DD Prod./SEDIF/Films A2–Artificial Eye.) Rel: 10 January 1992. 117 mins. Cert 18.

Mississippi Masala. Leisurely but moving and perceptive exploration of inter-racial relationships – and prejudice – in the deep South, where an Indian family, refugees from Idi Amin's Uganda, find fresh troubles when their pretty daughter falls in love with a local black. A charming and intelligent collector's piece – from the director of *Salaam Bombay*. The critics loved it. [FMS]

Cast: Denzel Washington (Demetrius), Sarita Choudbury (Mina), Roshan Seth (Jay), Sharmila Tagore (Kinnu), Charles S. Dutton (Tyrone), Joe Seneca (Williben), Ranjit Chowdhry (Anil), Konga Moandu (Okelo), Mohan Gokhale, Mohan Agashe, Tico Wells, Yvette Hawkins, Anjan Srivastava, Dipti Suthar, Varsha Thaker, Askok Lath, Natalie Oliver, Karen Pinkstron, Willy Cobbs.

Dir: Mira Nair. Pro: Nair and Michael Nozik. Co-Pro: Mitch Epstein. Ex Pro: Cherie Rodgers. Screenplay: Sooni Taraporevals. Ph: Ed Lachman. Ed: Robert Silvi. Pro Des: Mitch Epstein. M: L. Subrananiam. (Mirabi Films/Odyssey/Cinecome–Palace.) Rel: 17 January 1992. 114 mins. No cert.

Mobsters – The Evil Empire. Nicknamed *Young Buns With Tommy Guns* in the industry, this $23m epic is about as shallow as its sobriquet would suggest. Christian Slater top-bills as Charlie 'Lucky' Luciano, the top gun of a quartet of smooth young operators who calmly take over New York's underworld (1917–31). TV heart-throb Richard Grieco is Bugsy Siegel, the womaniser, and Patrick Dempsey and Costas Mandylor (the Australian foot-

Young Guns: Patrick Dempsey, Richard Grieco, Christian Slater and Costas Mandylor celebrate a successful breakthrough into organised crime in UIP's flashy Mobsters – The Evil Empire.

baller) co-star as Meyer Lansky and Frank Costello, respectively, each a killer down to his Guccis. A serious examination of the birth of crime this is not, but as a pop video exploiting the joys of sex and violence, it is surprisingly well-made by commercials director Michael Karbelnikoff in his film debut. Forget the historical accuracy. (Previously known as *Gangsters*.) [JC-W]

Also with: F. Murray Abraham (Arnold Rothstein), Lara Flynn Boyle (Mara Motes), Michael Gambon (Don Faranzano), Anthony Quinn (Don Masseria), Christopher Penn (Tommy Reina), Andy Romano (Antonio Luciano), Bianca Rossini (Rosalie Luciano), Robert Z'Dar (Rocco), Leslie Bega (Anna Lansky), Nicholas Sadler (Mad Dog Coll), Titus Welliver (Al Capone), Rodney Eastman, Clark Heathcliffe Brolly, Leonard Termo, Carmen Twillie, Seymour Cassel, Frank Collison, Joe Viterelli, James Michael, Russ Fega, Bill Bastiani, John Chappoulis.

Dir: Michael Karbelnikoff. Pro: Steve Roth. Ex Pro: C. O. Erickson. Screenplay: Michael Mahern and Nicholas Kazan. Ph: Lajos Koltai. Ed: Scott Smith and Joe D'Augustine. Pro Des: Richard Sylbert. M: Michael Small. Costumes: Ellen Mirojnick. (Universal–UIP.) Rel: 1 May 1992. 121 mins. Cert 18.

Monster in a Box. Spalding Gray, an actor and self-confessed 'hardcore Freudian existentialist', talks to a small audience (at London's Riverside Studios) about his attempts to complete a 1,800-page autobiographical novel – *Impossible Vacation* – which he now keeps in a box. Along the way he describes his adventures at a Soviet film festival and on a fact-finding stint in Nicaragua (for Columbia Pictures), and his obsession with catching AIDS. As a raconteur, Mr Gray can hold the attention well enough, which is more than can be said for this fidgety documentary which distracts the viewer with fussy camera moves. Follow-up to

Monster mouth: Spalding Gray talks in his diverting one-man show Monster in a Box *(from ICA).*

Gray's one-man show *Swimming to Cambodia*, filmed in 1987 by Jonathan Demme. [JC-W]

Dir: Nick Broomfield. Pro: Jon Blair. M: Laurie Anderson. (ICA.) Rel: 1 November 1991. 90 mins. No cert.

Mortal Thoughts. A New Jersey housewife (Demi Moore) is brought

in for questioning by tough, pensive copper Harvey Keitel. Over the next hour and a half she tells him about the murder of her best friend's husband, a robust thief, rapist and drug addict played with relish by Bruce Willis. This flash-back technique robs the film of any potential tension, while Alan Rudolph's heavy direction swamps it in pretension (beware the close-ups of TV cameras, screens, microphones etc). In short, a phony thriller with its plot and technique showing – and without a sympathetic character in sight. Not Mr Rudolph's genre. Ms Moore co-produced. [JC-W]

Cast includes: Demi Moore (Cynthia Kellogg), Glenne Headly (Joyce Urbanski), Bruce Willis (James Urbanski), John Pankow (Arthur Kellogg), Harvey Keitel (Det. John Woods), Frank Vincent (Dominic Marino), Crystal Field (Jeanette Marino), Christopher Scotellaro (Joey Urbanski), Kelly Cinnante (Cookie), Billie Neal, Karen Shallo, Maryanne Leone, Elain Graham, Thomas Quinn.

Dir: Alan Rudolph. Pro: John Fielder and Mark Tarlov. Ex Pro: Taylor Hackford and Stuart Benjamin. Co-Pro: Demi Moore. Screenplay: William Reilly and Claude Kerven. Ph: Elliot Davis. Ed: Tom Walls. Pro Des: Howard Cummings. M: Mark Isham. Costumes: Hope Hanafin. Sound: Gary Alper. (Columbia Tri-Star.) Rel: 25 October 1991. 102 mins. Cert 15.

Femmes fatales Glenne Headley and Demi Moore find themselves in a spot of husband trouble in Alan Rudolph's disappointingly phoney Mortal Thoughts *(from Columbia Tri-Star).*

Baby boom: Macaulay Culkin and Anna Chlumsky hoist the cute factor in Howard Zieff's sentimental black comedy My Girl *(from Columbia).*

My Girl. 1972, Pennsylvania. Not so much a movie, more a massage of the eye ducts – and a clumsy one at that. Following the success of *Home Alone* and other child-orientated movies, Columbia Pictures ploughed good money into this plotless weepie about an 11-year-old girl who looks like an ad for Kodak. Her mother's dead, and her father isn't interested, so the precocious Vada Sultenfuss (newcomer Anna Chlumsky) hangs around with little Thomas J. – uugghh! – a boy. Moronic music and shaky acting don't help. And why's it all set in 1972? [JC-W]

Also with: Dan Aykroyd (Harry Sultenfuss), Jamie Lee Curtis (Shelly DeVoto), Macaulay Culkin (Thomas J. Sennett), Richard Masur (Phil Sultenfuss), Griffin Dunne (Mr Bixler), Ann Nelson (Gramoo Sultenfuss), Glenda Chism (Thomas J.'s mother), Peter Michael Goetz, Jane Hallaren, Anthony Jones, Tom Villard, Lara Steinick, Kristian Truelsen, Dave Caprita, Nancy L. Chlumsky, Bill Cordell.

Dir: Howard Zieff. Pro: Brian Grazer. Ex Pro: Joseph M. Caracciolo and David T. Friendly. Screenplay: Laurice Elehwany. Ph: Paul Elliott. Ed: Wendy Green Bricmont. Pro Des: Joseph T. Garrity. M: James Newton Howard; numbers performed by The Temptations (*My Girl*), Creedence Clearwater Revival, Sly and The Family Stone, The Flamingos, Ravi Shankar, Artie Shaw, Chicago, The Fifth Dimension etc.

Road to ruin: River Phoenix sleeping his way to the bottom in Gus Van Sant's My Own Private Idaho *(from Electric).*

Costumes: Karen Patch. (Columbia.) Rel: 31 January 1992. 102 mins. Cert PG.

My Own Private Idaho. Borrowing its title from the B–52s' song and its plot from Shakespeare's *Henry IV*, this is a quirky road movie that is touching and funny when it's not showing off. River Phoenix stars as a narcoleptic gay prostitute in search of his mother who hooks up with co-hustler Keanu Reeves, a modern Prince Hal. Along the way they team up with a Falstaffian vagrant, indulge in erotic foursomes and get stranded in Idaho. There's plenty of original, surreal touches and illuminating interviews with real street hustlers, but the Shakespearean passages smack of pretentiousness. Ultimately there are just too many movies here, all wrestling for centre stage. [JC-W]

Cast includes: River Phoenix (Mike Waters), Keanu Reeves (Scott Favor),

James Russo (Richard Waters), William Richert (Bob Pigeon), Rodney Harvey (Gary), Chiara Caselli (Carmella), Tom Troupe (Jack Favor), Udo Kier (Hans), Michael Parker, Jessie Thomas, Flea, Grace Zabriskie, Sally Curtice, Oliver Kirk, Bryan Wilson, Tiger Warren, Mario Stracciarolo, Rain Phoenix.

Dir, Ex Pro and Screenplay: Gus Van Sant. Pro: Laurie Parker. Ph: Eric Alan Edwards and John Campbell. Ed: Curtiss Clayton. Pro Des: David Brisbin. M: Numbers performed by Bill Stafford, Rudy Vallee, Udo Kier, Aleka's Attic, Madonna, Elton John, The Pogues etc. Costumes: Beatrix Aruna Paszter. (New Line Cinema–Electric.) Rel: 27 March 1992. 105 mins. Cert 18.

Naked Lunch. 1953, New York/'Interzone'. David Cronenberg, who helped transform Jeff Goldblum into *The Fly*, has taken William S. Burroughs's unfilmable novel and mutated it into his own variation on a theme. Treading in the slime marks of Kafka's *Metamorphosis*, the film stars Peter Weller as William Lee, a pest exterminator who discovers that his wife is mainlining bug powder. Trying out the drug himself, Lee is plunged into a hallucino-

genic world of malevolent typewriters, sexually deviant centipedes and alien double agents. Ex-junkie Burroughs's breakthrough, semi-autobiographical novel is brought to vivid life through Cronenberg's obsession with the corporeal, but slides into smug pretentiousness when not affronting our sensibilities. A bad trip for sick intellectuals. [JC-W]

Also with: Judy Davis (Joan Frost/Joan Lee), Ian Holm (Tom Frost), Julian Sands (Yves Cloquet), Roy Scheider (Dr Benway), Monique Mercure (Fadela), Nicholas Campbell (Hank), Michael Zelniker (Martin), Robert A. Silverman (Hans), Joseph Scorsiani, Yuval Daniel, John Friesen, Sean McCann, Kurt Reis.

Dir and Screenplay: David Cronenberg. Pro: Jeremy Thomas. Co-Pro: Gabriella Mantinelli. Ph: Peter Suschitsky. Ed: Ronald Sanders. Pro Des: Carol Spiers. M: Howard Shore; numbers performed by Ornette Coleman, Thelonious Monk, Les Paul and Mary Ford. Costumes: Denise Cronenberg. Creature SFX: Chris Walas Inc. (Jeremy Thomas–First Independent.) Rel: 24 April 1992. 115 mins. Cert 18.

Naked Tango. Pseudo-erotic tosh about a gamine Parisian bride who decides to escape her older husband during a luxury cruise to Buenos Aires. Taking on the identity of a mail-order bride from Poland, stupid Stephanie becomes embroiled with a gang of Tango-obsessed Jewish no-goods, who adopt her as a slave. Stephanie, no big-amist by nature, admits in her voice-over, 'I had never intended to go this far, but I had never seen a Jewish wed-ding.' Laughable, offensive and ulti-mately very boring, *Naked Tango*'s message seems to be that sado-maso-chistic sex is better than the love of a caring old man. [JC-W]

Cast includes: Vincent D'Onofrio (Cholo), Mathilda May (Stephanie/Alba), Esai Mor-ales (Zico Borenstein), Fernando Rey (Judge Torres), Cipe Lincovski (Zico's mama), Josh Mostel (Bertoni the jeweller), Constance McCashin, Patricio Bisso, Sergio Lerer, Marco Woinski, Ruben Szuchmacher.
   Dir and Screenplay: Leonard Schrader. Pro: David W. Eisman. Ex Pro: Henry W. Holmes Jr and Jane Holzer. Ph: Juan Ruiz-Anchia. Ed: Debra McDermott and Lee Percy. Pro Des: Anthony Pratt. M: Thomas Newman. Costumes: Patricio Bisso. Chor-eography: Carlos Rivarola. Sound: Jose Luis Diaz. (Sugerloaf/Gotan/Towa/Praesens-Film AG/Grupo Baires–Blue Dolphin.) Rel: 16 August 1991. 93 mins. Cert 18.

Necessary Roughness. Now, you may not believe this, but the oddest set of college athletes you ever did see turn out to be a pretty promising football team after all. Oops, you weren't meant to guess that. Still, in spite of the over-powering predictability of this football version of *Major League* (1989), there is *some* entertainment value for the undemanding. [CB]

Cast includes: Scott Bakula (Paul Blake), Robert Loggia (Coach Rig), Harley Jane Kozak (Suzanne Carter), Sinbad (Andre Krimm), Hector Elizondo (Coach Gennero), Larry Miller (Dean Elias), Jason Bateman (Jarvis Edison), Fred Dalton Thompson (Carver Purcell), Rob Schneider, Chris Berman, Andrew Bryniarski, Duane Davis, Michael Dolan, Peter Navy Tuiasosopo, Marcus Giamatti, Kathy Ireland, Drew Kahn, Andrew Lauer, Louis Mandylor, Dick Butkus, Jim Kelly.
   Dir: Stan Dragoti. Pro: Mace Neufeld and Robert Rehme. Ex Pro: Howard W. Koch Jr. Screenplay: Rick Natkin and David Fuller. Ph: Peter Stein. Ed: John Wright and Steve Mirkovich. Pro Des: Paul Peters. M: Bill Conti; numbers performed by George Strait, DSK, Hank Williams Jr etc. Costumes: Dan Moore. Sound: J. Paul

Writer's camp: Peter Weller as William S. Burroughs's alter ego in David Cronenberg's brave attempt at translating the unfilmable – Naked Lunch *(from First Independent).*

Huntsman. (Paramount–UIP.) Rel: 27 March 1992. 108 mins. Cert 12.

Neil Simon's Broadway Bound – see *Broadway Bound*.

New Jack City was the *only* film to make a profit in the US in the spring of 1991. Shot for $8.5 million, the picture looks terrific, and in spite of its familiar storyline of New York cops infiltrating a drug-financed crime ring (this time run by gold medallion-choked Afro-Americans), *New Jack City* offers a heady cocktail of commercial ingredi-ents: young stars, rap music, sex, vio-lence and rap artist Ice T in his (impressive) film debut. First-time director Mario Van Peebles displays an energetic innovative style, which almost makes up for his grand larceny

Copz N The Hood: Judd Nelson and Ice-T fight crime in the New Jack City *(from Warner).*

New year story: The remarkable Maggie Jakobson in Henry Jaglom's idiosyncratic New Year's Day *(from Contemporary).*

of other pictures. This would make a case study of movie plagiarism, as *The Untouchables* gives way to *The Krays* in one particularly derivative scene. *Jaws*, *Juggernaut*, *The Godfather* – they're all here, and this is no *Naked Gun*. Still, there is plenty to admire, not least a bloody *a cappella* montage sequence (partly lifted from *The Godfather*), and a strong anti-drug message. As embittered cop Judd Nelson exclaims, 'This drug thing – it's not a black thing, it's not a white thing – it's a death thing.' [JC-W]

Cast includes: Wesley Snipes (very impressive as Nino Brown), Ice-T (Scotty Appleton), Allen Payne (Gee Money), Chris Rock (Pookie), Mario Van Peebles (Stone), Michael Michele (Selina), Bill Nunn (Duh Duh Duh Man), Russell Wong (Park), Bill Cobbs (old man), Christopher Williams (Kareem Akbar), Judd Nelson (Nick Peretti), Vanessa Williams, Tracy Camilla Johns, Anthony DeSando, Nick Ashford, Phyllis Yvonne Stickney, Thalmus Rasulala, John Aprea, Fab 5 Freddy, Flavor Flav, Laverne Hart, Eek-A-Mouse, Keith Sweat, Kelly Jo Minter.
Dir: Mario Van Peebles. Pro: Doug McHenry and George Jackson. Screenplay: Thomas Lee Wright and Barry Michael Cooper. Ph: Francis Kenny. Ed: Steven Kemper. Pro Des: Charles C. Bennett. M: Michel Colombier; numbers performed by Ice T, Guy, Keith Sweat, Johnny Gill, Christopher Williams, Troop and Levert, Color Me Badd, 2 Live Crew, F.S. Effect, Essence, Danny Madden, Doug E. Fresh

and The Get Fresh Crew, Redhead Kingpin and the FBI, and NWA. Costumes: Bernard Johnson. Sound: Franklin D. Stettner. (Warner.) Rel: 30 August 1991. 101 mins. Cert 18.

New Year's Day. Unable to cope with his disintegrating personal life in Los Angeles, 46-year-old writer Drew (Henry Jaglom) returns to his roots in New York, where he has sub-let a flat. There, exhausted from his flight, he overlaps with the apartment's three previous tenants. And he thought *he* had problems. Written and directed by Jaglom (*Always*, *Someone to Love*) from real-life experience, *New Year's Day* is an amusing, perspicacious look at a day in the life of a New York apartment, in particular examining the hopes, dreams and disappointments of three young women. Talky, spontaneous, touching and highly naturalistic cinema – from the master of the intellectual home movie. [JC-W]

Also with: Maggie Jakobson (Lucy), Gwen Welles (Annie), Melanie Winter (Winona), David Duchovny (Billy), Milos Forman (Lazlo), Michael Emil (Jaglom's real-life brother, as Dr Stadthagen), Harvey Miller (Lucy's father), Irene Moore (Lucy's mother), James DePreist (Lucy's shrink), Tracy Reiner, James Hurt, Robert Hallak, Katherine Wallach, Kristina Loggia, Rodger Parsons.
Dir and Screenplay: Henry Jaglom. Pro: Judith Wolinsky. Assoc Pro: Phyllis Curott. Ph: Joey Forsyte. Ed: Ruth Zucker Wald. M: various. (Jagfilm/International Rainbow Pictures–Contemporary.) Rel: 14 December 1991. 90 mins. No cert.

Noce Blanche. Aimless screen vehicle for French pop star Vanessa Paradis (*Joe le Taxi*). However, the camera appears to love her as much as her legion of fans do, and she makes a tantalising *femme fatale* in this otherwise ponderous romantic drama. The reliable Bruno Cremer plays Francois Hainault, a philosophy teacher at a secondary school in St Etienne, France. Annoyed by the habitual absenteeism of one of his students – the 17-year-old Mathilde Tessier – Hainault digs into her past and discovers a hornet's nest of pain. But what he hadn't bargained for was a student of brilliant mind and resources. Anyway, Mathilde seduces Hainault's mind before aiming for the body, and this awkward romance turns into a psychological drama. Plodding, but interesting. [JC-W]

Also with: Ludmila Mikael (Catherine Hainault), Francois Negret, Jean Daste, Veronique Silver, Philippe Tuin.
Dir and Screenplay: Jean-Claude Brisseau. Pro: Margaret Menegoz. Ph: Romain Winding. Ed: Maria-Luisa Garcia. M: Jean Musy. Sound: Georges Prat. (Les Films du Losange/La Sept/La Corciere Rouge/Sofia Investimage/Investimafe 2–Gala.) Rel: 12 July 1991. 92 mins. Cert 15.

Nothing But Trouble. Four wealthy, youngish New Yorkers are waylaid in a toxic, backwater police state when they take the picturesque route off the New Jersey Turnpike. There, they encounter a demented 106-year-old judge and a menagerie of deadly weirdos. Dan Aykroyd, who scripted, describes the story as 'a direct outgrowth of my personal observations and actual experiences'. Unfortunately, Aykroyd also directs (for the first time) and may never get the chance again. Described as an American Gothic comedy, *Nothing But Trouble* lived up to its name and became a major career embarrassment for its four stars. It really is appallingly bad. Previously known as *Git* and *Valkenvania*. [JC-W]

Cast includes: Chevy Chase (Chris Thorne), Dan Aykroyd (Justice of the Peace Alvin Valkenheiser/Bobo), John Candy (Sheriff Dennis Purda/Eldona), Demi Moore (Diane Lightson), Valri Bromfield (Miss Purdah), Taylor Negron (Fausto), Bertila Damas (Renalda), Raymond J. Barry, Brian Doyle Murray, John Wesley, Peter Aykroyd, Daniel Baldwin, John Daveikis (as L'il Debbull), Humpty Hump.
Dir and Screenplay: Dan Aykroyd; from a story by Peter Aykroyd. Pro: Robert K.

Weiss. Ph: Dean Cundey. Ed: Malcolm Campbell and James Symons. Pro Des: William Sandell. M: Michael Kamen; numbers performed by Ray Charles, digital underground, Bertila Damas, Frankie Valli and The Four Seasons, Hank Williams Jr, Jack Teagarden, Michael Kamen etc. Costumes: Deborah Nadoolman. Sound: Don H. Matthews. (Applied Action–Warner.) Rel: 23 August 1991. 94 mins. Cert 12.

The Object of Beauty. Jake and Tina are trapped in a luxurious London hotel, unable to pay their bill. Jake's latest business venture lies at the bottom of the sea, and the only way the American couple can make ends meet is to sell Tina's beloved Henry Moore bronze. Tina says she'll hide it and collect the insurance, Jake says he'll flog it straight away. And then it disappears. A beautifully constructed morsel this, a witty morality tale that never lets you know where it's going while always spitting out interesting ideas. Lolita Davidovich co-stars as Tina's best friend, taking over the part after Elizabeth Perkins fell ill. [JC-W]

Cast includes: John Malkovich (Jake Bartholomew), Andie MacDowell (Tina Leslie Bartholomew Oates), Joss Ackland (Mr Mercer), Lolita Davidovich (Joan), Rudi Davies (Jenny), Bill Paterson (Victor Swayle), Ricci Harnett (Steve), Peter Riegert (Larry Oates), Jack Shepherd (Mr Slaughter), Roger Lloyd Pack (Frankie), Rosemary Martin, Andrew Hawkins, Pip Torrens, Stephen Churchett, Jeremy Sinden, Ginger Corbett.
Dir and Screenplay: Michael Lindsay-Hogg. Pro: Jon S. Denny. Ex Pro: Cary Brokaw. Ph: David Watkin. Ed: Ruth Foster. Pro Des: Derek Dodd. M: Tom Bahler. Costumes: Les Lansdown; Giorgio Armani. (Avenue Pictures/BBC–Samuel Goldwyn/Winstone.) Rel: 27 September 1991. 103 mins. Cert 15.

Off and Running. Florida and New York. Predictable 'crazy' caper about a Madonna wannabe (Cyndi Lauper) pursued by an assassin after she witnesses the murder of her boyfriend. Along the way she meets up with an antisocial golf-pro and a precocious 10-year-old boy. For fans of Cyndi Lauper only. (Previously known as *Moon Over Miami*). [CB]

Cast includes: Cyndi Lauper (Cyd Morse), David Keith (Jack Cornett), Johnny Pinto (Pompey), David Thornton (Reese), Richard Belzer (Milt Zoloth, Jose Perez, Anita

Morris, Hazen Gifford, Linda Hart, Tracy Roberts, Dana Mark, Jodi Wilson.
Dir: Edward Bianchi. Pro: Aaron Russo and William C. Carraro. Screenplay: Mitch Glazer. Ph: Andrzej Bartkowiak. Ed: Rick Shaine. M: Mason Daring; numbers performed by Chris Montez, Cyndi Lauper, Anita Morris, Tommy James & The Shondells etc. Sound: Stan Bochner. (Rank.) Rel: 12 June 1992. 90 mins. Cert 12.

Chevy Chase and Demi Moore drive into their worst nightmare in Dan Aykroyd's staggeringly unfunny Nothing But Trouble *(from Warner).*

The object of money: John Malkovich and Andie MacDowell in a gilt-edged hell in Michael Lindsay-Hogg's piquant The Object of Beauty *(from Goldwyn/Winstone).*

Oedipus wrecked: John Candy and Maureen O'Hara suffer breakfast in Chris Columbus's Only the Lonely *(from Fox).*

Omen IV: The Awakening. Made for American TV, but had a brief cinema showing in Britain. In this sequel, a young couple adopt a little girl, only to find they've got more than they bargained for when the little weirdo reveals her demonic nature. [FDM]

Cast: Faye Grant (mother), Michael Woods (father), Asia Vieira (demon child), Michael Lerner, Madison Mason, Ann Hearn, Jim Byrnes, Don S. Davis, Megan Leitch, Joy Coghill.
  Dir: Jorge Montesi and Dominique Othenin-Girard. Pro: Harvey Bernhard. Co-Pro: Robert Anderson. Screenplay: Brian Taggert. Ph: Martin Fuhrer. Ed: Frank Irvine. Art: Lawrence Pevec. M: Jonathan Sheffer. (FNM Co–Fox.) Rel: 29 November 1991. 89 mins. Cert 15.

Once Upon A Crime. Rome/Monte Carlo, 1991. More Americans descend on Europe to wreak havoc and behave badly in this Hollywoodisation of the 1960 Italian comedy *Crimen* (which starred Alberto Sordi, Vittorio Gassman and Nino Manfredi). Here, two pairs of stupid Americans become involved in a murder case involving a dachshund called Napoleon and a stolen suitcase with a body in it. Everybody acts very funny indeed in a desperate attempt to disguise the absence of wit, except for Giancarlo Giannini who, perhaps, wasn't told it was a comedy. (Formerly known as *Returning Napoleon* and *Criminals*.) [JC-W]

Cast includes: John Candy (Augie Morosco), James Belushi (Neil Schwary), Cybill Shepherd (Marilyn Schwary), Sean Young (Phoebe), Richard Lewis (Julian), Ornella Muti (Elena Morosco), Giancarlo Giannini (Inspector Bonnard), George Hamilton (Alfonso de la Pena), Joss Ackland, Ann Way, Geoffrey Andrews, Elsa Martinelli.
  Dir: Eugene Levy. Pro: Dino De Laurentiis. Ex Pro: Marthe De Laurentiis. Screenplay: Charles Shyer, Nancy Meyers and Steve Kluger. Ph: Giuseppe Rotunno. Ed: Patrick Kennedy. Pro Des: Pierluigi Basile. M: Richard Gibbs. Costumes: Molly Maginnis. (Entertainment.) Rel: 6 March 1992. 94 mins. Cert PG.

Only the Lonely. Sentimental romantic comedy with John Candy as a big-hearted Chicago cop dominated by his mother. When he starts up an affair with a mortuary beautician, his mother (Maureen O'Hara) turns into an acid-tongued boa constrictor, fortifying her apron strings and preying on Candy's good nature and guilt. A breakaway vehicle for Candy, *Only the Lonely* was actually conceived as a New York story about an Italian-American. Still, Candy is surprisingly sweet and charming as an Irish-American *Marty*, while Maureen O'Hara makes a triumphant comeback after an absence of eighteen years. [JC-W]

Cast includes: John Candy (Danny Muldoon), Maureen O'Hara (Rose Muldoon), Ally Sheedy (Theresa Luna), Anthony Quinn (Nick), James Belushi (Sal), Kevin Dunn (Patrick Muldoon), Milo O'Shea (Doyle), Bert Remsen (Spats), Joe V. Greco, Marvin J. McIntyre, Macaulay Culkin, Allen Hamilton, Teri McEvoy, Bernie Landis, John M. Watson Sr.
  Dir and Screenplay: Chris Columbus. Pro: John Hughes and Hunt Lowry. Ex Pro: Tarquin Gotch. Ph: Julio Macat. Ed: Raja Gosnell. Pro Des: John Muto. M: Maurice

Jarre; numbers performed by Roy Orbison, Dean Martin, Van Morrison, Etta James and Mario Lanza. Costumes: Mary E. Vogt. Sound: Jim Alexander. (Fox.) Rel: 13 September 1991. 104 mins. Cert 12.

Oscar. 1931, New York. Old-fashioned, rather well structured farce starring Sylvester Stallone as a Mafia don attempting to go straight in order to fulfil his father's dying wish. One month later he's woken at the crack of dawn by his love-struck accountant with some startling news. The following chain of events includes the old switched case routine, mistaken identities and a dictionary-ful of malapropisms. A sparkling script – tightly controlled by director John Landis – is given much oomph by a crowded supporting cast bent on stealing each other's scenes. Very broad, energetic entertainment. Based on the French play and 1967 film of the same name. [JC-W]

Cast includes: Sylvester Stallone (Angelo 'Snaps' Provolone), Ornella Muti (Sofia Provolone), Don Ameche (Father Clemente), Peter Riegert (Aldo), Vincent Spano (Anthony Rossano, CPA), Tim Curry (Dr Poole), Chazz Palminteri (Connie), Richard Romanus (Vendetti), Kurtwood Smith (Lt Toomey), Joycelyn O'Brien (Nora), Marisa Tomei (Lisa Provolone), Martin Ferrero (Luigi Finucci), Harry Shearer (Guido Finucci), Elizabeth Barondes (Theresa), Jim Mulholland (Oscar), Joey Travolta, Paul Greco, Richard Foronjy, Yvonne De Carlo, Arleen Sorkin, Eddie Bracken, Tony Munafo, Robert Lesser, Art LaFleur, William Atherton, Mark Metcalf, Ken Howard, Sam Chew Jr, Kai Wulff, Linda Gray, Marshall Bell, Rick Avery, Joe Dante, Kirk Douglas (Provolone Sr).
  Dir: John Landis. Pro: Leslie Belzberg. Ex Pro: Alex Ponti and Joseph S. Vecchio. Screenplay: Michael Barrie and Jim Mulholland; based on the play by Claude Magnier. Ph: Mac Ahlberg. Ed: Dale Beldin. Pro Des: Bill Kenney. M: Elmer Bernstein; Rossini. Costumes: Deborah Nadoolman. Sound: William B. Kaplan. (Touchstone–Warner.) Rel: 6 September 1991. 110 mins. Cert PG.

Other People's Money. Smart, high-concept financial comedy adapted from the off-Broadway play by Jerry Sterner. Danny DeVito stars as the avaricious Wall Street 'businessman' who loves money 'more than the things it can buy'. When he proposes to take over the unprofitable (but debt-free) New

Sylvester Stallone takes elocution lessons from Tim Curry in John Landis's fast-paced comedy Oscar *(from Warner).*

England Wire and Cable Company, he comes up against some sturdy, home-grown values. He also meets his match in the chief executive's daughter (Penelope Ann Miller, replacing Michelle Pfeiffer), a high-flying lawyer who, like him, might care 'more about the game than the players'. Very funny, polished, up-to-the-minute (yet strangely old-fashioned) comedy – with teeth beneath the candyfloss. [JC-W]

Money talks: Penelope Ann Miller and Danny DeVito bicker over love and a few billion, in Norman Jewison's old-fashioned look at new business – Other People's Money *(from Warner).*

Cast includes: Danny DeVito (Lawrence 'Larry the Liquidator' Garfield), Gregory Peck (Chief Executive Andrew 'Jorgy' Jorgenson), Penelope Ann Miller (Kate Sullivan), Piper Laurie (Beau Sullivan), Dean Jones (William 'Bill' J. Coles), R. D. Call (Arthur), Mo Gaffney (Harry), Bette Henritze (Emma), Leila Kenzle (Marcia), Tom Aldredge (Ozzie).
  Dir: Norman Jewison. Pro: Jewison and Ric Kidney. Ex Pro: Ellen Krass and Davina Belling. Screenplay: Alvin Sargent. Ph: Haskell Wexler. Ed: Lou Lombardo. Pro Des: Philip Rosenberg. M: David Newman. Sound: Jeff Wexler. (Yorktown–Warner.) Rel: 15 November 1991. 101 mins. Cert 15.

Out for Justice. Another opportunity – the third – to see the martial arts prowess of Steven Seagal. This time around Seagal's an Italian cop who grimly pursues his partner's murderer,

Out of the mouths of children: Thora Birch and Elijah Wood attend a farmyard coupling in Mary Agnes Donoghue's slice of designer emotion, Paradise *(from Warner).*

wiping out anyone who stands in his way. Well orchestrated mayhem. [FDM]

Also with: William Forsyth (Richie), Jerry Orbach (Ronnie), Jo Champa (Vicky), Shareen Mitchell, Sal Richards, Gina Gershon, Jay Avocone.

Dir: John Flynn. Pro: Seagal and Arnold Kopelson. Ex Pro: Julius R. Nasso. Screenplay: David Lee Henry. Ph: Ric Waite. Ed: Robert A. Ferretti and Donald Brochu. Pro Des: Gene Rudolf. Art: Stephen M. Berger. Sound: R. R. Rutledge. M: David Michael Frank. (Arnold Kopelson and Steven Seagal–Warner.) Rel: 4 October 1991. 91 minutes. Cert 18.

Over Our Dead Bodies. Documentary by Stuart Marshall, a filmmaker who specialises in lesbian and gay history, on the social and cultural impact of AIDS. [FDM]

Dir: Stuart Marshall. (ICA.) Rel: 13 November 1991. 84 mins. No cert.

Paradise. Take a magical French tale of childhood, move it to the picturesque coast of South Carolina, slow the

Justice or murder? Dennis Hopper, the accused, and Ed Harris, his lawyer, exert a little prejudice on a small Southern town in Stephen Gyllenhaal's powerful Paris Trout *(from Palace).*

rhythm down to a snail's pace and then drown it in pretty music and you have *Paradise*. Photogenic Elijah Wood (*Avalon*) stars as Willard Young, a lied-to 10-year-old dumped on a couple of grumpy grown-ups for the summer by his mother. There, the boy learns a few home truths from his 9-year-old neighbour, Billie Pike (the photogenic Thora

Birch), and in turn teaches his new guardians some life lessons. The photography is lovely. [JC-W]

Also with: Melanie Griffith (Lily Reed), Don Johnson (Ben Reed), Sheila McCarthy (Sally Pike), Eve Gordon (Rosemary), Louise Latham (Catherine Reston Lee), Rick Andosca (Ernest Parkett), Greg Travis, Sarah Trigger, Richard K. Olsen, Timothy Erskine.

Dir and Screenplay: Mary Agnes Donoghue; from the film *Le Grand Chemin*. Pro: Scott Kroopf and Patrick Palmer. Ex Pro: Jean Francois Lepetit, Ted Field and Robert W. Cort. Ph: Jerzy Zielinski. Ed: Eva Gardos and Debra McDermott. Pro Des: Evelyn Sakash and Marcia Hinds. M: David Newman. Costumes: Linda Palermo Donahue. Sound: Richard E. Yawn and Gordon Ecker. (Touchstone/Touchwood Pacific Partners/Interscope Communications–Warner.) Rel: 19 June 1992. 111 mins. Cert 12.

Paris Trout. Georgia, USA, 1949. A hard-working storekeeper and respected pillar of the community, Paris Trout (Dennis Hopper), believes he is above the common law. When a young black man reneges on his commitment to pay Trout for a second-hand car, the latter's code of justice is brutal indeed . . . Hopper delivers yet another variation on his whacko character, turning in an authentic, chilling portrayal of insanity and evil. TV director Stephen Gyllenhaal makes an impressive theatrical bow, but cannot prevent the film from falling flat in its final third. [JC-W]

Also with: Barbara Hershey (Hanna Trout), Ed Harris (Harry Seagraves), Ray McKinnon (Carol Bonner), Tina Lifford (Mary Sayers), Darnita Henry (Rosie Sayers), Eric Ware (Henry Ray Sayers).

Dir: Stephen Gyllenhaal. Pro: Frank Konigsberg and Larry Sanitsky. Ex Pro: Diana Kerew. Screenplay: Pete Dexter; based on his novel. Ph: Robert Elswit. Ed: Harvey Rosenstock. Pro Des: Richard Sherman. M: David Shire. Costumes: Mary Rose (Palace.) Rel: 16 August 1991. 100 mins. Cert 18.

The People Under the Stairs. The latest nightmare from Wes Craven, the man who turned Elm Street into a shrine for insomniacs. The twist here is that them creatures 'neath the stairway are actually innocents (with their bad bits hacked out), held captive by grotesque murderers Mommy and Daddy (who also happen to be sister-

Meet the parents: Wendy Robie and Everett McGill entertain The People Under the Stairs *in Wes Craven's frenzied trip from UIP.*

and-brother mercenary landlords of a black ghetto). Enter spunky ghetto youth (Brandon Adams, the kid in Michael Jackson's *Moonwalker*), who is determined to steal back what is rightfully his. Silly boy. This is a genuinely nightmarish concoction that conjures up the same level of hysteria as *The Texas Chain Saw Massacre* did seventeen years earlier – but with a few laughs amid the mayhem. [JC-W]

Cast includes: Brandon Adams (Fool Pointdexter), Everett McGill (Daddy), Wendy Robie (Mommy), A. J. Langer (Alice), Ving Rhames (LeRoy), Sean Whalen (Roach), Bill Cobbs (Grandpa Booker), Kelly Jo Minter, Jeremy Roberts, Conni Marie Brazelton.

Dir and Screenplay: Wes Craven. Pro: Marianne Maddalena and Stuart M. Besser. Co-Pro: Dixie J. Capp. Ex Pro: Craven and Shep Gordon. Ph: Sandi Sissel. Ed: James Coblentz. Pro Des: Bryan Jones. M: Don Peake. Costumes: Ileane Meltzer. (Alive Films/Universal–UIP.) Rel: 26 December 1991. 102 mins. Cert 18.

The Playboys. County Cavan, Ireland, 1957. A headstrong, independent beauty, Tara Maguire (Robin Wright), gives birth to an illegitimate son in a small village stifled by old-world hypocrisies. Refusing to name the father,

Hollywood Babylon: Tim Robbins and Greta Scacchi in Robert Altman's mercilessly enjoyable The Player *(from Guild).*

Irish stew: Albert Finney in a rare screen appearance as the local constable up against unrequited love and the IRA, in the Irish-American The Playboys *(from Goldwyn-Winstone).*

Tara finds herself the subject of local ridicule, while aggressively courted by the local police sergeant and a handsome travelling actor. A film of enormous texture and beauty, *The Playboys* (named after the nomadic actors) is enriched by a strong central performance from Ms Wright, who took the role when Annette Bening deserted the project (and was subsequently sued). Only Albert Finney seems somewhat out of place, his overbearing demeanour dwarfing the pathetic little policeman he is trying to portray. [JC-W]

Also with: Albert Finney (Sergeant Brendan Hegarty), Aidan Quinn (Tom), Alan Devlin (Father Malone), Milo O'Shea (Freddie), Niamh Cusack (Brigid), Ian McElhinney (Cassidy), Adrian Dunbar (Mick), Stella McCusker, Niall Buggy, Anna Livia Ryan, Lorcan Cranitch, Killian McKenna, Tony Rohr, Mark Mulholland, Niall O'Brien.
    Dir: Gillies Mackinnon. Pro: William P. Cartlidge and Simon Perry. Screenplay: Shane Connaughton and Kerry Crabbe. Ph: Jack Conroy. Ed: Humphrey Dixon. Pro Des: Andrew Harris. M: Jean-Claude Petit. Costumes: Consolata Boyle. Sound: Peter Lindsay. (Samuel Goldwyn Co.–Winstone.) Rel: 5 June 1992. 108 mins. Cert 12.

The Player. Hilarious, beautifully crafted, biting satire on Hollywood, marking Robert Altman's come-back as a director to be reckoned with. Scripted by Michael Tolkin from his own novel which, in turn, was fuelled by his humiliation at the hands of Tinseltown, *The Player* is the story of a studio executive, Griffin Mill (Tim Robbins), who receives threatening postcards from a frustrated screenwriter. In a fit of drunken anger, Mill kills his stalker, only to discover it is the wrong man. Still, the story is a great concept for a movie . . . Altman made this superior, suspenseful black comedy-thriller for a mere $8 million, but you'd never believe it, particularly with the number of stars in supporting roles and cameos (see below). A favourite at Cannes (both Altman and Robbins won prizes), *The Player* also proved to be popular with the public, although the plethora of in-jokes would have been lost on them. The shallowness and powerplay of Hollywood has seldom been so skilfully captured on film before, and *never* so accurately. [JC-W]

Also with: Greta Scacchi (June Gudmundsdottir), Fred Ward (Walter Stuckel), Whoopi Goldberg (Detective Susan Avery), Peter Gallagher (Larry Levy), Brion James (Joel Levison), Cynthia Stevenson (Bonnie Sherow), Dean Stockwell (Andy Civella), Richard E. Grant (Tom Oakley), Sydney Pollack (Dick Mellen), Lyle Lovett (Detective Paul DeLongpre), Randall Batinkoff (Reg Goldman), Dina Merrill, Angela Hall, Leah Ayres, Gina Gershon, Margery Bond, Michael Tolkin, Stephen Tolkin. As themselves: Steve Allen, Richard Anderson, Rene Auberjonois, Harry Belafonte, Shari Belafonte, Karen Black, Michael Bowen, Gary Busey, Robert Carradine, Charles Champlin, Cher, James Coburn, Cathy Lee Crosby, John Cusack, Brad Davis, Paul Dooley, Peter Falk, Felicia Farr, Louise Fletcher, Dennis Franz, Teri Garr, Scott Glenn, Jeff Goldblum, Elliott Gould, Joel Grey, David Alan Grier, Buck Henry, Anjelica Huston, Kathy Ireland, Steve James, Sally Kellerman, Sally Kirkland, Jack Lemmon, Marlee Matlin, Andie MacDowell, Malcolm McDowell, Jayne Meadows, Martin Mull, Nick Nolte, Bert Remsen, Burt Reynolds, Julia Roberts, Mimi Rogers, Annie Ross, Alan Rudolph, Jill St John, Susan Sarandon, Rod Steiger, Joan Tewkesbury, Lily Tomlin, Robert Wagner, Ray Walston, Bruce Willis, Marvin Young.

Dir: Robert Altman. Pro: David Brown, Michael Tolkin and Nick Wechsler. Ex Pro: Gary Brokaw. Co-Pro: Scott Bushell. Assoc Pro: David Levy. Screenplay: Tolkin; based on his novel. Ph: Jean Lepine. Ed: Geraldine Peroni. Pro Des: Stephen Altman. M: Thomas Newman. Costumes: Alexander Julian. Sound: Michael Redbourn. (Spelling Films–Guild.) Rel: 26 June 1992. 124 mins. Cert 15.

The Pleasure Principle. Embarrassing British sex comedy with Peter Firth as Dick, an unattractive womaniser. This blighter, a medical journalist, has his greasy hands on a brain surgeon, an unbridled solicitor and a vulnerable, whining divorcee. Meanwhile, he still harbours feelings for his ex-wife, a lesbian. That somebody as blatantly double-dealing as this Dick could deceive such professional women is an insult to the work force. Amazingly, director-producer-writer David Cohen persuaded the manager of a high street bank to fork out the film's £200,000 budget. [CB]

Also with: Lynsey Baxter (Sammy), Haydn Gwynne (Judith), Lysette Anthony (Charlotte), Sara Mair-Thomas (Anne), Ian Hogg (Malcolm), Francesca Folan (Mrs Malcolm), Laim McDermott, Stephen Finlay, Gordon Warnecke, Cliff Parisi, Patrick Tidmarsh, Chris Knowles, Lauren Tauben, Mark Carroll, Sarah Campbell, Chloe Davies, Tim Mason, Guy Lowe.

Dir, Pro and Screenplay: David Cohen. Ex Pro: Stephen Woolley and Robert Jones. Co-Pro: Joe McAllister, Jan Euden and Alistair Spellar. Ph: Andrew Spellar. Ed: McAllister. Pro Des: Cecelia Bretherton. M:

Game, set and macho: Keanu Reeves becomes a man in Kathryn Bigelow's adrenalin-booster, Point Break *(from Fox).*

Sonny Southon. Costumes: Jackie Parry. Sound: Albert Bailey. (Psychology News–Mayfair Palace.) Rel: 7 February 1992. 96 mins. Cert 18.

Point Break. A classy, strapping thriller-adventure set in the disparate worlds of 'radical' surfers and dedicated members of the police force. Keanu Reeves, in his most adult role to date, plays a fast-talking rookie cop who teams up with 'over-the-hill burn-out' Gary Busey. Their mission is to solve a series of bank robberies conducted by a gang who call themselves 'the ex-Presidents', a deadly quartet who wield shotguns and masks of Ronnie, Jimmy,

Futurelust: Patricia Arquette and Corey Haim ignore The Prayer of the Roller Boys (*from First Independent*).

Tricky Dickie and LBJ. Busey believes they're surfer dudes, so Keanu goes undercover as a wave-chaser and befriends athletic Zen idealist Patrick Swayze. This is formula stuff, charged up with some energetic direction, a lively screenplay and some adrenalin-pumping stunts (both on the waves and in the skies). Tense, funny, thrilling escapism. Previously known as *Johnny Utah* and *Riders on the Storm*. [JC-W]

Cast includes: Patrick Swayze (Bodhi), Keanu Reeves (Johnny Utah), Gary Busey (Pappas), Lori Petty (Tyler), John C. McGinley (Ben Harp), James Le Gros (Roach), John Philbin, Bojesse Christopher, Julian Reyes, Daniel Beer, Chris Pedersen, Vincent Klyn, Sydney Walsh, Julie Michaels.

Dir: Kathryn Bigelow. Pro: Peter Abrams and Robert L. Levy. Ex Pro: James Cameron. Screenplay: W. Peter Iliff; from a story by Iliff and Rick King. Ph: Donald Peterman. Ed: Howard Smith. Pro Des: Peter Jamison. M: Mark Isham; numbers performed by Ratt, Concrete Blond, Jimi Hendrix, Westworld, Public Image Limited etc. (Largo Entertainment–Fox.) Rel: 22 November 1991. 120 mins. Cert 15.

Poison. Unpleasant, gimmicky first feature from Todd Haynes, interweaving three stories and cinematic styles exploring aberrant behaviour. In *Hero*, a low-budget documentary, a 7-year-old boy shoots his father dead. In *Horror*, a black-and-white parody of '50s sci-fi, a handsome scientist accidentally reduces himself to a sexual leper. And in *Homo*, Haynes takes us into the brutal, homosexual world of a men's prison, inspired by the writing of Jean Genet. Undeniably a truly original film, shot on a minuscule budget of $255,000, *Poison* is often quite witty and was a winner of the Grand Jury Prize at the 1991 Sundance Film Festival. [JC-W]

Cast includes: *Hero*: Edith Meeks (Felicia Beacon), Millie White (Millie Sklar), Buck Smith (Gregory Lazar), Anne Giotta, Lydia Lafleur, Ian Nemser, Rob LaBelle, Evan Dunsky. *Horror*: Larry Maxwell (Dr Graves), Susan Norman (Nancy Olsen), Al Quagliata, Michelle Sullivan, Parlan McGaw, Frank O'Donnel. *Homo*: Scott Renderer (John Broom), James Lyons (Jack Bolton), John R. Lombardi (Rass), Tony Pemberton, Andrew Harpending, Tony Gigante, Douglas F. Gibson, Damien Garcia.

Dir and Screenplay: Todd Haynes. Pro: Christine Vachon. Ex Pro: James Schamus and Brian Greenbaum. Assoc Pro: Lauren Zalaznick. Ph: Maryse Alberti; b/w ph: Barry Ellsworth. Ed: Haynes and James Lyons. Pro Des: Sarah Stollman. M: James Bennett. Costumes: Jessica Haston. (Bronze Eye/NY State Council on the Arts/National Endowment for the Arts/Jerome Foundation/NY Foundation for the Arts/Art Matters Inc–Mainline.) Rel: 11 October 1991. 86 mins. Cert 18.

Prayer of the Roller Boys. We are back in the 21st century and hating it. Graffiti is everywhere, pizza delivery boys carry machine guns and Germany has just bought Poland. A gang of young, white supremacists decides to take the law into its own hands, and glides around on designer rollerskates in long Sergio Leone raincoats. To finance their operation, the gay blades extort protection money from local businesses and market a lethal narcotic they call 'Heaven-mist'. Enter outsider Griffin (Corey Haim), who's leant on by the impoverished police force to act as a mole in the gang. Basically, this is nothing more than teen-orientated video fodder, but the film does display some comic verve and Patricia Arquette, as an undercover cop, gives it more sex appeal than it deserves. [JC-W]

Also with: Patricia Arquette (Casey), Christopher Collet (Gary Lee), J. C. Quinn (Jaworski), Julius Harris (Speedbagger), Devin Clark (Miltie), Mark Pellegrino (Bingo), Morgan Weisser (Bullwack), G. Smokey Campbell, Jake Dengel, John P. Connolly, Cynthia Gates.

Dir: Rick King. Pro: Robert Mickelson. Ex Pro: Tetsu Fujimara, Martin F. Gold, Richard Lorber and Robert Baruc. Screenplay: W. Peter Iliff. Ph: Phedon Papamichael. Ed: Daniel Loewenthal. Pro Des: Thomas A. Walsh. M: Stacy Widelitz. Costumes: Merrily Murray-Walsh, Sound: Craig Felburg. (JVC/TV Tokyo–First Independent.) Rel: 2 August 1991. 90 mins. Cert 15.

The Prince of Tides. Overlong, rambling and self-indulgently 'pretty' screen adaptation of Pat Conroy's best-selling novel about the trapped pain of childhood memory. Barbra Streisand directs, produces and co-stars as Dr Susan Lowenstein, the New York psychiatrist who tries to unlock the emotional malaise of the suicidal Savannah Wingo (Melinda Dillon) – through her sole surviving brother, Tom (Nick Nolte). Tom has a few ghosts of his own, and some lessons to

Chic meets hick: acclaimed violinist Jeroen Krabbe attempts to embarrass country boy Nick Nolte – in Barbra Streisand's epic weepie, The Prince of Tides *(from Columbia).*

teach Dr Lowenstein. A complex story, this, with many interlinking character threads and emotional highs and lows, some of which hit their mark, some of which don't. Nolte is *almost* convincing as the Southern hick – bad diction and all – and looks great, having lost thirty pounds for the part (both Robert Redford and Warren Beatty were originally pencilled in for the role). [JC-W]

Also with Blythe Danner (Sallie Wingo), Kate Nelligan (superb as Lila Wingo Newbury, Tom's mother), Jeroen Krabbe (Herbert Woodruff), George Carlin (Eddie Detreville), Jason Gould (Bernard Woodruff), Brad Sullivan (Henry Wingo), Lindsay Wray (Jennifer Wingo), Brandlyn Whitaker, Justen Woods, Bobby Fain, Trey Yearwood, Tiffany Jean Davis, Nancy Atchison, Kiki Runyan, Bob Hannah, Rebecca Fleming, Sandy Rowe, Alan Sader, Frederick Neumann.

Dir: Barbra Streisand. Pro: Streisand and Andrew Karsch. Ex Pro: Cis Corman and James Roe. Screenplay: Pat Conroy and Becky Johnston. Ph: Stephen Goldblatt. Ed: Don Zimmerman. Pro Des: Paul Sylbert. M: James Newton Howard; numbers performed by George Michael, Soul II Soul, Carl Perkins etc. Costumes: Ruth Morley. Sound: Kay Rose. (Columbia Tri-Star.) Rel: 21 February 1992. 131 mins. Cert 15.

Privilege. Yvonne Rainer's very personal and semi-documentary lecture on how women should treat the menopause and its effects advises treating this change of life as liberation. The lecture's a pretty wide-ranging affair, in which writer-director-producer Rainer rambles freely into other subjects, throwing up some slyly amusing moments. [FDM]

Dir, Pro, Screenplay and Editor: Yvonne Rainer. Ph: Mark Daniels. Sound: Antonio Arroyo. Art: Anne Stuyler and Michael Selditch. (ICA.) Rel: 23 October 1991. 103 mins. No cert.

Problem Child II. Not so much a movie, more a form of mental torture. Junior Healy (the limited and unappealing Michael Oliver repeating his old role) is now in favour of keeping his adopted dad (John Ritter) and teams up with a young bitch from hell (the delightful Ivyann Schwan, from *Parenthood*). Moronic, cheap, poorly-made, tasteless, juvenile, below-the-belt farce. Enough said? [CB]

Cast includes: John Ritter (Ben Healy), Michael Oliver (Junior Healy), Jack Warden (Big Ben Healy), Laraine Newman (LaWanda Dumore), Amy Yasbeck (Annie Young), Ivyann Schwan (Trixie Young), Gilbert Gottfried (Mr Peabody), Paul Wilson (Smith).

Dir: Brian Levant. Pro: Robert Simonds. Screenplay: Scott Alexander and Larry Karaszewski; based on their original characters. Ph: Peter Smokler. Ed: Lois Freeman-Fox. Pro Des: Maria Caso. M: David Kitay. Costumes: Robert Moore. Sound: John M. Stacy. (Imagine Films Entertainment/Universal–UIP.) Rel: 14 February 1992. 90 mins. Cert PG.

Blind faith: Celia (Genevieve Picot) pores over snapshots of her would-be lover, her blind employer – in Jocelyn Moorhouse's intelligent Proof *(from Artificial Eye).*

The Wizard of Odd: John Gielgud as Prospero-as-Shakespeare in Peter Greenaway's extraordinary Prospero's Books.

Proof. First-time director Jocelyn Moorhouse was once told of a blind photographer and has fashioned this story about a bitter, blind Melbourne man who asserts his identity through taking snapshots. Trapped within his own distrust of the sighted, Martin keeps his besotted housekeeper at arm's length. In return, she plays malicious tricks on him, and attempts to come between him and his new friend Andy. Andy is the only person Martin will allow to see and describe his photographs. A surprisingly assured first feature, *Proof* is a mature, compulsive psychological drama – dusted with dark humour – that keeps us guessing. [JC-W]

Cast includes: Hugo Weaving (Martin), Genevieve Picot (Celia), Russell Crowe (Andy), Heather Mitchell (Mother), Jeffrey Walker (young Martin), Saskia Post (waitress), Frank Gallacher, Frankie J. Holden, Daniel Pollock, Cliff Ellen.
  Dir and Screenplay: Jocelyn Moorhouse. Pro: Lynda House. Ph: Martin McGrath. Ed: Ken Sallows. M: Not Drowning, Waving. Sound: Lloyd Carrick. (Films Pty Ltd/Australian Film Commission/Film Victoria–Artificial Eye.) Rel: 29 November 1991. 90 mins. Cert 15.

Prospero's Books. If you were to be stranded on a desert island, which 24 books would you take with you? Prospero, wizard and exiled Duke of Milan, takes magical volumes on language, geometry, astronomy, games, pornography, architecture, husbandry –

anything and everything to manipulate the inhabitants of his island and to concoct a terrible revenge on his enemies. Sir John Gielgud, arguably the century's pre-eminent Prospero, has long wanted to transplant his performance to the screen – he has contemplated asking Kurosawa to direct, and even wrote to Bergman. Peter Greenaway has taken up the challenge, persuading Gielgud to voice *all* the characters in Shakespeare's *The Tempest* ('my instant reaction was that he must be mad', the actor says now), and has consequently created a film of great aural tedium. However, Greenaway's visuals are so spellbinding (including superimposed images, hundreds of naked extras, recreated masterpieces by Rembrandt etc), that the eye is swamped, the mind boggled. In fact, the pictorial content of the film is *so* overpowering that the narrative is completely submerged. An intriguing, controversial, infuriating and unforgettable work from a master filmmaker – an intellectual's LSD trip. [JC-W]

Also with: Isabelle Pasco (Miranda), Michael Clark (Caliban), Michel Blanc (Alonso), Erland Josephson (Gonzalo), Tom Bell (Antonio), Kenneth Cranham (Sebastian), Mark Rylance (Ferdinand), Gerard Thoolen (Adrian), Pierre Bokma (Francisco), Jim Van Der Woude (Trinculo), Michiel Romeyn (Stephano), Orpheo (Ariel 1), Paul Russell (Ariel 2), James Thierree (Ariel 3), Emil Wolk (Ariel 4), Marie Angel (Iris), Ute Lemper (Ceres), Deborah Conway (Juno).

Dir and Screenplay: Peter Greenaway. Pro: Kees Kasander. Ex Pro: Kasander and Denis Wigman. Ph: Sacha Vierny. Ed: Marina Bodbyl. Pro Des: Ben Van Os and Jan Roelfs. M: Michael Nyman. Costumes: Dien Van Straalen. Sound: Chris Wyatt. Choreography: Karine Saporta. (Allarts/ Cinea/Camera One/Penta/Elsevier Vendex Film/Film Four Int/VPRO Television/Canal Plus/NHK–Palace.) Rel: 30 August 1991. 120 mins. Cert 15.

Pump Up the Volume. The coolest American teen movie since *Heathers*, with Christian Slater repeating his role as the anarchic high school outsider. This time he plays Mark Hunter, a shy, bespectacled New York kid who's just moved to Paradise Hills, a 'white bread' suburb of Arizona. At precisely ten o'clock every evening Mark is transmogrified into Happy Harry Hard-on, a rebellious voice of the airwaves, a talk-show host who can vocalise Mark's most intimate thoughts and feelings

Agony uncle: Christian Slater reads a troubled letter over the air in Allan Moyle's spot-on teen satire, Pump Up the Volume *(from Entertainment).*

with impunity. Or so he thinks. Mark's liberal chatter and music become a cult attraction in his neighbourhood, producing idolatry, pirated tapes and, eventually, police intervention. While Christian Slater has never been better (dispensing with his Jack Nicholson mannerisms), the script, score and direction all contribute to a film of wit, style and message. Director Allan Moyle's last feature was *Times Square*, starring Tim Curry as a New York DJ. [JC-W]

Also with: Annie Ross (Loretta Creswood), Samantha Mathis (Nora Diniro), Ellen Greene (Jan Emerson), Scott Paulin (Brian Hunter), Mimi Kennedy (Marta Hunter), Keith Stuart Thayer (Luis Chavez), Cheryl Pollack (Paige), Robert Schenkkan (David Deaver), Clayton Landy (Shep Sheppard), Lala Sloatman, Seth Green, Ahmet Zappa, Billy Morrissette, Chris Jacobs, Holly Sampson, Nolan Hemmings, Robert Harvey, James Hampton, Juliet Landau.

Dir and Screenplay: Allan Moyle. Ex Pro: Sara Risher, Nicolas Stiliadis and Syd Cappe. Pro: Rupert Harvey and Sandy Stern. Ph: Walt Lloyd. Ed: Janie Hampton and Larry Bock. Pro Des: Robb Wilson King. M: Cliff Martinez; numbers performed by The Beastie Boys, Leonard Cohen, Stan Ridgeway, MC Five, Sly Stone, The Cowboy Junkies, Sonic Youth, The Pixies, Was (Not Was), Soundgarden, Concrete Blonde, The Descendants, Above The Law, Peter Murphy, Ivan Neville. Sound: Russell C. Fager. (New Line–Entertainment.) Rel: 30 August 1991. 102 minutes. Cert 15.

A Rage in Harlem starts promisingly enough, with some powerful set-pieces, neat character delineations and a superb cameo from Screamin' Jay Hawkins – all laid on with a sure directorial hand by actor-director Bill Duke. But the shoot-outs, the shouting, the profanity, the sex and the broad comedy routines never ease off as the film escalates into a kind of wild parody of everything black. Filmed in the streets of Cincinnati to double for Harlem, this is a good-looking, sweaty and hard-hitting gangster pic that eventually expires in its own overkill. However, as gang-

Robin Givens (right) *seduces Forest Whitaker in Bill Duke's forceful* A Rage in Harlem *(from Palace).*

ster's moll Imabelle, Robin Givens is sensational, while Forest Whitaker makes a sweet, *Marty*esque hero as the God-fearing Jackson unwittingly involved in a plot surrounding a stolen box of gold. [JC-W]

Also with: Gregory Hines (Goldy), Zakes Mokae (Big Kathy), Danny Glover (Easy Money), Badja Djola (Slim), John Toles-Bey, Ron Taylor, Samm-Art Williams, Stack Pierce, Willard E. Pugh, Helen Martin, T. K. Carter, Reynaldo Rey, James Spinks.
 Dir: Bill Duke. Pro: Stephen Woolley and Kerry Boyle. Ex Pro: Nik Powell, Harvey Weinstein, Bob Weinstein, William Horberg and Terry Glinwood. Co-Pro: Forest Whitaker and John Nicolella. Line Pro: Thomas A. Razzano. Screenplay: John Toles-Bey and Bobby Crawford; from the novel by Chester Himes. Ph: Toyomichi Kurita. Ed: Curtiss Clayton. Pro Des: Steven Legler. M: Elmer Bernstein. Costumes: Nile Samples. (Miramax–Palace.) Rel: 27 September 1991. 110 mins. Cert 18.

Raise the Red Lantern – Dahong Denglong Gaogao Gua. Northern China, the 1920s. Here, the red lantern is used both as a *leitmotiv* and as a metaphor. A rich master of the Chen clan houses four mistresses in his beautiful mansion, in which each occupies her own wing. The Master favours one mis-

tress at a time, laying on little luxuries (like a foot massage), the preparation of her favourite food and the kudos of raising red lanterns outside her quarters. Each mistress plots against the others to win the Master's interest in a savage, virtually subliminal fight to gain superiority. The Master himself is portrayed as a cipher (without close-ups), while the lanterns fail to shed anything

China blues: Gong Li is given the red carpet, only to have it taken away – in Zhang Yimou's poetic Raise the Red Lantern *(from Palace).*

but a false light on the women's folly. Zhang Yimou, the Chinese director of *Red Sorghum* and *Ju Dou*, improves with each film, and here proves to be a true master of his craft. Few filmmakers in the West have grasped this well the techniques of long shot, close-up and minimal camera movement. A poignant, beautiful, richly-layered film. A Chinese-Hong Kong co-production. [JC-W]

Cast includes: Gong Li (Songlian), Ma Jingwu (the Master), He Caifei (Meishan), Cao Cuifeng (Zhuoyun), Jin Suyuan (Yuru), Kong Lin (Yan'er), Ding Weimin, Cui Zhihgang, Chu Xiao.
 Dir: Zhang Yimou. Pro: Chiu Fu-Sheng. Ex Pro: Hou Hsiao-Hsien and Zhang Wenze. Screenplay: Ni Zhen. Ph: Zhao Fei. Ed: Du Yuan. Art: Cao Jiuping and Dong Huamiao. M: Zhao Jiping. Costumes: Huang Lihua. Sound: Li Lanhua. (ERA International/China Film Co.–Palace.) Rel: 21 February 1992. 120 mins. Cert PG.

Rambling Rose. Eloquent, well-acted film version of Calder Willingham's autobiographical novel of Southern gentility and sexuality. Set in 1935 in Glenville, Georgia, during the Depression, the film looks at the effect a young nymphomaniac has on the Hillyer household. It is a tale of mutual, multi-layered love, as the leggy, innocent Rose (Laura Dern) is taken in by hotel manager Daddy Hillyer (Robert Duvall, excellent as usual), his wife and three children. The eldest boy, Buddy (Lukas Haas), is particularly struck by the new arrival – and narrates the story

A Rose by any other name would still seduce the trousers off the South: Laura Dern and Lukas Haas dabble in tenuous sexuality in Martha Coolidge's restrained tale of lust, Rambling Rose *(from Guild).*

in flashback – but nobody is immune to Rose's charms. Filmed in North Carolina. [JC-W]

Also with: Diane Ladd (Mother Hillyer), John Heard (grown-up Buddy Hillyer), Kevin Conway (Dr Martinson), Robert Burke (Dave Wilkie), Lisa Jakub (Frances 'Doll Baby' Hillyer), Evan Lockwood (Warren 'Waski' Hillyer), Matt Sutherland (Billy).

Dir: Martha Coolidge. Pro: Renny Harlin. Ex Pro: Mario Kassar and Edgar Scherick. Screenplay: Calder Willingham. Ph: Johnny Jensen. Ed: Steven Cohen. Pro Des: John Vallone. M: Elmer Bernstein. Costumes: Jane Robinson. Sound: Richard Van Dyke. (Midnight Sun–Guild.) Rel: 1 November 1991. 112 mins. Cert 15.

Rebecca's Daughters. Riotous romp based on a little-known real-life incident, 'adapted' from a long-lost screenplay by Dylan Thomas. Set in picturesque Wales in 1843, the film focuses on the enormous tollgate fees set by the imperious British. Taking the law into his own hands, a local anglicised toff disguises himself as the rebellious Rebecca and leads a revolt against the turnpikes. Although both the comedy and acting is decidedly broad, the period detail is colourful and a lot of the silliness rather endearing. If Henry Fielding were Welsh . . . [JC-W]

Cast includes: Peter O'Toole (Lord Sarn), Paul Rhys (Anthony Raine/Rebecca), Joely Richardson (Rhiannon), Simon Dormandy (Capt. Marsden), Dafydd Hywel (Rhodri Hughes), Sue Roderick (Sarah Hughes), Gwenllian Davies (Sara Jane), Robert Blythe (Sgt Bridges), Keith Allen, Desmond Barrit, Eiry Palfrey, Clive Merrison, Ray Gravell, Peter Hugo Daly, Alan Devlin, Lucy Jenkins.

Dir: Karl Francis. Pro: Chris Sievernich. Co-Pro: Ruth Kenley-Letts. Ex Pro: Ruth Caleb, Faramarz Ettehadieh and Gert Oberdorfer. Screenplay: Guy Jenkin; from the screenplay-novel by Dylan Thomas. Ph: Russ Walker. Ed: Roy Sharman. Pro Des: Ray Price. M: Rachel Portman. Costumes: Mecheal Taylor. Sound: Jeffrey North.

Welsh dresser: Peter O'Toole in drag as Queen Elizabeth I in Karl Francis's startling Rebecca's Daughters *(from Mayfair Entertainment).*

Mikki Allen and Harrison Ford, as daughter and father, compare scars in Mike Nichols's sentimental yet riveting Regarding Henry *(from UIP).*

(Astralma Erste Filmproduktion/Delta Film/BBC Wales/British Screen–Mayfair Entertainment.) Rel: 24 April 1992. 90 mins. Cert 12.

Recollections of the Yellow House – Recordacoes de la Casa Amarela.
Dreary Portuguese piece about a penniless, sleazy drop-out, a rapist and much else, played with anti-heroic enthusiasm by director Joao Cesar Monteiro. [FDM]

Also with: Manuela de Freitas, Sabina Sacchi, Inez de Medeiros, Teresa Calado, Ruy Fertado, Henrique Viana Luis, Miguel Cintra, Maria Angela de Oliveira, Violeta Sarzedas.

Dir and Screenplay: Joao Cesar Monteiro. Pro: Joao Pedro Benard and Joaquim Pinto. Ph: José Antonio Loureiro. Ed: Helena Alvis and Claudio Martinez. Art: Luis Monteiro. M: Schubert, Vivaldi, Mozart etc. (Invicta Films–Artificial Eye.) Rel: 9 August 1991. 122 mins. Cert 18.

Regarding Henry. Harrison Ford is Henry Turner, a hard-edged, work-motivated, hotshot New York lawyer. He's also a husband, father and very wealthy man who, because he's nurturing a sensational legal career, has little time for family life. One night he's shot in the head and loses everything. Henry has to re-learn to walk, speak and read and to reconsider the ethics of adulthood. Except Henry Turner is now a child, with a man's responsibilities . . . This is an expertly crafted, adult and compassionate drama, that reassesses our values in a materialistic, speeded-up world – all the more remarkable as the script was written by a 23-year-old. A powerfully moving, thought-provoking film. [JC-W]

Also with: Annette Bening (Sarah Turner), Bill Nunn (Bradley), Mikki Allen (Rachel Turner), Donald Moffat (Charlie), Aida Linares (Rosella), Elizabeth Wilson (Jessica), Robin Bartlett (Phyllis), Bruce Altman (Bruce), Rebecca Miller (Linda Palmer), Julie Follansbee (Mrs Matthews), Peter Appel, Harsh Nayyer, John Leguizamo, Cynthia Martells, May Quigley, Jeffrey Abrams.

Dir: Mike Nichols. Pro: Nichols and Scott Rudin. Ex Pro: Robert Greenhut. Screenplay and Co-Pro: Jeffrey Abrams. Ph: Guiseppi Rotunno. Ed: Sam O'Steen. Pro Des: Tony Walton. M: Hans Zimmer; Mozart, The Police. Costumes: Ann Roth. Sound: James Sabat and Gene Cantamessa. (Paramount–UIP.) Rel: 13 September 1991. 107 mins. Cert 12.

The Rescuers Downunder. Fine sequel to the 1977 Disney cartoon about a couple of members of the all-mouse Rescue Aid Society who free an orphan girl from a terrible fate in Florida. Here, Bernard (again voiced by Bob Newhart) is about to propose to the lovely Miss Bianca (Eva Gabor, again) when they are both called on to liberate a kidnapped boy in Australia. Whereas in the original they had to contend with the evil Medusa and the alligators of the bayou, here they're up against the evil poacher McLeach (George C. Scott) and the crocodiles of the outback (and a giant lizard called Joanna). Orville, the albatross and rodent 'airline', is replaced here by his brother Wilbur (voiced by John Candy), but is just as clumsy and lovable. There are gags galore, spectacular aerial effects and, thankfully, no dance routines. Due to the advance of computer graphics, the animation is of a very high quality, which makes the diction of some of the actors appear even more slapdash. This is the 29th animated Disney feature. [JC-W]

With the voices of: Tristan Rogers (Jake), Adam Ryen (Cody), Wayne Robson (Frank), Douglas Seale (Krebbs), Bernard Fox (Chairmouse/doctor), Peter Firth (Red), Billy Barty (Baitmouse).

Dir: Hendel Butoy and Mike Gabriel. Pro: Thomas Schumacher. Assoc Pro: Kathleen Gavin. Screenplay: Jim Cox, Karey Kirkpatrick, Byron Simpson and Joe Ranft; based on characters created by Margery Sharp. Ed: Michael Kelly. Art: Maurice Hunt. M: Bruce Broughton. (Silver Screen Partners IV/Walt Disney.) Rel: 18 October 1991. 77 mins. Cert U.

Return to the Blue Lagoon. A mistaken effort to squeeze a few more pennies from De Vere Stacpoole's original idyllic story of two innocent castaways on a desert island, learning about life and love by instinct and not by the book. The Brooke Shields version in 1980 was a remake of the 1949 original. Now the son of the original castaways coincidentally finds himself marooned on the same island with a pretty girl . . . Glorious scenery and attractive castaways – but is that enough? [FDM]

Cast: Milla Jovovich (the girl), Brian Krause (the boy), Lisa Pelikan (Sarah Hargrave), Courtney Phillips, Garette Patrick Ratliffe, Emma James, Jackson Barton, Nana Coburn, Brian Blain, Peter Hehir.

Dir and Pro: William A. Graham. Ex Pro: Randal Kleiser. Co-Pro: Peter Bogart. Screenplay: Leslie Stevens. Ph: Robert Steadman. Ed: Ronald J. Fagan. Pro Des: Jon Dowding. Art: Paul Ammitzboll. M: Basil Poledouris. (Columbia.) Rel: 9 August 1991. 98 mins. Cert PG.

Rhapsody in August. Grandmother Kane (Sachiko Murase) lives in the countryside outside Nagasaki, and has her four grandchildren to stay for the summer. During their sojourn she receives a letter from a brother in Hawaii, who is dying. He begs her to visit, but being one of at least eleven children, she cannot remember him and is afraid to leave her haven. Her grandchildren, dressed in American T-shirts, jeans and baseball caps, discover another side to the dilemma and together explore the pain barely

Summer of discontent: Sachiko Murase surrounded by her grandchildren – Hidetaka Yoshioka, Mie Suzuki, Tomoko Ohtakara and Mitsunori Isaki – in Akira Kurosawa's gentle polemic, Rhapsody in August *(from Palace).*

beneath the surface of modern Nagasaki. Meanwhile, Grandmother Kane must reconcile herself to her memory – and to her memories of America – and explain the realities of war to her wards. It is hard to believe that this ineffectual, contemporary fable is from the great Japanese filmmaker Akira Kurosawa, now aged 81, but the film does project

Daredevil Jake and the lovely Miss Bianca harness the ophidian Frank in Disney's entertaining The Rescuers Down Under.

an admirable simplicity, while digging up some serious questions with a clean knife. [JC-W]

Also with: Tomoko Ohtakara (Tami), Mitsunori Isaki (Shinjiro), Hidetaka Yoshioka (Tateo), Mie Suzuki (Minako), Richard Gere (Clark), Hisashi Igawa, Narumi Kayashima, Toshie Negishi, Choichiro Kawarasaki.

Dir and Screenplay: Akira Kurosawa; from the novel *Nabe-No-Naka* by Kiyoko Murata. Pro: Hisao Kurosawa. Ex Pro: Toru Okuyama. Ph: Takao Saito and Masaharu Ueda. Art: Yoshiro Muraki. M: Shinichiro Ikebe; Schubert, Vivaldi. Sound: Kenichi Benitani. (Shochiko/Kurosawa Productions–Palace.) Rel: 27 September 1991. 104 mins. Cert U.

Ricochet. Nick Styles (Denzel Washington) is a bright cop who fools a ruth-

Alan Rickman transforms ham into an art form and wins the acting honours in Warner's otherwise bland Robin Hood: Prince of Thieves. *Mary Elizabeth Mastrantonio looks on.*

less gunman and becomes a local hero. While the gunman, Earl Talbot Blake (John Lithgow on chilling form), plots his revenge in prison, Styles works his way up to become assistant district attorney and a popular figurehead of the people. Blake is not interested in killing Styles – he just wants to humiliate him, drug him, give him VD, kill his family and friends, have him arrested and drive him insane. With the combined talents of producer Joel Silver (*Lethal Weapon, Die Hard*), director Russell Mulcahy (*Highlander*) and scripter Steven E. De Souza (*48 HRS, Die Hard*), this colourfully written, heart-pounding thriller could not fail to hit all the right buttons. It is, however, a surprisingly unpleasant outing for such a high-profile production. [JC-W]

Also with: Ice T (Odessa), Kevin Pollack (Larry Doyle), Lindsay Wagner (DA Priscilla Brimleigh), Josh Evans (Kim), Victoria

Dillard (Alice), John Cothran Jr (Farris), John Amos, Mary Ellen Trainor, Linda Dona, Matt Landers, Jesse Ventura, Tom Finnegan, Mark Phelan.

Dir: Russell Mulcahy. Pro: Joel Silver and Michael Levy. Ex Pro: Barry Josephson. Co-Pro: James Herbert and Suzanne Todd. Screenplay: Steven E. De Suza; from a story by Fred Dekker and Menno Meyjes. Ph: Peter Levy. Ed: Peter Honess. Pro Des: Jay Hinkle. M: Alan Silvestri; numbers performed by The Pointer Sisters, The Fabulous Thunderbirds, Shanice Wilson, Crystal Waters, Chic, Ice T, Donald D, Seal. Costumes: Marilyn Vance-Straker. Sound: Martin Maryska. (HBO/Cinema Plus LP–First Independent.) Rel: 24 April 1992. 110 mins. Cert 18.

Rigoletto. The Verdi opera brought to the screen, with Luciano Pavarotti as the Duke of Mantua and Ingvar Wixell in the title role. Filmed in Italy, with the sound track recorded in Vienna. A real musical treat. [FDM]

Also with: Edita Gruberova, Ferruccio Furlanetto, Bernd Weikl, Louis Otey, Remy Corazza, Kathleen Kuhlmann, Roland Bracht, Victoria Vergara, Fedora Barbieri.

Dir: Jean-Pierre Ponnelle. Ex Pro: Horant H. Hohlfeld. Set Design: Gianni Quaranta. Ph: Pasqualino de Santis. Music

performed by the Vienna Philharmonic Orchestra conducted by Riccardo Chailly, with the chorus of the Vienna State Opera. (A Unitel Opera.). Rel: 26 December 1991. 118 mins. Cert PG.

Robin Hood: Prince of Thieves. Imagine Indiana Jones in Merrie Olde England, and you have a rough idea of what this is about. Opening with a man having his hand cut off in Jerusalem, the film hurtles back to England and never stops. Witchcraft, comic villains and large-scale battles fill the screen until your head aches. Kevin Costner is an unsympathetic Robin (never thinking twice about putting an arrow through a colleague's hand), Morgan Freeman appears decidedly uncomfortable as a Moor without a country and Christian Slater looks odd as a squinting Will Scarlett with street cred. Technically the film tries far too hard to impress, the music barely pauses for an instant, the editing is over-impatient and the camera seldom stops moving. Another overblown, overscored, overbudgeted Hollywood excess story. Where's the charm? [JC-W]

High-flyer: Rocketeer *Bill Campbell is assisted by Alan Arkin in Disney's charming, guileless summer flop.*

Also with: Morgan Freeman (Azeem), Alan Rickman (Sheriff of Nottingham), Mary Elizabeth Mastrantonio (Marian), Geraldine McEwan (Mortianna), Micheal McShane (Friar Tuck), Brian Blessed (Lord Locksley), Michael Wincott (Guy of Gisborne), Nick Brimble (Little John), Soo Drouet (Fanny), Daniel Peacock (Bull), Jack Wild (Much), Daniel Newman, Walter Sparrow, Harold Innocent, Marc Zuber, Jimmy Gardner, Pat Roach, John Tordoff, Susannah Corbett, Richard Strange.

Dir: Kevin Reynolds. Pro: John Watson, Pen Densham and Richard B. Lewis. Ex Pro: James G. Robinson, David Nicksay and Gary Barber. Screenplay: Densham and Watson. Ph: Doug Milsome. Ed: Peter Boyle. Pro Des: John Graysmark. M: Michael Kamen; numbers performed by Bryan Adams and Jeff Lynne. Costumes: John Bloomfield. Sound: Chris Munro. (Morgan Creek–Warner.) Rel: 19 July 1991. 143 mins. Cert PG.

Rock-a-Doodle. Technically brilliant British feature cartoon from expert animator Don Bluth; rockin' rooster Chanticleer brings the sun up on his farm with his morning cry but when he leaves, disaster follows . . . Good fun and wonderful effects in this superior piece of animation. [FDM]

Narrator: Phil Harris. Chanticleer's voice: Glen Campbell.

Dir: Don Bluth. Co-Dir: Gary Goldman, Dan Kuenster. Pro: Bluth, Goldman, John Pomeroy. Ex Pro: G. A. Walker and Morris F. Sullivan. Screenplay: David N. Weiss. Ed: Bernard Caputo, Fiona Trayler, Lisa Dorney, Joe Gall. Pro Des: Dave Goetz. Art: Don Moore, Terry Pritchard. M: Robert Folk and T. J. Kuenster. (Goldcrest in assoc with Sullivan Bluth Studios Ireland Ltd–Rank.) Rel: 2 August 1991. 74 mins. Cert U.

Rocketeer. Disney's Big Summer Movie of 1991 turns out to be an immensely likable, tongue-in-cheek and occasionally charming live-action comic-strip adventure in the nature of Buck Rogers, Indiana Jones and the ilk. Button-nosed newcomer Bill Campbell plays Cliff Secord, the daredevil stunt flier who stumbles across a mysterious rocket pack in 1938 California. With the help of his trusty partner Peevy (a wonderfully restrained Alan Arkin as the inevitably eccentric sidekick), Secord adapts the pack to propel him around LA to uncover a Nazi plot. Any movie that has the gall to combine Howard Hughes, W. C. Fields, Clark Gable and a small army of Nazis can't be all bad. *Rocketeer's* strengths are that it doesn't take itself seriously for a moment, and that it boasts some superb aerial sequences and a terrifying henchman who's charged straight out of Disney's *Dick Tracy*. The story also works on a simple, straightforward trajectory without letting the special effects get in the way. Even James Horner's soaring score *carries* the movie rather than drowns it. Campbell is winning enough in the title role (a part variously discussed for Dennis Quaid, Kurt Russell and Johnny Depp), although he lacks the dash of Harrison Ford's Han Solo, and Timothy Dalton makes a divine villain as the silkily evil matinee idol, Neville Sinclair. The kids should love it, and there are enough in-jokes to keep the adults happy as well. [JC-W]

Also with: Jennifer Connelly (Jenny), Paul Sorvino (Eddie Valentine), Terry O'Quinn

(Howard Hughes), Ed Lauter (Fitch), James Handy (Wooly), Jon Polito (Bigelow), Tiny Ron, Robert Guy Miranda, John Lavachielli, Eddie Jones, William Sanderson, Don Pugsley, Nada Despotovich, Margo Martindale, Clint Howard, Julian Barnes, Rick Overton, Lori Lynn Ross.

Dir: Joe Johnston. Pro: Lawrence Gordon, Charles Gordon and Lloyd Levin. Ex Pro: Larry Franco. Screenplay: Danny Bilson, Paul De Meo and William Dear; based on the 'graphic novel' *The Rocketeer* by Dave Stevens. Ph: Hiro Narita. Ed: Arthur Schmidt. Pro Des: Jim Bissell. M: James Horner; numbers performed by Artie Shaw & His Orchestra. Costumes: Marilyn Vance-Straker. Sound: Thomas Causey. (Walt Disney/Silver Screen Partners IV– Disney.) Rel: 2 August 1991. 120 mins. Cert PG.

Ruby. Chicago/Dallas/Cuba/New Orleans/Washington DC, 1963–7. Workmanlike factionalisation of the last years of mobster and strip-club owner Jack

Relative theory: Lee Harvey Oswald (Willie Garson) is gunned down by Jack Ruby (Danny Aiello) in John Mackenzie's thoughtful reconstruction of the Kennedy brouhaha (from Rank).

Ruby (Danny Aiello) – before his murder of Lee Harvey Oswald. Stirring together fact, fiction and supposition, this is nevertheless a straightforward look at a man who dealt in dirty deeds without losing his dignity. Sherilyn Fenn (*Twin Peaks, Two-Moon Junction*) co-stars as the apocryphal girlfriend who draws out Ruby's more tender characteristics, providing the film with its most gratifying moments. The acting is polished, but the action neither engages the adrenalin nor intellect. Based on the play *Love Field*, first performed at London's Bush Theatre. [JC-W]

Also with: Sherilyn Fenn (Candy Cane), Arliss Howard (Maxwell), Tobin Bell (Ferris), David Duchovny (Officer Tippit), Richard Sarafian (Proby), Joe Cortese (Louie Vitali), Marc Lawrence (Santos Alicante), Willie Garson (Lee Harvey Oswald), Joe Viterelli (Joseph Valachi), Frank Orsatti, Jane Hamilton, Leonard Termo, Gerard David, Patrick Jude, Kevin Wiggins.

Dir: John Mackenzie. Pro: Sigurjon Sighvatsson and Steve Golin. Ex Pro: Michael Kuhn. Co-Pro: Jay Roewe. Screenplay: Stephen Davis; based on his play. Ph: Phil Meheux. Ed: Richard Trevor. Pro Des: David Brisbin. M: John Scott; numbers per-

formed by Sherilyn Fenn, Patrick Jude, The Robins, Judy Collins etc. Costumes: Susie DeSanto. Sound: Paul Clay. (Manifesto/ Polygram/Propaganda Films–Rank.) Rel: 29 May 1992. 111 mins. Cert 15.

Rush. Texas, 1975. Grim drama based on the semi-autobiographical novel by former policewoman Kim Wozencraft, the story of a couple of undercover narcotic officers who become engulfed by the drug world they inhabit. Very slow in parts and unrelentingly bleak, *Rush* is enhanced by a naked and forceful performance from Jennifer Jason Leigh as the cop who just manages to hang on to her sanity and honour. [JC-W]

Cast includes: Jason Patric (Jim Raynor), Jennifer Jason Leigh (Kristen Cates), Sam Elliott (Larry Dodd), Max Perlich (Walker), Gregg Allman (Will Gaines), Tony Frank, William Sadler, Special K. McCray, Dennis Letts, Dennis Burkley, Glenn Wilson, Merrill Connally, Connie Cooper, Cynthia Scott, John Ray Harrison.

Dir: Lili Fini Zanuck. Pro: Richard D. Zanuck. Screenplay: Pete Dexter; based on the novel by Kim Wozencraft. Ph: Kenneth MacMillan. Ed: Mark Warner. Pro Des: Paul Sylbert. M: Eric Clapton; numbers performed by Clapton (*Tears in Heaven, Help Me Up*), Terrell, Robin Trower, Patsy Cline, Freddie Fender, Lynyard Skynyrd, Bob Dylan, Jimi Hendrix, Bonnie Raitt, The Charlie Daniels Band etc. Costumes: Colleen Atwood. Sound: Gary Rydstrom. (MGM–UIP.) Rel: 5 June 1995. 120 mins. Cert 18.

Salmonberries. German filmmaker Percy Adlon, continuing his fancy for offbeat casting (witness *Bagdad Café* and *Rosalie Goes Shopping*), pitches Canadian singer k. d. lang, German stage actress Rosel Zech and Hollywood heavy Chuck Connors together in an off-centre drama set in remotest Alaska. The androgynous lang stars as Kotz, an enigmatic drifter in search of her roots who pesters German librarian Roswitha (Frau Zech) to distraction. Gradually, *very* gradually, the two women come to terms with each other and discover themselves through their friendship. [JC-W]

Also with: Chuck Connors ('Bingo' Chuck), Jane Lind (Noayak), Oscar Kawagley (Butch), Wolfgang Steinberg (Albert).

Dir and Screenplay: Percy Adlon. Pro: Eleanore Adlon. Line Pro: Jame Beardsley. Ph: Tom Sigel. Ed: Conrad Gonzalez. Pro

Hee-haw: the groom (James Wilder), the father-in-law (Leland Crooke) and the bride (Emily Lloyd) act up a storm in Rank's lamentable Scorchers.

Des: Amadeus Capra. M: Bob Telson, Beethoven, *Barefoot* performed by k. d. lang. Costumes: Cynthia Flynt. Sound: Jose Araujo. (Pelemele FILM GmbH Prod.–Electric.) Rel: 10 April 1992. 94 mins. Cert 12.

Scorchers. Deep in bayou country a cast of agitated characters (a whore, a drunk, a virgin) yell and scream at each other and pour out some home-spun philosophy. Based on the play by David Beaird, and adapted and directed by the same, *Scorchers* is a fine example of how a bad play can make an even worse film. Intended as a poignant look at love and sexuality in steamy Louisiana, this is hokey, preachy stuff, over-acted by a cast past their sell-by date and directed with the ineptitude of a man who doesn't know how to impress. However, Emily Lloyd's Southern accent is faultless. [JC-W]

Cast includes: Emily Lloyd (Splendid, the virgin), James Earl Jones (Bear, the barman), Denholm Elliott (Howler, the drunk), Faye Dunaway (Thais, the whore), Jennifer Tilly (Talbot, the jilted wife), James Wilder (Dolan, the groom), Anthony Geary (the preacher), Leland Crooke (Jumper, the narrator), Luke Perry (Ray Ray), Kevin Michael Brown, Michael Covert, Carter Burwell.

Dir and Screenplay: David Beaird. Pro: Morrie Eisenman and Richard Hellman. Ex Pro: John Quested, Richard Becker and John La Violette. Co-Pro: Steven J. Wolfe. Ph: Peter Deming. Ed: David Garfield and David Blewitt. Pro Des: Bill Eigenbrodt. M: Carter Burwell. Costumes: Heidi Kaczenski. Sound: Richard E. Yawn and Gordon Ecker. (Goldcrest–Rank.) Rel: 15 May 1992. 88 mins. Cert 18.

Shaking the Tree. Chicago; December, 1989. Four best friends approaching their late twenties – and 1990 – each goes through a crisis that

Playing adults: Arye Gross and Christina Haag discover mutual incompatibility in Duane Clark's labour of love, Shaking the Tree *(from HoBo).*

tests their friendship and enriches it. Heart-felt as this movie may be, it just doesn't ring true. Besides, these guys are so unalike that they would never be friends in a million years. Clichés clog the script, and some of the dialogue is unbelievable – which is a shame, as this is a labour of love that the scriptwriters made themselves. Check out the video of *Diner* instead. [JC-W]

Cast includes: Arye Gross (Barry), Gale Hansen (Sully), Doug Savant (Michael), Steven Wilde (Duke), Courteney Cox (Kathleen), Christina Haag (Michelle), Michael Arabian (Nickel), Ron Dean (Duke's father), Brittney Hansen (Bridgette), Dennis Cockrum, Nathan Davis, Terry 'Turk' Muller, John Malloy, Mick Scriba.

Dir: Duane Clark. Pro: Robert J. Wilson. Ex Pro: Anthony J. Tomaska and Richard Wagstaff. Screenplay: Clark and Steven Wilde. Ph: Ronn Schmidt. Ed: Martin L. Bernstein. Pro Des: Sean Mannion. M: David E. Russo. Costumes: Susan Michel Kaufman. (Blue Ridge/Filmtrust-HoBo.) Rel: 15 November 1991. 107 mins. Cert 15.

Shattered. Successful San Francisco property developer Dan Merrick (Tom Berenger) awakes from a coma with psychogenetic amnesia. He knows who the president of the United States is, but he cannot remember his own wife, Judith (Greta Scacchi). She carefully nurtures her husband back to reality – but she isn't telling him everything. Who *was* Dan Merrick before he lost his memory? *Shattered*, based on Richard Neely's novel *The Plastic Nightmare*

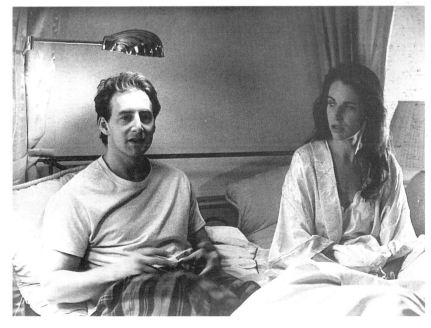

It'll be alright on the daytime: Sally Field confides in Whoopi Goldberg in Michael Hoffman's very funny Soapdish *(from UIP).*

(which was earlier announced to be filmed with William Hurt and Sissy Spacek), is blessed with an ingenious corkscrew plot, but is butchered by hamfisted, melodramatic direction straight out of a Fifties B-movie. When Berenger and Scacchi's love-making scene is superimposed over thundering surf you *know* you're in trouble. [JC-W]

Also with: Bob Hoskins (as the American Gus Klein), Corbin Bernsen (Jeb Scott), Joanne Whalley-Kilmer (Jenny Scott), Debi A. Monahan (Nancy Mercer), Bert Rosario, Jedda Jones, Scott Getlin, Kellye Nakahara, Theodore Bikel.

Dir and Screenplay: Wolfgang Petersen. Pro: Petersen, John Davis and David Korda. Ex Pro: Larry Sugar and Michel Roy. Ph: Lazslo Kovacs. Ed: Hannes Nikel and Glen Farr. Pro Des: Gregg Ponseca. M: Angelo Badalamenti. Costumes: Erica Edell Phillips. (Dieter Geissler Willi Baer Capella Films Prod/Palace.) Rel: 8 November 1991. 106 mins. Cert 15.

Shining Through. Lavish, old-fashioned WWII spy romance based on the 1988 best-selling novel by Susan Isaacs. Melanie Griffith is Linda Voss, a smart Irish-Jewish working girl infatuated with Hollywood spy movies. She's certainly too smart for her boss, attorney Ed Leland (Michael Douglas), whom she immediately spots as a spy. Still, they fall in love, the Japs bomb Pearl Harbor and Linda insists on being sent to Berlin to infiltrate a top Nazi household. The dialogue is crisp, funny and self-knowing, the story well-plotted and the production values first-rate. This is entertaining soap opera, although the flash-back structure of the film almost cripples it. John Gielgud, as a grumpy German, is wildly miscast. Filmed in East Germany, Austria and at Pinewood Studios by Dolly Parton's Sandollar Productions. [JC-W]

Also with: Liam Neeson (Franze-Otto Dietrich), Joely Richardson (Margrete Von Eberstien), John Gielgud ('Sunflower'), Francis Guinan (Andrew Berringer), Ludwig Haas (Adolf Hitler), Clement Von Franckenstein (BBC interviewer), Patrick Winczewski, Anthony Walters, Victoria Shalet, Sheila Allen, Stanley Beard, Sylvia

Syms, Ronald Nitschke, Hansi Jochmann, Mathieu Carriere, Deirdre Harrison, Wolf Kahler, William Hope, Jay Benedict, Tusse Silberg.

Dir and Screenplay: David Seltzer. Pro: Howard Rosenman and Carol Baum. Ex Pro: Seltzer and Sandy Gallin. Co-Pro: Nigel Wooll. Ph: Jan De Bont. Ed: Craig McKay. Pro Des: Anthony Pratt. M: Michael Kamen. Costumes: Marit Allen. (Peter V. Miller Investment Group/Sandollar Prods–Fox.) Rel: 20 March 1992. 132 mins. Cert 15.

Soapdish. A lively, spot-on and occasionally very funny spoof of daytime TV melodrama, *Soapdish* boasts a terrific line-up of stars on top form. Sally Field, cast against type, top-bills as Celeste Talbert, 42-year-old star of *The Sun Also Sets* and a 'buffet of bad news'. When the show's ratings plummet, Celeste's own private life becomes inseparable from the soap. Meanwhile, insiders plot to oust her – only to watch her popularity spiral upwards. Pacy direction, sturdy construction and some wonderful one-liners lift this into the realms of high farce. Oh yes, and there's a wonderful homage to *Tootsie* at the film's climax. [JC-W]

Also with: Kevin Kline (Jeffrey Anderson/ Dr Rod Randall), Robert Downey Jr (David Barnes), Cathy Moriarty (Montana Moorehead/Nurse Nan), Whoopi Goldberg (Rose Schwartz), Elisabeth Shue (Lori Craven/ Angelique), Kathy Najimy (Tawny Miller, the costume designer), Garry Marshall (Edmund Edwards), Teri Hatcher, Paul Johansson, Arne Nannestad, Tim Choate, Carrie Fisher, Costas Mandylor, Robert Camiletti, Michael Berkowitz, Sheila Kelley, Phil Leeds, Herta Ware, Clive Rosengren, Leeza Gibbons, John Tesh, Stephen Nichols.

Dir: Michael Hoffman. Pro: Aaron Spelling and Alan Greisman. Ex Pro: Herbert Ross. Co-Pro: Victoria White and Joel Freeman. Screenplay: Robert Harling and Andrew Bergman. Ph: Ueli Steiger. Ed: Garth Craven. Pro Des: Eugenio Zanetti. M: Alan Silvestri; *El Sol Tambien En Pone* performed by Ludar. Costumes: Nolan Miller. Sound: Petur Hliddal. (Paramount–UIP.) Rel: 23 August 1991. 96 mins. Cert 12.

Split Second. *Alien* visits the London Underground – in the year 2008. Thanks to global warming, England's capital is flooded and overrun by plague, rats and killer smog. Rutger Hauer plays Harley Stone, a leather-clad, maverick cop ('addicted to anxiety, chocolate and coffee') on the trail of a serial killer. The look of the film (shot in back alleys, night clubs

Global warning: Rutger Hauer sets the record straight for Pete Postlethwaite, in Tony Maylam's futuristic comedy-thriller, Split Second *(from Entertainment).*

and in the Underground) is impressive, but the script is so derivative that it's guilty of grand larceny. Still, the grim humour does a lot to compensate for the clichés. [JC-W]

Also with: Kim Cattrall (Michelle), Neil Duncan (Dick Durkin), Michael J. Pollard (the Rat Catcher), Alun Armstrong (Thrasher), Pete Postlethwaite (Paulsen), Ian

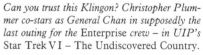

Can you trust this Klingon? Christopher Plummer co-stars as General Chan in supposedly the last outing for the Enterprise *crew – in UIP's* Star Trek VI – The Undiscovered Country.

Dury (Jay Jay), Roberta Eaton, Tony Steedman, Steven Hartley, Sarah Stockbridge, Colin Skeaping, Ken Bones, Dave Duffy, John Bennett, Tina Shaw.

Dir: Tony Maylam. Pro: Laura Gregory. Ex Pro: Keith Cavele and Chris Hanley. Screenplay: Gary Scott Thompson. Ph: Clive Tickner. Ed: Dan Rae. Pro Des: Chris Edwards. M: Stephen Parsons and Francis Haines; numbers performed by The Moody Blues and Cab Calloway. Costumes: Antoinette Gregory. Subway Train and additional sequences directed by: Ian Sharp. Sound: Mark Auguste. Creature FX and Design: Stephen Norrington. (Muse Productions BV/Challenge–Entertainment.) Rel: 5 June 1992. 90 mins. Cert 18.

Star Trek VI: The Undiscovered Country. Stardate 8679.14. On the recommendation of Spock, Captain James Tiberius Kirk finds himself escorting Klingon leader Chancellor Gorkon (David Warner) to Earth for peace talks. The Klingon moon Plaxus has exploded, leaving the hostile planet with 50 earth years before extinction. Kirk is uncomfortable with his new role as escort, and has every right to be . . . The final outing in the successful screen series for the original TV crew, *The Undiscovered Country* is more an extended small-screen episode than a movie, but the Shakespeare-themed dialogue is priceless (if a trifle whimsical). [JC-W]

Also with: William Shatner (Captain Kirk), Leonard Nimoy (Mr Spock), DeForest Kelley (Dr Leonard H. 'Bones' McCoy), James Doohan (Montgomery Scott), Walter Koenig (Commander Pavel Andreivich Chekov), Nichelle Nichols (Commander Uhura), George Takei (Captain Hikaru Sulu), Kim Cattrall (Vulcan Lt Valeris), Christopher Plummer (General Chang), Mark Lenard (Ambassador Sarek), Brock Peters (Admiral Cartwright), Rosana DeSoto (Azetbur), Grace Lee Whitney, Leon Russom, Kurtwood Smith, John Schuck, Michael Dorn, Paul Rossilli, Robert Easton, W. Morgan Sheppard, Iman, Todd Bryant, Christian Slater.

Dir: Nicholas Meyer. Pro: Ralph Winter and Steven-Charles Jaffe. Ex Pro: Leonard

Tip for tap: Liza Minnelli leads the class in Lewis Gilbert's entertaining goulash of styles in Stepping Out *(from UIP). Left to right: Jane Krakowski, Bill Irwin, Minnelli, Julie Walters, Sheila McCarthy and Ellen Greene.*

Nimoy. Screenplay: Meyer and Denny Martin Flinn; from a story by Nimoy, Lawrence Konner and Mark Rosenthal, based on characters created by Gene Roddenberry. Ph: Hiro Narita. Ed: Ronald Roose. Pro Des: Herman Zimmerman. M: Cliff Eidelman. Costumes: Dodie Shepard. Sound: Gene Cantamessa and George Waters II. (Paramount–UIP.) Rel: 14 February 1992. 109 mins. Cert PG.

Stepping Out. Americanisation of the long-running London play by Richard Harris about a motley gaggle of would-be tap dancers. Liza Minnelli, once again playing an amateur above her station, is the dance teacher out to make dreams happen. Not in the same class as director Lewis Gilbert's former hymns to the changing female spirit (*Educating Rita* and *Shirley Valentine*), this is nevertheless a heart-warming tale (set in Buffalo, filmed in Toronto) which is not as predictable – or as sentimental – as it could've been. However, there *is* an interesting clash of acting styles, from Minnelli's naturalistic cinematic approach to Julie Walters's pantomimic parody. [JC-W]

Cast includes: Liza Minnelli (Mavis Turner), Shelley Winters (Mrs Fraser), Bill Irwin (Geoffrey), Ellen Greene (Maxine), Julie Walters (Vera), Robyn Stevan (Sylvia),

Jane Krakowski (Lynne), Sheila McCarthy (Andy), Andrea Martin (Dorothy), Carol Woods (Rose), Luke Reilly (Patrick), Nora Dunn (Pam Leichner), Eugene Robert Glazer, Geza Kovacs, Raymond Rickman, Michael De Sadeleer.

Dir and Pro: Lewis Gilbert. Co-Pro: John Dark. Ex Pro: Bill Kenwright. Screenplay: Richard Harris; from his own play. Ph: Alan Hume. Ed: Humphrey Dixon. Pro Des: Peter Mullins. M: Peter Matz; *Stepping Out* by Fred Ebb and John Kander. Costumes: Candice Paterson. Choreography: Danny Daniels. (Paramount–UIP.) Rel: 20 September 1991. 105 mins. Cert PG.

Stone Cold. Harley Davidsons, explosions, swearing, black leather jackets and tattoos form the basics of *Stone Cold*. This formulaic thriller marks the debut of American footballer Brian Bosworth as an undercover cop who infiltrates a bevy of horrid bikers. Bosworth's hefty physical presence is just one more reason why 15-year-olds will love this action flick. [KK]

Cast includes: Brian Bosworth (Joe Huff/John Stone), Lance Henriksen (Chains), William Forsythe (Ice), Arabella Holzbog (Nancy), Sam McMurray (Lance), Richard Gant (Cunningham), Paulo Tocha, David Tress, Evan James, Kevin Page, Laura Albert.

Biker heaven: Brian Bosworth and the ton-up boys, in Craig R. Baxley's workmanlike Stone Cold *(from Columbia).*

Dir: Craig R. Baxley. Pro: Yoram Ben Ami. Ex Pro: Walter Doniger and Gary Wichard. Screenplay: Doniger. Ph: Alexander Gruszynski. Ed: Mark Helfrich. Pro Des: John Mansbridge and Richard Johnson. M: Sylvester Levay; numbers performed by The Doobie Brothers, Wire Train, Cryer etc. Costumes: Tammy Mor. Sound: Stacy Brownrigg. (Stone Group/Mace Neufeld–Columbia Tri-Star.) Rel: 19 June 1992. 92 mins. Cert 18.

Stop! Or My Mom Will Shoot. Not even the sight of Estelle Getty (Sophia Petrillo in TV's *The Golden Girls*) threatening baddy Roger Rees with 'I'll be back' is enough to conjure up a smile in this limp, cloying action-comedy. Sylvester Stallone continues his assault on the comedy genre as a macho LA cop who teams up with his li'l ol' 'mom' to unmask the identity of a gang of gunrunners. Even sillier than its title. [JC-W]

Cast includes: Sylvester Stallone (Joe Bomowski), Estelle Getty (Tutti), JoBeth Williams (Gwen Harper), Roger Rees (Parnell), J. Kenneth Campbell (McCabe), Dennis Burkley (Mitchell), Martin Ferrero, Gailard Sartain, John Wesley, Al Fann, Ella Joyce, Nicholas Sadler, Jane Arnold, Richard Schiff, Vanessa Angel, Joey DePinto, Patti Yasutake, Ving Rhames, Ernie Lively.
Dir: Roger Spottiswoode. Pro: Ivan Reitman, Joe Medjuck and Michael C. Gross. Ex Pro: Joe Wizan and Todd Black. Screenplay: Blake Snyder, William Osborne and William Davies. Ph: Frank Tidy. Ed: Mark Conte and Lois Freeman-Fox. Pro Des:

Charles Rosen. M: Alan Silvestri. Costumes: Marie France. Sound: Larry Kemp and Lon E. Bender. (Northern Lights/Universal–UIP.) Rel: 17 April 1992. 87 mins. Cert PG.

Straight Talk. Chicago, 1992. Bighearted romantic comedy about a friendly chatterbox who accidentally becomes a celebrity agony aunt on the radio. Dolly Parton – looking better than ever – is perfect as the homegrown sage dispensing gems of wisdom ('Get down off your cross, honey, someone needs the wood'), but James Woods is wildly miscast as the gooey-eyed reporter covering her story. The plot stinks, but the *bonhomie* is irresistible. [JC-W]

Cast includes: Dolly Parton (Shirlee Kenyon), James Woods (Jack Russell), Griffin Dunne (Alan Riegert), Michael Madsen (Steve Labell), Philip Bosco (Milo Jacoby), Deirdre O'Connell, John Sayles, Teri Hatcher, Spalding Gray, Jerry Orbach, Charles Fleischer, Keith MacKechnie, Jay Thomas, Amy Morton, Paula Newsome, Ralph Foody, Paul Dinello, Barnet Kellman, Domenica Cameron-Scorsese.
Dir: Barnet Kellman. Pro: Robert Chartoff and Fred Berner. Ex Pro: Sandy Gallin, Carol Baum and Howard Rosenman. Screenplay: Craig Bolotin and Patricia Resnick. Ph: Peter Sova. Ed: Michael Tronick. Pro Des: Jeffrey Townsend. M: Brad Fiedel; numbers written and performed by Dolly Parton. Costumes: Jodei Tillen. Sound: Glenn Williams. (Hollywood Pic-

Chat radio: straight-talkin', all-singin' Dolly Parton in Barnet Kellman's enjoyable soufflé, Straight Talk *(from Warner).*

Fings ain't wot they used to be: Steve Brooks (Ellen Barkin) has to contend with the body of a beautiful woman, assisted here by Joe Flood – in Blake Edwards's amusing Switch *(from Columbia Tri-Star).*

tures/Touchwood Pacific Partners/Sandollar–Warner.) Rel: 12 June 1992. 91 mins. Cert PG.

Strip Jack Naked – Nighthawks 2. British documentary of specialised interest and uneven technical qualities. Director Ken Peck's account of the making of his film *Nighthawks* and of his life as a gay. [FDM]

Dir, Pro and Script: Ken Peck. Ex Pro: Kate Ogborn. Ph: Peck and Christopher Hughes. Ed: Peck and Adrian James Carbutt. (BFI in assoc with Channel 4.) Rel: 31 July 1991. 90 mins. No cert.

Suburban Commando. Pretty silly (though occasionally amusing) sci-fi spoof, in which wrestler and would-be actor Hulk Hogan plays a visitor from outer space who boards with a conventional suburban couple. [FDM]

Rest of cast: Christopher Lloyd (Charlie Wilcox), Shelley Duvall (Jenny Wilcox), Larry Miller, William Ball, Joann Dearing, Jack Elam, Roy Dotrice, Christopher Neame, Michael Faustino, Tony Longo, Mark Calaway.

Dir: Burt Kennedy. Pro: Howard Gottfried. Ex Pro: Hulk Hogan, Kevin Moreton and Deborah Moore. Screenplay: Frank Cappollo. Ph: Bernd Heinl. Pro Des: Ivo Cristante. Ed: Terry Stokes. Sound: Jeffrey Douglas. (New Line/H. Gottfried–Entertainment.) Rel: 20 December 1991. 90 mins. Cert PG.

Switch. Steve Brooks (Perry King) is a male chauvinist pig who abuses and exploits women to fuel his ego. Murdered by a trio of his hurt conquests, Steve cannot get into heaven until he's proved to God that at least *one* female likes him. So he's returned to Earth – as a *woman.* Ellen Barkin is Steve Brooks, aka Amanda, in Blake Edwards's best film in aeons. Barkin is simply hypnotic as the macho stud trapped inside a model's body, and Edwards has some very pertinent points to make about male–female relationships. Funny, well-acted and sentimental tosh. But why does the

Devil always have an English accent in American movies? [JC-W]

Also with: Jimmy Smits (Walter Stone), JoBeth Williams (Margo Brofman), Lorraine Bracco (Sheila Faxton), Tony Roberts (Arnold Freidkin), Bruce Martyn Payne (the Devil), Lysette Anthony, Victoria Mahoney, Basil Hoffman, Catherine Keener, Kevin Kilner, David Wohl, Jim J. Bullock, Diana Chesney, Joe Flood, Emma Walton, Tea Leoni, Rick Aiello.

Dir and Screenplay: Blake Edwards. Pro: Tony Adams. Ex Pro: Arnon Milchan and Patrick Wachsberger. Assoc Pro: Trish Caroselli Rintels. Ph: Dick Bush. Ed: Robert Pergament. Pro Des: Rodger Maus. M: Henry Mancini: numbers performed by Paul Young and Clannad, Bruce Hornsby & The Range, Ronnie Milsap, Lyle Lovett, The Jets, Jody Watley, Billie Holiday etc. Costumes: Ellen Mirojnick. (Odyssey/Regency/HBO/Cinema Plus/Beco–Columbia Tri-Star.) Rel: 22 November 1991. 103 mins. Cert 15.

Tales from the Darkside – The Movie. Omnibus horror film of three grisly tales, developed and expanded from the TV series. 'The film brings moviegoers the stories that, frankly, we couldn't make for television,' explains producer Richard P. Rubinstein. 'Lot 249', adapted from the short story by Sir Arthur Conan Doyle, stars Christian Slater in an old-fashioned tale of revenge and a giant mummy; 'Cat from Hell', from the pen of Stephen King, features David Johansen as a hitman hired to eliminate an evil cat; and 'Lover's Vow', by Michael McDowell, stars James Remar as a New York artist who makes a pact with an evil gargoyle. A fourth story ties the other three together, in which a young boy becomes storyteller in order to delay his imminent demise from being cooked alive. Gruesome fun, enhanced by great special effects. [JC-W]

Cast includes: *The Wraparound Story*: Deborah Harry (Betty), Matthew Lawrence (Timmy); *Lot 249*: Christian Slater (Andy Smith), Steve Buscemi (Edward Bellingham), Robert Sedgwick (Lee), Julianne Moore (Susan Smith); *Cat from Hell*: David Johansen (Halston), William Hickey (Drogan); *Lover's Vow*: James Remar (Preston), Rae Dawn Chong (Carola), Robert Klein (Wyatt).

Dir: John Harrison. Pro: Richard P. Rubinstein and Mitchell Galin. Co-Pro: David R. Kappes. Screenplay: Michael McDowell and George A. Romero. Ph: Robert Draper. Ed: Harry B. Miller III. Pro Des: Ruth Ammon. M: Harrison, Donald A. Rub-

The Gargoyle from Hell: a potpourri *of horror in John Harrison's almanac of the grotesque,* Tales from the Darkside – The Movie *(from Columbia Tri-Star).*

instein, Jim Manzie, Pat Regan and Chaz Jankel. Costumes: Ida Gearon. Special Effects: Dick Smith and the KNB EFX Group. (Motion Picture Group/Paramount–Columbia Tri-Star.) Rel: 15 November 1991. 93 mins. Cert 18.

Teenage Mutant Ninja Turtles II: The Secret of the Ooze. The jolly pizza-guzzling, mutated reptilian dudes are back in another slambang adventure aimed squarely at the pocket and the pre-school market. Casey Jones is gone, but TV news reporter April O'Neil is back (in the guise of newcomer Paige Turco) and the dreaded Shredder returns from his certain death in the first film. This time ol' Shred has his greasy claws on the green ooze that transformed our heroes fifteen years earlier – and is threatening to use it where he will. Chaotic, raucous, noisy and unphotographic escapism for the braindead. Hardly radical and far from bodacious. [JC-W]

Also with: David Warner (Professor Jordan Perry), Ernie Reyes Jr (Keno), Michelan Sisti (Michaelangelo), Leif Tilden (Donatello), Kenn Troum (Raphael), Mark Caso (Leonardo), Kevin Clash (Splinter), Francois Chau (Shredder), Toshishiro Obata (Tatsu), Mark Ginther (Rahzar), Kurt Bryant (Tokka), Mark Doerr (Freddy), Kevin Nash, Michael Pressman, Sasha Pressman, David Pressman, Vanilla Ice, Earthquake. Voices: Laurie Faso (Raphael), Robbie Rist (Michaelangelo), Brian Tochi (Leonardo), Adam Carl (Donatello), Kevin Clash (Splinter), Frank Welker (Rahzar/Tokka), Michael McConnohie (Tatsu), David McCharen (Shredder).

Dir: Michael Pressman. Pro: Thomas K. Gray, Kim Dawson and David Chan. Ex Pro: Raymond Chow. Screenplay: Todd W. Langen. Ph: Shelly Johnson. Ed: John Wright and Steve Mirkovich. Pro Des: Roy Forge Smith. M: John Du Prez. Costumes: Dodie Shepard. Sound: David Kirschner, Gregg Landaker, Steve Maslow and Rick Kline. Animatronic Characters: Jim Henson's Creature Shop. (Golden Harvest-Fox.) Rel: 9 August 1991. 87 mins. Cert PG.

Teen Agent (US: *If Looks Could Kill*). High-school washout Michael Corben (Richard Grieco) is mistaken for an American secret agent on a school trip to France. Far-fetched hokum platforming heartthrob Grieco's move from the small screen (*21 Jump Street, Booker*) to the large: efficiently performed and enjoyable as a kindergarten James Bond. However, Grieco is given little to do (other than flex his pecs), while the storyline eventually deteriorates into high farce. [JC-W]

Also with: Linda Hunt (Ilsa Grunt), Roger Rees (Augustus Steranko), Robin Bartlett (Mrs Grober), Gabrielle Anwar (Mariska), Michael Siberry (Richardson), Carole Davis (Areola Canasta), Roger Daltrey (Blade), Geraldine James, Frederick Coffin, Tom Rack, Oliver Dear, Cyndy Preston, Michael Sinelnikoff, Travis Swords, Gerry Mendecino, Susan Dear, William Dear.

Dir: William Dear. Pro: Craig Zadan and Neil Meron. Ex Pro: Elliot Schick. Screenplay: Darren Star; from a story by Fred Dekker. Ph: Doug Milsome. Ed: John F. Link. Pro Des: Guy J. Comtois. M: David Foster; numbers performed by Glenn Medeiros, Kylie Minogue, The Fixx, Robin McAuley, Contraband etc. Costumes: Mary McLeod. Sound: Bill Phillips. (Warner.) Rel: 20 September 1991. 89 mins. Cert PG.

Terminator 2: Judgment Day. When Arnold Schwarzenegger declared 'I'll be back' in the $6 million 1984 sci-fi classic, *The Terminator*, he meant it. Seven years later, on a budget of $100-million plus, Arnold returns as the virtually indestructible cyborg from the

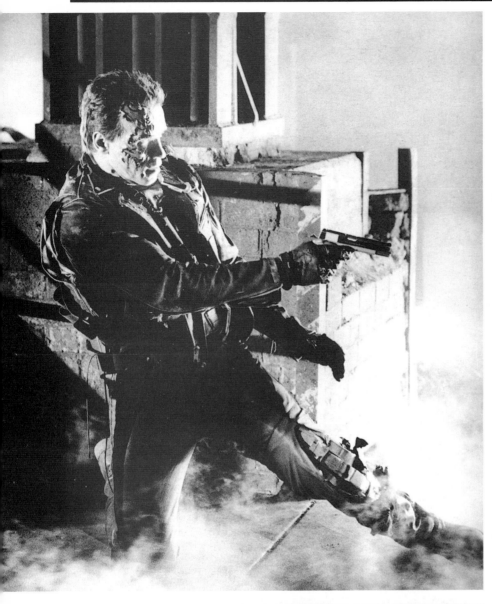

future, bent on changing history. This time he's after a young boy, who, at a later date, is destined to lead rebel forces against the killer machines. If the boy is eliminated now, the machines will be able to rule the world in AD 2029. Heady stuff, unrolled at breakneck speed, the humour and stunning special effects jostling for centre stage. From the very opening scene in which Arnold walks into a biker cafe stark naked and starts beating the waste matter out of the clientele, we are hooked. This is what cinema is all about: escapism, humour, action, and state-of-the-art special effects that will blow your mind. Also, most of the budget can be seen on the screen (except the Gulfstream G-III jet reputedly paid to Arnold as part of his salary). Photography, music, editing, production design – all exceptional. [JC-W]

Cast includes: Arnold Schwarzenegger (Terminator, model T–800), Linda Hamilton (Sarah Connor), Edward Furlong (John Connor), Robert Patrick (Terminator, model T–1000), Earl Boen (Dr Silberman), Joe Morton (Miles Dyson), S. Epatha Merkerson (Tarissa Dyson), Danny Cooksey (Tim), Jenette Goldstein (Janelle Voight), Xander Berkeley (Todd Voight), Castulo Guerra, Leslie Hamilton Gearren (Sarah Connor double), Robert Winley, Jim Palmer, Dan Stanton.

Dir and Pro: James Cameron. Ex Pro: Gale Anne Hurd and Mario Kassar. Co-Pro: B. J. Rack and Stephanie Austin. Screenplay: Cameron and William Wisher. Ph: Adam Greenberg. Ed: Conrad Buff, Mark Goldblatt and Richard A. Harris. Pro Des: Joseph Nemec III. Special Make-Up & Terminator Effects: Stan Winston. M: Brad Fiedel; numbers performed by Guns 'N' Roses, George Thorogood & The Destroyers and Dwight Yoakam. Costumes: Marlene Stewart. Sound: Lee Orloff. (Carolco–Guild.) Rel: 16 August 1991. 136 mins. Cert 15.

Tesuo: The Iron Man. Japanese cyberpunk horror film: hit-and-run car accident victim rebuilds his body, only to find when he sets out for revenge that his prey has also mutated into a metal man. One critic labelled this 'the world's first post-industrial hardcore movie'. Tough stuff. [FDM]

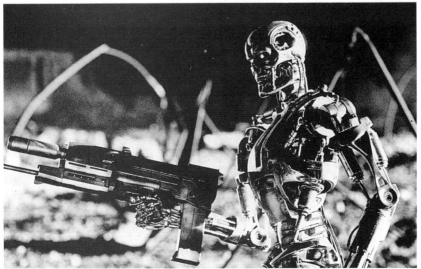

Images of a dark future: Arnold Schwarzenegger (above) *and a relative* (left) *fight the war of the machines in James Cameron's electrifying* Terminator 2: Judgment Day *(from Guild).*

Cast includes: 'Tomorrow' Taguchi, Fujiwara Kei.

Dir: Shinya Tsukamoto. (ICA.) Rel: 6 September 1991. 67 mins. Cert. to be fixed.

Thelma & Louise. When obedient housewife Thelma Dickinson (Geena Davis) and impulsive coffee waitress Louise Sawyer (Susan Sarandon) take an impromptu weekend away from the drudgery of their lives, they discover how to live. On their first stop-off in Arkansas, Thelma is near-raped in the parking lot by a diner and Louise shoots her attacker. Now Thelma and Louise are on the run – and the adrenalin tastes good. This is a heart-warming, heart-pounding 'buddy movie' with a difference, particularly surprising from Ridley Scott, a filmmaker more associated with dark, glossy state-of-the-art thrillers. Here, Scott gives centre stage to his actors, but dresses them in some of the most stunning photography ever to light America's South-Midwest. A moving, funny, gripping experience, backed up by exemplary filmmaking. [JC-W]

Also with: Harvey Keitel (Hal), Michael Madsen (Jimmy), Christopher McDonald (Darryl), Stephen Tobolowsky (Max), Brad Pitt (J. D.), Timothy Cathart (Harlan), Lucinda Jenny, Jason Beghe, Marco St John, Ken Swofford, Stephen Polk.

Dir: Ridley Scott. Pro: Scott and Mimi Polk. Co-Pro: Dean O'Brien and Callie Khouri. Screenplay: Khouri. Ph: Adrian Biddle. Pro Des: Norris Spencer. M: Hans

Easy riders: Susan Sarandon and Geena Davis take on the male population of the American Midwest in Ridley Scott's thrilling Thelma & Louise *(from UIP).*

Zimmer; numbers performed by Kelly Willis, Martha Reeves, Charlie Sexton, Tammy Wynette, Glenn Frey, The Temptations, Michael McDonald, Marianne Faithfull, Johnny Nash, B. B. King etc. Costumes: Elizabeth McBride. Sound: Keith A. Wester. (Pathe–UIP.) Rel: 12 July 1991. 130 mins. Cert 15.

Till There Was You. Described as an Australian *Romancing the Stone*, this is a cod piece of filmmaking, reminiscent of some of the more enterprising Bs

Poleaxed: Mark Harmon is given a royal escort in John Seale's cheesy adventure yarn, Till There Was You *(from Rank).*

of the 1960s. Mark Harmon, looking uncomfortably smart-ass, is a New York playboy and saxophonist invited to the South Pacific island of Vanuatu by his long-lost brother. Once there, Harmon finds his sibling dead, some police animosity and a beautiful woman. There's also gold, a hot-blooded villain and lots of naked natives. The scenes with the Bunlap tribe are by far the most interesting, in particular the sequence in which Harmon is forced to make the ceremonial leap (the Pentecost Jump) off a giant banyan tree, with only a vine attached to his ankle to stop his fall. The film's misleading title refers to the Meredith Willson song from *The Music Man*. [JC-W]

Cast includes: Mark Harmon (Frank Flynn), Deborah Unger (Anna Vivaldi), Jeroen Krabbe (Robert 'Viv' Vivaldi), Shane Briant (Rex), Ivan Kesa, Chief Telkon Watas, Lech Mackiewicz, Meriana Obed, Kristina Nehm, Ritchie Singer, Char Fontaine, Kate Ceberano, Willy Roy, Mathew Kamaly, Francine Bell.

Dir: John Seale. Pro: Jim McElroy. Screenplay: Michael Thomas. Ph: Geoff Simpson. Ed: Jill Bilcock. Pro Des: George Liddle. M: Graham Revell; Johann Strauss. Costumes: David Rowe. (Sovereign/Five Arrows–Rank.) Rel: 20 March 1992. 95 mins. Cert PG.

Too Hot to Handle (US: *The Marrying Man*). The off-set heat of Kim Basinger and Alec Baldwin fails to ignite their

Alec Baldwin and Kim Basinger fail to capture the magic of the old screwball romantic comedy in Warner's heavy-going Too Hot to Handle.

Dreams are made of this: Thomas (Thomas Godet) plots his revenge over a lifetime, in Jaco Van Dormael's delightfully unconventional Toto the Hero *(from Electric).*

Simon's customary wit and banter, but even this wise-cracking quartet cannot salvage the biggest flop of Simon's career. [JC-W]

Cast includes: Kim Basinger (Vicki Rosemary Anderson), Alec Baldwin (Charley Raymond Pearl), Robert Loggia (Lew Horner), Elisabeth Shue (Adele Horner), Armand Assante (Bugsy Siegel), Paul Reiser (Phil), Fisher Stevens (Sammy), Peter Dobson (Tony), Steve Hytner (George), Jeremy Roberts, Big John Studd, Tony Longo, Tom Milanovich, Tim Hauser, Clarke Gordon, Gretchen Wyler.
  Dir: Jerry Rees. Pro: David Permut. Screenplay: Neil Simon. Ph: Donald A. Thorin. Ed: Michael Jablow. Pro Des: William F. Matthews. M: David Newman; numbers performed by Kim Basinger, Tim Hauser, Billie Holiday, Charlie Parker etc. Costumes: Ruth Myers. Sound: Tim Cooney. (Hollywood Pictures/Silver Screen Partners IV–Warner.) Rel: 5 July 1991. 117 mins. Cert 15.

Toto the Hero – Toto le Héros. An engaging collage of flashbacks, flash-forwards and fantasy sequences, in which an old man looks back at his life while plotting the perfect murder. Thomas (Michel Bouquet, *inter alia*) is born shortly before a hospital fire, and in the ensuing confusion is saved by his neighbour. Brought up in a poor household, Thomas knows that his real parents live next door – and are bringing up his foster parents' child. Only in old age, in 2027, does Thomas decide to even the score. A real original, this, a powerful work from first time Belgian director Jaco Van Dormael, who won the Camera d'Or at the 1991 Cannes festival. A Belgian–French–German co-production. [JC-W]

Cast includes: Michel Bouquet, Jo De Backer and Thomas Godet (as Thomas), Gisela Uhlen and Mireille Perrier (as Evelyne), Sandrine Blancke (Alice), Peter Bohlke, the voice of Michel Robin, Didier Ferney and Hugo Harold Harrison (Alfred), Fabienne Loriaux (Thomas's mother), Klaus Schindler and the voice of Patrick Waleffe (as Thomas's father), Pascal Duquenne, the voice of Francois Toumarkine and Kerim Moussati (Celestin), Didier De Neck (Mr Kant), Christine Smeysters (Mrs Kant).
  Dir and Screenplay: Jaco Van Dormael. Pro: Pierre Drouot and Dany Geys. Ph: Walther Van Den Ende. Ed: Susana Rossberg. Art: Hubert Pouille. M: Pierre Van Dormael; *Boom* by Charles Trenet. Sound: Dominique Warnier and Jean-Paul Loublier. (Iblis/Les Productions Philippe

on-screen scenes in this limp romantic comedy. Baldwin is the $30-million toothpaste heir and playboy who repeatedly falls for lounge singer Basinger, girlfriend of gangster Bugsy Siegel. While B & B pant and pout, a Greek chorus of Hollywood hopefuls observe the proceedings with Neil

Dussart/Metropolis Filmproduktion/RTBF/
Jacqueline Pierreux/FR3/ZDF/Canal Plus–
Electric.) Rel: 15 November 1991. 90 mins.
Cert 15.

Toy Soldiers. Stirring dramatic thriller
that should've been an enormous hit
but wasn't. A school for rich, trouble-
some kids is held to ransom by a gang
of Colombian drug terrorists, the leader
of whom wants his father released from
prison. Determined and ruthless, the
killers have the army by their privates,
but hadn't bargained on the resourcefulness of their captives. Often teeter-
ing on the predictable and the sentimental, *Toy Soldiers* always veers off in
the nick of time, creating moments of
genuine tension and humour. The cast
is excellent and the script cohesive,
although the violence must have put
off many viewers for whom this was
intended. Only the music occasionally
reduces this to the level of pap entertainment. The director, Daniel Petrie
Jr, previously wrote *Beverley Hills Cop*.
[JC-W]

Cast includes: Sean Astin (Billy Tepper),
Whil Wheaton (Joey Trotta), Keith Coogan
(Snuffy Bradberry), Andrew Divoff (Luis
Cali), R. Lee Ermey (General Kramer),
Mason Adams (Deputy Director Brown),
Denholm Elliott (headmaster), Louis Gos-
sett Jr (Dean Parker), Georges Perez
(Ricardo Montoya), T. E. Russell (Hank
Giles), Shawn Phelan (Derek), Michael
Champion (Jack Thorpe), Jesse Doran
(Enrique Cali), Tracy Brooks Swope, Max
Maxwell, Joe Inscoe, Jerry Lyden, Rene
Gatica.
  Dir: Daniel Petrie Jr. Pro: Jack E. Freed-
man, Wayne S. Williams and Patricia Her-
skovic. Ex Pro: Mark Burg and Chris
Zarpas. Screenplay: Petrie Jr and David
Koepp; from the novel by William P. Ken-
nedy. Ph: Thomas Burstyn. Ed: Michael
Kahn. Pro Des: Chester Kaczenski. M:
Robert Folk. Costumes: Betsy Cox. (Colum-
bia Tri-Star.) Rel: 11 October 1991. 112
mins. Cert 15.

True Identity. In his first American
showcase, Lenny Henry seems somewhat subdued by the size of the project,
although he definitely has his moments.
Lenny stars as Miles Pope, a struggling
New York actor (à la *Tootsie*), who's
tired of being the understudy and playing fruit in commercials. When a supposedly dead mobster (Frank Langella)
reveals his true identity to Miles during
a near-fatal plane crash – and survives
– Miles finds himself in major jeopardy.
After several attempts have been made

*R. Lee Ermey, Louis Gossett Jr and Mason
Adams look on as the delinquents of Regis High
fight for their freedom from terrorists in Daniel
Petrie Jr's satisfying caper* Toy Soldiers *(from
Columbia Tri-Star).*

on his life, the actor goes undercover
as a white man – but before he can
revert to his true identity he has to
convince Langella that he's dead and
the FBI that Langella isn't. There's
plenty of good material here, but it's
all too sloppy, too improbable and too
flabby to gel into great entertainment.

*Lenny Henry in Touchstone's pleasant comedy
of switched personas,* True Identity.

Director Charles Lane (of the cult *Side-
walk Stories* fame) co-stars as Miles's
best friend, but lacks sufficient *oomph*
as a director to get this gentle comedy
out of first gear. [JC-W]

Also with: Frank Langella (Frank Luchino/
Leland Carver), Charles Lane (Duane), J.
T. Walsh (Craig Houston), Anne-Marie
Johnson (Kristi Reeves), Andreas Katsulas
(Anthony), Michael McKean (Harvey
Cooper), Peggy Lipton (Rita Carver), Bill
Raymond (Grunfeld), James Earl Jones (as
himself), Darnell Williams, Christopher
Collins, Melvin Van Peebles, Ruth Brown,
Joyce Meadows, Lynne Griffin.
  Dir: Charles Lane. Pro: Carol Baum and
Teri Schwartz. Ex Pro: Sandy Gallin and
Howard Rosenman. Screenplay: Andy
Breckman. Ph: Tom Ackerman. Ed: Kent
Beyda. Pro Des: John DeCuir. M: Marck
Marder; numbers performed by Ziggy
Marley, Gladys Knight, Ruth Brown etc.
Costumes: Abigail Murray. Sound: Russell
Williams. (Silverscreen Partners/Touch-
stone–Warner.) Rel: 13 September 1991. 95
mins. Cert 15.

True Love. The Bronx, 1989. Donna
(Annabella Sciorra) is a strong-willed,
conservative Italian-American prepar-
ing for her marriage to wild seed
Michael (Ron Eldard). There is jewel-
lery to be chosen for the bridesmaids
and grooms, the colour of the mashed
potato is to be determined and myriad
problems to be ironed out. Meanwhile,
Donna and Michael are having second
thoughts . . . Weddings really can be
like this, but usually the groom is a
little more sympathetic. You'd have

107

Seen a ghost? Well, actually, yes. Juliet Stevenson and Alan Rickman break the rules of the supernatural in Anthony Minghella's delightful Truly, Madly, Deeply *(from Samuel Goldwyn/Winston).*

more fun looking at your neighbours' wedding album. *True Love* marked Ms Sciorra's film debut. [JC-W]

Also with: Aida Turturro (Grace), Roger Rignack (Dom), Star Jasper (J. C.), Michael J. Wolfe (Brian), Kelly Cinnante (Yvonne), Rick Shapiro, Suzanne Costallos, Vinny Pastore, Marianne Leone, Nicky Sciorra, Angela Walshe.
Dir: Nancy Savoca. Pro: Richard Guay and Shelley Houis. Assoc Pro: Jeffrey Kimball. Screenplay: Savoca and Guay. Ph: Lisa Rinzler. Ed: John Tintori. Pro Des: Lester W. Cohen. Costumes: Deborah Anderko. Sound: Matthew Ebert. (Forward Films-Oasis Films.) Rel: 20 December 1991. 104 mins. Cert 15.

Truly, Madly, Deeply. Touching, quirky supernatural romance that deals with bereavement in a fresh and surprising way. Nina is, in the words of one of her many suitors, 'the most beautiful woman in London', but her

Highgate flat is a mess, she has rats, her walls have subsidence and her tap water is brown. Worse still, she has lost the man of her dreams to an unexpectedly fatal cough. But things could be worse – he could return to love her, haunt her, drive her from reality . . . In a part especially written for her, Juliet Stevenson is sensational at conveying a mixture of confusion, grief and passion in what could be the very best performance by a British actress this year. Magic realism with a human touch, that picked up a number of prestigious awards. Previously known as *Cello*. [JC-W]

Cast includes: Juliet Stevenson (Nina), Alan Rickman (Jamie), Bill Paterson (Sandy), Michael Maloney (Mark), Christopher Rozycki (Titus), David Ryall (George), Jenny Howe, Carolyn Choa, Keith Bartlett, Stella Maris, Deborah Findlay, Ian Hawkes, Arturo Venegas, Richard Syms, Mark Long, Teddy Kempner, Graeme DuFresne, Tony Bluto.
Dir and Screenplay: Anthony Minghella. Pro: Robert Cooper. Ex Pro: Mark Shivas. Ph: Remi Adefarasin. Ed: John Stothart. Pro Des: Barbara Gasnold. M: Barrington Pheloung. Costumes: James Keast. Sound: Jim Greenhorn. (BBC/Lionheart–Samuel

Goldwyn/Winston.) Rel: 16 August 1991. 106 mins. Cert PG.

Trust. Off-beat, low-budget romantic comedy about two lost souls whose problems mirror and complement each other's. Maria Coughlin, 17, has been made pregnant by her insensitive, football-crazy boyfriend and the news has given her father a fatal heart attack. Matthew Slaughter, who repairs computer terminals, is the most feared man in town, but is terrified of his own father. Meeting up, these two refugees from normality embark on a path of recovery. 'But', Matthew warns Maria's sadistic mother, 'a family is like a gun. If you point it in the wrong direction, you're gonna kill someone.' *Trust*, from the same team that brought us *The Unbelievable Truth*, is occasionally slow, sometimes aimless, but is so unusual and unpredictable that you have to cheer it to the finishing line. [JC-W]

Cast includes: Adrienne Shelly (Maria Coughlin), Martin Donovan (Matthew Slaughter), Merritt Nelson (Jean Coughlin), John MacKay (Jim Slaughter), Edie Falco

Trick or tryst? Adrienne Shelly and Martin Donovan in Hal Hartley's deliciously oblique Trust *(from Palace).*

(Peg Coughlin), Gary Sauer, Matt Malloy, Suzanne Costollos, Jeff Howard, Marko Hunt.

Dir and Screenplay: Hal Hartley. Pro: Bruce Weiss. Ex Pro: Jerome Brownstein. Ph: Michael Spiller. Ed: Nick Gomez. Pro Des: Dan Ouellette. M: Phil Reed. (True Fiction Pictures/Zenith–Palace.) Rel: 20 September 1991. 106 minutes. Cert 15.

Turtle Beach. Fascinating subject, not a terribly good film. Focusing on the plight of the Vietnamese boat people, *Turtle Beach* is the story of an Australian photojournalist 'finding' herself in Kuala Lumpur. In the midst of a crumbling marriage, Judith Wilkes (Greta Scacchi trying out a series of accents) goes after a story involving a Vietnamese barmaid now married to the Australian Ambassador to KL. As the two women's friendship strengthens, the true horror of the Asian refugees comes to a head, changing Ms Wilkes forever. Unfortunately, the drama is hamstrung by stilted acting, clumsy action, corny plotting and a dumb love scene. Apparently the director, Stephen Wallace (*Stir, Blood Oath*), was fired during the post-production, while the Australian government dissociated itself from the film. [JC-W]

Also with: Joan Chen (Lady Minou Hobday), Jack Thompson (Ralph Hamilton), Art Malik (Kanan), Norman Kaye (Sir Adrian Hobday), Victoria Longley (Sancha Hamilton), Martin Jacobs (Richard), William McInnes, George Whaley, Andrew Ferguson, Celia Wong.

Dir: Stephen Wallace. Pro: Matt Carroll. Ex Pro: Graham Burke and Greg Coote. Line Pro: Irene Dobson. Screenplay: Ann Turner; based on the novel by Blanche d'Alpuget. Ph: Russell Boyd. Ed: William Anderson. Pro Des: Brian Thomson. M: Chris Neal. Costumes: Roger Kirk. Sound: Peter Townend. (Village Roadshow Pictures–Warner.) Rel: 5 June 1992. 88 mins. Cert 15.

Twenty-One purports to be a realistic picture of sex in the 1990s, but by failing even to mention AIDS, it shoots itself in the foot before leaving the bedroom. A de-glossed Patsy Kensit stars

Greta Scacchi and Joan Chen struggle to rescue the boat people in Stephen Wallace's Turtle Beach *(from Warner).*

Better Jake than never: Jack Nicholson returns as Jake Gettes seventeen years after Chinatown. Harvey Keitel – as Jake Berman – and Nicholson, in Blue Dolphin's The Two Jakes.

Turn of the corkscrew plot: Kenneth Cranham and Liam Neeson with crime on their hands in Simon Moore's Under Suspicion *(from Rank).*

as Katie, a 21-year-old Shirley Valentine who directly addresses the camera while sitting on the loo. Set in London, but narrated from exotic New York (huh?), *Twenty-One* is neither witty nor realistic enough to engage our sympathy or even our interest. There are a few good scenes, and a refreshing score, but ultimately the film comes across like a bloodhound without teeth. [JC-W]

Cast includes: Patsy Kensit (Katie), Jack Shepherd (Kenneth), Patrick Ryecart (Jack), Maynard Eziashi (Baldie), Rufus Sewell (Bobby), Sophie Thompson (Francesca), Susan Wooldridge, Julia Goodman, Julian Firth, Guy Oliver-Watts, Robert Bathurst, Ben Murphy, Rebecca Cardinale, Kim Kindersley.

Dir: Don Boyd. Pro: Morgan Mason and John Hardy. Ex Pro: Mike Curb, Lester Korn and Carole Curb. Screenplay: Zoe Heller and Don Boyd. Ph: Keith Goddard and Colin Corby. Ed: David Spiers. Pro Des: Roger Murray-Leach. M: Michael Berkeley and Phil Sawyer. Costumes: Susannah Buxton. (Curb Communications–Entertainment.) Rel: 1 November 1991. 101 mins. Cert 15.

The Two Jakes. Trouble-plagued sequel to *Chinatown*, sixteen years on, with Jack Nicholson recreating his role as private detective Jake 'J.J.' Gettes. Planned to start filming on 30 April 1985, under scripter Robert Towne's direction, with Nicholson, producer Robert Evans, Kelly McGillis, Cathy Moriarty and Dennis Hopper starring, the production folded when Evans's acting – as the other Jake – was not up to scratch. Finally, Nicholson took over the directing chores (with Harvey Keitel replacing Evans), and has produced a film of enormous style and muddled content. Conceived as part of a trilogy on the making of Los Angeles, *The Two Jakes* is a complex story of murder, corruption, oil and infidelity. In a superb voice-over narration scripted by Towne, Gittes/Nicholson drones, 'I suppose it's fair to say that infidelity has made me what I am today.' However, his fortunes take a turn for the worse when his cuckolded client, Jake Berman, shoots his wife's lover dead. A beautifully made film – but too slow, confusing and overlong for most tastes. Nicholson has the makings of a great director, yet he may well have shot himself in the foot with this turkey. The film, budgeted at $19 million, was a box-office bomb. [JC-W]

Also with: Meg Tilly (Kitty Berman), Madeleine Stowe (Lillian Bodine), Eli Wallach (Cotton Weinberger), Ruben Blades (Mickey Nice), Frederic Forrest (Newty), David Keith (Loach), Richard Farnsworth (Earl Rawley), Perry Lopez (Capt. Escobar), Tracey Walter (Tyrone Otley), Joe Mantell (Walsh), James Hong, Jeff Morris, Rebecca Broussard, Paul A. DiCocco Jr, Luana

Anders, Tom Waits and the voice of Faye Dunaway.

Dir: Jack Nicholson. Pro: Robert Evans and Harold Schneider. Screenplay: Robert Towne. Ph: Vilmos Zsigmond. Ed: Anne Goursaud. Pro Des: Jeremy Railton and Richard Sawyer. M: Van Dyke Parks. Costumes: Wayne Finkelman. (Paramount–Blue Dolphin.) Rel: 22 November 1991. 137 mins. Cert 15.

Under Suspicion. Brighton, 1957–9. Tony Aaron, a down-at-heel private investigator, can help you with your divorce. All you need is a woman, a photograph . . . and Tony Aaron. In the days when a faked adultery was the window to a quick divorce, men like Aaron thrived. But when Aaron uses his actress wife as a stand-in mistress, both she and his wealthy client are murdered. The police are now on to Aaron's game – worse still, they suspect him of the murder . . . They don't make films like this anymore? Old-fashioned, a little creaky around the edges, perhaps, but an ideal diversion

Politics and poetry: Gerard Depardieu dominates the acting honours in Claude Berri's wordy fable, Uranus *(from Artificial Eye).*

for a rainy afternoon. Previously known as *The Other Woman, Prime Suspect* and *Dark Horizon*. [JC-W]

Cast includes: Liam Neeson (Tony Aaron), Laura San Giacomo (Angeline), Kenneth Cranham (Frank), Maggie O'Neill (Hazel Aaron), Michael Almaz (Stasio), Alphonsia Emmanuel (Selina), Stephen Moore (Roscoe), Malcolm Storry, Richard Graham, Pamela Sholto, Alan Stocks, Nicolette McKenzie, Lee Whitlock, Alex Norton, Danny Schiller.

Dir and Screenplay: Simon Moore. Pro: Brian Eastman. Ph: Vernon Layton. Ed: Tariq Anwar. Pro Des: Tim Hutchinson. M: Christopher Gunning. Costumes: Penny Rose. Sound: Ken Weston. (Columbia/LWT–Rank.) Rel: 27 September 1991. 95 mins. Cert 18.

Until the End of the World. Wim Wenders, after exploring the conflict between reality and the video image in his small-scale and dreary *Notebook on Cities and Clothes*, expands on the idea in this ambitious road movie-cum-love story. Originally six hours in length, the production began gestation in 1977 and ended up being filmed in fifteen cities in seven different countries – before settling down in the middle of the Australian outback. Set in 1999, the film opens in Venice and wends its way to France where Claire (Solveig Dommartin, Wenders's 'companion') meets an enigmatic American, Trevor McPhee (William Hurt). Obsessed by this man, Claire follows him to Lisbon, Berlin, Moscow, Beijing, Tokyo, San Francisco and beyond, herself followed by her former lover, Eugene (Sam Neill), who narrates the story. There's also a private detective, an Aborigine bounty hunter and a Nice bank robber, all of whom keep popping up all over the world. This part of the film is extremely tedious, and a waste of its locations. It's not until we are brought to the Outback (and to the genesis of the film's concept) that *Until the End of the World* falls into place. Here, 'Professor' Max Von Sydow is working on a camera that can see for the blind, a dangerous device that feeds our addiction for imagery. Will the world end in a nuclear blast or in a cultural vacuum centred on the intransigence of the image? Wenders plays around with many mind-boggling concepts, but his means defeats his end. However, the all-original soundtrack is a knockout (see music credits). [JC-W]

Also with: Max Von Sydow (Dr Henry Farber), Rudiger Vogler (Philip Winter), Jeanne Moreau (Edith Farber), Ernie Dingo (Burt), Chick Ortega (Chico), Eddy Mitchell, Adelle Lutz, Allen Garfield, Lois Chiles, David Gulpilil, Charlie McMahon.

Dir and Co-Pro: Wim Wenders. Pro: Jonathan Taplin and Anatole Dauman. Screenplay: Wenders and Peter Carey; from an idea by Wenders and Solveig Dommartin. Ph: Robby Muller. Ed: Peter Przygodda. Pro Des: Thierry Flamand and Sally Campbell. M: Graeme Revell; original numbers performed by Talking Heads, REM, Lou Reed, Nick Cave, Crime and the City Solution, Can, Neneh Cherry, T-Bone Burnett, Depeche Mode, Robbie Robertson, Blue Nile, Elvis Costello, Daniel Lanois, Peter Gabriel, U2, Patti and Fred Smith, Jane Siberry, k. d. lang, Julee Cruise. Costumes: Montserrat Casanova. Sound: Barbara von Weiterhausen. (Road Movies/Argos Films/Village Roadshow–Entertainment.) Rel: 24 April 1992. 158 mins. Cert 15.

Uranus. Spring, 1945. A small town in France is in ruins and its occupants are at each other's throats. The Communist government is now in power and it is determined to flex its muscle. Leopold (Gerard Depardieu), who runs the local bistro, is unimpressed by all this hypo-

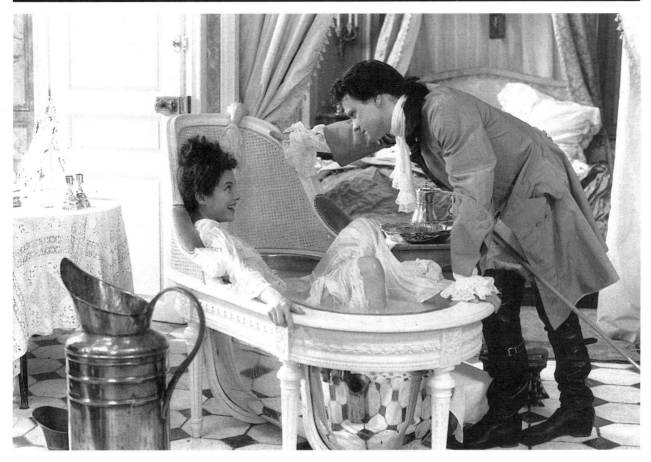

Sumptuous corruption: Annette Bening and Colin Firth plot the degradation of the virtuous, in Milos Forman's stunning Valmont *(from Artificial Eye).*

crisy and is more interested in his discovery of poetry. But he is bound to become a catalyst in a society savaged by war and rife with treachery. A robust, talky saga from Claude Berri (*Jean de Florette*), who might have had a better film if he'd reined in his actors' tendency to over-emote. Although Depardieu's bravura performance as the Herculean Bard is a towering accomplishment, he is more than matched by Philippe Noiret as a good-natured, eternally happy teacher whose wife was bombed in her lover's arms. [JC-W]

Also with: Michel Blanc (Geigneux), Jean-Pierre Marielle (Archambaud), Philippe Noiret (Watrin), Gerard Desarthe (Maxime Loin), Michel Galabru (Monglat), Daniele Lebrun (Mme Archambaud), Daniel Prevost (Rochard), Florence Darel (Marie-Anne), Fabrice Luchini, Myriam Boyer, Alain Stern.
 Dir: Claude Berri. Ex Pro: Pierre

Grunstein. Screenplay: Berri and Arlette Langmann; from the novel by Marcel Ayme. Ph: Renato Berta. Ed: Herve De Luze. Art: Bernard Vezat. Costumes: Caroline De Vivaise. Sound: Louis Gimel and Dominique Hennequin. (Renn Prods/Films A2/DD Prods/Soficas Sofi-Arp/Sofica Invest-image 2 et 3–Artificial Eye.) Rel: 11 October 1991. 100 mins. Cert 15.

Urga. Poetic portrayal of the life of a Mongolian shepherd who wishes to sire more than the three children he is allowed by law. Winner of the Golden Lion at the 1991 Venice Film Festival, *Urga* is a salute to the link between man and his natural environment. Although set in the steppes of Chinese Mongolia, the film was financed by French money (from the profits of *Cyrano de Bergerac*) and made by the Russian Nikita Mikhalkov, brother of Andrei Konchalovsky (director of *Tango and Cash* and *Runaway Train*). [CB]

Cast includes: Bayaertu (Gombo), Badema (Pagma, Gombo's wife), Vladimir Gostu-khikn (Sergei), Babushka (Grandma), Larissa Kuznetsova, Jon Bochinski, Bao Yong-yan, Wurinile, Wang Zhiyong.
 Dir: Nikita Mikhalkov. Pro: Michel Sey-

doux. Ex Pro: Jean-Louis Piel. Assoc Pro: Rene Cleitman. Screenplay: Roustam Ibra-guimbekov; from an idea by Mikhalkov. Ph: Villenn Kaluta. Ed: Joelle Hache. Pro Des: Aleksei Levtchenko. M: Eduard Artemiev. Costumes: Irina Guinno. Sound: Jean Goud-ier. (Palace.) Rel: 7 February 1992. 120 mins. ﹖rt PG.

Valmont. Sumptuous, intelligent and human version of the Choderlos de Laclos novel *Les Liaisons Dangereuses*, delayed by two years and ten months to let the dust settle over the Glenn Close–John Malkovich version. This is actually the better of the two films, with director Milos Forman opting for a more realistic, sympathetic approach. Here, the scheming Vicomte de Valmont and Marquise de Merteuil are in their mid-twenties, an age difference that makes their double-dealings far more palatable and likely, being the result of hot-headed youth. The put-upon, innocent and preciously virginal Cecile really *does* look fifteen here, making her corruption all the more plausible, terrible and wanton. Forman chose to make the film because he wanted to try to breathe life into the calculating chess pieces of Laclos' novel. This he does, even making us believe in Valmont's love for the guarded Madame de Tourvel. Suddenly, *Les Liaisons Dangereuses* all makes sense. Because Valmont seriously confuses the need for conquest with love, we are as disappointed by his disillusion as he is. Colin Firth is both charming and human as the young Valmont, while Annette Bening eschews the mannered charm and evil that Glenn Close doled out as Merteuil. As Cecile, Fairuza Balk (Dorothy in *Return to Oz*) is surprisingly touching *and* funny, helping to make this opulent, adult film a rare treasure. Music, photography, production design, costumes and script are all top notch, too. An Anglo-French co-production. [JC-W]

Also with: Meg Tilly (Madame de Tourvel), Sian Phillips (Madame de Volanges), Jeffrey Jones (Gercourt), Henry Thomas (Danceny), Fabia Drake (Madame de Rosemonde), T. P. McKenna, Isla Blair, Ian McNeice, Aleta Mitchell, Ronald Lacey, Vincent Schiavelli, Sandrine Dumas.
 Dir: Milos Forman. Pro: Paul Rassam and Michael Hausman. Screenplay: Jean-Claude Carriere. Ph: Miroslav Ondricek. Ed: Alan Heim and Nena Danevic. Pro Des: Pierre Guffroy. M: Christopher Palmer and John Strauss, conducted by Sir Neville Marriner. Costumes: Theodor Pistek. Choreography: Ann Jacoby. (Renn Prods/Timothy Burrill Prods/Claude Berri–Artificial Eye.) Rel: 22 November 1991. 140 mins. Cert 15.

Van Gogh. The fifth cinematic incarnation of Vincent Van Gogh and, like Robert Altman's *Vincent and Theo*, a slow-moving, over-long, intelligent and detailed portrait of the artist leading up to his death. Where this version differs is in its leisurely depiction of the life and times that conflicted with and guided Van Gogh's outlook and character. Jacques Dutronc, who won the Cesar for his performance, is suitably compelling and enigmatic, and makes the painter a shade more human this time round. The film is also remarkable in that it is a period piece that doesn't feel like a history lesson, but a totally believable real-life drama. [JC-W]

Also with: Alexandra London (Marguerite Gachet), Gerard Sety (Dr Gachet), Bernard Le Coq (Theo Van Gogh), Corinne Bourdon (Johahnna Van Gogh), Elsa Zylberstein (Cathy), Leslie Azzoulai, Jacques Vidal, Lise Lametrie, Chantal Barbarit, Claudine

Cop out: Kathleen Turner as V. I. Warshawski, *in Warner's disappointing, slipshod detective drama.*

Ducret, Didier Barbier, Damien Saubestre.
 Dir and Screenplay: Maurice Pialat. Pro: Daniel Toscan du Plantier and Sylvie Danton. Ph: Emmanuel Machuel, Gilles Henri and Jacques Loiseleux. Ed: Yann Dedet and Nathalie Hubert. Pro Des: Philippe Pallut and Katia Vischkof. Costumes: Edith Vesperini. Sound: Jean-Pierre Duret. (Erato Films/Studio Canal/Films 2/Les Films du Livradois, etc–Artificial Eye.) Rel: 8 May 1992. 158 mins. Cert 12.

V. I. Warshawski. A tough-talking but beautiful cop is what we wanted from Kathleen Turner. From a promising smart-mouthed start (where Warshawski takes a few in the face), this soft-hearted *policier* spins out into family mush, rather than staying professional to the end. A disappointing film from a brilliant idea. [KK]

Cast includes: Kathleen Turner (V. I. 'Vic' Warshawski), Jay O. Sanders (Murray), Charles Durning (Lt Mallory), Angela Goethals (Kat Grafalk), Nancy Paul (Paige), Frederick Coffin (Horton), Charles McCaughan, Stephen Meadows, Wayne Knight, Lynnie Godfrey, Anne Pitoniak, Stephen Root, Robert Clotworthy, Tom Allard, John P. Marsh.
 Dir: Jeff Kanew. Pro: Jeffrey Lurie. Ex Pro: Penney Finkelman Cox and John P. Marsh. Screenplay: Edward Taylor, David Aaron Cohen and Nick Thiel; based upon the *V. I. Warshawski* novels by Sara Paretsky. Ph: Jan Kiesser. Ed: C. Timothy O'Meara. Pro Des: Barbara Ling. M: Randy Edelman. Costumes: Gloria Gresham. Sound: Tom McCarthy and Roxanne Jones. (Chestnut Hill/Hollywood Pictures/Silver Screen Partners–Warner.) Rel: 3 January 1992. 89 mins. Cert 15.

Volere Volare. An unusual, charming Italian fantasy about a shy little man, Maurizio (co-director Maurizio Nichetti), who dubs wacky sound effects for cartoons. When he meets the romantic realisation of his dreams, Martina (Angela Finocchiaro), Maurizio is so shell-shocked that he turns into a cartoon. In the tradition of *Roger Rabbit* (and, perhaps, more accurately Ralph Bakshi's *Cool World*), *Volere Volare* (rough translation: *Wishing to Fly*) is a unique fusion of animation and live

Incredible journey: Sam Shepard as Walter Faber, a man escaping from himself in Volker Schlondorff's hypnotic Voyager *(from Palace).*

with the same woman. Walter's worst fear is the unexplained, and when he becomes trapped in 'a train of coincidences' he struggles to calculate the probabilities of chance. More threatening still, he becomes attracted to a beautiful, joyful girl who may or may not hold a key to his past . . . In the tital role, Sam Shepard is a compelling, intellectual presence, well matched by the incandescent Julie Delpy as his angel of mercy. A fascinating voyage. [JC-W]

Also with: Barbara Sukowa (Hannah), Dieter Kirchlechner (Herbert Henke), Traci Lind (Charlene), Deborah-Lee Furness (Ivy), August Zirner (Joachim), Thomas Heinze, Bill Dunn, Lorna Farrar.

Dir: Volker Schlondorff. Pro: Eberhard Junkersdorf. Screenplay: Schlondorff and Rudi Wurlitzer; based on the novel by Max Frisch. Ph: Yorgos Arvanitis and Pierre L'Homme. Ed: Dagmar Hirtz. Pro Des: Nicos Perakis. M: Stanley Myers. Costumes: Barbara Baum, Giorgio Armani. (Mayfair Entertainment.) Rel: 17 April 1992. 117 mins. Cert 15.

action, and slips into the history books for displaying the first sex scene between a cartoon character and a real, live woman. [CB]

Also with: Mariella Valentina (Martina's friend), Patrizio Roversi (Maurizio's brother), Remo Remotti (the child), Mario and Luigi Gravier, Renato Scarpa, Massimo Sarcheilli, Mario Rardi.

Dir and Screenplay: Maurizio Nichetti and Guido Manuli. Pro: Ernesto di Sarro, Mario Cecchi Gori and Vittorio Cecchi Gori. Ex Pro: di Sarro. Ph: Mario Battistoni. Ed: Rita Rossi. Art and Costumes: Maria

Pio Angelini. M: Manuel De Sica. Sound: Amedeo Casati. Animation: Quick Sand. (Italtoons Corporation/Bambu/Penta Film–Metro.) Rel: 8 May 1992. 92 mins. Cert 15.

Voyager. 1957; Venezuela, Mexico, New York, the Atlantic, Paris, Germany, Italy, Greece. Although spread over three continents, *Voyager* is essentially a character study. Walter Faber is a peripatetic, sought-after engineer who has rid his life of emotional ties. At times insensitive and downright brutal to others, he has formed the perfect existence – revelling in his travelling, workaholism and the accelerating development of science. He is not a man who reads fiction, never dreams and seldom spends more than four days

Wayne's World. Smash-hit film version of the recurrent ten-minute sketch from TV's *Saturday Night Live*. Mike Myers and Dana Carvey repeat their original roles as the party animals who host their own access cable TV show from Wayne's basement. Enter smarmy, two-timing TV executive Rob Lowe who buys the show and sells the boys downriver. Infantile, self-consciously trendy comedy with only sporadic flashes of ingenuity that borrows generously from the *Bill & Ted* films. Still, there's an infectious wackiness about it all, with plenty of babes, heavy metal music, star cameos and TV injokes. [JC-W]

Cast includes: Mike Myers (Wayne Campbell), Dana Carvey (Garth Algar), Rob Lowe (Benjamin Oliver), Tia Carrere (Cassandra), Brian Doyle-Murray (Noah Vanderhoff), Lara Flynn Boyle (Stacy), Kurt Fuller (Russell), Colleen Camp (Mrs Vanderhoff), Donna Dixon (dream babe), Meat Loaf (Tiny), Alice Cooper (himself), Michael DeLuise, Dan Bell, Lee Tergesen, Sean Gregory Sullivan, Frederick Coffin, Chris Farley, Ed O'Neill, Ione Skye, Robert Patrick.

Dir: Penelope Spheeris. Pro: Lorne Michaels. Ex Pro: Howard W. Koch Jr. Screenplay: Mike Myers, Bonnie Turner and Terry Turner. Ph: Theo Van de Sande. Ed: Malcolm Campbell. Pro Des: Gregg

Fonseca. M: J. Peter Robinson; with numbers performed by Queen, Ugly Kid Joe, Tia Carrere, Gary Wright, Soundgarden, Eric Clapton, Cinderella, Red Hot Chilli Peppers, Kik, Jimi Hendrix, Alice Cooper, Black Sabbath, Wayne & Garth etc. Sound: John Benson. (Paramount–UIP.) Rel: 22 May 1992. 95 mins. Cert PG.

Welcome Home, Roxy Carmichael. Wonderful little film, buried in distribution hell and drowned in a wave of 'bigger' movies. Winona Ryder, again playing the off-centre, 'profound' teenager she essayed in *Beetlejuice* and *Mermaids*, is Dinky Bossetti, an adopted child of designer, *nouveau riche* parents, and an outcast in the parochial community of Clyde, Ohio. But even Dinky cannot help being caught up by the excitement of the imminent arrival of the legendary Roxy Carmichael. Fifteen years earlier, Roxy upped sticks to become famous and left behind a trail of broken hearts and one illegitimate baby. What became of the baby nobody knows, but Roxy is a celebrity now and the town is painting itself red in anticipation of her arrival. A darkly comic drama of dreams and expectations, *Roxy Carmichael* is both touching and amusing while dealing with ideas seldom touched on in the American cinema. [JC-W]

Also with: Jeff Daniels (Denton Webb), Dinah Manoff (Evelyn Whittacher), Sachi

Parker (Libby), Laila Robbins (Elizabeth Zaks), Thomas Wilson Brown (Gerald), Frances Fisher (Rochelle Bossetti), Graham Beckel (Les Bossetti), Joan McMurtrey (Barbie Webb), Robby Kiger (Beannie), Stephen Tobolowski (Bill Klepler).

Waiting for Roxy: the superb Winona Ryder winning hearts and alienating adults in the charmingly dark, unusual Welcome Home, Roxy Carmichael *(from Castle Premier).*

Dir: Jim Abrahams. Pro: Penney Finkelman Cox. Ex Pro and Screenplay: Karen Leigh Hopkins. Ph: Paul Elliott. Ed: Bruce Green. Pro Des: Dena Roth. M: Thomas Newman; *In Roxy's Eyes* written and performed by Melissa Etheridge. Costumes: Betsy Heimann. Sound: David Kelson. (ITC–Castle Premier.) Rel: 6 September 1991. 95 mins. Cert 12.

Wendy Cracked a Walnut This feeble romantic comedy-fantasy is yet another vehicle for the forced playful antics of Rosanna Arquette. Oddly cast as an Australian housewife, Arquette is the Wendy of the title, who is bored by her dead-end factory job and inattentive husband. Thus, she starts hallucinating, dreaming up various Mills & Boon fantasies featuring an inexplicably sleazy Hugo Weaving. A gloomy, inept comedy that not only fails to elicit any

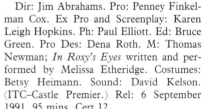

Party on: Dana Carvey and Mike Myers as the dudes with a purpose, in Penelope Spheeris's phenomenally successful Wayne's World *(from UIP).*

laughs, but is completely devoid of logic or credibility. [CB]

Also with: Bruce Spence (Ronnie, Wendy's husband), Hugo Weaving (Jake), Kerry Walker (Deidre), Doreen Warburton (Elsie), Desiree Smith (Cynthia), Susan Lyons (Caroline), Betty Lucas (Mrs Taggart), Dennis Hoey, Douglas Hedge, Barry Jenkins.

Dir: Michael Pattison. Pro: John Edwards. Ex Pro: Brian Rosen and Sandra Levy. Screenplay: Suzanne Hawley. Ph: Jeffrey Malouf. Ed: Michael Honey. Pro Des: Leigh Tierney. M: Bruce Smeaton. Sound: Nick Wood. (Classic Films P/L–Pacific Pictures.) Rel: 22 November 1991. 87 mins. Cert PG.

What About Bob? Bob Wiley (Bill Murray), a mentally paralysed, multiphobic personality, is terrified of leaving his front door. As he lives in the heart of New York, this is hardly surprising, but Bob cannot function without a psychiatrist within reach. So when Dr Leo Marvin (Richard Dreyfuss) goes on vacation with his family,

Mad to the bone: Richard Dreyfuss and Bill Murray switch insanities in Frank Oz's dissatisfying What About Bob? *(from Warner).*

he is not amused when Bob comes too. The trouble is, the Marvin family *like* Bob. The story of the doctor driven mad by his patient is a familiar one (cf. *The Couch Trip*), and this manic addition to the genre adds no new insights. A disappointing vehicle for Murray and Dreyfuss, *What About Bob?* is relentlessly unfunny due to a combination of obvious situations, broad caricatures and telegraphed jokes. [JC-W]

Also with: Julie Hagerty (Fay Marvin), Charlie Korsmo (Siggy Marvin), Kathryn Erbe (Anna Marvin), Marcella Lowery (Betty, the switchboard operator), Doris Belack (Dr Tomsky), Tom Aldredge, Susan Willis, Roger Bowen, Fran Brill, Brian Reddy, Melinda Mullins, Margot Welch, Barbara Andres, Aida Turturro, Reg E. Cathey, Tom Stechschutlte, Richard Fancy, Joan Lunden.

Dir: Frank Oz. Pro: Laura Ziskin. Co-Pro: Bernard Williams. Screenplay: Tom Schulman; from a story by Alvin Sargent and Laura Ziskin. Ph: Michael Ballhaus. Ed: Anne V. Coates. Pro Des: Les Dilley. M: Miles Goodman. Costumes: Bernie Pollack. (Touchstone–Warner.) Rel: 15 November 1991. 110 mins. Cert PG.

Who Needs a Heart. Fact and fiction merge in this evocation of black con-

sciousness in 1960s London, when Malcolm X's influence was at its height. Limited appeal only. [FDM]

Cast includes: Caroline Burghard, Treva Ettiene, Ruth Gemmell, Caroline Lee Johnson.

Dir: John Akomfrah. Pro: Lina Gopaul. Screenplay: Akomfrah and Eddie George. Ph: Nancy Schiesari. Ed: Brand Thumin. (Black Audio Film Collection.) Rel: 11 November 1991. 80 mins. No cert.

Whore. Broadly comic, grotesque film version of the play *Bondage*, a series of theatrical anecdotes inspired by conversations with prostitutes working London's King's Cross district. Here, David Hines's play is given the kiss of death by Ken Russell's cartoonish approach, re-setting the film in Los Angeles and directing Theresa Russell in her broadest, most embarrassing performance to date. Speaking directly to the camera, Theresa mugs shamelessly, while the director's flashback sequences border on pantomime. Although played for laughs, the film is definitely *not* funny, and is a degrading experience for both sexes. No doubt that was the original idea, but there must be a *few* sympathetic characters who work and live on the street. [JC-W]

Cast includes: Theresa Russell (Liz), Benjamin Mouton (Blake), Antonio Fargas (Rasta), Sanjay, Elizabeth Morehead, Michael Crabtree, John Diehl, Robert O'Reilly, Charles McCaulay, Jason Kristofer, Jack Nance, Frank Smith, Jason Saucier.

Dir: Ken Russell. Pro: Dan Ireland and Ronaldo Vasconcellos. Ex Pro: Mark Amin. Screenplay: Ken Russell and Deborah Dalton; based on the play *Bondage* by David Hines. Ph: Amir Mokri. Ed: Brian Tagg. Pro Des: Richard Lewis. M: Michael Gibbs. Costumes: Leonard Pollack. Sound: Tom Brandau. (Trimark–Palace.) Rel: 19 July 1991. 81 mins. Cert 18.

Why Has Bodhi-Dharma Left for the East? This very unusual, highly personal film took its South Korean producer, director, writer, editor and photographer Bae Yong-Kyun five years to make. Totally static, and set in glorious scenery, the film develops a hypnotic calm and stillness as an old monk teaches his two pupils the tenets of Zen Buddhism. The stillness will either infuriate or fascinate, but either way this is a unique piece of filmmaking. [FDM]

Designer politics: Andrew McCarthy and Sharon Stone face the grim realities of a hackneyed script in John Frankenheimer's Year of the Gun *(from First Independent).*

Cast: Pan-Yong Yi, Won Sop-Sin, Hae-Jin Huang, Su-Myong Ko, Hae-Yong Kim.

Dir, Pro, Screenplay, Ed, Ph: Bae Yong-Kyun. M: Kyu-Young Chin. (Bae Yong-Kyun–ICA.) Rel: 11 October 1991. 135 mins. No cert.

Year of the Gun. Rome, 1978. Deadly sincere, structurally flabby thriller with Andrew McCarthy unlikely casting as a political journalist living in Italy. The Red Brigade is in its prime, and David Raybourne (McCarthy) mines the terrorist unrest for a commercial novel that ends up in the wrong hands. Director John Frankenheimer is usually a dab hand at this kind of thing (*The Manchurian Candidate, Black Sunday*), but cannot build on his tepid script here, and is not helped by an uncharismatic turn from McCarthy. [JC-W]

Also with: Valeria Golino (Lia Spinelli), Sharon Stone (Alison King), John Pankow (Italo Bianchi), George Murcell (Pierre Bernier), Mattia Sbragia (Giovanni), Carla Cassola (Lena), Aldo Mengolini (Aldo Moro), Roberto Posse, Thomas Elliot, Lou Castel, Dick Cavett, Fiammetta Baralla.

Dir: John Frankenheimer. Pro: Edward R. Pressman. Ex Pro: Eric Felner. Screenplay: David Ambrose and Jay Presson Allen; from the novel by Michael Mewshaw. Ph: Blasco Giurato. Ed: Lee Percy. Pro Des: Aurelio Crugnola. M: Bill Conti. Costumes: Ray Summers. (J & M Entertainment/Initial Films–First Independent.) Rel: 10 January 1992. 111 mins. Cert 15.

Young Soul Rebels. Remember green pound notes, The Sex Pistols and the Queen's Silver Jubilee? It's 1977 in London and Chris and Caz, black, seventeen and British, are running Soul Patrol, a pirate radio station in the East End. But nobody's interested in black music and punk is king. Worse still, the National Front is flexing its muscle and fellow soul rebel T.J. is murdered in the park. Winner of the Critics' Prize at Cannes (1991), *Young Soul Rebels* bites off more than it can chew, but must be applauded as an *attempt* at realising an essential black cinema in Britain. Raw, but earnest. [JC-W]

Cast includes: Valentine Nonyela (Chris), Mo Sesay (Caz), Dorian Healy (Ken), Frances Barber (Ann), Sophie Okonedo (Tracy), Jason Durr (Billibud), Debra Gillett (Jill), Shyro Chung (T.J.), Gary McDonald, Eamon Walker, James Bowyers, Billy Braham, Wayne Norman, Danielle Scillitoe, Ray Shell, Nigel Harrison.

Dir: Isaac Julien. Pro: Nadine Marsh-Edwards. Ex Pro: Colin McCabe and Ben Gibson. Screenplay: Julien, Paul Hallam and Derrick Saldaan McClintock. Ph: Nina Kellgren. Ed: John Wilson. Pro Des: Derek Brown. M: Simon Boswell; numbers performed by Mica Paris, The Blackbyrds, X-Ray Spex, War, Funkadelic, The O'Jays, The Players Association, Sylvester etc. Costumes: Annie Curtis Jones. Sound: Ronald Bailey. (BFI/Film Four Int/Sankofa Film & Video/La Sept/Kinowelt/Iberoamericana–BFI.) Rel: 23 August 1991. 103 mins. Cert 18.

Souled out: Valentine Nonyela and Mo Sesay in Isaac Julien's Young Soul Rebels *(BFI), all about being seventeen, black and gay in seventies London.*

Letter from Hollywood

ANTHONY SLIDE

The sanitised version of Hollywood Boulevard can be found not in Hollywood but in Florida, at Disney World. Here there is a recreation of what Hollywood Boulevard *should* be – if all the prostitutes, drug addicts, homeless, boarded-up shops, cheap emporiums and other detritus of 1990s society and life were removed. At least the Disney Organisation has tried to do its part in cleaning up the real-life Hollywood Boulevard, with the acquisition of the old Paramount movie theatre and its renovation, or restoration to its original 1926 name of El Capitan.

Located almost directly across the street from the Chinese Theatre complex, the new El Capitan opened on 19 June 1991 with the premiere of Disney's *Rocketeer*. The company has furnished the theatre with uniformed ushers and a live stage presentation at evening performances. A multi-curtain light show precedes every performance, and this several-minute opening of the curtains and light extravaganza spotlighting twinkling stars and an art deco dancing couple is more impressive than many of the films which follow it – certainly far more appealing than *Rocketeer*. The El Capitan proved a natural setting for the premiere of *Beauty and the Beast*, a great theatre and a great movie to light up Hollywood Boulevard.

When it opened in 1926, the El Capitan was a legitimate theatre, with its initial presentation being an American version of *Charlot's Revue*. That show marked the West Coast debut of three great British stars of the era, Gertrude Lawrence, Beatrice Lillie and Jack Buchanan, all of whom were subsequently signed to Hollywood movie contracts. The last stage presentation at the El Capitan, in December 1941, was *Springtime for Henry*, starring Edward Everett Horton. In the intervening years, the theatre stage had been home to Will Rogers in *Ah, Wilderness*, Billie Burke in Noel Coward's *The Marquise*, and George Murphy and Shirley Ross in *Anything Goes*.

Two blocks west of the Chinese Theatre, the General Cinema chain opened a new six-screen complex in December 1991, with its combined seating capacity of 2400 making it the largest theatre complex on the Boulevard. (The El Capitan has 1100 and the Chinese 1392 seats.) The General Cinema complex Galaxy 6 had some problems in finding new films for its opening days, but, hopefully, its addition to the five other movie theatres at the west end of Hollywood Boulevard will bring back some of the glamour to Hollywood, and encourage cinemagoers to turn their attentions there, rather than look for an evening's entertainment in the Westwood area of Los Angeles (close to the UCLA campus).

With that end in sight, eight blocks of Hollywood Boulevard were dedicated as the Hollywood Cinema District on 17 June 1991. Unfortunately fewer than 100 people showed up for the dedication, and there were no personalities in attendance – a sad reflection on how those in the community feel towards the district which has given the film industry its generic name.

There is still talk of a Hollywood Museum, with the new site announced in November 1991 as the Pacific Warner Theatre, half a mile east of the Chinese Theatre on Hollywood Boulevard. So far, $3 million has been spent on the project, with another $10 million needed before it becomes reality. The organisers, a consortium of political figures and tired Hollywood names, have announced that the museum will be unique, but, in reality, it sounds exactly like the concept at London's Museum of the Moving Image. One can only ponder what that initial $3 million dollars could have done to help improve the lives of the poor and homeless on the Boulevard.

The opening of the Galaxy 6 is indicative of a major increase in new theatre openings in the Los Angeles area. Everyone may be staying home and watching video tapes and discs, but there are still, apparently, enough moviegoers to warrant the building of a number of multiplex theatres with a combined capacity of more than fifty screens. Between the autumn of 1991 and the spring of 1992, Old Pasadena 8 opened in downtown Pasadena; Glendale Central, with five screens, opened in downtown Glendale; the AMC Media Center, with four screens, and the AMC Burbank, with fourteen, opened in the centre of Burbank; Fullerton 10 opened in the city of that name to the south of Los Angeles; also in the Southland the LaCosta 6 and the Pierside Pavilion, with five screens, opened in Huntington Beach; and the Sunset 5 in West Hollywood opened as a multi-screen 'art house'.

The only major studio to have been located in Hollywood since its opening is Paramount, and on 1 May 1991, stage 10 on the lot (which was once part of the neighbouring RKO lot) was the site of the 50th anniversary celebration for *Citizen Kane*. Among the invited guests were actors Joseph Cotten, Ruth Warwick, William Alland, Buddy Swan (who played Kane at the age of eight), Robert Wise (who edited the film) and Linwood Dunn (who was responsible for the visual effects). The star turn of the evening, however, was not the original Rosebud sleigh hanging by wires over the lavish buffet but Ted Turner, owner of this and all other

RKO features. With his usual bluntness, Turner pointed out that he had not been involved in the film's production, and he had not colourised it. But if anyone had asked his opinion at the time he would have told them it *should* have been shot in colour, and if RKO had known how famous the film was to become, it would have been shot in colour.

Much maligned, Ted Turner is, in reality, deserving of praise for his company's continued efforts to preserve the RKO, MGM and Warner Bros films which he now controls. He put up the money for the *Citizen Kane* restoration, and also approved Robert Wise's hiring to oversee the project. Few in or out of the industry realise that Turner's colourisation of black-and-white films also results in their improved preservation or restoration, because in order to colourise a film it is necessary first to obtain the best possible black-and-white print, and that can only be accomplished by manufacturing the highest quality master elements. Indirectly, Turner's activities have also resulted in members of the creative Hollywood community seeking permanent control over their work, to prevent any tampering such as colourisation. In December 1991, Steven Spielberg, George Lucas, Stanley Kramer and others announced the formation of the Artists Rights Foundation. Lucas pointed out that filmmakers such as himself who specialise in state-of-the-art special effects know what the future can hold:

'Unless we are able to obtain protection of moral rights under the Berne Convention, the agony of filmmakers who have suffered as their work has been chopped, tinted and compressed, is nothing to what is going to be happening in the future. Releasing entities have gained experience through the video market and colourisation and it's not going to be long in the future before an actor, who has become unacceptable for whatever reason of politics or marketability, might be electronically replaced by another actor.'

The inter-relationship between Hollywood and politics was very apparent on 4 November 1991, when the Ronald Reagan Presidential Library was opened in Simi Valley, a community to the northeast of Los Angeles, with five US presidents – Reagan, Bush, Carter, Ford and Nixon – in attendance. The

Los Angeles *Times* described the event as 'A perfect mix of Hollywood and Washington,' with the former represented by Bob Hope, Merv Griffin, James Stewart, and Eva and Zsa Zsa Gabor. The last has been popping up everywhere, having recently published her autobiography. She was at the March 1992 opening of the Hungarian Consulate in Los Angeles, and if she is the best Hungary can do as an example of its contribution to world cinema, it does not bode well for the new republic.

1992 is the year of US presidential politics, and, as usual, the Democrats have all the best stars if not the best candidates. The Republican Party relies on the old guard, represented by Bob Hope, James Stewart and Charlton Heston, and a couple of 'clean-cut' all-American leading men in the shapely forms of Kevin Costner and Arnold Schwarzenegger. Of course, the last is really Austrian, but he does have the distinction of heading President Bush's physical fitness programme.

Bob Hope was in the news for the sale of some 7989 acres of land in the Santa Monica Mountains (which runs through and beyond the city of Los Angeles) to a conservation trust which will ensure its preservation as public parkland. The deal gave Hope $29.5 million, somewhat less than the $56 million he wanted. For British-born Hope, whose personal wealth is more than $200 million, that is considered generous.

As always the Hollywood year was replete with awards, tributes and presentations. The major salute from the Academy of Motion Picture Arts and Sciences was to writer-director Joseph L. Mankiewicz, on 6 May 1991. On hand were Karl Malden, Roddy McDowall, Vincent Price, Michael Caine and Elizabeth Taylor, who, of course, had to make a grand entrance at the evening's conclusion. Michael Caine again proved that he is as elegant and witty a commentator as he is a first-rate actor, hailing Mankiewicz as 'The most civilised man I ever met in the cinema.' The 82-year-old Manciewicz was presented with life membership of the Academy, and responded, 'At my age to be given a life membership in anything is small potatoes.'

On 8 July 1991, 30-year-old Eddie Murphy received the Lifetime Achievement Award from the Los Angeles

chapter of the National Association for the Advancement of Colored People. Murphy used a four-letter word to describe his work, and many in the gay community would probably agree with the homophobic Murphy's estimation of his career. A more worthwhile Lifetime Achievement Award to a far more deserving black actor was the American Film Institute's honouring of Sidney Poitier in March 1992. Poitier was the first black American to win an Oscar and, appropriately, the first black American to be honoured by the American Film Institute. On hand for the star-studded event were Richard Widmark, Louis Gossett Jr, Tony Curtis, Walter Matthau, Jack Lemmon, John Singleton, Danny Glover, Quincy Jones, Morgan Freeman, Stanley Kramer, Rod Steiger, Dan Aykroyd and Bill Cosby. The last received the biggest laugh of the evening – not a notably hilarious event – by appearing in a baseball cap and sneakers and asking, 'Where's the car? You promised to send a car for me.' Of Poitier, Cosby said, 'When we first met, I didn't know who he was, because he was no one at the time.'

The Western contribution to cinema was remembered in August 1991 with the 9th annual Golden Boot Awards, which raise money for the Motion Picture and Television Fund. Honourees this year included John Agar, Brian Keith, Phil Harris, Alice Faye, Hugh O'Brien and Maureen O'Hara. Some eyebrows might be raised at the inclusion of Harris and Faye, who are not exactly noted as cowboy stars. Buddy Rogers made his usual generous donation to the fund, this year presenting a cheque for $50,000. Bob Hope was the master of ceremonies, expressing mystification at the cowboy heroes: 'They jump off a porch and on to a horse, ride away and sing in a normal voice. How do they do that?'

Actor George Montgomery is well regarded for his superb sculptings of Western Art, and in December 1991 and January 1992 he was honoured with a major exhibit at the Gene Autry Western Heritage Museum. On hand to pay tribute to Montgomery were Autry, Iron Eyes Cody and Montgomery's former wife Dinah Shore.

On 14 September 1991, the American Cinema Awards Foundation honoured Donald O'Connor on his 65th anniversary in show business. Gene

Left to right: *Tony Curtis, Mrs Jack (Victoria Horne) Oakie, Jack Lemmon and Walter Matthau at the SAG Foundation's First Annual Jack Oakie Award for Comedy in Motion Pictures, held on 27 February 1992 at the Directors' Guild Theatre.*

Kelly and Bob Hope paid tribute, and there were additional appearances by the Nicholas Brothers, Buddy Ebsen, George Murphy and Petula Clark. (Whatever happened to Petula Clark?) Bob Hope and Cyd Charisse were honoured by the Professional Dancers Society on 22 March 1992. Ruby Keeler, who received a warm and much deserved standing ovation, presented the award to Hope, assisted by Jane Russell. Cyd Charisse flew in from New York, where she is starring on Broadway in *Grand Hotel*, for this, the society's sixth annual awards luncheon. Others in attendance included Janet Leigh, Milton Berle, Janis Paige, Janet Blair, Margaret O'Brien, Cesar Romero, Tony Martin and Giselle McKenzie.

On 29 September, Billy Wilder was the recipient of the Preston Sturges Award, presented jointly by the Writers Guild of America West and the Directors Guild of America. Among those praising Wilder were Walter Matthau, Tony Curtis, Walter Mirisch and Robert Wise, while Wilder, in turn, praised fellow writer-director Sturges, noting, 'He was the kind of a guy who was arrogant, but he had the right to

be arrogant. He had a number of things to be arrogant about.' The following month, Roddy McDowall was the 44th recipient of the Motion Picture and Television Fund's Silver Medallion Award of Honor; more than 120 celebrities (or so it was claimed) were on hand for the luncheon ceremony, among their number being Carol Burnett, Gene Autry, Janet Leigh, Jill St John, Robert Wagner and Vincent Price.

Posthumous tribute was paid to actor Michael Chekhov on 19 November 1991, with a ceremony hosted at the American Film Institute by the Screen Actors Guild Conservancy. Russian-born and trained, Chekhov came to England in 1935 at the behest of actress Beatrice Straight, whose parents ran Dartington Hall. Ms Straight was on hand to honour Chekhov, representing a group of students which included Gregory Peck, Marilyn Monroe, Jack Palance, Yul Brynner and Anthony Quinn.

Martha Raye has been in the news quite a bit in the last year. She complained that the Bette Midler movie *For the Boys* was based on her life, and that she was entitled to financial compensation. On 23 September 1991, in Las Vegas, Raye married Mark Harris, a man more than thirty years her junior, and the actress's daughter then sought guardianship of her financial estate. Harris and Raye were remarried at Friars Club Wedding Roast in January

1992, with Cesar Romero giving the bride away and Anne Jeffreys serving as matron of honour. Because this was a roast, Raye received a proclamation from Abraham Lincoln in recognition of her work in entertaining the troops during the Civil War.

Hollywood hypocrisy was never more visible than at the Second Annual Hollywood Hunger Banquet, sponsored by Oxfam America. Various Hollywood names, including Amy Madigan, Mike Farrell and Lou Diamond Phillips, paid $150 each to attend the banquet held on a sound stage at the Sony Studios (formerly MGM) in Culver City. In order to show their solidarity with the world's starving masses, 60 per cent of the celebrities sat on the floor and ate rice, 25 per cent sat on benches and ate rice and beans, and 15 per cent enjoyed a banquet. Cybill Shepherd posed for photographers sitting on a straw mat and eating rice with her fingers. At least she was not wearing the fur coat she refuses to give up despite protests from animal rights activists, and while she was willing to talk about world hunger she did not answer questions regarding her highly paid stint as spokeswoman for L'Oréal.

Those celebrities starving themselves for a few hours could take comfort in Warner Bros opening a new canteen on its Burbank studios lot two weeks earlier. I can report that studio employees will dine on superb food in pleasing surroundings.

There is a tragi-comic quality to Hollywood charity, and it segues rather nicely into comedy for comedy's sake. In December 1991, a statue of Lucille Ball was unveiled at the new headquarters of the Academy of Television Arts and Sciences in North Hollywood. Ball's husband Gary Morton was there, along with Milton Berle, Jayne Meadows and her husband Steve Allen. A couple of months later, Allen was the recipient of the first Lifetime International Award from the International Humor Institute, and also received the 'Golden Nose' award at the same highly publicised ceremony. The big question on everyone's lips was, what *is* the International Humor Institute?

There is no question as to the identity of Hal Roach, and he was the much deserving recipient of a tribute from the Motion Picture and Television Fund on 12 January 1992, in recognition of his 100th birthday. The only individual present to have worked for Roach was Anita Garvin, a wheelchair-bound resident of the Motion Picture Country House, who appeared as Stan Laurel's wife. She tells me she still receives much fan mail from British Laurel and Hardy fans – and loves it! While promoted as a 100th birthday celebration, the event was a little premature, as Roach pointed out: 'I've got two days more to go. I can talk about being ninety-nine all afternoon.'

Certainly one of the most delightful comedy-oriented evenings of the year took place on 27 February 1992, when the Screen Actors Guild hosted the first annual Jack Oakie Award for Comedy in Motion Pictures. Heavily funded and promoted by Oakie's widow, former actress Victoria Horne, the event was a tribute not only to Jack Oakie but also to the first recipient of the award, Walter Matthau. Naturally, Matthau received his award from Jack Lemmon, and master of ceremonies Carl Reiner pointed out that the clips used to highlight Matthau's career could just as easily be used to pay tribute to Lemmon, whom Reiner hoped would be the 1993 recipient of the award.

Reiner, who has been successful as both an actor (*It's a Mad Mad Mad Mad World* etc.) and a writer (*The Dick Van Dyke Show* etc.), proved a brilliant MC. Working with one of the sophisticated teleprompter devices, he mused that these were now used by everyone from presidents to 'goofballs', and thanks to their introduction any 'goofball' could become president. He challenged the audience to tell when he was himself and when he was reading from the teleprompter, and offered a prize to the best speaker adept at using the teleprompter. The prize went to Tony Curtis, the only actor present to have worked with both Oakie and Matthau.

Labor Day Weekend (the American equivalent of August Bank Holiday in the UK) is a good time for film buffs to be in Hollywood, for it is then the Society of Cinephiles holds its annual Cinecon convention at the Hollywood Roosevelt Hotel. The 1991 convention proved to be a star-studded event. Fay Wray presented an award to visual effects expert Linwood Dunn, with whom she first became acquainted when they both worked on *King Kong*. Lew Ayres was on hand for a screening of the 1936 feature *Hearts of Bondage*, which he directed, and also to present

an award to the film's leading lady Mae Clarke, who died on 29 April 1992 (see In Memoriam).

I hosted an afternoon of vaudeville on film and was happy to welcome as my guest Fayard Nicholas of the Nicholas Brothers, who later that same year were recipients of a Kennedy Center Award in Washington, DC. The question most people in the audience had for Fayard Nicholas was, did it hurt doing the adventurous splits for which the brothers are noted. The answer: not if you know how to do it properly. The awards banquet on Sunday evening honoured Cesar Romero (receiving his award from Anne Jeffreys), George Sidney (receiving his award from fellow director Andre de Toth) and Anna Lee. Miss Lee spoke at length on her close relationship with the British royal family, who are apparently her greatest fans. I am sure I was not the only person in the audience to wonder why the Queen had not flown in personally to award Miss Lee – but she didn't even send a telegram!

Anna Lee's defence of all things English is well known in Hollywood; each St Patrick's Day, she would fly the Union Jack over her house with a banner announcing, 'God Bless Ulster, God Save the Queen, Death to the IRA.' One Englishman in Hollywood of whom Miss Lee does not approve is

Anna Lee and Cesar Romero receive their awards at the 1991 Cinecon Convention.

Ian Whitcomb, the former rock star and current ragtime aficionado who a few years ago poked fun at the British community with his BBC documentary *Hollywood My Home Town*.

Illustrating yet another side to his career, Whitcomb adapted his novel *Lotusland* into a ragtime-jazz musical comedy for radio, and it was performed live on 9 February 1992, over station KPCC. It was a unique event, probably the first-ever musical comedy written specifically for American radio and certainly the first to be performed live. Set in Southern California in the period 1918–29, the show featured Whitcomb as a ragtime-crazed Englishman, supported by, among others, Leslie Easterbrook (best known for her performances in the *Police Academy* series) and Kathleen Freeman (*Singin' in the Rain*, *The Nutty Professor* etc.), who just about stole the show with her energy and vitality. Also in the cast was professional Irishman Sean McClory, suitably miffed that this presentation of *Lotusland* had forced postponement of his presentation of *The Informer*. There was obviously little love lost between McClory and the very English Ian Whitcomb.

At least in Hollywood the age-old battle between English and Irish cultures is fought out with no harm to either side. America may be the melting pot of world cultures, but in Hollywood – as the Academy Awards with its various protesting groups well illustrates – they remain apart.

Movie Quotations of the Year

'I was their number one child, but they treated me like number two.'
An unloved Penguin (Danny DeVito) in *Batman Returns*.

Street protester (Emma Walton) to fur-coated JoBeth Williams: 'Do you know how many animals died to make that coat?' Ms Williams: 'Do you know how many animals I fucked to get this coat?'
From Blake Edwards's *Switch*.

Doctor: 'I'm afraid you have a growth.' Patient: 'I want a second opinion.' Doctor: 'OK. You're ugly.'
A little joke related by William Hurt as *The Doctor*.

'Don't torture yourself, Gomez. That's my job.'
A loving Anjelica Huston to husband Raul Julia in *The Addams Family*.

Angelica Huston, in The Addams Family

'Rumours are always true, you know that.'
Showbusiness attorney Sydney Pollack to Tim Robbins in Robert Altman's *The Player*.

'I don't know whether to shoot her or fall in love.'
Security guard on encountering Michelle Pfeiffer's Catwoman in *Batman Returns*.

'Jeez, I don't know whether to look at him or read him.'
Robert Mitchum on encountering Robert De Niro's tattooed torso in *Cape Fear*.

'How's it hangin', Death?'
Keanu Reeves to The Grim Reaper, in *Bill & Ted's Bogus Journey*.

Enraged TV star Celeste Talbert (Sally Field) to disruptive autograph-hunter: '*Excuse me*, I'm having a life!'
From *Soapdish*.

Chevy Chase and Daryl Hannah smooching in the ladies' room; Daryl, breathlessly: 'Howard, what are we doing?' Chase: 'I hope it's foreplay.' Daryl, breathlessly: 'Let's not do anything cheap and meaningless.' Chase: 'OK. How much do I owe you?'
From *Memoirs of an Invisible Man*.

'Do you ever get the feeling America is all fucked up?'
Opening words in *Pump Up the Volume*, c/o Christian Slater.

William Hurt, in The Doctor

Christian Slater, in Pump Up the Volume

'That's it – call off Christmas!'

An incensed Sheriff of Nottingham (Alan Rickman) depriving the poor of their festive rights after finding out they have sided with *Robin Hood: Prince of Thieves*.

'What's a war for if not to hold on to what we love?'

Melanie Griffith to her swain, Michael Douglas, on the airstrip – in *Shining Through*.

Melanie Griffith, in Shining Through

'We'll fuck like minks, raise rug rats and live happily ever after.'

Michael Douglas's maxim for a happy-ever-after scenario in *Basic Instinct*.

The year's best threats and insults:
'Your wife is so fat, her high school picture was an aerial photograph.'

An insolent Bruce Willis, on his knees, to back alley mugger Badja Djola, in *The Last Boy Scout*.

'Marianne needed an instruction manual to chew gum.'

Barbara Williams on the IQ of an old school acquaintance, in *City of Hope*.

'If you insult Natalie again I'll hit you so fucking hard your dog will bleed.'

Ed O'Neill threatening Christopher McDonald, ex-husband of his new girlfriend, in *Driving Me Crazy*.

'You have not discovered Shakespeare until you've read him in the original Klingon.'

David Warner as Klingon St John Talbot in *Star Trek VI – The Undiscovered Country*.

'Me? Lie? Never! The truth is much too fun!'

Dustin Hoffman as Captain James Hook.

'Thank God I'm me!'

Jeff Bridges in *The Fisher King*.

Onlooker: 'He thinks he's the last Coca-Cola in the desert.' Cathy Moriarty: 'He is.'

Two women ogling Armand Assante on the dance floor in *The Mambo Kings*.

'Roses are red/Violets are blue/I'm a schizophrenic/And so am I.'

Mad patient Bill Murray in *What About Bob?*

'Marriage is punishment for shoplifting in some countries.'

Mike Myers extemporising in *Wayne's World*.

'Why don't you run outside and jerk yourself a soda?'

Annette Bening offering some advice to Warren Beatty – in *Bugsy*.

'The cop couldn't find his cock with two hands and a map.'

Ed Harris summing up an officer of the law in *Glengarry Glen Ross*.

'I'm gonna suck his eyes out through his nose.'

Mel Gibson making a far from idle threat in *Lethal Weapon 3*.

'I insist.'

Arnold Schwarzenegger in *Terminator 2: Judgment Day*.

'Nobody's dressed up in my underclothes since the day my late husband died.'

Gwenllian Davies, reluctant to give up her petticoats, in Dylan Thomas's *Rebecca's Daughters*.

'I've lost track of how many I've had. Must be miles.'

Liz, the prostitute played by Theresa Russell in *Whore*, contemplating the number of male organs she has encountered.

The year's most ludicrous line:
'I'm not of woman born, Mikey – and I'm gonna kill ya.'

Peter Boyle mixing Shakespeare with New Yorkese in *Men of Respect*, William Reilly's update of *Macbeth*.

The year's most provocative threat:
'Miaow.'

Michelle Pfeiffer as Catwoman in *Batman Returns*.

The year's most irritating line:
'OK. OK. OK. OK. OK. OK. OK.'
Joe Pesci in *Lethal Weapon 3*.

Annette Bening, in Bugsy

TV Feature Films of the Year

F. MAURICE SPEED

In this section you will find listed all the made-for-television movies shown for the first time in the UK during the year 1 July 1991 to 30 June 1992. Films shown during the year which have been previously televised in the UK are not listed, but can be found in the edition of *Film Review* for the year when they were first shown. The date given in brackets after each title is the year when the movie was made or originally shown (often in the US).

In a few cases, despite being first shown on television, these films may have been made originally for the cinema.

When a film made for American TV receives its first UK showing in a cinema, it is of course reviewed in the 'Releases of the Year' section.

Acceptable Risk (1986). Lacklustre if topical film about the fight to stop the developers building houses next to a toxic chemical plant. A just about acceptable production. With Brian Dennehy, Cicely Tyson. Dir: Rick Wallace. BBC2, 5 February 1992.

Act of Love (1980). Mickey Rourke, paralysed after a motor-bike smash, persuades his brother (Ron Howard) to finish him off – but then the mercy killer has to fight a murder charge. Dir: Jud Taylor. Channel 4, 8 October 1991.

Adam (1983). True story about the fight by parents of an abducted and murdered child to make the FBI reveal their records of such cases to other worried parents. A sincere and absorbing drama which aroused public support. With Daniel Travanti, JoBeth Williams. Dir: Michael Tuchner. Channel 4, 24 September 1991.

Adam Bede (1991). New adaptation of the George Eliot story about a tragic triangle, with Bede (Iain Glen) and the Squire (James Wilby) both competing for the hand (and more) of a pretty milkmaid (Patsy Kensit). Made with all the BBC's usual expertise for period (1859) pieces. Dir: Giles Foster. BBC1, 1 January 1992.

Adam: His Song Continues (1986). Anti-climactic follow-up to the 1983 *Adam*. With Daniel J. Travanti, JoBeth Williams. Dir: Robert Markowitz. Channel 4, 14 January 1992.

Agatha Christie's Murders With Mirrors (1985). One of Miss Marple's earlier outings: when her host is murdered under her nose, she sniffs out the killer. Helen Hayes delightful as Miss M, with Bette Davis as the victim (her first film after the stroke which the doctors said would prevent her ever acting again!) and John Mills. ITV, 23 September 1991.

Agency (1981). Somewhere here was a good, original idea about an American politician (Robert Mitchum) who employs an advertising agency to get subliminal ads on TV in order to help his career. But it just didn't finish up as good entertainment. Also with Lee Majors. Dir: George Kaczender. BBC1, 6 September 1991.

Alive and Kicking (1991). Lenny Henry and Robbie Coltrane in hard-hitting drugs 'comedy' with plenty of four-letter words. Dir: Robert Young. BBC1, 13 October 1991.

American Harvest (1987). The tough life of the itinerant Mid-West wheat harvesters, with a concentration on the feudin' families involved. With Wayne Rogers. Dir: Dick Lowry. ITV, 11 September 1991.

André's Mother (1990). Moving and realistic story of a mother coming to terms with her son's death from AIDS. With Richard Thomas, Sada Thompson. Dir: Deborah Reinisch. BBC2, 1 December 1991.

The Ann Jillian Story (1988). Biopic about a star singer/actress more famous in her native USA than in the UK. Details her rise to fame, fight against breast cancer, and subsequent triumphant return to the limelight. Occasionally interesting. With Ann Jillian, Tony Lobiaco, Viveca Lindfors. Dir: Corey Allen. ITV, 12 January 1992.

Babycakes (1989). Odd little romance between a lonely mortuary cosmetician and an underground worker. With Ricki Lake. Dir: Paul Schneider. ITV, 26 December 1991.

Baby Makes Three (1988). Romantic comedy about the stress caused to a happy marriage when the wife decides she wants a child and her husband – who is 20 years older than her – decides it's a bad idea. With Dabney Coleman, Jane Curtin. Dir: Tom Moore. ITV, 30 December 1991.

Baywatch. Two feature length films to introduce the popular series about lifeguards on the sunny beaches of Los Angeles. *Panic at Malibu Beach* (1989) and *The Nightmare Bay* (1991). With David Hasselhoff. ITV, 30 August 1991 and 12 October 1991.

Bejeweled (1990). Comedy with Emma Samms and others trying to recover some priceless stolen jewels. Dir: Terry Marcel. ITV, 21 December 1991.

Benny's Place (1982). J. Rufus Caleb's prize-winning play fits nicely into the small screen, thanks largely to Lou Gossett Jr, playing an honest trader of mellow years who finds time and younger men are catching up with him, and decides he needs a helpmate. Very watchable. Also with Cicely Tyson, Anna Maria Horsford. Dir: Michael Schultz. Channel 4, 11 June 1992.

BFG. Animated film of Roald Dahl's best-selling children's book. ITV, 28 December 1991.

The Best of Friends (1991). TV version of Hugh Whitmore's stage play with John Gielgud, Patrick McGoohan and Wendy Hiller as Sir Sydney Cockerell, G. B. Shaw and a Benedictine Abbess – three pen friends who over 50 years discuss a very wide-ranging span of subjects. Unusual but fascinating. Dir: Alvin Rakoff. Channel 4, 28 December 1991.

Blood Vows: The Story of a Mafia Wife (1987). *Godfather* territory: a disillusioned young wife discovers her husband's law practice covers a Mafia connection. Strong stuff, with polished production and good performances. With Melissa Gilbert, Joe Penny. Dir: Paul Wendcos. BBC1, 30 July 1991.

Bluffing It (1987). Drama about a works foreman who hides his Archilles heel of not being able to read or write by his tough talking – until the day of reckoning. With Dennis Weaver. Dir: James Sadwith. Channel 4, 10 March 1992.

Bonnie and McCloud (1976). Another routine Marshal Mac episode-feature which is well up to the entertaining standard. With Leigh Taylor-Young, Dennis Weaver. Dir: Steven Stern. ITV, 31 May 1992.

A Breed Apart (1984). Wealthy collector Donald Pleasence hires mountain climber Powers Boothe to steal the eggs of a rare Bald Eagle, and Rutger Hauer swoops to the bird's defence. Nice Blue Ridge Mountains scenery. (Nobody seems able to make their minds up whether this was originally intended as a TV or cinema film!) Dir: Philippe Mora. BBC1, 15 October 1991.

Bret Maverick (1981). James Garner at his likeable and amusing best as the TV cowboy looking to hang up his guns in the comfortable little town of Sleepwater, until some baddies turn up to change his mind. Very watchable performance by Stuart Margolin – who also directed. BBC2, 3 March 1992.

Bridesmaids (1989). Bright and fluffily entertaining TV movie about four old friends reunited as bridesmaids at the wedding of the fifth. With Shelley Hack, Sela Ward, Stephanie Faracy. Dir: Lila Garrett. BBC2, 21 October 1991.

Brotherhood of Justice (1986). Powerful story about a group of teenagers who form a vigilante force to clean up their school but find they are becoming more violent than the thugs they are up against. With Keanu Reeves, Kiefer Sutherland. Dir: Charles Braveman. BBC2, 9 February 1992.

By Dawn's Early Light (1989). From cable TV (for which it was made), an edge-of-the-seat story about two US airmen faced with the responsibility of 'going nuclear' and thereby starting the apocalyptic World War III. With Powers Boothe, James Earl Jones, Rebecca de Mornay. Dir: Jack Sholder. BBC1, 24 August 1991.

The Care of Time (1989). Fairly lavish but routine and familiar spy drama – a second-drawer Bond familiar – that moves around the world and has authentic backgrounds but never impresses. With Michael Brandon, Christopher Lee. Dir: John Davies. ITV, 24 August 1991.

Case Closed (1988). Veteran cop Charles Durning is lured back on the beat by the enthusiasm of young cop Byron Allen, who wants help to solve a murder connected with the theft of one of the world's largest diamonds. Durning makes it all very watchable. Dir: Dick Lowry. ITV, 1 January 1992.

The Child Saver (1987). Well-intentioned advertising executive Alfre Woodard puts her career and even her life in peril when she decides to save a 7-year-old dope peddler. Pretty routine stuff. Dir: Stan Latham. Channel 4, 29 October 1991.

Choices (1986). Anti-abortionist judge George C. Scott (a good performance) faces a dilemma when his wife and daughter (Jacqueline Bisset and Melissa Gilbert) both become unacceptably pregnant. Contrived and generally soapy. Dir: David Lowell Rich. BBC2, 28 October 1991.

Christmas Comes to Willow Creek (1987). Simple seasonal tale about two warring brothers set the task of getting Christmas cheer from California to a remote town in Alaska. With *Hazard* stars John Schneider and Tom Wopat. Dir: Richard Lang. BBC1, 24 December 1991.

Christmas Gift (1984). Architect John Denver is seduced by the rural charms of a village due for unwelcome development, and switches sides to fight his former allies, the developers. Dir: Michael Pressman. ITV, 23 December 1991.

Codename: Dancer (1987). (Originally titled *Her Secret Life*.) Secret agent caper about a housewife (ex-agent) who, when the call comes to free a buddy from a Cuban hell-hole, drops her apron and takes off, to the puzzlement of her husband. Silly but quite acceptable. With Kate Capshaw. Dir: Buzz Kulik. (Made for American Cable TV.) Channel 4, 4 February 1992.

Colour Scheme (1978). George Baker as New Zealand cop Roderick Alleyn in one of four Ngaio Marsh detective stories he made there in the 1970s. Routine – but very watchable. ITV, 28 September 1991.

Columbo: Now You See Him (1975). Note the date: no wonder he's been looking so much the worse for wear recently. He'll have to be pensioned off soon, despite his continuing popularity with viewers. With Peter Falk. BBC1, 12 January 1992.

A Cop for the Killing (1990). Routine but fast-paced cops and drugs melodrama, based on an actual case. With James Farentino. Dir: Dick Lowry. BBC1, 10 April 1992.

The Count of Sola (1991). Extremely interesting BBC TV feature, made in France, about a deaf lad who 200 years ago was taken under the wing of the Abbé de l'Epée, who invented the first sign language in order to communicate with him. The boy is played by the stone-deaf 14-year-old Tyron Woolie. Fascinating viewing. Dir: Tristram Powell. BBC2, 2 February 1992.

Custody (1987). TV movie from Down Under, an interesting if unsuccessful attempt to weld fact and fiction in the story of a marriage on the rocks and the struggle to gain custody of the unfortunate offspring. Some uncomfortable improvised dialogue. With Judith Stratford, Peter Browne. Dir: Ian Munro. Channel 4, 30 July 1991.

Dallas: The Early Years (1986). Lively 'prequel' to the famous series with Larry Hagman explaining how it all started. Great stuff for the fans. Dir: Larry Ellikan. BBC1, 13 October 1991.

A Dangerous Man – Lawrence After Arabia (1992). A mistaken but not wholly unsatisfactory small-screen effort to follow in the footsteps of the classic cinema film *Lawrence of Arabia*. With Ralph Fiennes, Dennis Quilley, Nicholas Jones, Siddig El Fadil. Dir: Christopher Menaul. ITV, 18 April 1992.

Daughter of Darkness (1989). Uninvolving and finally uninteresting vampire thriller set in the land of the classic bloodsuckers – Romania. With Mia Sara, Anthony Perkins. Dir: Stuart Gordon. ITV, 15 April 1992.

A Deadly Silence (1989). Macabre true-life story of a sexually abused schoolgirl who pays a pal to kill the culprit – her own father. With Heather Fairfield. Dir: John Patterson. Channel 4, 3 September 1991.

The Defiant Ones (1985). Another mediocre and feeble attempt to re-make a good cinema film (1958, with Sidney Poitier) about two convicts – one white and racist, the other black – who escape despite being chained together. The original was a good moral lesson. With Robert Urich and Carl Weathers. Dir: David Lowell Rich. BBC2, 2 September 1991.

The Deliberate Stranger (1986). Top-class (if over-long by 20 minutes) TV movie about handsome but horrific serial killer 'Ted' Bundy (Mark Harmon) and the dedicated team of cops who never give up until they have nailed their man and put an end to the slaughter. A true story, of course. With Frederic Forrest, M. Emmet Walsh. Dir: Marvin J. Chomsky. BBC1: Part 1, 6 August 1991; Part 2, 7 August 1991.

Doctors' Private Lives (1978). Missable pilot feature for a series that lasted just four episodes. Soap opera hospital tale that no operation could have saved. With John Gavin, Donna Mills, Ed Nelson. Dir: Steven Hilliard Stern. ITV, 16 March 1992.

The Dollmaker (1984). Jane Fonda deservedly won an Emmy award for this, her first TV movie, playing a woman who sustains her family during the difficult days of the war. Commended. Also with Levon Helm, Geraldine Page. Dir: Daniel Petrie. BBC2, 29 March 1992.

Dottie (1987). She's been suffering from agoraphobic symptoms since her hubbie died a couple of years back but is now forced back into the New York world by her estranged sister's fatal illness. With Elizabeth Franz, Betty Miller, Margaret Gibson. Dir: David Gelfand. Channel 4, 27 September 1991.

Dying Room Only (1973). Oddly familiar (*The Vanishing*?) story of a husband who vanishes when he enters the 'comfort station' of a seedy wayside res-taurant. Tightly scripted, well directed and altogether superior TV thriller. With Cloris Leachman. Dir: Philip Leacock. Screenplay: Robert Matheson. BBC1, 12 July 1991.

Easy Prey (1986). Nasty but true story about a psychopath who abducts a teenager and takes her on a ride of terror. Missable. With Gerald McRaney, Shawnee Smith. Dir: Sandor Stern. BBC1, 5 October 1991.

Ellis Island (1984). Epic-scale TV film about immigrants arriving in America (circa 1907) to find the streets not all paved with gold, and the great American dream all too easily turning to a nightmare. With Richard Burton, Claire Bloom, Faye Dunaway. Dir: Jerry London. ITV: Part 1, 5 July 1991; Part 2, 12 July 1991.

Embassy (1985). A first-rate cast are somewhat wasted in this spy story about secret plans hidden in a kid's candy bar! With Nick Mancuso, Eli Wallach, Sam Wanamaker, Blanche Baker. Dir: Richard Michael Lewis. ITV, 27 November 1991.

Escape (1971). Superficial (cardboard characters – unbelievable dialogue) but not unamusing story of a stage magician who becomes a spy, and is up against a mastermind villain with plans to become a world dictator. Comical comic-strip stuff. With Christopher George, William Windom, Marilyn Mason. Dir: John Llewellyn Moxey. ITV, 18 August 1991.

Evil in Clear River (1987). Strong, honest and thoughtful racial tension drama set in a small Canadian town, with performances measuring up to the general high standard. With Randy Quaid, Lindsay Wagner. Dir: Karen Arthur. Channel 4, 16 March 1992.

Family of Spies (1990). Ironically amusing true story of an American naval officer (Powers Boothe) who over 20 years found selling US secrets to the Russians so lucrative that he recruited his own family to help him! But mistakenly padded out to make two parts.

Dir: Stephen Gyllenthal. ITV, 1 and 2 September 1991.

Farewell Miss Freedom (US: *Goodbye Miss 4th of July*) (1988). Disney 'real-life' story of a Greek family who come to America for peace and security only to find racial prejudice from the Ku Klux Klan. Well-made drama. With Louis Gossett Jr, Roxana Zai, Chris Sarandon. Dir: George Miller. Channel 4, 15 October 1991.

Father Christmas (1991). Animated feature with the voice of Mel Smith. Dir: Dave Unwin. Channel 4, 24 December 1991.

A Father's Homecoming (1988). Deadly dull family portrait from life, love and all else at a New England private school. With Michael McKean. Dir: Rick Wallace. Channel 4, 7 May 1992.

Fear Stalks (1989). Routine, over-familiar story of a female TV producer pursued with evil intent by a mental case. With Jill Clayburgh. Dir: Larry Shaw. BBC1, 3 December 1991.

Filipina Dreamgirls (1991). Amusing new BBC comedy, with flashes of serious insight, about several optimistic Welshmen who go on holiday to Manila hoping to bring back the wives they have failed to find in their native Wales. With Bill Maynard giving a shining, full-blooded performance as philosophic matchmaker. Also with Charles Drake, Geoffrey Hutchings. Written by Andrew Davies. Dir: Les Blair. BBC1, 15 August 1991.

Flea Bites (1991). Leisurely, slight, but quite charming and even on occasion moving story of the efforts of a youngster and an old Polish emigré with whom he becomes friends to bring back up to scratch the latter's Flea Circus. An offbeat BBC telefilm. With Anthony Hill, Nigel Hawthorne. Dir: Alan Dossor. BBC2, 26 January 1992.

Forget About Me (1990). Heart-warming story about a couple of Scottish army lads and a local girl they pick up as they travel to see a Hungarian-staged

Simple Minds concert. Made in Budapest; lovely locations. With Bryan McCardie, Ewen Bremner, Zsuzanna Varronyi. Dir: Michael Winterbottom. Channel 4, 1 January 1992.

The Four Feathers (1976). A. E. W. Mason's story of 'cowardice' and bravery in the *Boy's Own Paper*, black-and-white style. Dated and delicious. With Beau Bridges, Robert Powell, Simon Ward. Dir: Don Sharp. ITV, 1 January 1992.

Foxfire (1987). Highly successful adaptation of the Broadway stage play about a widow who lives in a mountain home and keeps in contact with her dead husband. In spite of the unlikely story, thanks to delicate performances it works beautifully. See it next time around. With Jessica Tandy and real life hubbie Hume Cronyn. Dir: Jud Taylor. BBC2, 4 January 1992.

Galahad of Everest (1991). Actor Brian Blessed turns climber – and life risker – to recreate the famous ascent cf Everest by George Mallory, who died on the mountain in 1924. An original and fascinating TV film and a remarkable achievement by Blessed. BBC2, 9 December 1991.

The Games of Love (1989). Life in an American 'singles' bar, where various characters forgather to find a partner. Surprisingly fascinating. With Ken Olin, Ed Marinaro. Dir: Bobby Roth. Channel 4, 16 August 1991.

Go To the Light (1988). Well produced and acted true story about a schoolboy who contracts AIDS from a blood transfusion, and his mother's fight against subsequent prejudice. With Linda Hamilton, Richard Thomas. Dir: Mike Robe. BBC2, 2 December 1991. (Shown the day after the similar *The Ryan White Story*, also listed here.)

God Bless the Child (1988). Pleasantly unsoapy story of a young single mother caught in the poverty trap, who tries to fight her way out. Gripping and topical. With Mare Winningham, Dorian Harewood. Dir: Larry Elikann. Channel 4, 24 January 1992.

Golden Gate (1981). Another pilot for a series that never was. A widow and her family struggle to keep a San Francisco newspaper going. With Jean Simmons, Richard Kiley. Dir: Paul Wendkos. ITV, 4 November 1991.

Goldie and the Boxer (1979). Familiar, routine story of a black boxer (O. J. Simpson) and a cute little girl (Melissa Michaelson) who adopts him. Sackfuls of sentimentality. Channel 4, 18 June 1992.

Goliath Awaits (1983). Imaginative – and incredible – tale of a photographer who comes across a group of survivors leading an idyllic existence in their German-torpedoed luxury liner twenty years after the end of World War II. Cut from its original 240-minute length to 170 minutes – a mixed blessing. With John Carradine, Christopher Lee, Mark Harmon. Dir: Kevin Connor. ITV, 22 August 1991.

The Grass Arena (1991). Impressive, award-winning BBC production based on a true story about a promising young boxer who slips into the meths and cardboard bed category but is saved by his discovery that he can become an outstanding chess player. Well worth those awards. With Mark Rylance, Pete Postlewaite, Lynsey Baxter. Dir: Gillies MacKinnon. BBC2, 19 January 1992.

Hancock (1991). Excellent BBC film about the final phase of the great comedian's tragic life; his success, boozing, marriage, failure and final suicide in a small Australian hotel room. A remarkably sure performance by Alfred Molina. Also with Frances Barber as the ill-used wife. Dir: Tony Smith. BBC1, 1 September 1991.

Hands of a Murderer (1990). The sleuth of Baker Street rides again, with Edward Woodward enjoying himself immensely as Holmes, thwarting Prof. Moriarty's (Anthony Andrews, also excellent) plan to escape from jail. Add a pile of secret government papers, the nearing outbreak of the 1914 war and a brilliant script, and you have a real winner. Dir: Stuart Orme. ITV, 17 August 1991.

Harem (1986). Painfully dated melodrama about nasty Turk Omar Sharif kidnapping pretty Nancy Travis and adding her to his collection of luscious lovelies, though his No. 1 wife Ava Gardner isn't too pleased. Shades of Valentino and *The Sheik*! Dir: Billy Hale. ITV, 11 August 1991. (No relation to the 1985 cinema film with Ben Kingsley and Nastassja Kinski.)

Haunted (1984). No spooks or poltergeists – just the story of a woman trying to sort out the facts of her mysterious childhood. With Brooke Adams, Trish Van Devere. Dir: Michael Roemer. Channel 4, 2 April 1992.

A Hazard of Hearts (1987) Authoress Barbara Cartland reaches the screen, with a highly wrought period melodrama about a lovely young virgin sold by her father as a cardgame loss to a nasty old lecher. Super production and great stars – Helena Bonham Carter, Diana Rigg, Edward Fox, Stewart Granger, Christopher Plummer etc – make it great fun! Dir: John Hough. BBC1, 18 August 1991.

Heading Home (1991). Director David Hare wrote as well as directed this rather strange, certainly personal story of life in post-war London, where a girl from the provinces edges her way into literary as well as criminal circles. With Gary Oldman, Joely Richardson. BBC2, 18 December 1991.

Heart of a Champion: The Ray Mancini Story (1985). A young boxer fights for the championship which the war prevented his pugilist dad from winning. The fights are crunchingly realistic. With Doug McKeon (boxer), Robert Blake (Dad). Dir: Richard Michaels. ITV, 18 May 1992.

The Helicopter Spies (1967). The men from UNCLE up against a fanatical sect who plan to dominate the world. Familiar stuff, with Robert Vaughn and David McCallum. Dir: Boris Sagal. BBC2, 12 December 1991.

Hellinger's Law. Telly Savalas lifts this to a very watchable story of a lawyer who finds he is defending a member of the Mafia on a murder charge. Superior

tension-stretcher. Also with Rod Taylor. Dir: Lou Penn. ITV, 22 December 1991.

High School USA (1983). We've been here before . . . and more than once. The usual friction between bullies and good guys on the campus. Billed as a comedy, but my sides remain unsplit. With Michael J. Fox, Nancy Mickeon. Dir: Rod Amateau. ITV, 10 August 1991.

The Hillside Stranglers (1989). A cop who becomes obsessed with catching a ten-times killer. Inept story and treatment leaves one completely uninvolved. With Richard Crenna, Billy Zane. Dir: Steven Gethers. BBC1, 6 January 1992.

Hollywood Uncensored (1987). Amusing historical documentary about quirky film censorship decisions in America from silent days till now. ITV, 28 October 1991.

A Home of Our Own (1975). Biopic about the life work of Father William Wasson (Jason Miller), who founded a home for orphans in Mexico. Good intentions if nothing more. Dir: Robert Day. Channel 4, 4 June 1992.

Hostile Witness (US: *Terrorist on Trial*) (1988). Absorbing courtroom drama about a New York Jewish attorney defending a Palestinian terrorist (!). Superb performances by Sam Waterston, Ron Leibman and Robert Davi. Dir: Jeff Bleckner. This TV feature had a short cinema life in the US. BBC1, 21 September 1991.

How to Murder a Millionaire (1990). Joan Rivers as the wealthy wife who thinks her husband is planning to murder her. Not half as funny as it sets out to be. Also with Alex Rocco, Morgan Fairchild. Dir: Paul Schneider. ITV, 22 December 1991.

I Married a Centrefold (1985). Complications follow a young man's bet that he will get a date with a centrefold model. With Teri Copley, Diane Ladd. Dir: Peter Werner. ITV, 27 December 1991.

I'll Be Home for Christmas (1988). Shamelessly romantic but well-played

and warmly produced story about a New England couple waiting expectantly for their offspring to arrive for Christmas. Good seasonal entertainment. With Eva Marie Saint and Hal Holbrook. Dir: Marvin J. Chomsky. Channel 4, 23 December 1991.

In the Glitter Palace (1977). Investigator Chad Everett uncovers some pretty nasty surprises when he agrees to an old girl friend's pleas to help her lesbian lover who's become involved in a murder. Very sleazy. Also with Barbara Hershey, Howard Duff. Dir: Robert Butler. ITV, 13 April 1992.

The Immortal Story (1968). Orson Welles directed himself in this yarn about a very rich Macau merchant who pays a sailor to make love to his wife, Jeanne Moreau. A seldom seen and lesser Welles work. BBC2, 24 December 1991.

In Defence of Kids (1983). Softhearted Blythe Danner gives up a promising legal career in order to devote herself to helping teenagers up against the law. Also with Sam Waterston as her understanding husband. Dir: Gene Reynolds. Channel 4, 25 February 1992.

In Line of Duty: The FBI Murders (1988). Strong stuff – all based on fact. A couple of killers are tracked, cornered and killed by their FBI pursuers in a bullet-flying, body-falling climax. With David Soul, Michael Gross. Dir: Dick Lowry. BBC1, 9 July 1991.

Inherit the Wind (1988). Another sadly mistaken effort to re-make a big screen classic for the small screen. Kirk Douglas and Jason Robards make brave but futile efforts to re-create the magnificent performances of Spencer Tracy and Fredric March in the original 1960 courtroom drama about a teacher's defence of his explaining Darwin's theory of evolution to a Deep South class. Dir: David Green. BBC2, 16 August 1991.

Izzy and Moe (1985). Jackie Gleason (who also wrote the music) and Art Carney as a couple of vaudeville performers (circa 1920s) who are recruited into the FBI as Prohibition Enforcers in New York. Funny in flashes. Dir: Jackie Cooper. Channel 4, 16 April 1992.

J. Edgar Hoover (1986). Interesting biopic about the famous FBI director, who developed from dedicated young lawman to old and corrupt dictator. With Treat Williams, Rip Torn. Dir and Screenplay: Robert Collins. BBC1, 20 September 1991.

Jack the Ripper (1988). After a 20-year interval, Michael Caine returns to the small screen and obviously enjoyed himself as the Victorian detective given the notorious case to solve. A very controversial solution – but you'll probably share Caine's enjoyment. Also with Jane Seymour. Dir: David Wickes. ITV: Part 1, 13 January 1992; Part 2, 14 January 1992.

Jane of Lantern Hill (1990). Canadian TV film about young Jane's enforced stay with her grandmother during the Depression. With Mairon Bennett, Sam Waterston, Patricia Phillips. Dir: Kevin Sullivan. Channel 4, 24 December 1991.

Jazz Detective (1990). When jazz musician Daniel Webb becomes a murder suspect, he turns detective in order to clear his name. Also with Marella Oppenheim. Dir: Alan Clayton. ITV, 27 April 1992.

Jekyll and Hyde (1989). Another disastrous attempt to re-make a classic film, with Michael Caine trying to follow in the footsteps of Fredric March and Spencer Tracy, and failing painfully. Dir: David Wickes. ITV, 14 December 1991.

The Josephine Baker Story (1991). So-called biopic about the rise and subsequent slide of the famous black American dancer who shook up the blasé Folies Bergère audiences in Paris in the 1920s. A grand performance by Lynn Whitfield. Dir: Brian Gibson. ITV, 24 May 1992.

Justice Denied (1989). Canadian TV film based on a sensational miscarriage of justice, with Billy Merasty as the victim and the real-life parents playing themselves. Sadly uninvolving. Dir:

Paul Cowan. Channel 4, 12 November 1991.

Kate's Secret (1986). She's suffering from compulsive overeating! All very routine stuff. With Meredith Baxter Birney. Dir: Arthur Seidelman. BBC1, 3 December 1991.

Killer at Hell's Gate (1981). A group of river trippers find they are facing some real bullets when they shoot the rapids! Forget the routine story and enjoy the exciting backgrounds of wild waters and narrowing cliffs. With Robert Urich, Deborah Raffin, Lee Purcell. Dir: Jerry Jameson. BBC1, 21 February 1992.

A Kind of Anger (1984). Unworthy German adaptation of the complex Eric Ambler spy novel. Dir: Ulrich Edel. ITV, 26 March 1992.

Kojak: The Marcus-Nelson Murders (1973). Based on a true story, this Kojak documentary-style investigation pre-dates the series and carried off an award. With Telly Savalas, José Ferrer, Marjoe Gortner. ITV, 20 April 1992.

Kung Fu (1972). The original pilot feature for the very successful cult film series that followed, with its mixture of Western and martial arts. It did no harm to David Carradine as the star performer. Good fun. Dir: Jerry Thorpe. BBC1, 15 March 1992.

Lady Mobster (1988). Fairly routine piece about a girl who's brought up by a gangster family and becomes a tough cookie lawyer. With Susan Lucci. Dir: John L. Moxey. Channel 4, 3 March 1992.

Lassie: Adventures of Neekda (1968). The famous dog is reunited with a young Indian friend. Dir: Dick Moder and Richard Hively. BBC2, 5 September 1991.

Lassie: Flight of the Cougar Three shortish Lassie episodes – shown between 1954 and 1972 – edited into a feature film showing the intelligence of the wonder dog. Dir: William Beaudine, Jack Hively and Dick Moder. BBC1, 14 September 1991.

Lassie's Great Adventure (1964). Four of the old Lassie series stitched together to make a pleasantly entertaining family film. BBC2, 19 January 1992.

Lassie: Well of Love (1970). When a beloved dog dies, Lassie gallantly steps in to present the bereaved owners with one of her pups. Dir: Jack Hively. BBC2, 6 September 1991.

The Last Innocent Man (1987). Marital mix-up. Lawyer Ed Harris finds out he is having an affair with the estranged wife of his murder-rap client. Gripping stuff; excellent cast, including Roxanne Hart and David Suchet. Dir: Roger Spottiswoode. BBC1, 27 May 1992.

The Law Lord (1991). Political drama about the government's attempt to take over and run the British legal system. Slow and ultimately too close to a bore for comfort. With Anthony Andrews, Bernard Hill. Dir: Jim Goddard. BBC2, 22 March 1992.

The Lion of Africa (1987). Less-than-thrilling African adventure with Brian Dennehy and Brooke Adams sharing a Kenyan safari . . . of a kind. Missable. Dir: Kevin Connor. BBC1, 4 April 1992.

Little Girl Lost (1988). Highly charged, true story of the obstacles that have to be overcome by the foster-parents of a little American girl (Marie Martin), when they want to adopt her. Also with Tess Harper, Frederic Forrest. Dir: Sharron Miller. BBC2, 18 May 1992.

Little White Lies (1989). Familiar romantic tale about a girl – in this case a cop – on holiday who pretends to be a millionairess but regrets the pose when she falls in love and fears the truth will out! With Ann Jillian, Tim Matheson. Dir: Anson Williams. ITV, 23 December 1991.

The Littlest Victims (1989). Tim Matheson as a New York doctor doing his best for children with AIDS. Sombre and sad. Dir: Peter Levin. ITV, 1 December 1991.

Long Time Gone (1986). Rescued from the shelf (where it spent its first two years sadly neglected), this feature introduction to an unmade series deserved better, for it is a very watchable story about an unsuccessful private eye who suddenly has to look after his young son while he's involved in a tricky missing person case. With Paul LeMat, Al Dusenberry, Wil Wheaton. Dir: Robert Butler. BBC2, 14 October 1991.

The Longshot (1986). A quartet of cosy crooks plan to make a killing on the horses but then put the – borrowed – small fortune on the wrong gee-gee, with disastrous results. Smutty dialogue and general sleaziness made this unenjoyable and even offensive to me – and I'm sure to others. No relation to the cinema film with same title. With Tim Conway, Jack Weston, Stella Stevens. Dir: Paul Bartel. BBC2, 24 March 1992.

Looking for Miracles (1990). Comedy-drama about a teenager bluffing his way into a summer camp (with his younger brother) as a counsellor – with the expected complications. Set during the great American Depression. With Grey Spottiswoode, Zachary Bennett. Dir: Kevin Sullivan. Channel 4, 29 December 1991.

Love and Hate: A Marriage Made in Hell (1989). At its heart, an absorbing courtroom drama. Two-faced rancher/politician (Kenneth Walsh), with a seemingly perfect alibi, fights the accusation that as a result of a custody battle he murdered his wife. Well-made edge-of-seat stuff. Also with Kate Nelligan. Dir: Francis Mankiewicz. BBC1 Part 1, 13 August 1991; Part 2, 14 August 1991. (A Canadian production based on a true story.)

Love on the Run (1985). Mediocre film supposedly based on a true story about a female lawyer who falls in love with a murderer client, helps him escape from jail and goes on the run with him. Missable. With Stephanie Zimbalist, Alec Baldwin. Dir: Gus Trikonis. ITV, 8 December 1991.

Madigan: The Manhattan Beat (1972). Moviegoers with memories of the original 1966 cinema film may be affronted by the liberties taken everywhere in this TV spin-off series. But at least brilliant veteran star Richard Widmark retains the title role of the weary, seen-everything, done-everything New York cop. BBC1, 9 August 1991. **The Midtown Beat** (1972). A party stops being fun when a youngster steps into the festivities with a cocked gun and looks as if he might use it. Extra bonus: veteran 'scat' singer Cab Calloway in full song. BBC1, 16 August 1991. **The Lisbon Beat** (1973). Madigan on unfamiliar territory trying to grab an escaped prisoner in Portugal. BBC1, 23 August 1991. **The Naples Beat** (1973). The world-wandering Madigan has the hazardous job of bringing a big-time Mafia squealer back to the States. Filmed in Rome and Naples. BBC1, 30 August 1991.

The Magic Flute (1974). Ingmar Bergman's wonderful TV film of the Mozart opera. Magic in every sense. Beautifully sung, imaginatively staged; one of the finest of all filmed operas. (Sung in Swedish; with English subtitles.) BBC2, 29 December 1991.

A Man for All Seasons (1988). Charlton Heston both directs and stars as Sir Thomas More in this TV version of Robert Bolt's powerful play and cinema film. An honest, very careful production, but just that bit longer than is good for it. Also with Vanessa Redgrave as Lady More, Adrienne Thomas as Margaret More, John Gielgud as Wolsey and Martin Chamberlain as King Henry VIII. BBC1, 10 November 1991.

The Man Who Lived at the Ritz (1988). An American (a rich art student) in wartime Paris finds things getting tough when Goering moves into his hotel and he can no longer ignore the Nazi menace. With Perry King, Joss Ackland, Leslie Caron, David McCallum, Cherie Lunghi. Dir: Desmond Davis. ITV: Part 1, 11 August 1991; Part 2, 18 August 1991.

Manhunt for Claude Dallas (1986). Shameful true story about a hunter who shot two game wardens when they tried to arrest him for illegal hunting, and became something of a folk hero to some Americans. With Matt Salinger, Claude Akins. Dir: Jerry London. ITV, 11 December 1991.

The Marvellous Land of Oz (1986). Animated sequel to the classic *Oz* film. It lacks the voice of Judy Garland at her girlish best . . . but it's still fun. Channel 4, 1 January 1992.

Matt Helm (1975). Anthony Franciosa as a Bond-ish investigator hired to solve one case, but stumbling on a much bigger black market operation. A mixture of thrills and chuckles. Also with Ann Turkel. Dir: Buzz Kulik. ITV, 22 April 1992.

Matt Houston (1982). Though this pilot feature was a pretty mediocre effort, the series it introduced, about an incredible Texan amateur sleuth, ran for years! With Lee Horsley, Barbara Carreras, Dale Robertson, Jill St John. Dir: Richard Lang. BBC2, 17 March 1992.

McCloud: A Cowboy in Paradise (1978). Good old Mac takes a trip to Hawaii to help his chief who's been framed for murder. With Dennis Weaver, Martha Hyer. Dir: Jerry Paris. ITV, 16 May 1992.

McCloud: The Great Taxicab Stampede (1976). Routine Mac episode with the marshal now facing an accusation of murder. With Dennis Weaver. Dir: Ivan Dixon. ITV, 23 May 1992.

McCloud: Lady on the Run (1974). Mariette Hartley as the running lady, Clu Galager as the killer on her heels and Dennis Weaver as dependable Mac. ITV, 20 June 1992.

McCloud: The Million Dollar Round-up (1973). This time Marshal Mac (Dennis Weaver) is on the trail of a stolen gem-encrusted statue. Routine stuff, but well done. Dir and Screenplay: Douglas Heyes. ITV, 2 May 1992.

Memento Mori (1992). Star-studded BBC feature adaptation of Muriel Spark's witty novel about a group of friends who get threatening telephone calls. With Maggie Smith, Michael Hordern, Renee Asherson. Dir: Jack Clayton. BBC2, 19 April 1992.

Michigan Melody (1986). French–Canadian TV feature, a romance between a girl who needs a husband within 24 hours and a truck driver who wants to remedy his disastrous marriage. With Anne Canovas, Edward Meeks. Dir: Bernard Toublanc-Michel. ITV, 6 January 1992.

Mickey Spillane's Mike Hammer: Murder Takes All (1989). Stacy Keach as the tough private eye picking his way past the corpses in Las Vegas and trying to convince the cops *he* isn't the killer. Far-fetched but amusing whodunnit. Also with Lynda Carter. Dir: John Nicolella. ITV, 19 August 1991.

Mirrors (1985). Familiar story about an out-of-town innocent in New York trying to make a ballet career for herself, forced into taking a chorus line job in a new musical to make ends meet; at the same time having to choose between romance and career. With Marguerite Hickey, Antony Hamilton, and nice to see Keenan Wynn, Patricia Morison and Signe Hasso. Dir: Harry Winer. BBC2, 18 November 1991.

Miss Delafield Wants to Marry (1986). Indomitable, indestructible Katharine Hepburn as a wealthy Gentile widow who decides to put the cat amongst the family pigeons by marrying a Jewish doctor. Another remarkable performance by the evergreen veteran, ably supported by Harold Gould. Dir: George Schaefer. BBC1, 7 May 1992.

Moonglobe (1988). Prize-winning Soviet feature documentary about a quartet of veteran Russian circus artistes who create a world of their own in a cellar deep below ground. A unique movie. Channel 4, 4 November 1991.

Murder COD (1990). Amusingly unreal thriller about a baddie (William Devane) who will bump off anyone for personal profit. Determined to see the villain brought to justice is dour, determined cop Patrick Duffy. Dir: Alan Metzger. BBC1, 8 May 1992.

Murder for Two (1984). Fairly original murder mystery about a train passenger who solves the killing of a woman he meets during the journey by finishing her crossword! With Michael Nouri, Glynis Johns, James Cromwell. Dir: Larry Elikann. ITV, 28 December 1991.

My Mother's Secret Life (1984). Banal piece about a daughter who comes home to find her mother is a prostitute. Switch-offable. With Noni Anderson, Paul Sorvino, Grace Zabriskie. Dir: Robert Markowitz. ITV, 7 June 1992.

My Sister's Wife (1992). The ramifications of a British Pakistani's decision to take a second wife. With Meera Syal, Paul Bhattachharjee. Dir: Lesley Manning. BBC2, 23 February 1992.

Nick Knight (1989). Yet another pilot for a series that was still-born. And judging by this, very understandably! Perish the thought of a series as bad as this suggests it would have been. With Rick Springfield. Dir: Farhad Mann. ITV, 8 November 1991.

Night of the Fox (1990). A fine, largely British cast wasted on a tired World War II story. With George Peppard, John Mills, Michael York, John Standing. Dir: Charles Jarrott. ITV: Part 1, 20 January 1992; Part 2, 21 January 1992.

The Night Strangler. Reporter Darren McGavin in Seattle on the trail of a 120-year-old serial killer! Plenty of macabre and gruesome killings, lots of thrills, and some splendid direction from Dan Curtis. (A follow-up to the previously shown *The Night Stalker*.) Also with Jo Ann Pflug. BBC1, 14 August 1991.

No Place Like Home (1989). There's plenty of topical relevance in this story of unemployment and homelessness. Depressing but good. With Christine Lahti, Jeff Daniels. Dir: Lee Grant. BBC2, 1 April 1992.

North Shore (1987). Silly and slim surf movie set against beautifully photographed background of wild Hawaiian wavescapes. With Matt Adler, Nia Peeples. Dir: William Phelps. BBC2, 18 March 1992.

Of Pure Blood (1986). Lee Remick as brilliant as ever as a very amateur investigator, a mother who goes to Germany to find out more about her son's puzzling death and finds some nasty things swept under the carpet. Very watchable. Also with Patrick McGoohan. Dir: Joseph Sargent. ITV, 20 October 1991.

The Old Man and the Sea (1990). A reinforcing lesson to prove how daft it is to try and re-make classic cinema films for the small screen. This new version of the Spencer Tracy triumph in the Hemingway story is, quite frankly, a complete bore. Anthony Quinn does his best in Tracy's shadow. Dir: Jud Taylor. ITV, 25 August 1991.

Old Scores (1991). An unlikely bonus for rugby fans. A Wales–New Zealand match is replayed 25 years later because the linesman admits on his deathbed to cheating over his judgements. With Robert Pugh, Glyn Houston, Alison Bruce and lots of old stars of the game. Dir: Alan Clayton. ITV, 25 September 1991.

Out on the Edge (1989). Former boy wonder Ricky ('Rocky') Schroder playing his age (teens) in more or less routine piece about the effects on a youngster of his parents' divorce. Also with Mary Kay Place. Dir: John Pasquin. Channel 4, 28 January 1992.

Pals (1987). Brilliant playing by Don Ameche and George C. Scott – ably supported by (very-welcome-back) Sylvia Sidney – as the two ex-Army buddies who come across a drugs baron's fortune and happily make free with it while pursued by the gangster. Delightful comedy. Dir: Lou Antonno. BBC2, 7 October 1991.

The Penthouse (1989). Silly girl Robin Givens (ex-wife of Mike Tyson) invites an old boyfriend into her father's lush apartment, unaware she's harbouring a psychopath. Pretty daft. Also with David Hewlett. Dir: David Greene. ITV, 6 July 1991.

Perry Mason: The Case of the Musical Murder (1989). Raymond Burr trying to find out who killed the director of a musical about to open on Broadway. Also with Debbie Reynolds, Barbara Hale. BBC1, 19 April 1992.

Pirate Prince (1991). Jack Prince (James Hazeldine) is a British rebel in the Caribbean helping the slaves fight for their freedom. An amusing larger-than-life swashbuckler. Also with Thandie Newton, Dearbhla Molloy. Dir: Alan Horrox. ITV, 26 December 1991.

Plain Clothes (1988). Comedy murder mystery with a schoolteacher victim, and a cop who goes back to the classroom to sort out the suspects and let his brother off the hook as suspect No. 1. With Arliss Howard, Diane Ladd. Dir: Martha Coolidge. BBC1, 4 March 1992.

Playing Away (1986). British comedy about a village cricket match. (Unclear whether it was made originally for TV or the cinema, but it did have a UK cinema release on 6 November 1987, and was fully reviewed in the 1988–9 *Film Review*.) Channel 4, 8 August 1991.

Poirot. Agatha Christie's famous Belgian private detective Hercule Poirot (David Suchet), with the help of his very English side-kick Captain Hastings (Hugh Fraser), solves a series of feature-length problem cases in a very civilised manner . . . all brains and no bashings. Very watchable and especially well acted. Screenplays: Clive Exton. **The Dream**. After annoyance at being asked to explain some suicidal dreams Poirot finds more in them than he or anyone else had suspected. Dir: Edward Bennett. ITV, 6 July 1991. **The Adventure of Johnnie Waverly**. Poirot, called in to protect a child from threatened kidnap, isn't as worried as everyone else when the 'criminals' succeed: he's solved the case in advance! Dir: Renny Rye. ITV, 13 July 1991. **The Veiled Lady**. Less of a lady than she looks, as she tries to help her co-conspirator pull off a big jewel robbery under Poirot's nose . . . unsuccessfully, of course. Dir: Edward Bennett. ITV, 20 July 1991. **The Theft of the Royal Ruby**. Poirot's plans for a quiet Christmas are thwarted by the Foreign Office, who recruit him to recover a priceless ruby stolen from the heir to the Egyptian throne. Dir: Andrew Grieve. ITV, 29 December 1991.

Poison Ivy (1985). Yet another failed attempt to re-make a cinema comedy; life in an American summer camp for youngsters. It wasn't that good as a cinema film, but now . . . With Michael J. Fox, Nancy McKeon, Robert Klein. Dir: Larry Elikann. ITV, 16 November 1991.

The Preppie Murder (1989). Somewhat hypocritical feature about the murder by a prep school graduate of a fellow student in New York's Central Park. At the same time as condemning the media for its salacious treatment of the case, it serves up plenty of salacity itself, leaving a nasty taste in the mouth. With William Baldwin, Danny Aiello, Lara Flynn Boyle. Dir: John Herzfeld. ITV, 13 July 1991.

Prince (1991). Good performances, direction and production cannot hide the switch-off silliness of this story of a man who prefers his snarling Alsatian dog to his pretty French wife. For me the terminal moment came when the dog-owner, on his way to a family day at the seaside, pulls the communication cord so he can rush back to his animal. With Sean Bean, Jackie McGuire. Dir: David Wheatley. BBC1, 6 October 1991.

The Prince and the Pauper (1962). Poor-relative, made-for-TV re-make (with a cinema release in the UK) of the historical Mark Twain story of Prince Edward VI switching roles with a look-alike. Not a patch on the 1937 Errol Flynn melo or even the less noteworthy earlier re-make. With Guy Williams, Laurence Naismith, Donald Houston. Dir: Don Chaffey. ITV, 18 August 1991.

Prison for Children (1986). Hackneyed story about the new superintendent of a minors' jail who tries to introduce reforms but is met with polite scorn. With John Ritter, Betty Thomas. Dir: Larry Peerce. BBC2, 19 August 1991.

Quantum Leap (1989). The original feature that launched two time-traveller series, which in spite of their leisurely pace have become cult viewing. Definitely amusing. With Scott Bakula, Dean Stockwell, Jennifer Runyon. BBC2, 4 November 1991.

A Question of Attribution (1991). BBC heavyweight production based on the Anthony Blunt affair which emerges as only intermittently gripping. James Fox as the titled renegade, Prunella Scales brilliant as Queen Elizabeth II. Screenplay: Alan Bennett. Dir: John Schlesinger. BBC1, 20 October 1991.

Quincy: Go Fight City Hall – to the Death (1976). TV's popular pathologist Quincy finds frustration and worse when he tries to explain to the authorities that their candidate for the hot chair, as the rapist killer, wasn't strong enough to have committed the crime. With Jack Klugman, Lynette Mettey, Garry Walberg. Dir: E. W. Swackhamer. ITV, 20 July 1991.

Rachel River (1987). Pamela Reed as the radio journalist whose regular programme about other people's lives makes her realise her own is reaching crisis point. Quite interesting, but oh so slow! Dir: Sandy Smolan. BBC2, 10 January 1992.

The Rating Game (1984). Very funny sharp satire on American TV and the struggle to bump up the ratings. Directed by and starring Danny De Vito. Also with Rhea Perlman (his real-life wife). Channel 4, 17 December 1991.

The Reluctant Agent (1989). Comedy spoof about an injured FBI agent persuading her waitress sister to stand in for her. Frothy fun. With Jackee, Richard Lawson. Dir: Paul Lynch. ITV, 3 January 1992.

Resting Place (1986). Racial prejudice in deep-South Georgia flares up when a Vietnam veteran tries to bury a black war hero in a white cemetery. With Morgan Freeman, M. Emmet Walsh. Dir: John Korty. BBC2, 11 May 1992.

The Richest Woman in the World (1987). A controversial title, as she surely wasn't wealthier than Queen Elizabeth II? Anyway, it takes a two-part feature to tell the story of the filthy-rich Woolworth heiress Barbara Hutton, for whom the money didn't bring happiness, in spite of seven husbands, one of them Cary Grant! And with all the fortune spent she died poor, drunk and doped in 1979. Only mildly enjoyable. With Farrah Fawcett, James Read, Burl Ives. ITV: Part 1, 15 August 1991; Part 2, 16 August 1991.

Riviera (1987). Another pilot that didn't lead anywhere. An American ex-agent finds plenty to keep him busy when he comes to Britain to re-open his late father's mansion. With Ben Masters, Elyssa Davalos, Richard Hamilton. Dir: John Frankenheimer. ITV, 6 November 1991.

Roe v. Wade (1989). Determinedly balanced drama about a legal battle over an abortion – set in America in the 1970s. With Holly Hunter, Amy Madigan. Dir: Gregory Hoblit. BBC1, 11 March 1992.

The Roommate (1984). John Updike's amusing story of a couple of mismatched students sharing a room in college in the 1950s. With Lance Guest and Barry Miller. Dir: Nell Cox. Channel 4, 28 May 1992.

The Rose and the Jackal (1990). Promising story of Pinkerton, founder of the famous detective agency, turns out to be less than interesting thanks to poor production qualities (Christopher Reeve sporting facial hair and funny Scots accent as Pinkerton), unconvincing American Civil War background and a feeling of general malaise. A letdown. Also with Madolyn Smith Osborne. Dir: Jack Gold. BBC1, 21 June 1992.

Roses Are for the Rich (1987). Turn off your incredulity and settle down to enjoy this totally unrealistic drama about an Appalachian coalminer's daughter out for revenge on her dad's boss, whom she blames for destroying the family. With Lisa Hartman, Bruce Dern. Dir: Michael Miller. BBC1: Part 1, 5 May 1992; Part 2, 6 May 1992.

Runaway! A train without brakes hurtles down a mountain to certain death and disaster. Familiar, of course, but still gripping. With Ben Murphy, Ben Johnson. Dir: David Lowell Rich. ITV, 27 December 1991.

The Ryan White Story (1989). About a boy who contracts AIDS through a faulty blood transfusion, and the subsequent prejudice displayed against him. Said to be a true story. With George C. Scott. Dir: John Herzfeld. ITV, 1 December 1991. (Shown the day before the similar *Go Toward the Light*, also listed here.)

Salvage (1979). Andy Griffith as the rag-and-bone man who has a plan to build a moon rocket from his junk and bring back enough abandoned goods from the moon to make his fortune. Also with Joel Higgins, Trish Stewart. Dir: Lee Philips. ITV, 29 June 1992.

Scandal Sheet (1985). Burt Lancaster brings some distinction to this otherwise unremarkable film about an unscrupulous magazine publisher who will stop at nothing in order to get a story and boost his circulation. (Seems familiar? Maybe you saw *Sweet Smell of Success*.) Also with Pamela Reed, Robert Urich, Lauren Hutton. Dir: David Lowell Rich. ITV, 26 April 1992.

The Secret Life of Kathy McCormick (1988). Cinderella-ish romantic comedy. With Barbara Eden. Dir: Robert Lewis. BBC2, 9 September 1991.

She Knows Too Much (1988). Pilot feature that didn't make the grade: about a golden-hearted female cat burglar and a flakey sort of secret agent collaborating to solve the murders. Some critics – including me – thought it was good enough to justify a series. Likeable, amusing performances by Meredith Baxter Burney, Robert Urich. Dir: Paul Lynch. BBC1, 26 November 1991.

Sherlock Holmes in New York (1976). Roger Moore as the famous sleuth sorting out his old enemy Moriarty (John Huston) in the Big Apple. Good chuckly entertainment. Dir: Boris Sagal. ITV, 29 March 1992.

Side by Side (1988). Amusing little comedy about three old friends who, bored with life, start up a firm selling sportswear for the over 65s and do so surprisingly well they spark off a reaction from another fashion house. With

Milton Berle, Sid Caesar, Danny Thomas. Dir: Jack Bender. ITV, 26 December 1991.

Single Bars, Single Women (1984). Far too serious for its subject, so if it were not for some good work from an excellent cast (Tony Danza, Paul Michael Glaser, Shelley Hack etc.) this would lose interest – and its audience – along the way. Dir: Harry Winer. Channel 4, 11 February 1992.

Six Against the Rock (1987). No dancing here; but a story about Alcatraz in 1946 and six optimists who plan to break out. The would-be escapees include David Carradine, Jan Michael-Vincent and Richard Dysart. Dir: Paul Wendkos, who does a very professional job. Channel 4, 5 November 1991.

A Small Dance (1991). Gloomy British film about a teenage girl who finds herself pregnant and has a pretty rough time of it. Set in the Fens of East Anglia. Winner of a Prix Europa special prize, awarded by the Council of Europe. With Kate Hardie, James Hazeldine. Dir: Alan Horrox. ITV, 3 June 1992.

Some Other Spring (1991). Young mother Jenny Seagrove kidnaps her daughter from her ex-husband, flees to Istanbul, where her boyfriend should have met her at the airport but doesn't, and is soon involved in a terrorist plot. A handsome and mysterious South American and lots of watching eyes keep up the tension. A major production budget, fascinating locations, good technical quality and nice performances make it all very watchable. Also with Dinsdale Landen, Jean-Claude Dauphin. Dir and Screenplay: Peter Duffell. ITV, 23 July 1991.

Spectre (1977). Polished production and attention to detail plus an amusing performance by Gig Young help to mitigate this daft story of Robert Culp's investigation into the weird goings-on at the home of wealthy John Hurt. Also with Gordon Jackson. Dir: Clive Donner. ITV, 19 January 1992.

Spies, Lies and Naked Thighs (1988). Really crazy, slapstick-filled comedy in which a house guest involves his bemused host in a murder case. With Ed Begley Jr, Harry Anderson, Linda Purl. Dir: James Frawley. BBC1, 3 August 1991.

A Stoning in Fulham County (1988). When the case of a farmer's child killed by teenagers comes to court it is complicated by the family's religious convictions. Predictable drama. With Ken Olin, Jill Eikenberry. ITV, 17 December 1991.

Strange Voices (1987). Probably sincere but less than convincing story of a mother who finds she has a schizophrenic daughter on her hands. With Valerie Harper, Nancy McKeon. Dir: Arthur Seidelman. ITV, 10 July 1991.

Stranger in My Bed (1986). Forget the children's story about the Three Bears; this is a deadly serious (if familiar) story about a housewife's accident resulting in loss of memory, even of her family. With Lindsay Wagner, Armand Assante. Dir: Larry Elikann. ITV, 2 January 1992.

Stuck with Each Other (1989). Enjoyable, fast-paced comedy-thriller with boss Richard Crenna and saucy secretary Tyne Daly (from *Cagney and Lacy*) trying to keep the million dollars that has fallen into their laps but which the crooks reckon is theirs. Start of chase! Dir: Georg Stanford Brown (Ms Daly's ex). ITV, 17 August 1991.

Taken Away (1989). Too many missed chances in this story about an overworked single-parent mother who struggles to regain her child after it is taken away from her by the authorities. With Valerie Bertinelli. Dir: John Patterson. Channel 4, 1 October 1991.

A Tale of Two Cities (1984). An animated version of the oft-filmed Charles Dickens classic about the French Revolution and the 'Far better thing . . .' of sacrificial Sidney Carton. ITV, 26 December 1991.

Target Harry (1968). Very much *The Maltese Falcon* in a different setting, but sadly failing to match that classic movie. With Vic Morrow, Suzanne Pleshette, Victor Buono. Dir: Henry Neill – aka Roger Corman. ITV, 5 April 1992.

The Tenth Man (1988). Not exactly compulsive viewing – but nicely produced. A rich Parisian lawyer pays another man to take his place in front of a Nazi firing squad, and after the war observes the effect of the switch on the dead man's family. Based on a Graham Green novella. With Anthony Hopkins. Dir: Jack Gold. ITV, 2 September 1991.

Terror Out of the Sky (1978). A follow-up to *Savage Bees* – and even sillier! With Efrem Zimbalist Jr, Dan Haggerty. Dir: Lee H. Katzin. ITV, 19 April 1992.

Things That Go Bump in the Night (1989). Courtroom whodunnit played out in style! The clothes are as important as this lady lawyer's cases. With Jacklyn Jellyn, Celeste Holm, Ralph Bellamy. Dir: E. W. Swackhammer. ITV, 28 June 1992.

This Child is Mine (1985). Story of a single mother who decides to allow her child to be adopted, but subsequently changes her mind, with all the legal and human snags involved. Familiar material. With Nancy McKeon, Lindsay Wagner, Chris Sarandon. Dir: David Greene. BBC2, 23 September 1991.

This Wife for Hire (1985). Daft – and the fact that it is based on a true story makes it no less so – story about a happily married housewife who announces she is for hire, as a housewife – with all the obvious complications! With Pam Dawber. Dir: Jim Blake. ITV, 29 September 1991.

Thornwell (1981). Absorbing true story about an ex-GI who sued the government for the lasting mental effects of the drugs administered to him during the war when he was suspected of being a spy. With Vincent Gardenia. Dir: Harry Moses. Channel 4, 18 February 1992.

Thunderboat Row (1988). The novelty in this otherwise familiar cops and drug smugglers melo is that the chases are all by fast boat instead of fast cars. Florida locations. With Chad Everett, Nick Corri. Dir: Thomas J. Wright. ITV, 17 August 1991.

A Time to Triumph (1984). Patty Duke is better than her material in this true story about a housewife who becomes a helicopter pilot when her husband has a heart attack and she is forced to become the family breadwinner. Also with Joseph Bologna. Dir: Noel Black. ITV, 12 February 1992.

To Each His Own (1988). True story about a hospital mix-up. When a couple discover that the child they nurtured as their own is somebody else's, they set out to find their own youngster. With Juli Watson, Hilton McRae, Robert Lang. Dir: Moira Armstrong. ITV, 5 August 1991.

To Heal a Nation (1988). True story about a veteran GI who, after two years in Vietnam, starts a campaign to build a Vietnam Veterans Memorial. With Eric Roberts. Dir: Michael Pressman. Channel 4, 23 April 1992.

Trenchcoat in Paradise (1989). When things get too hot for him in his native New Jersey, Dirk Benedict moves to Hawaii to carry on his private-eyeing, and finds the cases no easier to solve in his not very expert way. A tolerably entertaining comedy-thriller. Also with Catherine Oxenberg, Bruce Dern. Dir: Martha Coolidge. BBC1, 1 October 1991.

Two Fathers' Justice (1985). Temptingly switch-offable. Two ill-assorted dads join forces to take revenge on the baddies who killed their respective progeny. With Robert Conrad, George Hamilton. Dir: Rod Holcomb. ITV, 7 June 1992.

Two Friends (1987). Sensitive and charming Australian TV film about two teenager girlfriends struggling with the generation gap. Unusually (but in this case very effectively) the whole story is told backwards. A real refresher. With Emma Coles, Kris Bidenko. Dir: Jane Campion (who directed *An Angel at My Table*).

The Two Worlds of Jennie Logan (1979). Unhappy housewife Lindsay

Wagner discovers that when she dons an old dress she is able to escape into the world of a century ago, which doesn't prove to be the utopia she imagined. Also with Marc Singer. Dir: Frank de Fellita. BBC1, 3 September 1991.

Uncle Tom's Cabin (1987). Surprisingly this is the first time since 1927 that Harriet Beecher Stowe's classic story of slavery in the Deep South has been used as screen material. Sadly, a paceless picture but there are rewards in it for the patient viewer. With Avery Brooks, Phylicia Rashad, Bruce Dern. Dir: Stan Lathan. BBC2, 14 January 1992.

Vintage Murder. Routine whodunnit from New Zealand, written by Ngaio Marsh, about Det. Insp. Alleyn (that's good old George Baker) making a train journey with a group of scared theatricals. Will the female director's (Glynis McNicoll) hubbie be correct in thinking he is due to become a murder victim? ITV, 21 September 1991.

Voices Within (1990). Two-part true story about a woman who became nearly a score of different personalities as a result of a childhood trauma. With Shelley Long, Tom Conti. Dir: Lamont Johnson. BBC1. Part 1, 27 August 1991; Part 2, 28 August 1991.

Voyage of Terror: The Achille Lauro Affair (1989). Burt Lancaster as the unfortunate disabled passenger who was murdered and thrown overboard by Palestinian terrorists after they hijacked the Italian cruise liner *Achille Lauro*. Also with Eva Marie Saint. Dir: Alberto Negrin. ITV: Part 1, 8 September 1991; Part 2, 9 September 1991.

Where Pigeons Go to Die (1989) Shamelessly sentimental, overdone story of the relationship between a 10-year-old boy and his pigeon-fancying old grandad. With Michael Landon (who also directed), Art Carney, Robert Hy Gorman. BBC2, 19 March 1992.

The Writing on the Blotting Paper (1990). Disappointing French TV whodunnit about murder on the film set. Far too long for its own good. With Francois Perrot, Pascale Petit. Dir: Pierre Boutron. ITV, 27 February 1992.

The Yellow Wallpaper (1989). Ghost chiller. A young doctor and his wife find the bedroom of their new house, with its strangely coloured wallpaper, hardly conducive to sound sleeping. With Julia Watson, Stephen Dillane. Dir: John Clive. BBC2, 2 January 1992.

Video Releases

FILMS BETWEEN JULY 1991 AND JUNE 1992

ANTHONY HAYWARD

As British video dealers experienced a second depressed year, an American film executive was pronouncing home video Hollywood's 'saviour'. Peter Hoffman, president of Carolco Pictures, told the 1991 VSDA dealers' convention in Las Vegas that video had significantly lower marketing costs than cinema releases, which had quadrupled over the previous ten years. Actor Martin Sheen emphasised the importance of film's 'rival' medium by telling the convention that concluding a home video deal had become crucial before shooting a picture.

Suddenly, Hollywood was acknowledging the importance of video. But that was no consolation to British dealers, who had lost about a quarter of their rental trade in two years. British distributors responded by increasing their marketing budgets by a massive 23 per cent, to £13.3 million, during 1991.

The two most rented tapes of the year were *Ghost* and *Home Alone*, both summer releases that gave dealers a welcome boost. In previous years, many distributors had held back videos of box-office hits until the busier autumn period. Other top rental titles of 1991 included *Total Recall*, *Three Men and a Little Lady*, *Pretty Woman*, *Die Hard 2*, *RoboCop 2* and *The Silence of the Lambs*.

While rentals were disappointing, the 'sell-through' market of budget-price tapes experienced a boom, reaching an all-time high. More than 55 million were sold, an increase of 13 million on 1990. Market leader was Buena Vista, with its Disney classics continuing to find an eager market. The 51-year-old *Fantasia* became the biggest-selling British video ever, with sales of 3.2 million – almost double those of the previous No 1, *Lady and the Tramp*.

Like *Pinocchio, Sleeping Beauty* and *Lady and the Tramp* during the previous three years, *Fantasia* was released into the Christmas market for a limited period only. After the 99-day availability to dealers ended, Walt Disney Studios 'retired' some of the film's sequences and started work on adding new music and animation for a sequel to be known as *Fantasia Continued*, for cinema release in 1996 or 1997. This continuing development of the film was apparently Walt Disney's own original concept. Another, more recent Disney picture, *The Little Mermaid* – the cinema's most successful animated film ever – sold 1.5 million copies on tape during 1991, fresh from its £4 million success at the British box office.

One bone of contention in an industry that seems to thrive on controversy was the screening of *Home Alone* on BSkyB's Movie Channel just nine months after its video release. Some dealers were concerned that the reduction in the usual one-year satellite holdback would set a precedent, and several other 'early' screenings followed.

Absolute Strangers (First Independent) August

Aces Iron Eagle III (Guild) April

The Addams Family (Columbia Tri-Star) June

The Adventures of Milo and Otis (Virgin Vision) December

After Dark My Sweet (Virgin Vision) December

Aftermath (ITC) July

Against the Odds (New World/High Fliers) September

Air America (Guild) July

Aladdin (Genesis) September

Alice (20:20 Vision) February

Alien (wide-screen version) (FoxVideo) August

Aliens Special Edition (FoxVideo) April

Alligator/Alligator II: The Mutation (two films on one tape) (Braveworld) October

Almost an Angel (CIC) July

Always Remember I Love You (Odyssey) July

Ambulance (EV) September

American Friends (Virgin) November

American Graffiti (CIC) July

The Amityville Curse (Virgin Vision) October

Angel in Red (20:20 Vision) January

Angel of the Island (Moonlight) April

Another Pair of Aces (20:20 Vision) April

The Antagonist (CIC) March

Arachnophobia (Hollywood/Buena Vista) July

The Arrival (Braveworld) May

Au Pair (High Fliers) February

Awakenings (RCA/Columbia) September

Backdraft (CIC) March

Bad Attitude (ITC) October

Bad Girls from Mars (High Fliers) November

Beastmaster 2 (Medusa) October

Bed and Breakfast (EV) March

A Bed of Lies (Warner) May

Bethune (RCA/Columbia) October

The Big Picture (20:20 Vision) September

The Big Slice (RCA/Columbia) August

The Big Steal (Warner West Coast) August

Bill and Ted's Bogus Journey (20:20 Vision) June

Bite (Moonlight) June

Black Magic Woman (CIC) June

Black Star (Medusa) July

Black Widow (After Hours) July

Blackmail (CIC) June

Blind Judgement (New World/High Fliers) October

Blonde Forces (Moonlight) June

Blood Games (RCA/Columbia) August

Blood Moon (Capital) July

Blood Oath (RCA/Columbia) November

Blood Red (RCA/Columbia) August

Blood and Sand (First Generation) February
Body Parts (CIC) June
The Bonfire of the Vanities (Warner West Coast) September
Born to Fight (VPD) December
Born to Ride (Warner) November
Boyfriend from Hell (Warner East Coast) October
Boyz N the Hood (Columbia Tri-Star) April
Breakin' the Rules (Virgin Vision) July
Breathing Fire (VPD) August
The Bride (After Hours) July
Broken Badges (Columbia Tri-Star) April
Brother Future (Warner) June
Buddy's Song (FoxVideo) August
Bump in the Night (Odyssey) August
Bush Pilots (Silhouette) April
By the Sword (EV) May

Cafe Flesh (Silhouette) March
Caged Fury (RCA/Columbia) November
Camp Cucamonga (NBC/Ingram) August
Captain Power – The Legend Begins (Genesis/Excalibur) July
Captive (Capital) June
Carnal Crimes (Medusa) June
Carolina Skeletons (New Age) March
Cast a Deadly Spell (Warner) April
Champion Fighter (VPD) November
Chance of a Lifetime (Guild) March
The Chase (Capital) August
Chattahoochee (Columbia Tri-Star) April
Chernobyl – The Final Warning (First Independent) September
Child of Darkness, Child of Light (CIC) February
Child's Play II (CIC) September
Christmas on Division Street (Odyssey) March
Circle of Fear (Virgin Vision) June
City Slickers (First Independent) March
Class Action (FoxVideo) January
Close My Eyes (Artificial Eye) December
Cold Dog Soup (FoxVideo) September
Cold Justice (20:20 Vision) September
College Kickboxer (VPD) February
The Comfort of Strangers (20:20 Vision) July
Committed (RCA/Columbia) October
The Commitments (FoxVideo) April
The Company (Warner) September
The Company II: Sacrifices (Warner East Coast) November
Comrades in Arms (High Fliers) June
Conagher (First Independent) April
Conspiracy of Silence (Odyssey) February
Cover Up (Guild) September
Crackdown (RCA/Columbia) January
Crazy from the Heart (First Independent) February
Crazy People (CIC) August
Creepers (20:20 Vision) March
Crime Lords (Warner) November
Crimes of Passion (ITC) December
Criminal Justice (Warner) October
The Crossing (20:20 Vision) October
Cry in the Wild (Capital) December

Curse of the Catwoman (Silhouette) December
Cyrano de Bergerac (Artificial Eye) August

Daddy (VPD) March
Dance of the Damned (Virgin Vision) June
Dancing in the Forest (Virgin Vision) June
Dances with Wolves (Guild) November
Dangerous Passion (Capital) August
Dark Avenger (Columbia Tri-Star) April
Dark Secrets (Genesis) May
Dead End Brattigan (Columbia Tri-Star) April
Dead On (Warner) June
Dead Silence (FoxVideo) March
Dead Solid Perfect (Warner) October
Deadly Desire (CIC) August
Deadly Intentions . . . Again? (Warner) October
Deadly Revenge (ITC) July
Deadly Surveillance (First Independent) January
Deadspace (RCA/Columbia) March
Death Dealers (Genesis) September
Death Merchants II (Warner East Coast) August
Deathstalker (Braveworld) September
Deceptions (20:20 Vision) November
Defending Your Life (Warner East Coast) November
Delta Force 3 (Warner) September
Descending Angel (Warner East Coast) September
Desert Law (RCA/Columbia) December
Desperate Hours (FoxVideo) October
The Devil in Miss Jones 3 (After Hours) November
Die Hard (wide-screen version) (FoxVideo) August
Dillinger (Warner East Coast) July
Dinosaurs (Guild) October
Diplomatic Immunity (VPD) October
Disturbed (Warner) January
Do or Die (20:20 Vision) (starring Erik Estrada) April
Do or Die (Genesis) (starring Robert Urich) May
Doc Hollywood (Warner) April
Dogfight (Warner) April
Dollman (EV) June
Dolly Dearest (First Independent) November
The Doors (Guild) October
Double Crossed (Warner) April
Down the Drain (RCA/Columbia) September
Dragon Fight (Warner) December
Dragonfire (CIC) December
Dread's Revenge/Captain Power II (Genesis) December
Dream Machine (First Independent) September
Driving Me Crazy (FoxVideo) April
Driving Miss Daisy Crazy (After Hours) November
Drop Dead Fred (20:20 Vision) March
Dying Young (FoxVideo) March

Earth Angel (Genesis) November
Easy Kill (Genesis) February
Easy Wheels (Virgin Vision) March
Edge of Honour (First Generation/High Fliers) November
Edward Scissorhands (FoxVideo) February
Edward II (Palace) March
Emerald City (High Fliers) July
The Empire Strikes Back (wide-screen version) (FoxVideo) August
Empire City (Warner) June
Encounter at Raven's Gate (RCA/Columbia) October
Everybody Wins (Virgin Vision) October
Everybody's Fine (RCA/Columbia) February
Evil Toons (New Age) April

Fall from Grace (NBC/Ingram) September
False Arrest (Braveworld) February
False Identity (Virgin Vision) April
Fantasia (and deluxe boxed set) (Walt Disney/Buena Vista) (November)
Fantasy (RCA/Columbia) February
Fast Food (Genesis) April
Fatal Exposure (CIC) September
Fast Getaway (First View/First Independent) July
Fatal Sky (RCA/Columbia) July
Fear (First Independent) July
The Feud (High Fliers) January
Fever (20:20 Vision) May
Field of Fire (CIC) May
Fight for Freedom (Genesis) August
Filofax (Hollywood) October
The Final Alliance (EV) November
The Final Days (RCA/Columbia) November
The Final Sanction (20:20 Vision) October
The Finishing Touch (20:20 Vision) June
Fire, Ice and Dynamite (EV) November
Firehead (RCA/Columbia) March
Fires Within (Warner) May
The First Power (Warner West Coast) August
The Fisher King (20:20 Vision) May
Fist of Fury II (VPD) October
The Flash 2 – The Revenge of the Trickster (Warner) November
Flight of the Black Angel (CIC) November
Flight of the Intruder (CIC) August
Flirting (Warner) May
Flying Blind (NBC/Ingram) October
Force of the Dragon (VPD) June
The Forgotten One (Warner East Coast) November
Frame Up (High Fliers) March
Frankenstein General Hospital (Virgin Vision) August
Frankenstein Unbound (Warner West Coast) July
Freak Show (RCA/Columbia) September
FX2 – The Deadly Art of Illusion (RCA/Columbia) March

Gettysburg (Genesis) October
Ghost Writer (RCA/Columbia) September
The Godfather Part III (CIC) December

Going Under (Warner East Coast) August
Golden Years (Braveworld) April
Good Evening Vietnam (After Hours) February
Graveyard Shift (20:20 Vision) November
The Great LA Earthquake (Capital) August
Green Card (Buena Vista) September
Grizzly Adams, The Legend Continues (Braveworld) December
Guilty by Suspicion (Warner East Coast) November

Hamlet (20:20 Vision) October
Hangfire (20:20 Vision) January
Hangin' with the Homeboys (20:20 Vision) June
Happy Together (Guild) January
Harbour Beat (CIC) September
The Hard Way (CIC) April
Harley (High Fliers) October
Harley Davidson and the Marlboro Man (MGM/UA) April
Hate to See You Go (Silhouette) April
The Haunted (FoxVideo) November
He Said, She Said (CIC) December
Heaven Tonight (First Independent) August
H.E.L.P. (CIC) August
Highlander II – The Quickening (EV) October
The Hitman (Warner) June
Hollister (CIC) May
Home Alone (FoxVideo) July
Homer and Eddie (Virgin Vision) November
Homicide (First Independent) May
Hot in the City (Silhouette) May
Hot Shots! (FoxVideo) May
The Hot Spot (RCA/Columbia) July
Hotel California (After Hours) September
House 4: The Repossession (Medusa) September
Hudson Hawk (20:20 Vision) January
Human Shield (Warner) May
Hyper Sapien: People from Another Planet (Warner West Coast) November

Ice Pawn (River First/SGE) July
I'm Dangerous Tonight (CIC) September
The Immortaliser (20:20 Vision) October
Impromptu (RCA/Columbia) October
In the Best Interests of the Children (Odyssey) April
In Broad Daylight (New World) August
In a Child's Name (High Fliers) May
In a Stranger's Hand (Odyssey) May
In the Cold of the Night (CIC) October
In the Line of Duty (Genesis) August
In the Spirit (Warner West Coast) August
An Inconvenient Woman (Odyssey) January
Inner Sanctum (Columbia Tri-star) May
Intimate Stranger (Medusa) February
Invasion Force (20:20 Vision) April
Invisible Maniac (Medusa) November
Iron Maze (First Independent) June

Ironclads (First Independent) May
It (Warner East Coast) August
The Ivory Hunters (Warner) January

Jacob's Ladder (Guild) May
Jailbirds (Genesis) October
Jealous Eyes (New Age) April
Judgement (Warner) September
Jungle Fever (CIC) May

K2 (EV) March
Karate Cop (EV) February
The Keys (CIC) March
Kick Fighter (VPD) November
Kickboxer from Hell (VPD) July
Kickboxer King (VPD) December
Kickboxer 2 (EV) August
Kidnapped (Genesis) November
Kill Me Again (ITC) September
Killing Mind (20:20 Vision) May
Killing Streets (VPD) November
Kindergarten Cop (CIC) October
King of the Hill (Palace) December
King of New York (Palace) October
King Ralph (CIC) September
A Kiss Before Dying (CIC) February
Kiss Shot (New Age) February
Knight Rider 2000 (CIC) May
Kootenai Brown (New World) January
Kung Fu Genius (VPD) January
Kung Fu Kids (VPD) February

LA Story (Guild) December
Ladies' Game (SGE) July
Laid in Heaven (Silhouette) May
Leather Jackets (Medusa) December
Let Him Have It (First Independent) February
Liberty and Bash (SGE) August
Life Stinks (FoxVideo) March
The Lightning Incident (CIC) April
Lily Was Here (20:20 Vision) October
Line of Fire (Warner West Coast) August
The Little Mermaid (Buena Vista) (September)
Little Noises (Columbia Tri-star) May
Living a Lie (Odyssey) March
London Kills Me (Columbia Tri-star) June
The Long Walk Home (FoxVideo) June
Look Who's Talking Too (20:20 Vision) September
The Lookalike (CIC) December
Love and Betrayal (ITC) August
Love at Large (Virgin Vision) July
Love, Lies and Murder (Odyssey) October
Love or Money (RCA/Columbia) January
Lover (SGE) September
The Lust Potion of Dr F (After Hours) September

McBain (Warner) April
Mafia Kid (20:20 Vision) July
Mannequin on the Move (Warner) June

Mario and the Mob (Capital) February
Marked for Death (FoxVideo) January
Martians Go Home (Virgin Vision) May
Matters of the Heart (CIC) July
Maximum Security (High Fliers) December
Meet the Applegates (RCA/Columbia) September
Memories of Midnight (Genesis) December
Meeting Venus (Warner) March
Memphis (First Independent) March
Men at Work (EV) July
Mermaids (Virgin Vision) January
Miami Blues (Virgin Vision) September
Midnight (Braveworld) July
Midnight Fear (New World/High Fliers) July
Midnight Matinee (Virgin Vision) May
Miller's Crossing (FoxVideo) August
Miracle Mile (RCA/Columbia) July
Mirage (Silhouette) December
Mirror Images (Medusa) March
Misery (First Independent) October
Mission of the Shark (New Age/20:20 Vision) December
Mississippi Masala (Palace) April
Mob Boss (Vidmark/High Fliers) September
Mob Story (High Fliers) December
Mob War (RCA/Columbia) March
Modern Love (Medusa) June
Moonlusting (After Hours) July
Mortal Passion (Genesis) February
Mortal Thoughts (Columbia Tristar) April
The Most Dangerous Woman Alive (Braveworld) August
A Mother's Justice (Warner) April
Mr Destiny (Touchstone) September
Mr Johnson (Warner) September
Murder 101 (CIC) December
Murder in New Hampshire (Capital) June
Murderous Vision (CIC) December
Murphy's Fault (Virgin Vision) May
Mutronics the Movie (Medusa) May
My Son Johnny (Odyssey) April

Naked Gun 2½: The Smell of Fear (CIC) January
Naked Tango (Warner) March
Navy Seal (Virgin Vision) March
Near Mrs (Buena Vista) April
Necessary Roughness (CIC) June
Neon City (First Independent) April
Netherworld (CIC) June
The Neverending Story II: The Next Chapter (Warner West Coast) July
The New Adventures of Swamp Thing (CIC) March
New Jack City (Warner) February
Night Eyes (Big Pictures/High Fliers) July
Night of the Hunter (Capital) October
Night Raiders (High Fliers) April
Nightbreed (Warner West Coast) November
Nightmare (Genesis) October
Nightmare on the 13th Floor (CIC) July
Nightshift Nurses (Silhouette) April
9½ Ninjas (Virgin Vision) January
976-EVIL II: The Return (Medusa) January

Not of This World (CIC) November
Not Without My Daughter (MGM/UA) October
Nukie (20:20 Vision) January

O Pioneers (Warner) June
Object of Beauty (Buena Vista) January
Odd Ball Hall (EV) July
Oh What a Night (Silhouette) December
Omen IV: The Awakening (FoxVideo) February
Once Around (CIC) January
One Against the Wind (Odyssey) May
One Good Cop (Touchstone) February
1001 Nights (20:20 Vision) January
One Wild Night (Guild) August
Only the Lonely (FoxVideo) June
Operation Condor (EV) April
Opportunity Knocks (Guild) August
Oscar (Touchstone) April
Other People's Money (Warner) May
Out for Justice (Warner East Coast) December
Out of Time (Braveworld) November
Over Her Dead Body (First Independent) October
The Overthrow (VPD) September

Pacific Heights (FoxVideo) September
Palomino (VPD) May
Paradise Calling (Moving Pictures) April
Paris Trout (Palace) November
Party Favours (First View) June
The People Under the Stairs (CIC) June
The Perfect Bride (Virgin Vision) April
The Perfect Weapon (CIC) February
Perfectly Normal (Palace) July
Pink Cadillac (Warner West Coast) September
The Pit and the Pendulum (EV) October
The Platinum Triangle (Columbia Tri-star) April
Play Christy for Me (Silhouette) April
Playin' Dirty (Silhouette) March
The Pleasure Principle (Palace) April
Point Break (FoxVideo) May
Popcorn (Transatlantic) March
The Pope Must Die (RCA/Columbia) January
Postcards from the Edge (RCA/Columbia) August
Prayer of the Rollerboys (First Independent) January
Predator 2 (FoxVideo) November
Pretty Peaches – The Quest (After Hours) September
Prime Target (New Age) June
Prison Stories – Women on the Inside (Warner West Coast) August
Problem Child (CIC) November
Proof (Artificial Eye) March
Prospero's Books (Palace) March
Psycho IV (CIC) November
Pump up the Volume (20:20 Vision) February
Puppetmaster III (CIC) April
Pushed to the Limit (ITC) June

Q&A (Virgin Vision) August
Quest for the Mighty Sword (RCA/Columbia) October
Quick Change (Warner East Coast) October
Quicker Than the Eye (Genesis) April
Quiet Days in Clichy (Palace) September
Quigley Down Under (MGM/UA) October

Race for Glory (20:20 Vision) March
Racquel's Addiction (VPD) May
Rad (Warner West Coast) August
A Rage in Harlem (Palace) February
Rage of Innocence (Genesis) December
The Rain Killer (RCA/Columbia) September
Rainbow Drive (20:20 Vision) October
Rambling Rose (Guild) April
Raw Nerve (20:20 Vision) June
Real Men Eat Keisha (After Hours) November
Red Surf (Medusa) February
Red Wind (CIC) January
Regarding Henry (CIC) April
The Return of the Jedi (wide-screen version) (FoxVideo) August
The Return of Superfly (VPD) September
Return of the Tiger (VPD) August
Return to the Blue Lagoon (RCA/Columbia) February
Return to Justice (Genesis) February
Reunion (RCA/Columbia) December
Reversal of Fortune (20:20 Vision) July
Riding the Edge (EV) December
Riff Raff (Palace) September
Ring of Fire (VPD) April
Robin Hood (FoxVideo) September
Robin Hood: Prince of Thieves (Warner) January
Rocketeer (Buena Vista) March
Rocky V (MGM/Pathe) August
Romeo and Juliet (After Hours) July
Roots of Evil (Warner) May
A Row of Crows (CIC) February
Run (Hollywood) August
Runaway Dreams (Capital) February
Runaway Father (Odyssey) November
The Runestone (EV) June
Running Against Time (CIC) October
The Russia House (Warner West Coast) August

Sam's Son (Genesis) November
Satin Angels (After Hours) September
Scanners II: The New Order (Warner East Coast) October
Scenes from a Mall (Touchstone) November
Schizo (Medusa) May
Scissors (First Independent) August
Seeds of Tragedy (FoxVideo) October
Separate But Equal (Odyssey) November
Servants of Twilight (First Independent) May
Seven Minutes (Warner) September
Shades of LA (CIC) March
Shadow of a Doubt (CIC) May
Shattered (Columbia Tri-star) May
Short Time (20:20 Vision) August
Showdown in Little Tokyo (Warner) May

Sibling Rivalry (First Independent) November
The Silence of the Lambs (20:20 Vision) November
Silhouette (CIC) August
Sinset Boulevard (After Hours) November
The Sitter (FoxVideo) November
Ski School (First Independent) December
Sleeping with the Enemy (FoxVideo) October
Slick Honey (VPD) December
Soapdish (CIC) May
Soda Cracker (RCA/Columbia) November
Somebody Has to Shoot the Picture (CIC) July
Sometimes They Come Back (EV) May
Son of Darkness (First Generation) January
Son of Morning Star (Odyssey) October
Space Case (Moving Pictures) April
Spellcaster (RCA/Columbia) October
Spirit of the Eagle (SGE) July
Spirits (Big Pictures) August
The Spring (Braveworld) November
Star 90 (Silhouette) March
Star Wars (wide-screen version) (FoxVideo) August
Star Worms II (Virgin Vision) April
State of Grace (Virgin Vision) February
State Park (Virgin Vision) April
Stay the Night (New World) March
Staying Together (20:20 Vision) August
Stepfather III (ITC) April
Stepping Out (CIC) March
Stop at Nothing (First Independent) July
Stranger in the Family (New Age) June
Street Asylum (Medusa) November
Stroke of Midnight (Buena Vista) November
Suburban Commando (EV) April
Sunny After Dark (After Hours) February
Surefire (VPD) June
Survive the Savage Sea (Warner) March
Sweet Poison (CIC) January
Sweet Revenge (Buena Vista) November
Swingers Ink (Silhouette) March
Switch (Columbia Tri-star) June

Taking It All Off (First View) June
The Taking of Beverly Hills (Guild) June
Tales from the Dark Side: The Movie (Columbia Tri-star) May
Taste of Hemlock (Braveworld) July
Teen Agent (Warner) March
Teenage Mutant Ninja Turtles II – Secret of the Ooze (FoxVideo) December
The Ten Million Dollar Getaway (CIC) October
The Tender (EV) March
Terminal Bliss (Warner) February
Terminator 2: Judgement Day (Guild) February
Thelma and Louise (Warner) January
They Came from Outer Space (CIC) January
Thick as Thieves (Capital) September
This Gun for Hire (CIC) October
Three Men and a Little Lady (Touchstone) August
Thrill Street Blues (After Hours) February
'Til I Kissed Ya (Warner) January
Till Death Us Do Part (Odyssey) June

Time of the Beast (CIC) June
Time of the Gypsies (RCA/Columbia) September
Time to Kill (High Fliers) June
Time to Kill – In the Line of Duty III (Genesis) October
Timebomb (EV) January
Timescape (Medusa) April
To Catch a Killer (Odyssey) February
To My Daughter (Warner West Coast) November
Too Hot To Handle (Hollywood Pictures) January
Top Squad (VPD) July
Total Exposure (High Fliers) April
Touch and Die (ITC) February
Toy Soldiers (20:20 Vision) April
Trancers II (EV) September
Transylvania Twist (Warner East Coast) July
Triple Cross (American Imperial/VPD) January
True Colors (CIC) October
True Identity (Buena Vista) May
Truly, Madly, Deeply (Buena Vista) December

Trust (Palace) November
Turn Back the Clock (Ingram) July
The Two Jakes (CIC) April

Under Suspicion (20:20 Vision) June

Valentino Returns (High Fliers) March
Vampire's Kiss (20:20 Vision) July
Vestige of Honour (CIC) December
Victim of Beauty (Capital) (starring Sally Kellerman) January
Victim of Beauty (Odyssey) (starring William Devane) June
Victim of Love (Capital) November
Vigilante Cop (ITC) August
V. I. Warshawski (Hollywood) June

War Party (RCA/Columbia) October
Wedlock (EV) November
Welcome Home Roxy Carmichael (20:20 Vision) March
What About Bob (Buena Vista) June

Where Angels Fear to Tread (20:20 Vision) December
The Whereabouts of Jenny (Odyssey) December
Whispers (20:20 Vision) August
White Fang (Buena Vista) December
White Hunter, Black Heart (Warner East Coast) July
White Light (Columbia Tristar) May
White Palace (CIC) November
Who Will Love My Children? (Odyssey) May
Whore (Palace) August
Wild Texas Wind (Braveworld) June
Windprints (Virgin Vision) September
Wise Guys (Genesis) April
Wishful Thinking (Medusa) August
Women and Men (Warner West Coast) July
Writer's Block (CIC) April

Year of the Gun (First Independent) April
Young Soul Rebels (Braveworld) March

Zandalee (ITC) November
Zapped Again (RCA/Columbia) November

The Ten Most Promising Faces of 1992

JAMES CAMERON-WILSON

Halle Berry. Over the last handful of years a host of stunning Afro-American actresses have slunk seductively across our screens. Stand-outs include Shari Headley in *Coming to America*, the honey-voiced Cynda Williams in *Mo' Better Blues*, Anne-Marie Johnson in *True Identity*, Cynthia Bond in *Def by Temptation*, Robin Givens in *A Rage in Harlem*, Vanessa Williams in *Harley Davidson and the Marlboro Man* – and, oh, countless more.

But few have managed to combine an incendiary sex appeal with a talent to win over the critics. The exception to the rule is Halle Berry. Winner of various beauty pageants and the official Miss Teen All-American of 1985, Halle was determined to avoid typecasting from the outset. This she did by playing the role of the crack addict Vivian in Spike Lee's *Jungle Fever*. Besides frequenting crack houses with an undercover cop and discussing the pitfalls of addiction with junkies in rehab, the actress was allowed to direct her own scenes with co-star Samuel L. Jackson.

'Spike let Sam and me do it because we'd gone to the crack houses to see them,' she explains. 'Spike didn't go because he was scared to death.'

Halle was so convincing in the part that she found herself in danger of being typecast. 'You'd be surprised how many offers I've had to play crackheads,' she says. Fortunately, she's avoided the trap.

Raised in the suburbs of Cleveland, the 25-year-old actress won her first professional break on a three-week USO tour with Bob Hope. After a spot of real-life modelling she played a TV model in the sitcom *Living Dolls* and also appeared on *Knot's Landing* as Frank's girlfriend, Debbie Porter.

She then auditioned for the female lead in *Strictly Business*, but lost the role because the director, Rolando Hudson, was 'tired of people thinking that to be beautiful, you have to have fair skin'. Nevertheless, when Hudson was replaced by director Kevin Hooks, Halle got the part after all.

Introduced in soft-focus slow-motion as a vision of sensuality, Halle became an instant sex goddess for every heterosexual male lucky enough to see the

Halle Berry as stripper Cory, seen here with Damon Wayans, in Tony Scott's express-train of a comedy, The Last Boy Scout

film. The trade paper *Variety* glowed, 'Given a glamorous intro not unlike Bo Derek's in *10* . . . Berry is [the] pic's revelation as a sexy and intelligent young woman . . .'

Next, the goddess won the role of Damon Wayans's short-lived stripper girlfriend in *The Last Boy Scout* (a hit), and was then signed up to star alongside Eddie Murphy, no less, in the megabudgeted comedy *Boomerang*.

With so many black American films now being made, Halle admits, 'I feel lucky to be coming along at the time I am. Five years ago I'd have been suicidal.' We wish her luck.

Caroline Goodall

Caroline Goodall. Amid the confusion, special effects and star cameos of Steven Spielberg's *Hook*, one actress displayed a calm and a resolve that marked her out from the rest. Although playing the significant part of Robin Williams's wife, Moira Banning, Caroline Goodall was the only member of the adult cast who didn't have a hit movie attached to her name. As Mrs Banning represented the only anchor to reality in the entire epic fantasy, perhaps this was intentional on Spielberg's part.

And while the likes of Dustin Hoffman, Bob Hoskins and Maggie Smith chewed up the scenery whole, Caroline Goodall was quietly convincing, authoritative and moving as the wife caught up in a snowballing nightmare. She was also very beautiful, without sacrificing her maternal standing. She held her own.

Born in London, Caroline lived very near to Kensington Gardens as a child, where the statue of Peter Pan held a particular fascination for her. She was also interested in acting at an early age,

and joined the National Youth Theatre to prove it. Later, she graduated from Bristol University with an honours degree in drama and went on to tackle the classics in regional productions of *Romeo and Juliet* and *Twelfth Night*. In London, she played Susan in the Royal Court's controversial *Susan's Breasts* and appeared in *Command or Promise* at the National Theatre. As a member of the Royal Shakespeare Company she played Lady Anne to Antony Sher's *Richard III* and also appeared in *Misalliance* and *Heresies*. On TV she was seen in *After the War, Madly in Love* and in episodes of *Poirot* and *Rumpole of the Bailey*.

Visiting the country of her mother's birth, Australia, Caroline starred in the TV miniseries *Cassidy* (opposite Martin Sheen) and was nominated for an Australian Film Institute award. She also starred in the lavish Anglo-Australian four-part TV movie *Ring of Scorpio* (as an avenging angel), and played Amy Johnson in the Aussie miniseries *The Great Air Race*.

Also in the States, the actress appeared in episodes of *Remington Steele* and *Quantum Leap*, and had a

decent role (as Sally) in the film *Every Time We Say Goodbye*, with Tom Hanks.

However, it is her exposure in *Hook* that has opened the eyes of Hollywood. In her next film, the big-budget action-adventure *Cliffhanger*, she is in the estimable company of Sylvester Stallone and John Lithgow.

Woody Harrelson. For devotees of the long-running TV series *Cheers*, Woody Harrelson is already a star. As the endearingly dim-witted bartender Woody Boyd, Harrelson replaced Nicholas Colasanto in the sitcom when the latter died. Handsome, naive and charming, Woody's Boyd was a TV character created in heaven, a winning counterpoint to Ted Danson's worldly, scheming Sam Malone. It was a part that won Harrelson the title of 'best dumb blond on TV'.

'Actually, I've always considered Woody naive, not dumb,' the actor contests. 'If anything, he's an idiot savant. He has an amazing knowledge of trivia and can beat anybody at chess.'

However, popular as *Cheers* has been over the last ten years, it has failed to turn its regular supporting cast into overnight stars. Except for Woody. Swapping New York for LA to play a small part in the ill-fated Goldie Hawn comedy *Wildcats*, Woody auditioned for the part in 1985.

'I was twenty-three and had dreamed about doing Broadway,' he recalls. 'Suddenly I was being offered TV. I had never seen the show, so I watched a couple of episodes. I thought it was phenomenal.'

Two years later the actor was honoured with an American Comedy Award for his work and in 1989 won the Emmy as 'Outstanding Supporting Actor'.

Woody Harrelson has been wary of straying from the successful formula of his amiable bumpkin act.

'I have turned down roles – like a rapist, once – in which I would be too different from Woody. I've looked for parts that are an appropriate transition, like my character in *Doc Hollywood*. He had some of Woody's innocence, but he was *considerably* more in touch with his sexuality.'

Woody Harrelson's own sexuality is the stuff of Hollywood legend. He dated the actress Carol Kane, ten years his senior, for eighteen months; he was Brooke Shields's first public boyfriend; and, on a whim, he married Neil Simon's daughter, Nancy, in Mexico (they divorced shortly afterwards). He has also been romantically linked with Moon Unit Zappa and Ally Sheedy, and, in a fanfare of publicity, proposed to Glenn Close (*fourteen* years his senior) on his 30th birthday. It was a short-lived engagement.

'I thought I couldn't be happier than if I was having sex with a lot of women,' the star admitted. 'I spent almost a decade on that hedonistic bent.' He also enjoyed the occasional bar-room brawl. 'Violence was almost an aphrodisiac for me; I really loved it. I would smile when I was about to get into a fight.'

Indeed, Woody's father, Charles Harrelson, is currently serving two life sentences for killing a federal court judge.

But Woody's own life has come full circle. 'I wanted to be a minister,' he explains. 'I was the head of the youth group and used to lead Bible studies.' But, while studying theology at Hanover College on a Presbyterian scholarship, he made a sharp U-turn. 'I began to think it had become too much of a capitalistic enterprise. In doing so, I turned my back on some of the most important aspects of religion.'

All that changed in 1990 when Woody visited Machu Picchu, the Peruvian mountain city that doubles as a spiritual mecca. He came back a changed man, took up vegetarianism and began exploring, for him, the more consequential things in life. He is now an outspoken critic of the American government, was an active campaigner against the Gulf War and has followed in the footsteps of his *Cheers* co-star Ted Danson, contributing considerable energy (and money) in support of the environmental groups the Earth Communications Office and the American Oceans Campaign.

However, his forthright opinions have caused some backlash. An invitation to serve as grand marshal at the Mardi Gras parade in New Orleans was abruptly cancelled, as were a series of profitable TV commercials for Miller Beer.

Still, Woody Harrelson is his own man, and in 1992 his film career took off. Reportedly beating out Keanu Reeves to play the only white character in Ron Shelton's gritty basketball comedy *White Men Can't Jump*, Woody was something of a revelation. Again, he played the naive charmer, but his physical presence and expertise on the basketball court was the stuff of stardom-in-the-making. Wearing a wardrobe that would shame Russ Abbot, Harrelson played Billy Hoyle, a con artist who hid his street savvy behind baggy shorts and sagging socks.

'I remember my agent ragging on me to spend less time playing basketball and more time going up for movie roles,' Woody laughs now. 'But when *White Men Can't Jump* came along I was able to say, "See!" '

Yet, however slick Billy Hoyle is on the court, he cannot handle his girlfriend's emotional ups-and-downs. That's Woody Boyd all over for you.

But it's Harrelson's easy charisma and muscular build that puts him in the running for celluloid celebrity. Also, his good-natured one-upmanship with co-hustler Wesley Snipes was a joy to behold thanks, in part, to a rapid-fire screenplay from Shelton. As Hoyle attempts to comprehend the beat of the black heart, he is constantly snubbed by Snipes. Although he listens to Jimi Hendrix, he is told he cannot *hear* Jimi Hendrix. And then, in a whine worthy of Woody Boyd himself, Hoyle declares, 'I don't hustle with people who are dishonest.'

A black film that appealed equally to white audiences, *White Men Can't Jump* was a huge box-office hit, grossing almost $19 million in its first week in the US. Even more surprising was that *White Men* achieved this in the face of *Basic Instinct*'s simultaneous media onslaught.

Harrelson was then signed up to star in MGM-Pathe's *Benny and Joon*, but backed out to team up with Robert Redford and Demi Moore in Adrian Lyne's considerably hotter project *Indecent Proposal*. Subsequently, MGM brought a lawsuit against Harrelson for breach of contract, and brought in Aidan Quinn to replace him.

Woody Harrelson (right), *with Wesley Snipes, in Ron Shelton's gritty, fast-paced comedy* White Men Can't Jump

Samuel L. Jackson (left) with Willem Dafoe, in Roger Donaldson's White Sands

Samuel L. Jackson. While Wesley Snipes was accumulating all the media attention for his triple-punch at the box-office (*New Jack City, Jungle Fever, White Men Can't Jump*), another black actor was quietly rising up the ranks. Or not so quietly. In 1991 Samuel L. Jackson won the Cannes and New York Film Critics' Circle awards for Best Supporting Actor for his role as Gator Purify in Spike Lee's *Jungle Fever*. As the deranged junkie brother of Wesley Snipes, Jackson gave a chilling performance as a man emotionally blinded by the need for crack. Of all the supporting characters in the film, it is Jackson you remember. And in a year that made stars of such black actors as Snipes, Cuba Gooding Jr and Larry Fishburne, Samuel L. Jackson was the one winning the greatest critical kudos. And the work.

Born in 1943 in Georgia, Jackson has actually been acting for more than twenty years. A graduate of Atlanta's Morehouse College (like Spike Lee), he moved to New York in 1977 and has been performing solidly ever since. In the cinema Jackson has clocked up a prodigious gallery of roles, making his debut in 1981 in Milos Forman's *Ragtime*. Since then he's had small parts in Spike Lee's *School Daze, Coming to America, Eddie Murphy Raw, Sea of Love, A Shock to the System, Do the Right Thing, Mo' Better Blues, The Exorcist III* and *GoodFellas*. In the 1990s, with the breakthrough of black cinema, he has been even more in evidence.

In James Bond III's sharply written *Def by Temptation*, he played Minister Garth, Bond's fire-and-brimstone father; in the critically celebrated *Strictly Business*, he won good reviews as Monroe, the postroom supervisor; he took a secondary role in the would-be cult film *Jumpin' at the Boneyard*; and had telling cameos in the cult *Johnny Suede* and the runaway hit *Juice*.

However, it wasn't until the success of *Jungle Fever* that the big parts – and big movies – came along. First off, Jackson was signed up to play 'a straightlaced FBI man' on the trail of gunrunner Mickey Rourke in Roger Donaldson's *White Sands*. When Jackson originally read the script he presumed he was playing the bad guy (Rourke's part). 'Then they call me back and say, "No, you're Meeker, the FBI agent." What? I had to go back and read it again. And I liked the guy a lot. He's not obviously bad or obviously good. It was a stretch from Gator Purify to that character, and I really would like to display the fact that I have that range.'

According to director Donaldson, 'Sam's got enormous resources as an actor. Technically, he's extremely talented. He can do something on one take, then go back and build on it. He's spontaneous – but he's also well trained.'

From *White Sands* Jackson moved on to play Harrison Ford's partner in *Patriot Games*, the first of three sequels to *The Hunt for Red October* (all of which he's been signed up for). He then went on to star in *Amos & Andrew*, with Nicolas Cage and Dabney Coleman. In the latter, Jackson plays the central role of a black playwright who, working from an exclusive 'vacation island', is mistaken for a burglar in his own home. It's Jackson's first lead – and about time, too.

Anthony LaPaglia. Like so many overnight sensations, Anthony LaPaglia stole the notices on a couple of pictures and then worked himself to a frazzle keeping up with the movie offers.

'I've only been acting the last six, seven years, playing a lot of psychos and killers,' the actor notes. 'In TV I've played every guy that ever held a knife and a gun. When your last name ends in a vowel, that happens a lot.'

LaPaglia first caught the attention of the public (and critics) when he played the young Italian-American Stevie Dee in Alan Alda's *Betsy's Wedding*. It was only a supporting role (he was the shady, vain hood who courted Ally Sheedy's female cop Connie Hopper), but the actor made it his own and walked away with every scene he was in.

He won the part after being invited to join an informal reading of Alda's script with the cast. 'It was really good fortune,' he says now, 'because if I'd had to audition, I probably wouldn't have gotten it.'

His second scene-stealing turn was in the highly-acclaimed HBO movie *Criminal Justice*, in which he delivered a powerful performance as a legal aid attorney plagued by doubt.

LaPaglia has now cornered the market in playing tough Italian-American New Yorkers, and is frequently mistaken for Andy Garcia, Sam Waterston, Treat Williams, and both Alec and Billy Baldwin.

'Look,' he says ruefully, 'just look at the actors I've got to go up against: Alec Baldwin, Ray Liotta, Andy Garcia . . . Actually, there *is* no competition between us because I think that they win out every single time.' When his hair's slicked back, casting agents like to think of LaPaglia as 'the new De Niro', he says.

The joke is that Anthony LaPaglia isn't even American. He was actually born in Adelaide 34 years ago and grew up in Australia – working first as an elementary school teacher, then installing sprinkler systems and later selling shoes. His career prospects didn't look hopeful. His brothers were both doing well – one in medicine, the other running the family car dealership – when LaPaglia's girlfriend took him, aged 25, to see his first play, Congreve's *The Way of the World*. He enjoyed the experience, contemplating becoming an actor, but thought he was too old to start. When his application to enrol at Australia's National Institute of Dramatic Arts was rejected, he packed his bags and emigrated to New York.

'I felt more at home in New York in ten minutes than I ever did in Australia,' he says. He tried LA, stayed for two years, lassoed an agent, but then scuttled back to the Big Apple. Hollywood was . . . well, 'there's this rush to make it – by the time you're twelve.'

LaPaglia definitely was starting late. 'I still feel like I'm three steps behind,' he complains. 'I never feel like I've read enough, I never feel like I've seen enough theatre. I feel like I have a *lot* to catch up on. But,' he continues, 'that's not necessarily bad. It's a good driving force. When I'm working, I'm obsessed with what I'm doing.'

He made his first impression in the off-Broadway play *Bouncers*, in which he had to portray about eight different characters, and then came the predictable string of TV bits in such shows as *Magnum P.I., The Equalizer, Hunter*, and so forth.

Film-wise, he was Henry in James Ivory's *Slaves of New York*, had a small but telling part in *He Said, She Said* (as a TV crew member), and then played Michael Keaton's ill-fated partner in the tough crime drama *One Good Cop*.

Keaton was a fan. 'You can walk into

a scene with Anthony and say anything to him, and he doesn't get thrown. He's really fun to act with. And I think he will have to work at not getting jobs. He will actually have to go out of his way not to be employed.'

LaPaglia stayed right where he was and kept on accepting scripts. He starred opposite Danny Aiello in *29th Street*, which the actor describes as 'a cross between *Mean Streets* and *It's a Wonderful Life*'. The writer–director, George Gallo, enthused, 'Anthony's got something in his eyes that is just sort of magical. Another kind of actor would probably have come off as very unsympathetic in the role.'

In the HBO movie *Keeper of the City* LaPaglia was frighteningly convincing as a psychotic killer, and upstaged co-stars Louis Gossett Jr, Peter Coyote and Renee Soutendijk. He was then cast as an undercover cop working for the mob in John Landis's romantic horror movie, *Innocent Blood*, co-starring Anne Parrillaud as a salacious vampire. Next, he'll be seen alongside Annabella Sciorra in *Whispers in the Dark*, a psychodrama exploring the old story of the shrink sleeping with her patient. This time the patient turns out to be the suspect in a murder case. Ironically, Alan Alda has a supporting role, as one of Sciorra's colleagues.

LaPaglia's current obsession with his work was partly responsible for the break-up of his four-year marriage, although the actor is now trying to slow the work-load down. 'You have a life first,' he says, 'and acting comes second. Because all you bring to the screen is your experience as a person.' His background as an Australian has yet to be witnessed, although at the end of a long shoot the old vowels do surface. But, as far as his fans are concerned, Anthony LaPaglia is your regular New York psychotic.

Juliette Lewis. As is so often the case with star-laden films, it is the unknown who shines brightest. Indeed, this was the instance with *Cape Fear*, in which, in spite of the presence of Nick Nolte, Jessica Lange, Joe Don Baker, Martin Balsam, Robert Mitchum and Gregory Peck, it was the unfamiliar, 18-year-old Juliette Lewis who won an Oscar nomination alongside her co-star Robert De Niro.

As Danielle Bowden, the unsteady, faltering 15-year-old daughter of Nolte

Juliette Lewis huddles against her screen mother Jessica Lange, in Martin Scorsese's cuticle-chewing Cape Fear

and Lange, Lewis was unforgettable, reaching deep into her psyche to help ward off the convict from hell. Although the film's salient violence was much discussed, the scene most people remember is when De Niro's Max Cady confronts Danielle for the first time. It is the sequence when director Martin Scorsese finally keeps his camera still and lets Lewis and De Niro act their socks off. It is the sequence when we first see Danielle as a sexual being, weighing up the threat and attraction of the man in the shadows. It is the sequence when De Niro spontaneously slips his thumb into the girl's mouth.

'I didn't know that was going to happen,' the actress, now 19, explains. 'All Marty said was, "Bob's gonna do something before the kiss." I would have gone out of character if it was wrong for the scene. But it was totally right. Both Marty and Bob are such geniuses!'

It is a mutual admiration. 'I met her at the Beverly Hills Hotel for a preliminary chat,' recalls De Niro. 'And I had an interesting feeling about her. She had a natural thing.

'You have to have a certain kind of awareness of yourself to be an actor,' the star continued. 'And I was impressed with how she handled the highly emotional stuff in *Cape Fear*. It's not easy to pull that out of yourself, to know where to get it. Some people don't even know how to begin to do it.'

Of course, Juliette Lewis had had a head start. She is the daughter of popular character actor Geoffrey Lewis (*Every Which Way But Loose*, *The Lawnmower Man*), and started acting at the age of 12, cast in a leading role in the two-part cable movie *Home Fires* (1987). She then spent two years serving time in TV, appearing in the ill-fated sitcoms *I Married Dora* and, with Robert Mitchum, *A Family for Joe*, as the latter's adopted daughter. She also had a recurring role in *The Wonder Years* – but I wouldn't remind her of that if I were you ('sitcoms can demolish anyone of artistic creativity').

In the dire *National Lampoon's Christmas Vacation* (1989) she played Chevy Chase's offspring, Audrey Griswood, and had brief roles in *The Runnin' Kid* and *Meet the Hollowheads*, neither anything to write home about.

Luke Perry

However, there was plenty to be pleased with in the searing, true-life TV drama *Too Young to Die* (1990), in which the actress portrayed 'a fourteen-year-old, sexually abused runaway who gets involved in drugs and ends up killing her lover'. Besides winning decent reviews, the film introduced her to her famous boyfriend Brad Pitt (another of this year's Most Promising Faces).

Lewis, however, is less than complimentary about the experience, which shows that she can already think for herself.

'The whole movie was repulsive to me because it was cleaned up for TV. I decided I didn't want to do another based-on-a-true-story unless it was as gruesome as the real story was.'

Cape Fear was gruesome enough for her, and pulled no punches in the scene in which she hurls a pan of boiling water into De Niro's face. She changed track dramatically in her next film, *That Night*, a poignant tale of a young hood (C. Thomas Howell) who courts and impregnates a frisky teenage beauty (Lewis). Howell, who has worked with his share of famous leading ladies (Jamie Lee Curtis, Ann-Margret, Elizabeth Taylor), was ambivalent in his feelings for Lewis.

'The biggest problem was just getting around her,' he said. 'I mean, she sometimes wouldn't show up for

rehearsals. She's very talented, but she doesn't really know where it comes from or why. If you don't know what you're doing and that makes you feel uncomfortable, it makes everybody else feel uncomfortable.'

She was back amongst the stars in Woody Allen's latest (as yet unnamed) film, replacing Emily Lloyd at the eleventh hour, and joining the ranks of Woody himself, Mia Farrow, Liam Neeson and Judy Davis.

'I loved working with Woody,' she glows. 'He made my character very bright and confident and sort of unique. She's sort of a part of me – with a vocabulary. *And*,' she says with some emphasis, 'I play a twenty-one-year-old.'

Next, she stars opposite Brad Pitt in *Kalifornia*, in which the couple play Adele and Early, a lethal combination. He's a serial killer, she's a chatterbox. Could be interesting.

Luke Perry. TV phenomenons invariably spill on to the big screen, and in America there was no phenomenon bigger than Fox TV's *Beverly Hills 90210*. Premiered on 4 October 1990, the hour-long dramatic episodes became the bible of America's wannabe cool youth. Set in LA's West Beverly High School, the show launched a series of young faces into the gilt-edged stratosphere of overnight fame. Faces belonging to the likes of Jason Priestley, Shannen Doherty, Carol Potter and Luke Perry. These young TV stars epitomised the It generation, the wealthy, white and wise of urban *chic*. Every Thursday at 9 p.m., teenagers stayed in to watch the antics of their heroes and were unphased by the dramatic realism of interracial romance, teen suicide and pregnancy scares, not to mention talk of AIDS, drug abuse and breast cancer. Hell, with characters this attractive and hip, who cared if a little real life got in the way?

Actually, *Beverly Hills 90210* was extremely well plotted, the conversation dead on the button and the performances refreshingly naturalistic. These actors *deserved* to become instant icons. Still, the attention was somewhat overwhelming.

'It's a little strange to be screamed at when you walk down the street,' noted Ian Ziering, who plays Steve Sanders in the series. 'It's scary. It happens on the grocery line, at the stoplight, at the gym. It's like everyone seems to be watching this show.'

Luke Perry, perhaps the most visible member of the cast, provoked a rampage when he agreed to make an appearance at a Florida shopping centre. 'It's nice to get out and meet the people,' he volunteered, 'but seeing me is not worth getting injured for.'

Perry has found his way on to practically every cover of every teen magazine invented (and a few more serious publications into the bargain), and film fame is just a frame away.

Born on 11 October 1964, he is seriously older than the 17-year-old Dylan McKay he plays on the show, and he won't thank you for mentioning it. 'A woman from *Rolling Stone* asked me how old I was once, and I said, "I'll tell you, but then I'll have to kill you." Actually, I'm twenty-five,' he lied.

Unlike Dylan McKay, who is worth $100 million in the show, Perry had a poor upbringing, moving with his family from one small farm to another, across the plains of Ohio. Graduating from high school in Fredericktown, Ohio, aged 17, Perry bummed around for a while, visited Los Angeles, and then moved into a rented apartment in Harlem.

He paid his acting dues in two day-time soaps, *Loving* and *Another World*. On celluloid, he had a small role as a young buck – Ray Ray – in the truly dreadful *Scorchers*, with Emily Lloyd, and was handed his first starring role in *Buffy the Vampire Slayer*. The latter is a modern-day vampire thriller set in Los Angeles, with Perry joined by Kristy Swanson, Donald Sutherland, Rutger Hauer and Paul Reubens (better known as Pee-wee Herman). An unusual combination of horror, martial arts and teen comedy, the film was rushed into production by Fox to capitalise on their star's saturation following.

According to the film's producer, Howard Rosenman, Luke has 'got a great sense of humour. He has the humour of his generation, really. This project has been very interesting for me, because around him there is this whole bunch of people that are like satellites. It's true stardom. It reminds me of Sean Penn and the Brat Pack. But this is the next generation. On the set every single night, all these young, happening kids would show up.'

It only remains to be seen whether

Brad Pitt, the ultra-hip protagonist of Tom DiCillo's wryly amusing Johnny Suede

or not Luke Perry's legion of admirers will follow him into the multiplexes.

Brad Pitt. For every new Marilyn Monroe or Marlon Brando, there's a budding James Dean lurking in the Hollywood shadows. This year's Dean clone looks more promising than most, displaying a substantial acting talent and the sort of good looks that knock up the sales of smelling salts.

Brad Pitt is well aware of the label the media have slapped on him, and he's not happy about it.

'James Dean?' he sneers. 'That's crap. And it amazes me all these actors who try to impersonate James Dean instead of finding out who they are. They ride around on their Harleys trying to be Mickey Rourke and they won't bath. Why would you want to pattern your life after someone who wasn't a survivor?'

Nevertheless, Mr Brad Pitt leapt into the public eye (and women's hearts) as a character called 'JD' – in Ridley Scott's cult hit *Thelma & Louise*. JD was the charismatic hitchhiker who gave Geena Davis her first orgasm and took her last penny (a part William Baldwin was due to play until he walked off to take the lead in *Backdraft*). In a cast of despicable male characters, JD was at least an attractive bad guy, thanks to Brad Pitt's easy swagger, pale blue eyes and physical perfection (you could play the xylophone on his stomach muscles).

Liz Smith, the goddess of New York gossip, reported that Pitt and Davis had enjoyed an affair on the set, and the media moved in. Meanwhile the young Mr Pitt (born 18 December 1965) was already having discussions with Robert Redford about the lead in *A River Runs Through It*. Also, he'd already sharpened his acting teeth on a smattering of TV and movie parts, and had been caught dating Robin Givens a year earlier.

Born in Shawnee, Oklahoma, and raised in the city of Springfield, Missouri, Pitt took small parts in school musicals, and at the University of Missouri majored in journalism, but lost his degree. He moved to Los Angeles to attend art school, but instead worked as a chauffeur for Strip-O-Gram artistes and dressed up as a giant chicken to promote a fast-food chain.

After working as a film extra, Pitt landed his first TV role as 'an idiot boyfriend who gets caught in the hay' in *Dallas*, and then played another ne'er-do-well in the sitcom *Growing Pains*. He had a regular bit in the day-time soap *Another World*, and was Walker Lovejoy, a college dropout, in the short-lived series *Glory Days* (1990). Other TV parts included spots in *21 Jump Street* and *thirtysomething*, and a trio of TV films. He had a small role in the cable movie *The Image*, with Albert Finney, another bit in the highly-acclaimed *A Stoning in Fulham County*, starring Ken Olin and Jill Eikenberry, and then starred with Ms Eikenberry's husband, Michael Tucker, in *Too Young to Die*. In the last-named he played a junkie-pimp who brutalises a runaway girl, the latter portrayed by a 16-year-old Juliette Lewis. It was the start of a meaningful friendship.

'Yeah, it was quite romantic,' he recalls, 'shooting her full of drugs and stuff.' Anyway, the couple became inseparable, attending various prem-ieres (and the Oscar ceremony) together, becoming the hottest new double-act in Hollywood since Johnny Depp and Winona Ryder.

Film-wise, there were a few odds and ends for Mr Pitt, such as a part in Bozi-dar Nikolic's *Dark Side of the Sun* and a starring role (as an ace athlete) in the low-budget *Across the Tracks*. He had a supporting bit, as Brian, in the roman-tic comedy *Happy Together*, a bigger part in the Z-grade high-school slasher *Cutting Class* and popped up in Donald Petrie's *The Favor*, alongside Harley Jane Kozak and Elizabeth McGovern.

And then William Baldwin backed out of *Thelma & Louise*. Another (unnamed) actor was considered as a last-minute replacement, when Pitt was called in to audition. 'It just sparked,' the actor said of his reading with Geena Davis, and three days later he was strutting his stuff for his fifteen minutes of stardom (literally, in this case).

According to the film's casting direc-tor (who saw 400 hopefuls for the part of JD), 'there are stars that aren't great actors, but when I met Brad, I thought, "He's going to be a star *and* he can act." His career is going to be a capital BIG.'

'I could have walked in like an idiot,' reflects the actor, 'but Geena and Susan were really cool. They made me feel comfortable.'

'Cool' is Brad Pitt's favourite word, and before the word on *Thelma & Louise* was out, Pitt was up for his first title role as the incarnation of cool – in Tom DiCillo's cult exercise in New York postmodernism, *Johnny Suede*.

As JD was sexually smart and the stuff of rural machismo, so Johnny Cool was carnally ignorant and the victim of urban stress. In fact, the only thing these two characters had in common was their lust for women and their baby good-looks. For Pitt it was a stretch, and he carried it off with aplomb – combing his hair in the mirror, preening his outsize pompa-dour, singing simple love songs inspired by Ricky Nelson . . .

Although *Johnny Suede* only cost $1 million to film, director DiCillo still found it tough to go with Brad Pitt as his star. He had to fight for him.

'At the time I cast the movie, he was a complete unknown,' DiCillo explains. 'He read for the part, and there was no doubt that he was the one for the role. He was the only one to get that Johnny was this guy who has no idea what he's doing. It's not that I knew he was going to be a star the minute he walked in, but I did know there was a beautiful transparency to his work – whatever's going on inside Brad, you can see it.'

Pitt was also cast in one of the three central roles in *Cool World* (another film title that reflected his inherent flair) –

Marisa Tomei in Jonathan Lynn's hilarious My Cousin Vinny

alongside Kim Basinger and Gabriel Byrne. An X-rated tribute to *Roger Rabbit*, the semi-animated fantasy was directed by Ralph Bakshi, creator of *Fritz the Cat* and *Heavy Traffic*.

'I had seen about two hundred actors for the part,' Bakshi notes. 'Like *every-one*. Brad walked in the room, did a reading and blew me away. He was a cross between a young Alan Ladd and James Dean. Brad could walk across a floor and be sensual without even trying. He is a throwback to what I thought Americans *should* be like. Like the guys who hit the beach at Iwo Jima. He can also act. He's going to go places.'

Still *Thelma & Louise* hadn't opened. Next, Pitt pinned one of the leads in Robert Redford's *A River Runs Through It*, based on Norman Mac-Lean's classic novel. In the latter he plays Paul, the brother who can't fit in, in a cast that includes Craig Sheffer, Tom Skerritt and Emily Lloyd.

After that he plays another reprobate in the sinister story of a couple of hitchhikers, *Kalifornia*, paired with Juliette Lewis. And then he's to star opposite John Malkovich in *The Forget-Me-Knot*, a contemporary thriller directed by Damian Harris.

And now that *Thelma & Louise* has opened there is no stopping him.

Marisa Tomei. In spite of the coverage such megahits as *Batman Returns*, *Wayne's World* and *Sister Act* attracted in the press, one little film, virtually ignored by the media, chugged along happily and made a lot of money – at least $50 million, and then only from its domestic cinema release.

My Cousin Vinny was an unlikely candidate for success. The modest story of a hip, hopelessly inept lawyer from Brooklyn who ends up in Wahzoo City, Alabama, fighting for his little cousin's life, the film sounded possibly cute, but far from commercial. And the casting of the foul-mouthed Joe Pesci in the title role didn't alter anybody's prog-nosis of the movie's potential. Neither did the name Marisa Tomei. Who?

Marisa Tomei was third-billed in *My Cousin Vinny*, behind Joe Pesci and Ralph Macchio, but turned out to be the main reason for seeing the film. As Vinny's conflagrant Brooklyn girlfriend Lisa, Ms Tomei was a joy and a revel-ation. A master at comedy timing, the actress didn't so much *play* her character, as *ignite* her. Displaying an eye-catching, brain-numbing wardrobe with brash aplomb, Ms Tomei was funny *and* sexy, beautiful *and* intelligent, tough *and* feminine, and gave Oscar-winner Joe Pesci a run for his money. Hell, she stole the movie from everybody – including the scenery.

Naturally, Ms Tomei had been working hard on overnight fame. Born in Brooklyn, New York (in the early sixties), she studied acting while at college and made her professional debut in Garry Marshall's critical success *The Flamingo Kid* (1984).

'One line,' she explains. 'It was like, "Oh my God, you're so drunk." I don't consider that my big debut.'

Nevertheless, it was a start and led to a year and a half on the daytime soap *As the World Turns* (as a resident loony). After that she made her theatrical debut in *Daughters*, for which she won the 1986 Theatre World Award and a nomination from the Outer Critics Circle. She next played the role of 'Blue' in the off-Broadway production of *Beirut*, which transferred to Los Angeles and won her the 1987 Dramalogue Award for best actress.

TV followed with a regular part as Lisa Bonet's talkative roommate Maggie Lawton in the sitcom *A Different World*, and then the title role in the Emmy-winning ABC Special *Supermom's Daughter*. More theatre ensued, and then she captured the female lead in the Joel Silver-produced TV movie *Parker Kane*, starring Jeff Fahey. There was also a short film, *Two For Tijuana*, in which she starred opposite Woody Harrelson (qv).

The actress returned to the cinema with the role of Remy, Nicolas Cage's seductive floozy in the awful *Zandalee*, and then played Sylvester Stallone's zany daughter in John Landis's underrated comedy *Oscar*. In a film bursting with star cameos, Tomei's sex-starved Lisa Provolene was a scene-stealer and led to *My Cousin Vinny*.

Now that she has a true hit on her hands, Marisa Tomei can count herself a leading lady and is already getting to see better scripts. She has a small role in Richard Attenborough's much-anticipated, all-star Chaplin biography, *Charlie*, and appears alongside Matthew Modine, Lara Flynn Boyle, Lori Singer and Fred Ward in Alan Rudolph's well-acted, bittersweet ensemble drama *Equinox*.

Polly Walker as the elegant Lady Caroline, with Alfred Molina, in Mike Newell's Enchanted April

Milos Forman signed her up for the lead, as a 'young and immature wife', in his international romance, *Hell Camp*, but the film was cancelled when Japanese investors objected to the material.

However, Marisa promptly landed another lead – in *The Baboon Heart*, Tony Bill's unusual tale of a romantically-ignored waitress (Tomei) who falls for an orphan bus boy (Christian Slater) who believes he has the heart of a baboon. It sounds right up her street.

Polly Walker. In a year virtually devoid of British movies, Polly Walker made a considerable impact in one of the best of them, *Enchanted April*. In an outstanding cast, Ms Walker displayed an uncommon grace and beauty as the cool, sensible and aristocratic Lady Caroline Dester, reminiscent of a kindly Kristin Scott Thomas from *A Handful of Dust*.

Polly assures us that 'I don't come from an aristocratic background myself, not at all. But I've mixed with people like Caroline at college and at parties. Superficially, it seemed an easy part to play – floating around and looking attractive – but she could have become a caricature, one of those, "You rang, my lady?" types, and I didn't want that. I wanted to make her real.'

Obviously Polly made her mark, as she was snapped up for a leading role in the $42.5 million *Patriot Games*, the much-touted sequel to *The Hunt for Red October*. Polly played Annette, a beautiful, mysterious and ruthless member of the IRA who keeps Harrison Ford in a perpetual sweat. Donning a series of exotic disguises (including a risqué outfit of black lingerie), she manages to outwit the CIA while leaving a trail of dead bodies behind her.

After that the actress was cast as the sexually provocative Lenni in the BBC's large-screen adaptation of Franz Kafka's *The Trial*, alongside Kyle MacLachlan, Anthony Hopkins, Jason Robards, Juliet Stevenson, Jean Stapleton and Alfred Molina.

Born in Warrington, North Cheshire, Polly was educated at boarding school in Sussex and went on to the Ballet Rambert School. An injury forced her to think twice about dance as a career and she opted for acting instead, debuting as the second gravedigger in an RSC tour of *Hamlet*.

'I understudied everyone as well,' she says, 'but my Ophelia was terribly healthy! I hadn't done any professional work before, so it was a baptism by fire.' A stopover at the Old Vic (as Phoebe in *As You Like It*) and another stint at the RSC followed, before the actress landed the title role in the TV production of *Lorna Doone*. She has also appeared in the movies *Shogun Mayada* (with Sho Kosugi, David Essex and Christopher Lee!), *Les Equilibristes*, starring Michel Piccoli and based on a Moroccan episode in the life of Jean Genet, and Chris Menaul's *A Dangerous Man*, in which she plays Madame Dumont.

Film World Diary

JAMES CAMERON-WILSON

July

Terminator 2 – Judgment Day becomes the box-office hit of the summer ★ A man is killed and almost 30 people wounded in shootings across America at screenings of *Boyz N The Hood*. The film – which depicts gang warfare in Los Angeles – was intended to preach peace, but the plea went badly wrong. The film's director, **John Singleton**, denied responsibility for the shoot-outs, saying, 'It's just a reflection of the way our society is going right now.' Violence also accompanied the premiere screenings of *Harlem Nights* and *New Jack City* ★ **Audrey Hepburn** is held prisoner at gunpoint in Hanoi on a UNICEF charity mission. Released after five hours, she was told there were 'irregularities' on her exit visa ★ *Sleeping with the Enemy* grosses $100 million in the US – after 23 weeks on release ★ Following the cancellation of her wedding to **Kiefer Sutherland, Julia Roberts** moves in with actor **Jason Patric**, Kiefer's co-star from *The Lost Boys* ★ *Terminator 2* grosses $100 million in the US – in two weeks ★ **Alec Baldwin** proposes to **Kim Basinger** – who accepts ★ **Rob Lowe** marries make-up artist **Sheryl Berkoff** ★ **Kirk Cameron**, aged 20, marries actress **Chelsea Noble**, 26 ★ **Demi Moore**, 28, gives birth to a 5lb 15oz baby girl, Scout LaRue Willis ★ Following a remark accusing the unions of driving up the cost of movies, **Bruce Willis** is run off the road by an anonymous car. Worse still, he and Demi Moore receive a note threatening their 3-year-old daughter, Rumer. The couple hire bodyguards to protect their family ★ **Pee-wee Herman**, alias Paul Ruebens, is arrested for indecent exposure at a porn cinema in Florida, near his parents' home ★ *City Slickers* clocks up over

$100 million in the US, making it the most successful comedy of the year ★ *Terminator 2*, in just five weeks, has amassed $150 million Stateside ★ **Maria Shriver** and **Arnold Schwarzenegger** are the proud parents of a baby girl, Christina.

August

Julia Roberts collapses while filming *Hook*. Insiders say the actress has lost

Will you marry me? Alec Baldwin proposes to Kim Basinger – and stops playing Patriot Games

an inordinate amount of weight ★ **John Travolta**, 37, and fiancée **Kelly Preston**, 28, announce their first pregnancy ★ **Colleen Dewhurst**, 67, the great stage actress and former wife (twice) of George C. Scott, dies of cancer in South Salem, New York. Her film appearances included *The Nun's Story, Annie Hall, The Dead Zone* and *Dying Young* ★ **Sylvester Stallone** sues Montreal's *News Extra* for $25 million, contesting their story that he underwent penile implant surgery ★ *Terminator 2* breaks box-office records in the UK, knocking up $4,421,000 in its first three days, and $7,827,903 in its first week * **Tom Selleck** sues the American tabloid *Globe* for claiming that he was homosexual. He cites $20 million in damages, but settles out of court after an apology is printed * **Alec Baldwin**, who played Jack Ryan in *The Hunt for Red October*, walks off the $42.5 million sequel – *Patriot Games* – because of script delays. The hold-up would have forced the film's schedule to clash with the actor's Broadway appearance in *A Streetcar Named Desire*. **Harrison Ford** takes over as Ryan, after his own film, *Night Ride Down*, falls through * **Jack Nicholson** and girlfriend **Rebecca Broussard** announce their second pregnancy * **Frank Capra**, 94, dies.

September

Robin Hood: Prince of Thieves clocks up $150 million in the States * A cinema in Florida refuses to show *Pee-wee's Big Adventure* following **Paul Ruebens**'s arrest there for indecent exposure * **John Travolta** and **Kelly Preston** marry in secret – at midnight in Paris * **Brad Davis**, 41, star of *Midnight Express* and Fassbinder's *Querelle*, dies of AIDS in Los Angeles. He leaves a wife and daughter * **Alex North**, 81, the legendary film composer (*A Streetcar Named Desire*, *Spartacus*, John Huston's *The Dead*), dies in LA of pancreatic cancer * **Carol White**, 49, 1960s British star of *Poor Cow* and TV's *Cathy Come Home*, dies in Florida of liver failure * In Carmel, California, **Harry Hamlin** and **Nicolette Sheridan** finally tie the marital knot * After much controversy, the Papal farce *The Pope Must Die* has its title changed in America – to *The Pope Must Diet*. This was inspired by the actions of a graffiti artist who added the 't' to the London poster depicting the portly **Robbie Coltrane** as Pope * **Dennis Quaid** and **Meg Ryan** proudly announce their pregnancy * So do **Steven Spielberg** and **Kate Capshaw** * **George Pan Cosmatos**, director of *Rambo*, is sued to the tune of $50 million for failing to 'unequivocally' state that he will continue work on the Salkinds' troubled production of *Christopher Columbus: The Discovery*. Apparently, Cosmatos also breached his contract by failing to secure a completion bond * **Elizabeth Perkins** gives birth to a baby girl * **Chuck Vincent**, 51, dies of a heart attack in Florida. A prolific filmmaker,

who was in the middle of writing his first novel, Vincent directed such films at *Hot T-Shirts*, *Slammer Girls* and the hard-core *Sex Crimes 2084* * *Kindergarten Cop* passes the $200 million mark worldwide.

October

Yoram Globus, after severing all ties with **Giancarlo Paretti** and his ill-fated Pathé Communications Corporation, forms his own company, Melrose Entertainment * **Steven Spielberg** marries actress **Kate Capshaw** * *My Own Private Idaho* is the hit of the 29th New York Film Festival * **Elizabeth Taylor**, 59, is married for the eighth time (after being single for ten years and following two broken engagements) to carpenter **Larry Fortenski**, twenty years her junior. The ceremony, invaded by more than twenty media helicopters, is held at **Michael Jackson**'s Neverland ranch in California and is attended by **David Hockney, Dustin Hoffman, Eddie Murphy, Gregory Peck** and **Nancy Reagan** * **Sonny Bono** announces his candidacy for the United States Senate * **Paul**

Robbie Coltrane diets for the American market

Reubens joins the cast of *Batman Returns* * **George Pan Cosmatos** is replaced by **John Glen** as director of the Salkinds' *Christopher Columbus: The Discovery* * **Annie Potts** is pregnant. So is **Amanda Pays** (c/o **Corbin Bernsen**), **Greta Scacchi** (c/o **Vincent Phillip D'Onofrio**) and **Susan Sarandon** (c/o **Tim Robbins**) * **Marcello Mastroianni**, 67, leaves his wife – for the 26th time in 41 years. He is currently filming *Used People* in Toronto, opposite **Shirley MacLaine** * **Redd Foxx**, 68, the American comedian, dies of a heart attack in Los Angeles. He is probably best known for the TV series *Sanford & Son* (based on the BBC's *Steptoe & Son*), while his films number *Norman . . . Is That You?* and *Harlem Nights* * British black actors protest over the casting of African-American star **Forest Whitaker** as a black Londoner in Neil Jordan's *A Soldier's Wife* * **Jonathan Lynn**, who co-scripted the BBC's *Yes, Minister*, is signed up by Twentieth Century-Fox to a two-year directing deal. To date, Lynn has directed *Clue, Nuns on the Run* and *My Cousin Vinny* * *Terminator 2: Judgment Day* grosses $200 million in the United States – in seventeen weeks.

November

The ever-busy **Nick Nolte** separates from his wife, Becky ⋆ **Fred MacMurray**, **Gene Tierney**, producer **Irwin Allen**, British actor-playwright **Donald Churchill**, director **Tony Richardson**, **Yves Montand**, **Ralph Bellamy**, **Klaus Kinski**, director **Daniel Mann** and British Oscar-winning production designer **Anton Furst** (*Batman*) all pass on ⋆ *Beauty and the Beast* and *Cape Fear* wow the critics in New York ⋆ **Eddie Murphy** returns to work, starring in Paramount's big-budget comedy *Boomerang*. Absent from the screen since starring in the box-office bombs *Harlem Nights* (which he directed) and *Another 48 HRS*, Eddie is being paid $12 million this time round ⋆ **Alexander** and **Ilya Salkind** announce that they have signed **Marlon Brando** to play Torquemada in their film *Christopher Columbus: The Discovery*. The

Emily Lloyd (seen here in Scorchers*) is dismissed by Woody Allen*

little-known French-Greek actor **Georges Corraface** (*Impromptu*) is cast in the title role ⋆ **Emily Lloyd** is replaced by **Juliette Lewis** on **Woody Allen**'s latest (unnamed) picture, currently shooting in New York. The film also stars Woody, **Mia Farrow, Liam Neeson** and **Judy Davis**.

December

Ridley Scott's much-touted *Columbus* starts production, with **Gerard Depardieu** in the title role. Later, the film's title is changed to *1492*, and **Sigourney Weaver** is signed up to play the Queen of Spain ⋆ On a whim, **Richard Gere**, 42, marries supermodel **Cindy Crawford**, 25, in Las Vegas – at 11.30 p.m. Earlier that day neither anticipated that they would become husband and wife ⋆ **Giancarlo Parretti**, head of MGM-Pathé, is imprisoned in Sicily on charges of tax evasion ⋆ Fat-burning superstar **Jane Fonda**, 54, marries media mogul **Ted Turner**, 53, founder of Cable News Network. A few days later *Time* magazine names Turner

their Man of the Year ⋆ **Giancarlo Parretti** is ordered by a Delaware judge to hand over control of MGM-Pathé ⋆ A man posing as a film producer and extracting money from gullible would-be actors is arrested in New York City on charges of 'grand theft and three counts of forgery' ⋆ **Cassandra Harris**, 39, the beautiful Australian actress (*For Your Eyes Only*), dies of ovarian cancer. She is survived by her husband, **Pierce Brosnan**, and three children.

January

Dirk Bogarde is knighted in the New Year's honours ⋆ *Terminator 2: Judgment Day* officially becomes the highest-grossing film of 1991 ⋆ Mike Leigh's *Life Is Sweet*, filmed in Enfield, Middlesex, is voted best film of the year by America's National Society of Film Critics. The director's wife, **Alison Steadman**, is voted best actress and **Jane Horrocks** best supporting actress ⋆ **Warren Beatty** and **Annette Bening** become the proud parents of an 8lb

11oz baby girl, Kathlyn Beatty ⋆ *The Addams Family* grosses $100 million in the United States ⋆ Director **John Carpenter** and his producer wife **Sandy King** are signed up by Universal Pictures to develop a series of pictures, including a remake of the company's 1954 classic *The Creature from the Black Lagoon* ⋆ Universal also signs up director **Randa Haines** (*Children of a Lesser God, The Doctor*) to a non-exclusive, first-look agreement ⋆ **José Ferrer**, Oscar-winner for 1950's *Cyrano de Bergerac*, dies at the age of 80 ⋆ *Hook* grosses $100 million in six weeks in the States ⋆ *Beauty and the Beast* grosses $100 million after eleven weeks on release.

February

Bugsy sweeps the Oscar nominations, nabbing ten for itself. *The Prince of Tides* wins seven, but director **Barbra Streisand** is left out in the cold ⋆ **Donald Trump** files a lawsuit against financier **Meshulam Riklis** and his actress-singer wife **Pia Zadora** – for not paying the £70,000-a-month rent on their two apartments in Trump Tower. Riklis, formerly one of the richest men in the world, files for bankruptcy ⋆ **Barry Diller**, chairman of Twentieth Century-Fox Inc., hands in his resignation. **Rupert Murdoch**, who owns Fox, takes over as acting chief – much to the shock of Hollywood ⋆ **Warren Beatty** pays a surprise visit to the Oxford Union, inviting students to ask any questions they want. However, he avoids talking about his affair with **Madonna** ⋆ **Elizabeth Taylor** celebrates her 60th birthday at Disneyland, which is closed for the occasion. Celebrity guests include **Gregory Peck, Tom Selleck, George Harrison, Ringo Starr, David Bowie, Elton John, Jon Voight, Roddy McDowall, Barry Diller** and **Mickey Mouse** ⋆ In a dramatic attempt to economise, Tri-Star Pictures fires several senior production executives and virtually dismantles their story department. Earlier, the company had invested $70 million in Steven Spielberg's *Hook*.

March

Robin Williams is sued for $6 million by former girlfriend Michelle Tish Carter – for giving her herpes ⋆ The Oscar-winning actress **Sandy Dennis**,

Once again Barbra Streisand is ignored by the American Academy of Motion Picture Arts and Sciences

54, dies of ovarian cancer at her home in Connecticut ⋆ Spanish-Cuban cinematographer **Nestor Almendros**, 61, dies in New York. His most memorable films include *Claire's Knee, The Story of Adele H, Kramer vs Kramer, The Last Metro, Sophie's Choice, Places in the Heart, Billy Bathgate* and *Days of Heaven*, for which he won the Oscar ⋆ **Warren Beatty** and **Annette Bening** marry in private ⋆ Orion Pictures begins a massive staff lay-off. Of the company's 400-strong staff, 200 are expected to be released ⋆ **Richard Brooks**, 79, director of *The Blackboard Jungle, In Cold Blood* and *Looking for Mr Goodbar*, dies in Beverly Hills of congestive heart failure ⋆ Writer **Art Buchwald** is awarded $150,000 and producer **Alain Bernheim** $750,000 for their part in the success of Paramount's hit comedy *Coming to America*. However, the producer and writer had aimed to walk away with $6.2 million before the long-running, controversial case had ended. Initially, Paramount denied that they had plundered Buchwald's original story, and then denied that their film had made a profit – in spite of its US gross of $128 million ⋆ **Georges Delerue**, 67, the French film composer, dies in Hollywood. His scores for *Anne of the Thousand Days, The Day of the Dolphin, Julia* and *Agnes of God* were all nominated for Oscars, while his music for *A Little Romance* actually won the Academy Award ⋆ Walt Disney Studios decides to cut back on staff ⋆ **Greta Scacchi** gives birth to a baby girl, Leila George. The father is actor **Vincent Philip D'Onofrio**.

April

Favourite rubber-lipped Hollywood heavy **Neville Brand**, 70, dies in Sacramento, California. His films included *Riot in Cell Block 11*, *The Scarface Mob*, *That Darn Cat* and *Eaten Alive* ★ Euro-Disney unlocks its doors to the world, the opening gala attended by the likes of **Cher, Melanie Griffith, Don Johnson** and **Angela Lansbury** ★ The great Indian filmmaker **Satyajit Ray**, 71, dies of a heart attack in Calcutta ★ **Marlon Brando** moves to have his name removed from the credits of the Salkinds' *Christopher Columbus – The Discovery*. He objects to the inaccuracies in the film's script relating to the Indians, and is also angered over the non-payment of crew members. However, for *his* efforts Brando was paid more than $5 million for ten days' work ★ **Meg Ryan** and **Dennis Quaid** become the proud parents of young Jack Henry – born by caesarean section on 24 April ★ A cinema in Melbourne, Australia, offers a free showing of David Cronenberg's *Naked Lunch* for anybody who will turn up naked. Nobody does and the screening is cancelled ★ *Wayne's World* clocks up $104,088,904 in ten weeks in the US. Bodacious ★ **Emilio Estevez**, 29, marries pop star **Paula Abdul**, 28, in a secret courthouse ceremony. Only two witnesses were present.

May

MGM-Pathé Entertainment takes out a lawsuit against **Woody Harrelson** for breach of contract to star in their film *Benny & Joon*. **Aidan Quinn** takes over the role ★ The Cannes Film Festival kicks off with **Marlene Dietrich** emblazoned on the publicity and posters. A day before, the screen legend, 90, dies quietly in her Paris apartment ★ Filming starts in Washington on **Eddie Murphy**'s new big-budget, political comedy, *The Distinguished Gentleman*, directed by **Jonathan Lynn** ★ MGM-Pathé is auctioned off to its largest creditor, Credit Lyonnais in Paris, for $483,400,000. There were no other bidders ★ **Susan Sarandon** and **Tim Robbins** become the proud parents of their second child (and son), Miles Guthrie ★ As Warner Brothers' *Malcolm X* goes over-budget and the film's completion bond company prevents him from writing any more cheques, director **Spike**

Robert Redford: reducing his price to play a millionaire who tries to buy the sexual favours of Demi Moore

Lee pleads for financial help from black millionaires. To date, Lee has invested almost $3 million of his own salary into the project, and has won fiscal support from **Prince, Janet Jackson, Bill Cosby** and basketball legend, **'Magic' Johnson** ★ *Lethal Weapon 3* grosses $42,942,266 in its opening week in the US. The magic is back.

June

Basic Instinct clocks up $100 million in the United States ★ The beloved British actor and raconteur **Robert Morley**, 84, dies four days after suffering a stroke ★ In the US, *Lethal Weapon 3* grosses $100 million in 23 days ★

Robert Redford takes a substantial pay cut to star in Adrian Lyne's new drama, *Indecent Proposal*, filming in Las Vegas with **Demi Moore**. Redford's last film, *Havana*, was an unmitigated bomb ★ Former No. 1 box-office star **Burt Reynolds** reveals to the press that he is in debt. At one time, he admits, he owed eleven banks a total of $30 million and had to sell off practically everything he owned. Today he rents a house in Los Angeles ★ *Batman Returns* eats up box-office records in the States, where it grosses $47,720,711 in its opening weekend. In its first full week it grosses $1.4 million more than the first, record-breaking *Batman* did ★ **Mike Myers**, now a hot property after the success of *Wayne's World*, stars in his second film, *So I Married an Axe Murderer*. Shooting in San Francisco, the movie co-stars, of all people, Ireland's Brenda Fricker.

In Memoriam

Winner of the British Film Academy's 1952 Award for 'Most Promising Newcomer' (for her performance in *Mandy*), Australian-born **Dorothy Alison** died in London on 17 January 1952, at the age of 66. Filmgoers are most likely to recall her for her leading roles in *Georgie Girl* (1966), *Reach for the Sky* (1956) and *Turn the Key Softly* (1953).

Irwin Allen, who died on 2 November 1991 at the age of 75, was king of the disaster movies, with such masterpieces of the genre as *The Poseidon Adventure* (1972) and *The Towering Inferno* (1974). New York born, Allen started his career as a journalist and went to Holly-

Judith Anderson (left) *in* Rebecca, *with Joan Fontaine*

wood in the late 1930s as the editor of *Key* magazine. From there he graduated to radio and TV shows (and for a while was a literary agent) and in due course started to produce films, initially shorts, winning the 1953 Oscar for his production of the documentary *The Sea Around Us*. His first feature was *The Story of Mankind* in 1957. His two big disaster films made almost $100 million for Fox from the American box office alone. Apart from his cinema films Allen made many TV features and produced or directed a considerable number of series. Allen's other films, either as writer, producer or director, or as all three, included *Double Dynamite* (1951), *Dangerous Mission* (1954), *The Big Circus* (1959), *The Lost World* (1960), *Voyage to the Bottom of the Sea*

(1961), *Five Weeks in a Balloon* (1962), *The Swarm* (1978), *Beyond the Poseidon Adventure* and *When Time Ran Out* (his final film in 1980). His last work was five years later, when he made a two-part TV feature of *Alice in Wonderland*.

Ronald Allen, who died aged 56 on 18 June 1991, will be best recalled by most of the British public for his role of manager of the hotel in the long-running, popular British TV serial *Crossroads*. After provincial repertory in 1953, Allen went on to play classic roles in the Old Vic Company before his TV successes. His Hollywood films included a part in *Cleopatra*.

Although primarily a stage actress, Australian-born Dame **Judith Anderson** (real name Frances Anderson) – who died aged 94 on 3 January 1992 – made her mark in both television and films. Who could forget her remarkable performance as the malevolent housekeeper in Alfred Hitchcock's *Rebecca* (1940), for which she won an Oscar nomination? No less impressive was her work in such films as *Laura* (1944), *Cat on a Hot Tin Roof* (1958), *Ben Hur* (1959), *The Ten Commandments* (1956), *A Man Called Horse* (1970) and *Star Trek III* (1984). Her screen career began most unpromisingly: arriving in Hollywood in 1918 with a letter of recommendation to Cecil B. de Mille, she was rejected out of hand by him. Fifteen years later she made her screen debut in the gangster movie *Blood Money*. Heavily dramatic roles were her *forte*, and she claimed that she had played Lady Macbeth more times than any other actress. Her other films were *King's Row* (1942), Renoir's *The Diary of a Chambermaid* (1946), Ben Hecht's

Jean Arthur

Spectre of the Rose (1946) and Anthony Mann's psychological Western *The Furies* (1950).

Jean Arthur (real name Gladys Georgianna Greene), who died at the age of 90 on 19 June 1991, was one of Hollywood's most reluctant film stars. She loved acting but she hated the publicity and lack of privacy that came with it. Frank Capra once said she was so highly strung and nervous that between every scene she would rush back to her dressing room to be sick and to cry. This was during work on the films in which she gave her most brilliant performances; notably, the great Capra trio *Mr Deeds Goes to Town* (1936), *Mr Smith Goes to Washington* (1939) and *You Can't Take It With You* (1938).

Miss Greene (as she then was) began her professional life as a photographer's model, until Fox gave her a new name, a screen test and her debut role in John Ford's *Cameo Kirby* in 1923. Subsequently she was to be seen in a series of easily forgettable minor movies – she

was with Buster Keaton in his *Seven Chances*. But the talkies brought her a new popularity and better roles. The public grew to adore her special and unforgettable voice with its husky lilt, and the way she used it. After some two and a half years on the Broadway stage, her first big screen success came in John Ford's 1935 film *The Whole Town's Talking*. Her most popular roles with moviegoers were as the girl with the brassy, wisecracking exterior hiding a heart of gold, a role she was to repeat with variations in many of her movies. Her last screen role came in 1953 in *Shane*, after which she sat back and enjoyed her life, no longer having to face the Hollywood rigmarole she hated. Anyone who has never seen nor heard Jean Arthur has missed one of the most enjoyable experiences the cinema can offer.

Miss Arthur's list of films – in excess of 60 – also includes: *Drug Store Cowboy* (one of the seven she made in 1925), *The Cowboy Cop* (one of nine she made the following year), *The Masked Menace* (a serial) in 1927, *Sins of the Fathers* (1928), *The Mysterious Dr Fu Manchu* (1929), *Paramount on Parade*

(1930), *The Gang Buster* (1931), *Diamond Jim* (1935), *The Plainsman* (as Calamity Jane) and *History Is Made at Night* (1937), *Only Angels Have Wings* (1939), *Arizona* (1940), *The Devil and Miss Jones* (1941), *The Talk of the Town* (1942), *The More the Merrier* and *A Lady Takes a Chance* (1943) and *The Impatient Years* (1944).

(Jean Arthur's death was briefly noted in *Film Review 1991–2*.)

Frederick Llewellyn, better known as **Freddie Bartholomew**, was born in London or Dublin, according to different sources, and became a millionaire child star – though always an unassuming and natural one. His wealth was later considerably depleted by two major lawsuits (one over his film contract, the other brought by his parents, who wanted some of the cash his foster-parent aunt had helped him to amass), and he died, aged 67, on 23 January 1992. He will always be remembered for his performance in *Little Lord Fauntleroy* in 1936, but he began his career on the London stage at the age of 3 and by the age of 10 already had stage and screen experience – *Fascination* (1930) and *Lily Christine* (1932) were two of his films. At the age of 10, during a visit to New York with his formidable mentor Aunt Cissie, he was signed by David Selznick to star with

Freddie Bartholomew

W. C. Fields, Basil Rathbone and Edna May Oliver in *David Copperfield* (1934). He stayed in America to make some big successes such as *Anna Karenina* (1935), *Captains Courageous* (1937), *Kidnapped* (1938), and *Tom Brown's Schooldays* (1940). After these films he was reaching an awkward age for casting and his career accordingly began to slide downwards. He made three films in 1942 and then only three more before ending his screen career (with *The Town Went Wild*, *Sepia Cinderella* and *Benny the Dip*). He served in the USAF for a short time, and after his discharge performed in night clubs in Australia and toured America in vaudeville and the repertory theatres. He also worked considerably in television, where he acted, directed and produced. His other films included *Professional Soldier*, *The Devil Is a Sissy* and *Lloyds of London* (all 1936), *Spirit of Culver* and *Two Bright Boys* (1939), *Swiss Family Robinson* (1940) and *A Yank at Eton* (1942).

Robert Beatty, the Canadian actor who made Britain his home from the age of 30 and who died in London on 3 March 1992 at the age of 82, was one of those dependable actors who are often better than the roles they play. Despite his crooked, ready smile, rugged features, tough charm and Canadian accent

Robert Beatty

Ralph Bellamy

(which he doggedly retained in all his roles, and which made him ideal for playing American characters), he never achieved the major stardom for which he earlier seemed destined – partly, perhaps, because of his habit of taking long 'rests' between his assignments. Born in Toronto, and a graduate of Toronto University, he started out as a cashier. But his main interest was the theatre and his success in amateur dramatics led to an engagement with a local broadcasting station. Subsequently, on the advice of Leslie Howard (who was approached by Beatty's aunt) he came to England and enrolled at RADA. His professional debut was in a production of *Idiot's Delight* at the Apollo Theatre. At the same time he was an extra in several films; soon promoted to playing minor roles, as in *San Demetrio London* (1942), *49th Parallel* (1941) and *One of Our Aircraft Is Missing* (1942). He gave a fine performance as the friend of the fugitive James Mason in *Odd Man Out*. He also won major roles on radio and

TV, including an outstanding impersonation of Ronald Reagan in *Breakthrough at Reykjavik*. Other films included *Dangerous Moonlight* (1941), *Captain Horatio Hornblower* and *The Magic Box* (1951), *The Gentle Gunman* (1952), *Albert RN* (1953), *Tarzan and the Lost Safari* (1957), *The Shakedown* (1960), *The Amorous Prawn* (1962), *2001: A Space Odyssey* (1968), *Where Eagles Dare* (1969), *Pope Joan* (1972) and *The Spikes Gang* (1974).

Although he made more than 100 films and was a star for seven decades, **Ralph Bellamy**, who died aged 87 on 29 November 1991, is less memorable than many less distinguished players. This is no reflection on the quality of his performances, more on the roles he played: the man who doesn't quite get the girl in the end was a role he filled again and again. But there were some more memorable highlights, for instance in *The Awful Truth* (1937), which brought him a nomination for an Oscar. (Bellamy was finally awarded a special Oscar in 1987 for 'his distinguished service to the profession of acting'.)

Bellamy began his career by running away from home when he was 16 to join a group of travelling Shakespearean players, the first of fifteen such companies he toured with over ten years. In 1927 he formed his own company, before reaching Hollywood and trying the movies.

Apart from his 'other man' roles, Bellamy played everything from smooth killers to crooked tycoons and self-effacing heroes, then, as later, being content to play parts in B-movies as well as first features. But one day reading a casting script he came upon the pencilled note against one of the characters: 'charming but dull – a typical Ralph Bellamy type'. This so upset him that he deserted films for ten years, finding on Broadway the respect denied him by Hollywood. One of his stage triumphs during this period was his Tony award-winning role as Franklin D. Roosevelt in *Sunrise at Campobello* (a role he was subsequently to repeat when the play was filmed). Always deeply concerned about the welfare of his profession, Bellamy was one of the founders of the Screen Actors Guild and served four terms as President of American Actors Equity.

Among his films are: *The Magnificent Lie* (1931), *Rebecca of Sunnybrook Farm* (1932), *The Picture Snatcher* (1933), *Hands Across the Table* (1935), *Fools for Scandal* (1938), *His Girl Friday* and *Brother Orchid* (1940), several Ellery Queen features (1940–1), *Footsteps in the Dark* (1941), *The Ghost of Frankenstein* (1942), *The Court Martial of Billy Mitchell* (1955), *The Professionals* (1966), *Rosemary's Baby* (1968), *Doctors' Wives* (1971), *Cancel My Reservation* (1972), *Oh God!* (1977), and, notably, *Pretty Woman* (1990). In 1979 he published his autobiography, *When the Smoke Hit the Fan*.

Eleanor Boardman, who died in December 1991 at the age of 93, was initially famed as the Eastman Kodak Girl in the Kodak advertisements, and eventually became a popular star of the silent era. After some stage work Miss Boardman made her screen debut in *The Stranger's Banquet* (1928), but she gave her finest performance when directed by King Vidor (whom she married) in the classic movie *The Crowd* (1928). Other of her many films include *The Centaur* (1924), *Sinners in Silk* (1925), *Bardelys the Magnificent* (1926),

She Goes to War (1929), *Redemption* (1930) and *The Squaw Man* (1931). *The Big Chance*, of 1933, seems to have been her last screen appearance; the same year, she and King Vidor were divorced. She subsequently married the French director Henri d'Abaddis d'Arrast, and went to live in a *château* in the Pyrenees. Later she came to Paris to take up the post of Fashion Correspondent (all her life she made her own clothes) for *Harper's Bazaar* and other Hearst publications.

Going straight into the US Army from high school, veteran screen baddie **Neville Brand**, who died on 16 April 1992 at the age of 71, only started taking drama lessons after ten years of military service. (During his war service Brand became the fourth most decorated GI.) Brand achieved his first film success as a gunman in *DOA* and *Port of New York* (both in 1949). He played gangster boss Al Capone in two films and had a critical success in *Riot in Cell Block 11* in 1954. He also appeared in *Stalag 17* (1953), *Love Me Tender* (1956), *The Tin Star* (1957), *Cry Terror* (1958), *The Adventures of Huckleberry Finn* (1960), *The George Raft Story* (1961), *The Scarface Mob* and *Birdman of Alcatraz* (1962), *Three Guns for Texas* (1968), *The Desperadoes* (1969), *Tora! Tora! Tora!* (1970), *Cahill US Marshal* (1973), *Psychic Killer* (1975) and *Seven from Heaven* (1979). His only romantic film role was in 1954's *Return from the Sea*.

Neville Brand

One of Hollywood's most outstanding screenwriter/directors (and sometimes producer as well), **Richard Brooks** died at the age of 79 on 11 March 1992. Eight times nominated for an Oscar – three for direction, five for screenplay – Brooks finally won the award for his screenplay of *Elmer Gantry* in 1960. Among his considerable output of movies as writer, director or both, four stand out; his angry *Blackboard Jungle* in 1955, his two adaptations of the Tennessee Williams stage plays, *Cat on a Hot Tin Roof* in 1958 and *Sweet Bird of Youth* in 1962, and Truman Capote's *In Cold Blood* in 1967. Although he liked to make films with social themes, Brooks was very versatile, taking adaptations of literary work, light comedy and romance in his stride. In different ways he contributed to *Key Largo* (1948), *Crisis* (1950), *Deadline USA* (1952), *The Last Time I Saw Paris* (1954), *Something of Value* (1957), *The Brothers Karamazov* (1958), *Lord Jim* (1965), *The Professionals* (1966), *Bite the Bullet* (1975), *Looking for Mr Goodbar* (1977), *Wrong Is Right* (1982), *Fever Pitch* (1985), *50 Years of Action!* (1986) and *Listen Up* (1990).

Frank Capra, the cinema's stoutest champion of the Little Man struggling against Corruption and the machinations of ruthless Big Business, died at the age of 94 on 3 September 1991, after a heart attack brought to an end a long downhill battle against illness. Winner of three Oscars for Best Direction (*It Happened One Night* – which also gained four other awards: for Best Film, Best Actor – Clark Gable – Best Actress – Claudette Colbert – and Best Screenplay – Robert Riskin; *Mr Deeds Goes to Town*; and *You Can't Take It With You*), Capra achieved all this within a four-year period in the 1930s.

Originally from Palermo, he was the son of a vineyard worker who emigrated to America (where he became an orange picker) when Capra was seven. By working as a newspaper seller, as a banjoist in a local niterie, and many other odd jobs, Capra raised the money to pay for his own primary and further education and achieved a Chemical Engineering degree in 1918, promptly volunteering for US army service, teaching artillery officers ballistics. After the Army, unable to find a job, Capra took off on a three-year wander in America's Southwest, living hand-to-mouth by any odd jobs he could pick up along the way. Turning down an offer to make illicit stills for a prohibition gangster, he managed – without experience or credentials – to talk his way into directing a one-reel film melodrama, for which he received $75. With this credit he persuaded a studio to give him the job of props man, graduating to the cutting room in 1925. He left this to become a gag man for the 'Our Gang' comedies at the Hal Roach studios. From there it was a short leap to Mack Sennett, where he was given his first solo direction on a Harry Langdon comedy, *The Strong Man* (1926). Two years of unemployment followed after which he managed to persuade Harry Cohn of Columbia to give him a chance. This was to prove fruitful for all concerned, not least for the very difficult Cohn (with whom Capra, however, got along remarkably well) who was to see Capra raise Columbia from a producer of cheap quickies to a major force in Hollywood production status. Now with complete control over his films, Capra turned out in rapid succession some of the classic films of the 1930s. When World War II broke out, Capra re-joined the Army, this time as an official moviemaker, producing the much-lauded documentary series 'Why We Fight', the first of which, *Prelude to War*, won Capra the 1942 Best Documentary Oscar. Demobbed with the rank of colonel, Capra then took it increasingly easy, making only seven films between the mid–1940s and his death.

In his Preface to Capra's 1971 autobiography, *The Name Above the Title*, John Ford rightly wrote that Capra's story – from poverty to riches and fame – is 'An inspiration to all those who believe in The American Dream'.

Capra made some 50 films (including his documentaries), of which the main ones are: *Tramp, Tramp, Tramp* and *The Strong Man* (1926), *Long Pants* and *For the Love of Mike* (1927), *So This is Love, Submarine* and *The Power of the Press* (1928, three of the seven films he made during that year), *The Young Generation, Flight* and *The Donovan Affair* (1929), *Ladies of Leisure* and *Rain or Shine* (1930), *Dirigible, Miracle Woman* and *Platinum Blonde* (1931), *Forbidden* and *The American Madness* (1932), *The Bitter Tea of General Yen* and *Lady for a Day* (1933), *It Happened One Night* and *Broadway Bill* (1934),

Joan Caulfield

Mr Deeds Goes to Town (1936), *Lost Horizon* (1937), *You Can't Take It With You* (1938), *Mr Smith Goes to Washington* (1939); *Meet John Doe* (1941), *Arsenic and Old Lace* (1934), *It's a Wonderful Life* (1947), *Riding High* (1950), *Here Comes the Groom* (1951), *A Hole in the Head* (1959), and *A Pocketful of Miracles* (1960), a re-make – flop, incidentally – of *Lady for a Day* (1961). Capra's final stint behind the camera was for a 1964 short called *Rendezvous in Space*.

Starting her working life as a model before turning to acting, and appearing in several Broadway productions, Beatrice **Joan Caulfield**, who died aged 64 on 18 June 1991, made her screen debut in *Duffy's Tavern* in 1945 and appeared in three films the following year – *Blue Skies, Miss Susie Slagle's* and *Monsieur Beaucaire* – and quickly became one of Paramount's most popular players. Her other films include *Dear Ruth* (1947), *Dear Wife* (1950), *The Lady Says No* (1951), *The Rains of Ranchipur* (1955), *Cattle King* (1963), *Buckskin* (1968), *The Daring Dobermans* (1973) and *Pony Express Rider* (1976). After marrying producer Frank Ross

in 1950 (they were divorced ten years later), she made only rare appearances on the screen. However, she was to be seen regularly in the 1950s and 1960s on the small screen in a number of favourite series, and she also appeared on radio. (Joan Caulfield's death was briefly noted in *Film Review 1991–2*.)

Film fame is sometimes strangely won: although **Mae Clarke** (real name, Mary Klotz), who died on 29 April 1992 at the age of 81, had a career spanning

Mae Clarke

38 years and appeared in nearly 100 movies, she will always be known to film buffs as the actress who had a grapefruit squashed in her face by James Cagney in *The Public Enemy*. The daughter of a cinema organist, Mae Clarke started her professional career as a dancer in cabaret, switched to stage musicals and made her film debut in 1929 in two films, *Big Times* and *Nix on Dames*. She achieved stardom in such films as *The Front Page, Waterloo Bridge* and *Frankenstein* (1931). Her other films include *Magnificent Obsession* (1954), *Thoroughly Modern Millie* (1967), *Watermelon Man* (1970), *Annie Get Your Gun* (1950), *The Great Caruso* (1951) and *Singin' in the Rain* (1952).

Those in showbusiness – even on the fringes – will know the name of **Theo Cowan**, ace publicist to the stars, who died in late September 1991. Cowan knew everyone and everyone knew Cowan. Formidable of appearance, surprisingly frank for someone in his game, glasses glinting, he was to be seen everywhere. A former Rank publicist, he soon became confident enough to set up his own business and quickly built up a starry list of clients, including Peter Sellers, Dirk Bogarde, Michael Caine, Richard Attenborough and many more.

Ray Danton, who died on 11 February 1992 at the age of 60, was an actor and director who will be best recalled for the playing of the title role in *The Rise and Fall of Legs Diamond* in 1960, playing the same character again the following year in the Dutch Schultz biopic *Portrait of a Mobster*. Gangster roles were his *forte*, and he took the title role in the 1961 film *The George Raft Story*. Danton began his long career as a child actor in radio. After three years' service in the US Army during the Korean War he turned to TV, in which medium he continued to act and direct throughout his life. Danton made his film debut in three 1955 films: *Chief Crazy Horse, The Spoilers* and *I'll Cry Tomorrow*, firmly establishing him as ideal casting for villain. After appearing in several more films – *The Beat Generation* (1959), *The Longest Day* and *The Chapman Report* (1962) – Danton went to Italy, where he made his directing debut with *Corrida for a Spy*, going on the make sixteen more films there and

John Dehner (in The Boys from Brazil)

starting up his own production company. In 1975 he returned to America, where he was mostly employed on the stage and TV. One of his last films as director was *The Deathmaster* in 1972; and as actor, *Psychic Killer* (which he also co-scripted) in 1975.

Familiar as a 'baddie' **John Dehner** – real name John Forkumin – died in Santa Barbara in early March 1992 at the age of 76. When not playing villains, Dehner could often be seen as a stern, merciless upholder of the law, and his more than 100 films included many Westerns. Dehner's first contact with the movies was as an animator for Walt Disney, and he made his acting debut after World War II (in which he was a war correspondent following General Patton through Africa and Europe) in *Lake Placid Serenade* in 1944 – after having also worked as a disc jockey and a pianist. Some of his more familiar films include: *Ten Tall Men* (1951), *Apache* (1954), *Carousel* and *The Fastest Gun Alive* (1956), *The Left-Handed Gun* (1958), *Cast a Long Shadow* (1959), *The Canadians* (1961 – his only leading role), *The Chapman Report* (1962), *Support Your Local Gunfighter* (1971), *The Day of the Dolphin* (1973), *Fun With Dick and Jane* (1977) and *The Boys from Brazil* (1978).

It was Richard Burton who once said of **Sandy Dennis** – with whom he co-starred in *Who's Afraid of Virginia Woolf?* in 1966, the film which won Miss Dennis her supporting actress Oscar – 'She's one of the genuine eccentrics I've known.' Certainly Miss Dennis, who died aged 54 on 2 March 1992, was odd by Hollywood stan-

Sandy Dennis

dards, once admitting she never went to see films – even her own – preferring to stay at home and read a good book. Miss Dennis (real name Sandra Dale Dennis) was a product of the Actors Studio and belonged to the Method school of acting, making her film debut, after some stage experience, in *Splendor in the Grass* in 1961. More recently Miss Dennis (she never married, living for a long time with her mother) gave some excellent 'middle-aged' performances, her last film being *The Indian Runner* in 1991. Her other films were: *The Fox* and *Up the Down Staircase* (1967), *Sweet November* (1968), *That Cold Day in the Park* (1969), *The Out-of-Towners* (1970), *Mr Sycamore* (1974), *God Told Me To* and *Nasty Habits* (1976), *The Animals Film* and *The Four Seasons* (1981), *Come Back to the Five and Dime Jimmy Dean, Jimmy Dean* (1982), *976-EVIL* and *Another Woman* (1988). With her high-pitched voice, nervous twitchy actions and often strange demeanour, Sandy Dennis didn't please some critics, even if others found her style endearing. Apart from her Oscar, she won the Best Actress award at the Moscow Film Festival. Both on and off the screen and on stage, she was certainly unique in Hollywood.

J. G. (James Gerard) **Devlin** was in the great tradition of Irish character actors and was a popular, very versatile player, coping with anything from Beckett's *Waiting for Godot* to a role in TV's 'Z Cars'. He didn't make many movies (he had only just completed a role in *Far and Away* when he died) but they included *No Surrender*, *The Garnet Saga* and Neil Jordan's *The Miracle*. He died aged 84 on 17 October 1991.

Once, long ago and far away, I fleetingly met the lovely and formidable **Marlene Dietrich**, who represented for me, with her smoky voice, distinctive accent, and secret slow smile, the golden age of Hollywood glamour. A little more of that glamour ended with her death as a recluse in her tiny but smart Paris flat at the age of 90 on 6 May 1992.

Berlin-born Maria Magdalene Dietrich studied the violin and for a short time played it professionally before turning to the theatre and studying under Max Reinhardt, leading to a number of German films, starting with

Marlene Dietrich

The Little Napoleon in 1923. Josef von Sternberg, in Berlin to cast his film *The Blue Angel* (1930), saw Dietrich performing and became enthralled, casting her opposite Emil Jannings. Her performance as the cabaret singer Lola Lois and her singing of 'Falling in Love Again' swept her to major stardom overnight. Under von Sternberg's guidance, Dietrich went on to make a series of six films, *Morocco* (1930), *Dishonoured* (1931), *Shanghai Express* and *Blonde Venus* (1932), *Scarlet Empress* (1934) and *The Devil Is a Woman* (1935), the commercial failure of the last leading to the break-up of the partnership. All the outstanding directors worldwide were eager to work with her, including Clair, Lubitsch, Hitchcock, Welles, Lang and Wilder, co-starring her with the foremost male stars of the period. During World War II Dietrich devoted much time to entertaining the troops with her one-woman show: they

adored her and her song 'Lili Marlene'. After *Just a Gigolo* (1978), Dietrich decided her public appearances would in future be confined to her always immensely popular solo shows, and she made no further films. Reluctant to let her public see her as an old woman, she became increasingly reclusive, refusing to be seen on moving or still camera, confined to her tiny flat, largely alone; a sad ending to a great career. Far more than an actress, a singer and glamorous star, Dietrich will be remembered as one of the great personalities of her era and the last of a kind.

Dietrich's other films included *The Garden of Allah* (1936), *Knight Without Armour* (1937), *Destry Rides Again* (1939), *The Flame of New Orleans* (1941), *The Lady Is Willing* (1942), *Kismet* (1944), *Golden Earrings* (1947), *A Foreign Affair* (1948), *Jigsaw* (1949), *Rancho Notorious* (1952), *Around the World in 80 Days* (1956), *Witness for the Prosecution* (1957), *Touch of Evil*

(1958), *Judgement at Nuremberg* (1961), *The Black Fox* (1962) and *Paris When It Sizzles* (1963).

Bill Douglas's output was small, and gets little mention in the film reference books. But Douglas deserves his place in British film history for his trio of stark films about his youth in Scotland: *My Childhood, My Ain Folk* and *My Way Home*. In contrast to these very short features, *Comrades* (1987), Douglas's final film – he died from cancer at only 54 – was a marathon effort, about the Tolpuddle Martyrs, nineteenth-century heroes of the British trade union movement.

It is to fans of the B-Western that the name of **Oliver Drake**, who died after a long illness on 5 August 1991, aged 88, will be best known. A cattle rancher who began making short films with his trained horse in 1917, he then made some 28 Westerns, writing, directing and starring in them. Taking the sound film in his stride, he continued pouring out Western features for the big companies like RKO Radio, Monogram, Columbia and Republic. He provided endless vehicles for Autry, Rogers, Tex Ritter, Johnny Mack Brown and other boots-and-saddles stars. He also directed and sometimes produced films like *The Texas Tornado* in 1934, *Today I Hang* in 1941, and *Song of the Sierras* in 1947. In 1951 he succumbed to the lure of TV and here again his output was immense, with such shows as 'The Gene Autry Show', 'Annie Oakley', 'The Adventures of Wild Bill Hickok', 'Lassie' and 'Gunsmoke'. But in 1967 he retired, to write his autobiography *Written, Produced and Directed by Oliver Drake*. Despite all this Western work, his name is strangely omitted from many reference sources, even those entirely devoted to the Western.

Mildred Dunnock, who died at the age of 90 on 5 July 1991, may not be familiar to the majority of modern moviegoers, but she made more than 25 feature films during her career and won supporting actress Oscar nominations for two of them: *Death of a Salesman* in 1951 (following her acclaim in the stage play) and *Baby Doll* five years later. Initially a teacher, at her parents' insistence, she took part in many amateur productions. She turned professional in 1931 and nine years later achieved a

Mildred Dunnock

personal triumph as the Welsh school-teacher in the Emlyn Williams play *The Corn Is Green*, a role she repeated five years later when the play was filmed. She scored another hit when she played the wife in the original Broadway production of *Death of a Salesman*, repeating this success in the 1951 film and

José Ferrer

the TV adaptation in 1966. Other fine performances followed on stage, screen and TV, and she became a valuable asset to any production. Her other films included: *Kiss of Death* (1947), *I Want You* (1951), *Viva Zapata!* (1952), *The Jazz Singer* and *Bad for Each Other* (1953), *The Trouble With Harry* (1955), *Love Me Tender* (1956), *Peyton Place* (1957), *The Nun's Story* (1959), *The Story on Page One* and *Butterfield 8* (1960), *Something Wild* (1961), *Sweet Bird of Youth* (1962), *Behold a Pale Horse* and *Youngblood Hawke* (1964), *Seven Women* (1965), *Whatever Happened to Aunt Alice* (1969), *One Summer Love/Dragonfly* (1976), the re-make of *The Spiral Staircase* the same year, and – her last film, made a decade later – *Pickup Artist*.

Puerto Rican born **José Ferrer** (full name José Ferrer de Otero y Cintron), who died on 26 January 1992 at the age of 80, had a 50-year theatrical career as actor, director and producer with some triumphs along the way. His awards included two Tonys for acting (in *Cyrano de Bergerac* in 1947 and *The Shrike* in 1952) with a third for directing *Stalag 17*, *The Fourposter* and *The*

Shrike the same year. In the cinema he won an Oscar in 1950 in *Cyrano de Bergerac* as well as nominations for his 1948 screen debut in *Joan of Arc* and for his performance as Toulouse Lautrec in John Huston's *Moulin Rouge*. Originally intending to become an architect, Ferrer won a BA at Princeton University and then switched his sights to the theatre, getting a first job in 1935 as an assistant stage manager. From then on he worked almost continuously in the theatre (his preferred medium), on screen and television. In fact he worked right up to his death and was planning to appear on Broadway in a new play in March 1992. But his career, however successful overall, was not without its failures, and after the 1960s it went into a decline, particularly in the cinema, where he had to play small character roles. Despite this, his successes were notable, and he was possibly – until Gerard Depardieu – the greatest Cyrano of both stage and screen. His other films included *Miss Sadie Thompson* (1953), *The Caine Mutiny* (1954), *The Cockleshell Heroes* (which he also directed, 1956), *The*

Paul Henreid

Great Man (which he also directed and co-scripted, 1957), *I Accuse* (in which he played Dreyfus and also directed, 1958), *Lawrence of Arabia* (1962), *The Greatest Story Ever Told* (1965), *Cervantes* (1967), *Voyage of the Damned* (1976), *The Swarm* (1978) and *The Fifth Musketeer* (1979).

Virginia Field (Margaret Cynthia Field), who died in late January 1992 at the age of 74, made some 30 films during her career and appeared in a number of plays and musicals on Broadway, from where she was lured to Hollywood by the offer of a Fox contract, playing second leads, often as the heroine's best friend. The daughter of a London barrister, she was educated in Britain, Paris and Vienna. She made her stage debut in Reinhardt's *All's Well That Ends Well* and her screen bow in the 1934 British film, *The Lady Is Willing*. She made a trio of films under her Fox contract in 1936 including *Lloyds of London* and the following year appeared in five films including *London by Night*, *Think Fast Mr Moto* and *Charlie Chan in Monte Carlo*. Five more films came in 1939, including another Mr Moto episode, *The Sun*

Never Sets and *The Cisco Kid and the Lady*. And in 1940 she gave what was to be her most memorable performance, as Vivien Leigh's friend in *Waterloo Bridge*. Later titles included *Hudson's Bay* (1941), *Atlantic Convoy* (1942), *The Crystal Ball* (1943), *The Imperfect Lady* (1948), *A Connecticut Yankee in King Arthur's Court* (1949), *Appointment With a Shadow* (1958), *The Explosive Generation* (1961) and, back in Britain, *The Earth Dies Screaming* (1964).

One of the great ladies of the British theatre, Dame **Gwen Ffrangcon-Davies** died on 27 January 1992 at the age of 101. Her 80-year career included many triumphs but she was seldom tempted to the film studios and appeared in very few movies, and then only in supporting roles. Indeed, few of her obituaries even mentioned her work outside the theatre and the occasional TV appearance. Her most notable movie was John Boorman's *Leo the Last*, made in 1969.

James Franciscus, who died aged 57 on 8 July 1991, had two main interests in life: drama and sport. At Yale, where he studied English and Drama, he excelled at football, baseball and running. Also at Yale, he produced and acted in several of his own plays, acting in summer stock productions during the holidays. His first big success was in *Four Boys and a Gun* in 1957, and he subsequently appeared in – between his almost constant TV work – a score of feature films, among which were *I Passed for White* (1960), *The Outsider* (1962), *Youngblood Hawke* (1964), *Marooned* (1969) and *The Day the World Ended* (1970). His was the voice of the bird in *Jonathan Livingston Seagull*, and he also appeared in a couple of British films – *Hell Boats* and *Planet of the Apes* in 1970 – and the Italian production *Cat o' Nine Tails* in 1971. In the 1970s he started the James Franciscus Celebrity Tennis Tournament in aid of victims of multiple sclerosis, a disease from which his mother suffered. In recent years he had become disillusioned with acting, and after 1985 he concentrated entirely on screenwriting.

The son of a Swedish baron who became a prominent banker in Vienna, Paul George Julius Henreid Ritter von Wassel-Waldingua, or **Paul Henreid** as moviegoers knew him, died at the age

Donald Houston

of 84 on 29 March 1992. Starting his working career as an assistant in a Vienna publishing house, he was 'discovered' by Otto Preminger in 1933, and was soon playing leading parts in Max Reinhardt's Vienna productions. Two years later he came to England, where he played Prince Albert in the play *Victoria Regina*. He made films here, too, notably as a German professor in *Goodbye Mr Chips*. In 1940 Henreid made his New York stage debut in *Flight to the West*. Hollywood beckoned and in 1942 he appeared as a French pilot in *Joan of Paris*, and in 1942 made a big hit as the underground leader Victor Laszlo in the classic *Casablanca*. In 1948 he became a producer with *Hollow Triumph* and after more producing became a director for television, which kept him busy on both sides of the camera. In the 1960s and 1970s he appeared less often, only making the occasional film, and in 1977 made his final appearance in *Exorcist II: The Heretic*. Of the 50 films in which he appeared these are some of the more familiar: *Victoria the Great* (1937), *Now, Voyager* (1942), *Between Two Worlds* (1944), *The Spanish Main* (1945), *Of Human Bondage* (1946), *Rope of Sand* (1949), *Last of the Buccaneers* and *So Young, So Bad* (1950), *Pardon My French* (1951), *Thief of Damascus* (1952), *Mantrap* (1951), *Live Fast, Die Young* (1958), *Holiday for Lovers* (1959), *The Four Horsemen of the Apocalypse* (1962), *Operation Crossbow* (1965) and *The Madwoman of Chaillot* (1969). Henreid also collaborated on *On the Road to Hollywood* in 1984.

Although chubby comic **Benny Hill** (real name, Alfred Hawthorn Hill), who died aged 67 on 20 April 1992, became popular in some 80 countries (including Russia and China) he inexplicably never found film fame, appearing in only a handful of movies (*Who Done It?*, *Light Up the Sky*, *Those Magnificent Men in their Flying Machines*, *The Italian Job* and *Chitty Chitty Bang Bang*). Hill's recipe for success was simple: seaside postcard humour, mixed with slapstick, smutty jokes and lots of lightly clad pretty girls: simple but highly effective, more especially so in his expert hands. You might even call him a comedy genius.

Donald Houston, the thick-set boy from Tonypandy in South Wales, who died at his adopted home in Portugal on 13 October 1991 at the age of 67, was primarily a stage actor despite his 40 films. He loved the theatre and returned to it at every opportunity, after making his repertory debut in 1940. After a brief flirtation with the movies in *A Girl Must Live*, he joined the RAF, serving as rear gunner and radio officer. He then went back to the theatre, and after finding success as the narrator in Dylan Thomas's *Under Milk Wood* and *The Cocktail Party*, boosted his career further by playing the young castaway opposite Jean Simmons in the 1949 film of *The Blue Lagoon*. Some of his other films included *Dance Hall* (1949), *The Red Beret* (1953), *Doctor in the House* (1954), *Yangtse Incident* (1957), *Room at the Top* (1958), *The Longest Day* (1962), *Doctor in Distress* and *Carry on Jack* (1963), *633 Squadron* (1964), *Where Eagles Dare* (1969), *My Lover, My Son* and *Bushbaby* (1970) and *Voyage of the Damned* (1976). His final appearance on the screen was in 1980 in *Sea Wolves*. Never a major star in movies, Houston always gave solid, professional performances, but reserved his best work for the stage.

In the masterly hands – and tones – of **Frankie Howerd**, the simplest and most unlikely phrase ('Ooh, ah, yes; let's get comfy') became invariably and unforgettably hilarious. Francis Alex Howerd, who died on 19 April at the age of 70, was a beloved clown and in his special way a genius. He could make a dictionary sidesplittingly comic by his inflexions, his surprised innocence and innuendos. Although he did appear on the stage – in comedies like *A Funny Thing Happened on the Way to the Forum* and Shakespeare's *A Midsummer Night's Dream* (as Bottom) – he was at his best in his one-man stage and music hall performances . . . and of course on TV, a perfect medium for him. Howerd also enjoyed some film success, notably in his Roman riot *Up Pompeii* (and the two sequels, *Up the Chastity Belt* and *Up the Front*). Others of his films were: *The House in Nightmare Park*, *The Cool Mikado*, *Watch It Sailor*, *Up the Creek* and *Further Up the Creek*, *The Ladykillers*, *Mouse on the Moon*, *An Alligator Named Daisy*, *The Runaway Bus*, several of the *Carry On* films and *The Great St Trinians Train Robbery*. With Frankie Howerd's death we all lose a lot of laughter.

Many actors can boast of 100 films in a lifetime – few can lay claim to more than 150. Yet that was the tally of **John Ireland**, the feature player who died aged 78 on 21 March 1992. Canadian-born Ireland began his showbiz career by appearing as a professional swimmer in water carnivals, soon coming in out of the water to play parts in the theatre, both on and off Broadway. His early star status didn't last long and he drifted into the secondary roles which he was to play for the rest of his life. He never won an Oscar, though he was

John Ireland

nominated for one in 1949 for his role in *All the King's Men*. In the 1960s his career took a downward turn that was to persist throughout the 1970s and 1980s – in fact in 1987 he took out an advert in a trade paper which said, 'I'm an actor; PLEASE let me act.' (The result was a part in the telefilm *Bonanza: The Next Generation*.) Just a few of his 150-plus films were: *My Darling Clementine* (1946), *I Shot Jesse James* (1949), *The Return of Jesse James* (1950), *Little Big Horn* and *The Bushwackers* (1951), *Hurricane Smith* (1952), *Outlaw Territory* (1953, which he also co-directed and produced), *Southwest Passage* (1954), *Queen Bee* (1955), *Gunfight at the OK Corral* (1957), *Faces in the Dark* (which he made in Britain in 1960), *Spartacus* (1960), *55 Days at Peking* (1963), *The Fall of the Roman Empire* (1964), *Fort Utah* (1967), *Farewell my Lovely* (1975), *Tomorrow Never Comes* (1978) and *The Shape of Things to Come* (1979).

One can readily appreciate why Polish-born Gunther Nakszynski adopted the somewhat simpler name of **Klaus Kinski** when he started out on his acting career. Kinski, who died on 23 November 1991 at the age of 65, made – according to *Variety* – at least 170 screen appearances during his varied international showbiz career; his most sensational and enduring being those in the films of German director Werner Herzog, with whom he had a close but stormy relationship (they wouldn't even speak to each other for a period of two years). Drafted into the German Army at the age of 16 during World War II, Kinski was captured by the Allies and became a British POW. After the war, he returned to Germany and began performing in small halls – where he revived the art of the poetry recital – before appearing in cabaret in Berlin. Kinski broke into films in 1948 in *Morituri* but it was not until 1955 that his career took off with a trio of films he made that year; *Ludwig II, Kinder, Mutter und ein General* and *Sarajewo*. Thereafter he always seemed to be in front of the cameras in one country or another – Britain, the United States, Spain, Israel, Italy, Austria and France included – appearing in everything from horror thrillers to comedies and Spaghetti Westerns – including Sergio Leone's *For a Few Dollars More*. But it was in Herzog's

Klaus Kinski (in Fitzcarraldo)

productions that he gave his best work – who can forget his horrific performance in *Nosferatu, the Vampyre*? His films included *Dead Eyes of London* (1961), *Dr Zhivago* (1965), *A Rocket to the Moon* (1967), *Su-Muru* (1967), *Venus in Furs* (1969), *Count Dracula* (1971), *Aguirre, The Wrath of God* (1972), *Woyzeck* (1979), *The Little Drummer Girl* (1984) and *Fitzcarraldo* (1982). In lesser films Kinski could seem uninterested and automatic but in portraying madness, or near to it, he was unexcelled – maybe because he once spent 90 days locked up in a lunatic asylum.

Moviegoers of the 1930s and 1940s will surely remember the performance of **Ginette Leclerk** (real name Geneviève Menut) as the voluptuous, flirtatious wife in Marcel Pagnol's witty *La Femme du Boulanger – The Baker's Wife* (1938), in which the baker was played by that beloved French clown, Raimu. Mme Leclerk, who died in Paris on 1 January 1992 at the age of 79, also gave

a memorable performance in Henri-George Clouzot's *Le Corbeau – The Crow* (1943). Only some of her 100 or more films have ever been screened in Britain, but her output included *L'Enfant du Miracle* (her screen debut in 1932), *Prisons sans Barreaux – Prisons Without Bars* (1939), *Le Mistral* (1942), *Le Plaisir* (1952), *Les Magiciennes – Double Deception* (1960) and, her final film, *Spermula* in 1976. She also made one film in America, *Tropic of Cancer* in 1970. She blotted her French copybook during World War II when she continued to act during the Nazi Occupation, an error of judgement which at the end of hostilities brought her a year's prison sentence and a temporary ban on future work.

Tutte Lemko, who died in late November 1991 at the age of 73, will most easily be recalled as the agile violinist in the film of the musical play *Fiddler on the Roof* (1971) – a role for which he learned to play the violin from scratch. Born Isak Samuel Lemko in Sweden, he came of Russian Jewish stock and started his showbusiness career in a double tap-dancing act – The Lemko Brothers – as well as playing ice hockey professionally. But in his teens he decided to make a switch to ballet and started training with the Norwegian Ballet Company. Forced to flee when the Nazis invaded Denmark, Lemko walked to Sweden with all his worldly goods slung over his shoulder. He was soon dancing with the Swedish Ballet and appeared in their production, the first outside Russia, of Prokofiev's *Romeo and Juliet*. At this time he met and married a young Swedish actress, Mai Zetterling. He continued dancing in Madrid, Copenhagen and Paris before coming to England in 1947 to join the Ballet Rambert. But he became increasingly involved with film and stage choreography while at the same time finding himself wooed to play a number of straight character parts in films and plays, the former including roles in *Moulin Rouge* (1952), *Masquerade* (1964) and, more recently, *Raiders of the Lost Ark* (1981). He was associated with Peter Sellers in the production of *A Shot in the Dark* (1964)

Fred MacMurray

and *The Wrong Box* (1966) and, with Tony Shaffer, wrote the script for the TV series 'Thor the Viking'. (He was also the anonymous occasional contributor to the 'Show Talk' columns of *What's On in London*. Another of his lesser known facets was his training as a film editor under Roy Boulting, which stood him in good stead when he directed three full-length ballet films. Small, restless, endlessly gifted, he was always ready to take on new challenges, but was too volatile by nature ever to become an international star in any one area of showbusiness.

John Lund, who died aged 81 on 10 May 1992, never quite fulfilled the promise he showed in his early career, and he retired in the early 1960s after a number of minor roles. The son of a Norwegian-born glassblower, Lund did various manual jobs until he wound up in a New York advertising agency. At this point he was offered a part in one of the World's Fair shows and subsequently appeared on Broadway in a production of *As You Like It*. He also worked on radio, both as writer and

performer, and he wrote both book and lyrics for the Broadway revue *New Faces of 1943*. He made his film debut in *To Each His Own* in 1946 and went on to appear in *The Perils of Pauline* (1947), *Miss Tatlock's Millions*, *A Foreign Affair* and *The Night Has 1000 Eyes* (1948), *My Friend Irma* (1949), *The Mating Season* (1951), *The Battle of Apache Pass* (1952), *Latin Lovers* (1953), *Chief Crazy Horse* (1955) and *High Society* (1956). His final appearance was apparently in *If a Man Answers* in 1962.

One of the busiest and best supporting actresses in Hollywood – she won the Best Supporting Actress Oscar in 1944 for her performance in *Dragon Seed* – **Aline MacMahon** died on 12 October 1991 at the age of 92. Dark haired, with expressive, sad eyes, Miss MacMahon was not the routine Hollywood beauty – and so never became a regular star – but she had great presence and an impressive personality. She began her career in the theatre in 1920 and it wasn't until 1931 that she was tempted to Hollywood for a supporting role in *Five Star Final*. Thereafter she was seldom out of the studios for long, appearing in nearly fifty films, among which were: *Gold Diggers of 1933*, *Babbitt* (1934), *Ah! Wilderness* (1935), *The Lady Is Willing* (1942), *Dragon Seed* (1944), *The Flame and the Arrow* (1950), *Cimarron* (1960), *Diamond Head* and, in Britain, *I Could.Go on Singing* (1963).

Fred MacMurray, who died on 6 November 1991 at the age of 83, was essentially a 'nice guy' and light comedian, though paradoxically it was in *Double Indemnity* in 1944 that he gave his greatest performance, as a murderer opposite Barbara Stanwyck's scheming siren. A saxophonist and singer in his college days, MacMurray started his career as a member of night-club bands, leading to his debut as just that in the Broadway musical of 1930, *Three's a Crowd*. This led in turn to a screen test and contract with Paramount, and his screen debut in *Friends of Mr Sweeney* in 1934. Loaned to RKO Radio the following year, his performances in *Grand Old Girl* and, more particularly, opposite Claudette Colbert in the comedy *The Gilded Lily* made him a star, which he remained for his next fifty films, at the rate of between four and five a year. His career seemed to be tailing off in the 1950s but it rose again triumphantly when Walt Disney starred him in a series of family comedies starting with *The Shaggy Dog* (1959), although he followed this by unexpectedly playing the heel again – brilliantly – in *The Apartment* (1960). But he was soon back in his familiar role as the bemused family man in further Disney comedies such as *The Absent Minded Professor* (1961) and *Son of Flubber* (1963). The musical *The Happiest Millionaire* (1972) and *Charley and the Angel* (1973) were followed by MacMurray's final appearance in 1978 in *The Swarm*. Genuinely modest, he is on record as once saying 'I wouldn't walk around the corner to see any Mac-Murray films,' and 'I have always been scared stiff of performing in front of people for my whole life' – and meaning it. He is credited with somewhere between fifty and eighty films, among which were: *Alice Adams* (1935), *The Trail of the Lonesome Pine* and *The Texas Rangers* (1936), *Sing You Sinners* (1938), *Cafe Society* (1939), *Little Old New York* (1940), *Dive Bomber* and *One Night in Lisbon* (1941), *The Lady Is Willing* and *Star Spangled Rhythm* (1942), *Above Suspicion* (1943), *And the Angels Sing* (1944), *Murder He Says* and *Captain Eddie* (1945), *The Egg and I* (1947), *Never a Dull Moment* (1950), *Callaway Went Thataway* (1951), *The Caine Mutiny* (1954), *The Rains of Ranchipur* (1955), *There's Always Tomorrow* (1956), *Day of the Badman* (1958), *A Good Day for a Hanging* and *The Oregon Trail* (1959).

Marne Maitland lived in Rome (where he died in mid-March 1992 at the age of 76) since the early 1970s, but was born in India and then moved to England at an early age. He started acting while still at Magdalen College, Cambridge, and played numerous roles before the war. After six years in the British Army he returned to acting, joining the British Old Vic Company and doing a great deal of work for TV. His Indian appearance made him a natural for Eastern roles and he appeared in numerous films, among them *Bhowani Junction* (1956), *Camp on Blood Island* (1958), *Cleopatra* (1963), *Anne of the Thousand Days* (1969), *The Trail of the Pink Panther* (1982), *I'm Al Right Jack* (1959), *The Man with the Golden Gun* (1974) and

Yves Montand

many others. He continued working through a long illness, and only a few weeks before his death reluctantly turned down a film offer.

Daniel Mann (real name Clugerman), who died on 21 November 1991 at the age of 79, had a varied career including performing as a comedian and musician, and teaching drama, before becoming a prominent stage director and TV producer after the war. The acting in his films was always top class and it was in his *Come Back Little Sheba* (1952) that Shirley Booth won her Oscar; in *The Rose Tattoo* (1955) , that Anna Magnani won hers; and in *Butterfield 8* (1960) that Elizabeth Taylor won the first of hers. Mann's other films include *I'll Cry Tomorrow* (1955), *The Teahouse of the August Moon* (1956), *The*

Last Angry Man (1959), *Who's Been Sleeping In My Bed* (1963), *Our Man Flint* (1966), *For Love of Ivy* (1968), *Journey Into Fear* (1975) and, his final film, *The Incredible Mr Chadwick* (1980).

Popular French singer, actor and political personality **Yves Montand** (real name Ivo Livi) died aged 70 on 9 November 1991, while on location for a new film. Originally Italian, Montand made his stage debut in Marseilles in 1939, and during World War II worked as a docker while taking singing, dancing and English lessons. After the war he returned to the theatre and was taken under the wing – and into the bed – of Edith Piaf. He appeared on the screen for the first time in 1946 in *Etoile sans Lumière*. Three years later he met and married film star Simone Signoret, a marriage that was to last, in spite of his several well-publicised affairs, until her death in 1985. Originally active on the political left, as a communist, he later became firmly right-wing, and was once considered as a possible Presidential candidate.

Montand became an international star when he made Clouzot's thriller *The Wages of Fear – La Salaire de la Peur* in 1953 and from then on made movies in Hollywood as well as France and Italy, though he was not comfortably cast in some of his American work. It was just when his film career appeared to be waning that in 1986 he made the two films which capped his career and in which he achieved his greatest performances, as the artful, mean and yet finally dignified Provencal patriarch in Claude Berri's magnificent adaptation of Marcel Pagnol's stories *Jean de Florette* and *Manon des Sources*. He completed his last film in 1990, Jacques Deray's *Netchhiev Est de Retour*. Others of his 60-odd films include *L'Idole* (1948), *Souvenirs*

George Murphy

Perdus (1950), *Temi Nostri* (1953), *Napoleon et Les Heros Sont Fatigués* (1955), *Marguerite de la Nuit* (as Mephistopheles, 1956), *Uomini e Lupi* and *The Witches of Salem* (1957), *La Grande Strada Azzura* (1958), *La Loi – Where the Hot Wind Blows* (1959), *Let's Make Love* (1960), *Goodbye Again – Aimez-vous Brahms?* (1961), *My Geisha* (1962), *Is Paris Burning?* and *Grand Prix* (1966), *Le Diable par la Queue – The Devil by the Tail* and *Z* (1969), *On a Clear Day You Can See Forever* (1970), *La Folie des Grandeurs* (1971), *Tout va Bien* and *Cesar and Rosalie* (1972), *Vincent, Francois, Paul and the Others* (1975), *Le Grand Escogriffe* (1976), *Routes du Sud* (1978) and *Clair de Femme* (1979).

Always larger than life, **Robert Morley** died of a stroke on 3 June 1992 at the age of 84. (A keen fan of racing, he would have appreciated the irony of dying on Derby Day.) A great personality, who stamped his own mark on everything he did, Morley was very versatile: apart from his acting he wrote eight plays and five books, and contributed regularly to *Punch*, *Playboy* and other publications. Rotund, witty (he loved talking), and naturally wise in the mechanics of his profession, Morley early on in his career won the hearts of theatregoers and retained their affection all his life. Educated at Wellington School (which he hated; asked to go back to talk to the pupils, he said he would only return if he could burn the place down), he made his stage debut in 1929. In the same year he made his first film, playing the pathetic King Louis XVI in *Marie Antoinette* (Norma Shearer was the Queen) and gaining an Oscar nomination for the role, a unique distinction. He made well over 50 films (as well as all his plays and television appearances), some of which were: *Major Barbara* (1941), *Edward, My Son* (from his own play: 1948), *The African Queen* (1951), *Outcast of the Islands* (1951), *Melba* (1952), *Beau Brummell* (1954), *Quentin Durward* (1955), *Around the World in 80 Days* (1956), *The Doctor's Dilemma* (1958), *The Sheriff of Fractured Jaw* (1958), *Oscar Wilde* (1960), *The Old Dark House* (1963), *Of Human Bondage* (1964), *Topkapi* (1964), *Genghis Khan* (1965), *The Loved One* (1965), *Those Magnificent Men in their Flying Machines* (1965), *The Alphabet Murders* (1966), *Sinful Davey* (1969), *Cromwell* (1970), *Theatre of Blood* (1973), *The Blue Bird* (1976), *Who Is Killing the Great Chefs of Europe?* (1978), *The Human Factor* (1979), *High Road to China* (1983), *Second Time Lucky* (1984), *The Wind* (1987), *Little Dorrit* (1988) and *Istanbul* (1990).

Cabaret act, stage and screen star turned politician, **George Murphy** died of leukaemia aged 89 on 3 May 1992. His screen career began in 1934 when he was noticed by the talent scouts while playing second lead in the stage musical *Roberta*. The result was a supporting role in the Eddie Cantor musical *Kid Millions*. An agile dancer, with a cheerful and pleasant personality, Murphy quickly became a popular star of screen musicals. In 1943 he was elected President of the Screen Actors Guild, which he guided successfully through some very difficult times. He finally retired from acting in order to work on the business side of movies, including the position of Vice-President at Technicolor. In 1964 he stood for the California seat in the US Senate and won it against some stiff opposition. In 1950 he was awarded a special Oscar for his work in 'interpreting the film industry to the country at large'. Among Murphy's films are *The Broadway Melody* of 1938 and 1940, *Little Miss Broadway* (1938), *Risky Business* (1939), *Little Nellie Kelly* (1940), *Tom, Dick and Harry* (1941), *The Navy Comes Through, For Me and My Gal* and *This Is the Army* (1943), *Broadway Rhythm* (1945), *Up Goes Maisie* (1946), *Cynthia* (1947), *Tenth Avenue Angel* (1948), *Battleground* (1949), *It's a Big Country* and *Talk About a Stranger* (1952).

Laurence Naismith (real name, Laurence Johnson) was one of those dependable feature players who, though they never achieve actual stardom, are kept busy on screen, stage and television. Born in Surrey, he died in Southport, Australia, on 5 June 1992 at the age of 83 – still working. Naismith made his stage debut when he was eighteen, as one of the chorus in the 1927 musical *Oh, Kay*, but he didn't make his screen debut until 1948, when he had a role in *Trouble in the Air*. His many later movies included *Camelot* (1970), *Richard III* (1955), *Jason and the Argonauts* (1963), *Boy on a Dolphin* (1957), *Diamonds Are Forever* (1971), *The Trials of Oscar Wilde* (1960), *Sink the Bismarck!* (1960), *The Angry Silence* (1960), *Solomon and Sheba* (1959), *The Beggar's Opera* (1953), *Carrington VC* (1955) and *The Singer Not the Song* (1961).

An unfamiliar name to today's moviegoers, **Doriel Paget** (born Dorothy Elizabeth Paget), who died aged 93 in August 1991, appeared in many British silent films. Though primarily a singer and stage actress, she also appeared in concert parties during World War I, and later had a long and successful season at the famous Dublin Abbey Theatre with her husband, Colin Firth (who met his wife-to-be by knocking her down with his bicycle). At the insistence of her father she retired from public life before the 1939 outbreak of war in 1939. Miss Paget was one of the founder members of British Actors' Equity.

Producer of more than a hundred movies – almost all of them highly successful – **Joe Pasternak** died in Hollywood from Parkinson's Disease on 13 September 1991 at the age of 89. The secret of his success lay simply in familiar, innocent stories (which often brought a sniffy reaction from the critics), melodies that one came out of the cinema humming, and winning performances by the stars. Pasternak certainly used top stars, but often created them himself, such as Deanna Durbin (in *Three Smart Girls*, her screen debut; she went on to make ten movies with the maestro), Judy Garland, Esther Williams and Mario Lanza, all of whom he gave their first chance. He also turned Marlene Dietrich's faltering career into a bonanza when he starred her in his comedy Western classic *Destry Rides Again*, and with the Durbin films he transformed the ailing Universal Pictures into a new and highly successful major studio.

Born in a small village in Hungary (with a name he himself admitted was unpronounceable) Pasternak came to America as an immigrant determined to make movies, and achieved the first shaky rung of the ladder when he was employed as a dishwasher at Universal studios, soon rising to waiter. He climbed a further rung when he was appointed fourth assistant to a director. His own first film was a two-reel comedy starring comic El Brendel, which he both wrote and directed. It was successful enough for Universal to offer him the position of assistant director, which in turn led to his becoming associate producer. Visiting Europe for a Universal production, he stayed for six years, making movies in Germany (which he had to flee when the Nazis came to power – members of his family were sent to the gas chambers) and in his native Hungary. He returned to Hollywood in 1936 to continue his highly successful career at Universal. But in 1941 he accepted an offer from MGM, where he stayed for the next 27 years, as one of their top producers.

Pasternak's output was noteworthy for the charm and musical excellence of his films – 'Keep the people nice,' he was reported as saying. 'Even when I was a waiter I liked to keep things clean!' It's sad to have to recall that his final picture, a youth-oriented movie called *Sweet Ride*, was something of a flop; sad, too, was the fact that although the stars of his films won many Oscars he never achieved that accolade himself. His ghost-written autobiography, *Easy the Hard Way*, was published in 1956.

It's impossible to list every one of his films (variously claimed to be between 86 and 110) but the best known and best loved are: *Three Smart Girls* (1936, his Hollywood debut after several films in Europe), *100 Men and a Girl* (1937), *Mad About Music* and *That Certain Age* (1938), *Three Smart Girls Grow Up, First Love* and *Destry Rides Again* (1939), *A Little Bit of Heaven* and *Seven Sinners* (1940), *The Flame of New Orleans* and *It Started With Eve* (1941), *Seven Sweethearts* (1942), *Presenting Lily Mars* and *Thousands Cheer* (1943), *Song of Russia* and *Two Girls and a Sailor* (1944), *Music for Millions, Thrill of a Romance* and *Anchors Aweigh* (1945), *Holiday in Mexico* and *Two Sisters from Boston* (1946), *This Time for Keeps* and *The Unfinished Dance* (1947), *A Date with Judy, On an Island With You, Luxury Liner* and *The Kissing Bandit* (1948), *In the Good Old Summertime* (1949), *Summer Stock* and *The Toast of New Orleans* (1950), *The Great Caruso* (1951), *Skirts Ahoy* and *The Merry Widow* (1952), *Latin Lovers* and *Easy to Love* (1953), *The Flame and the Flesh* and *The Student Prince* (1954), *Hit the Deck* and *Love Me or Leave Me* (1955), *Meet Me in Las Vegas* (1956), *This Could Be the Night* (1957), *Party Girl* (1958), *Ask Any Girl* (1959), *Please Don't Eat the Daisies* (1960), *Girl Happy* (1965), *Made in Paris* (1966) and *The Sweet Ride* (1968).

French star **Suzy Prim**, often seen as a *femme fatale*, died at the age of 95 at the end of July 1991. With the real name of Suzanne Arduini, she made her stage debut in 1897 and reached cinema stardom in the 1930s. She made more than 50 films, among which was the original *Mayerling* directed by Anatole Litvak in 1935, *Tarakanova* (a very sexy Catherine the Great), Andre Cayatte's *Au Bonheur des Dames* (1947), Duvivier's *Au Royaume des Cieux* (1949), and Renoir's *Can-Can* (1955). By 1955 she had become deeply involved in production, but she continued taking the occasional acting role in films until 1976.

Just a month after being awarded a special Oscar for his films, **Satyajit Ray**, one of the world's greatest movie-

Lee Remick

makers, died aged 70 on 23 April 1992. Ray always generously credited the American film for its influence on his work, but his productions were as unlike the typical American movies as one could imagine. Leisurely, detailed, non-violent and psychologically subtle in their handling of Indian problems, they were perfect portraits of a people and way of life totally unlike the Western world. Made in the minority Bengali language, Ray's films never had the appeal in India that they had elsewhere.

For ten years Ray was lay-out artist and art director for the Calcutta branch of an English advertising agency, illustrating books as well. One of these was *Pather Panchali* which so fascinated him he decided to make a film of it. Unable to get any funding, he started to make it at weekends and in his spare time, but eventually succeeded in get-

ting a government grant, with which he completed it. The film went on to win the Special Jury Prize at the Cannes Film Festival. From this sprang the famous Apu trilogy, the second film of which, *Aparajito*, won the premier Golden Lion award at the 1956 Venice Film Festival. *The World of Apu* completed the trio in 1959. Ray called his movies 'chamber music films', and they were very much his own creations from start to finish, with Ray as director, writer, composer, casting director, cinematographer and all else in many of his productions, making the end results highly individual and personal. While working on *The Home and the World* in 1984 Ray suffered two heart attacks which forced him to stop all work for five years. But he returned in 1989 to make *An Enemy of the People*, completing two more films prior to his death, *The Branches of the Tree* (1990) and *The Stranger* (1991). Ray's other films included *Charulata* (1964), *Shakespeare*

Wallah (1965), *Days and Nights in the Forest* (1969), *The Adversary* (1971), *Company* (1972), *Distant Thunder* (1973), *The Chess Players* (1977), *The Elephant God* (1979) and *Deliverance* (1982).

Having lived in England for some thirteen years, **Lee Remick**, who died aged 55 on 2 July 1991, was almost regarded as an honorary Briton and indeed she called herself 'the resident American in England'. Lee Remick was one of the most versatile stars that Hollywood has produced, with a wide range of roles played beautifully and in general faultlessly. She was equally convincing playing straight or comic, seductive or ladylike; and equally effective on film, stage, television or radio, dividing her time fairly equally between the various mediums.

With original ambitions to become a dancer, she decided to become an actress after an invitation to join a summer stock company, though her subsequent debut on Broadway (as a wisecracking teenager in the flop *Be Your Age*) was hardly encouraging. Turning to TV, she was picked from there by Elia Kazan to star in his 1957 film *A Face in the Crowd*. Her performance persuaded Fox to offer her a contract, the first result of which was a sizzling performance in *The Long Hot Summer* (1958). After a Western, *These Thousand Hills* (1959), she gave a memorable performance in Otto Preminger's controversial courtroom drama *Anatomy of a Murder* in the same year, followed by an equally impressive in-depth portrait of a tragic habitual drunk in *Days of Wine and Roses* (1962). She then came to England to appear in Carol Reed's *The Running Man* (1963) and returned to the US theatre, to star in the 1964 musical *Anyone Can Whistle* and the thriller hit *After Dark*. Seeing the difficult 'in-between' years for a film star on the horizon, she switched to TV, where she had some big successes in series and telefeatures, including *The Blue Knight* (1973), which though made as a four-part mini-series in the US ended up as a cinema feature release in Britain. Then came Miss Remick's greatest TV success, playing Winston Churchill's mother in *Jennie*. A vast amount of small-screen work preceded and followed this career triumph and her output lessened only as her cancer grew worse. Her final appearance was on stage in the summer of 1990 in *Love Letters* at the Canon Theater in Beverly Hills.

Lee Remick, who admitted she was not tough enough to consistently face up to Hollywood – she called herself 'a housewife who only incidentally is an actress' – was one of the cinema's most accomplished and versatile stars, as her list of honours suggests: an Oscar nomination for *Days of Wine and Roses* (for which many people thought she should have won the award), seven Emmy nominations, the British Academy of Film and TV's 1975 Best Actress award (for *Jennie*) and the 1960 Tony prize for her role in *Wait Until Dark*. Others of her total of more than 25 films include *Sanctuary* (1961), *Experiment in Terror* (1962), *Baby the Rain Must Fall* and *The Hallelujah Trail* (1965), *The Detective* (1968), *Never Give an Inch* (1971), *Delicate Balance* (1973), *The Omen* (1976) and *Telefon* (1977). Her other British films (apart from Carol Reed's *Running Man*) were *A Severed Head* and *Loot* (1968), *Hennessee* (1975), *The Hunted* (1976), *The Medusa Touch* (1978) and James Ivory's *The Europeans* (1979).

Anti-establishment left-wing British director–producer **Cecil Anthony 'Tony' Richardson** died of AIDS at the age of 63 on 14 November 1991. Richardson made some 20 films, including his adaptation of Fielding's classic, *Tom Jones* (1963), which won him an Oscar. Initially a BBC producer, he became director of the Royal Court theatre and met playwright John Osborne while producing Osborne's play, *Look Back in Anger*. Osborne and Richardson together formed Woodfall Films, originally to make a film of the play (1959), but later to make several other movies including *Saturday Night and Sunday Morning* (1960), *A Taste of Honey* (1961), *The Entertainer* (1960) and *The Loneliness of the Long Distance Runner* (1962). This work led to his first, very disappointing, Hollywood film, *Sanctuary* (1961), but the riotous success of *Tom Jones* more than compensated for this. His gimmicky flop *The Charge of the Light Brigade* (1968) was followed by *Ned Kelly* (1970), starring Mick Jagger as the Australian bushranger. His last film, *Blue Skies*, is at the time of writing still unreleased. His other films include *The Loved One*

Gene Tierney

(1965), *Mademoiselle* (French/English, 1966), *Sailor from Gibraltar* (1967), *Hamlet* (1969), *A Delicate Balance* and *Dead Cert* (1973), *The Border* (1982), *Hotel New Hampshire* (1984) and *Hills Like White Elephants* (1989). Richardson was at one time married to Vanessa Redgrave, with whom he had two daughters, Natasha and Joely, both now actresses.

Viviane Romance (real name Pauline Ortman), who died in Nice in late October 1991 at the age of 79, was 'Miss Paris' of 1930 and entered the French film business as an extra the following year, reaching the peak of her success between the mid-1930s and the mid-1940s. Only a small number of her films reached Britain, among them Duvivier's *La Bandera* (1935), *La Belle Equipe* (1936) and *Carmen* (1943). During World War II she made many enemies by acting for the Germans.

Later films included *The Seven Deadly Sins* (1952), Henri Verneuil's *Mélodie en Sous-Sol* (1963) and Chabrol's *Nada*, which was to be her final screen appearance.

For an actress known more for her great, theatrical beauty than her acting prowess, **Gene Tierney**, who died aged 70 on 6 November 1991, nonetheless had the benefit of working with some of Hollywood's best directors, notably Fritz Lang, John Ford, von Sternberg, Rouben Mamoulian, Ernst Lubitsch, Otto Preminger and Joseph L. Mankiewicz. None of them succeeded in producing the electric performance that always seemed promised by this mysterious, green-eyed, dark-haired star, though she did win an Oscar nomination for her performance in the 1945 melodrama *Leave Her to Heaven*. Her private life was as sensational as any role she played on screen, her well-publicised liaisons with John F. Kennedy, Howard Hughes, Tyrone Power and Aly Khan keeping her constantly in the

Regis Toomey

of his theatrical career firmly on the stage (including a tour of England in *Little Nelly Kelly*), and it wasn't until 1929 that he turned to films, with two minor roles that year in *Alibi* and *Illusion*. His more familiar other films include: *The Light of Western Stars* (1930), *Shopworn* (1932), *State Trooper* (1933), *G-Men* (1935), *Big City* and *Shadows of the Orient* (1937), *Union Pacific* (1939), *His Girl Friday*, *Northwest Passage* and *North West Mounted Police* (1940), *Meet John Doe* and *They Died with Their Boots On* (1941), *The Forest Rangers* (1942), *Jack London* (1943), *Spellbound* (1945), *The Big Sleep* and *The Bishop's Wife* (1947), *The Boy with Green Hair* (1948), *Show Boat* (1951), *The High and the Mighty* (1954), *Guys and Dolls* (1955), *Warlock* (1959) – and the list goes on. In addition to his vast number of films, Toomey was a great TV favourite, and he was a gift to casting directors, who knew whatever the role he would do it impeccably.

While there may be some excuse for leaving **Thorley Walters** out of Katz's (American) *Film Encyclopedia*, it is wholly unforgivable that his name is omitted from *Who's Who in British Films*, for Walters, who died at the age of 78 on 6 July 1991, appeared in some 60 films during a career that lasted 57

Thorley Walters

headlines. Just as newsworthy was her parents' fight against her marriage to dress designer Count Oleg Cassini. She contracted measles while she was pregnant in 1943, and her daughter (one of two by Cassini) was born severely retarded, one of the main causes of Miss Tierney's traumas that followed, leading to her becoming a patient in a mental home. In 1970 these incidents were included in a film made about her life.

Among her 40-odd films were: *The Return of Jesse James* (her screen debut in 1940), *Hudson's Bay* and *Tobacco Road* (1941), *Belle Starr* (1941), *Shanghai Gesture*, *Rings on Her Fingers*, *Son of Fury* and *Thunder Birds* (all 1942), *China Girl* and *Heaven Can Wait* (1943), *Laura* (1944), *A Bell for Adano*

(1945), *Dragonwyck* and *The Razor's Edge* (1946), *The Ghost and Mrs Muir* (1947), *The Iron Curtain* (1948), *The Mating Season* and *On the Riviera* (1951), *Never Let Me Go* (1953), *Personal Affair* – her one British film – and *The Egyptian* (1954), *The Left Hand of God* (1955), *Advise and Consent* (1962), and her final film, *The Pleasure Seekers* (1964). She did make some subsequent appearances on TV. Her own story of her tempestuous life, *Self Portrait*, was published in 1979.

It is said that in all his 200-plus films, **Regis Toomey** – who died aged 93 on 12 October 1991 – never gave anything but a very good performance; certainly Hollywood knew him as a dependable, versatile and very professional performer. Changing plans in mid-stream (he was originally set on the law) the young Toomey spent the first five years

years. The son of a priest, Walters made his acting debut in a London production of Shaw's *The Admirable Bashville* in 1933. Thereafter he was seldom not working, either on the stage, in the film studios or in front of the TV cameras. He established himself as a brilliant young light comedian in the Cicely Courtneidge/Jack Hulbert *Under the Counter* which after some 700 performances in England crossed the Atlantic to chalk up a similar success in the United States. Walters's films include *Private's Progress* (1956), *Blue Murder at St Trinians* (1957), Hammer's own version of *The Phantom of the Opera* (1962), *Dracula Prince of Darkness* (1965), *Rotten to the Core* (1965), *The Wrong Box* (1966), *Oh! What a Lovely War* (1969), *Trog* (1970), *There's a Girl in My Soup* (1970), *Mr Forbush and the Penguins* (1970), *Young Winston* (1972), *The Adventures of Sherlock Holmes's Smarter Brother* (1967), *The Wildcats of St Trinians* (1980), *A Walk in the Sun* (1945), *Spider's Web* (1960) and *The Little Drummer Girl* (1984). Handsome, with a winning personality, a wide range of performances, a perfect sense of comic timing, and a smooth overall polish which he brought to every role he played, Walters was one of the most welcome names in any cast list.

Essentially a stage actor and TV favourite who made the occasional film, **Alan Wheatley**, who died at the age of 84 on 30 August 1991, is probably most widely known and admired for his early radio and TV success in the early 'Sherlock Holmes' series and, more recently, *The Adventures of Robin Hood*, *The Avengers* and the *Doctor Who* series. Among his films were Gabriel Pascal's *Caesar and Cleopatra* (1945), *Conquest of the Air* (1961), *Brighton Rock* (1947), *The Rake's Progress* (1945) and *Shadow of the Cat* (1980). Wheatley was praised for his work on the BBC's World Service during World War II.

London-born **Carol White**, who died aged 49 in late September 1991 of liver failure at her Florida home, had a less than happy life. She never recaptured the success of her early career, when she starred in a number of 'kitchen-sink' dramas on film, radio and TV, such as *Up the Junction* and *Cathy Come Home* (TV, 1965), and *Poor Cow* (film, 1967). Her performance in *The Fixer* in 1968 won her a Hollywood contract,

Carol White

the first result of which was *Daddy's Gone a-Hunting* (1969). But Hollywood didn't prove easy for her (she once said, 'I came to America thinking I was at the top, but pimps, pushers, liars and ex-husbands brought me crashing down') and she was soon making headlines for her personal life rather than her performances, with stories about her romances, marriages, divorces, drinking and drugs. She was last in the UK in 1982, when she was hired to appear in the stage play *Steaming*, only to be sacked because of missed performances. Her seventeen or so films included: *Circus Friends* (her screen debut in 1956), *Carry on Teacher* (1959), *Linda* (1960), *Gaolbreak* (1962), *Ladies Who Do* (1963), *Slave Girls* (1966), *I'll Never Forget Whatsisname* (1967), *The Man Who Had Power Over Women* (1970), *Dulcima* (1971), *Made* (1972) and *The Squeeze* (1977). Her last two film appearances were in *The*

Spaceman and King Arthur (1979) and *Nutcracker* (1982). Carol White wrote two books: *Carol Comes Home* (memoirs) and *Forever Young*, a book about beauty. In a final tribute, writer Jeremy Sandford said: '. . . Carol, besides being pure and straight, was always reckless, always something of a life gambler.'

Others who have died during the year include:

British musical comedy and straight actress **Adele Dixon**, in April 1992, at the age of 83. Though essentially a stage actress, Miss Dixon did appear in a number of films including *Uneasy Virtue* (1931), *Calling the Tune* (1936) and *Woman to Woman* (1947).

Art Babbitt, film animator and creator of the Goofy character in so many Disney cartoons. He was 84 when he died in Hollywood in May 1992. Babbitt animated Donald Duck for his screen debut in 1934.

Bookshelf
A selection of the year's books on cinema

IVAN BUTLER

Recession or not, the torrent of cinema books shows no sign of drying up. To attempt to cover anything like all of them in detail would be impossible in this space, but I have this year introduced a simple additional listing by title of books worth mentioning, but which there was no room to review.

This year has seen a large number of excellent film books published, particularly biographies and works of reference. My personal choice from these would include Kate Fleming's delightful life of her sister, *Celia Johnson*, Richard VanDerBeet's sensitive study of *George Sanders*, Scott Eyman's *Mary Pickford* and the autobiography of *Fred Zinnemann*; and of the reference works, William Darby's *Masters of Lens and Light*, George A. Katchmer's *Eighty Silent Film Stars* and the invaluable *Virgin International Encyclopedia of Film*, about to be joined imminently by *The Virgin Film Guide*.

Andrew Marton, interviewed by Joanne d'Antonio; Scarecrow Press, dist. Shelwing, £39.40
Hopalong Cassidy, Bernard A. Drew; Scarecrow Press, dist. Shelwing, £24.40
Screen Gems, Jed. H. Perry; Scarecrow Press, dist. Shelwing, £31.90

Three more volumes from the extensive Scarecrow library exploring the less travelled avenues of the film and television world.

Andrew Marton is an 'Oral History', in which Marton talks about his long career, mainly as 2nd Unit director on such pictures as the 1959 *Ben-Hur* (the famous chariot race), *The Red Badge of Courage* and *The Longest Day*. He is an articulate and frank interviewee and the book is full of fascinating sidelights on the making of movies.

Hopalong Cassidy is a comprehensive and detailed reference book on the career of the famous fictional Westerner in novels, the cinema and television. It includes a 32-page list of 'resources' and is a welcome handbook for his many devotees.

Screen Gems is a complete history of the astonishing output of Columbia Pictures Television from 1948 to 1983, with full casts and credits of all the series, 'telefeatures' and pilots, plus a chronology and list of awards. Many names familiar from feature films appear, and also titles such as *Mr Deeds Goes to Town, From Here to Eternity* and *Gidget*.

Arthur Jacobson, Irene Kahn Atkins (interviewer); Scarecrow Press, dist. Shelwing, £22.15

The Directors Guild of America Oral History series, of which this is Number 11, specialises in selecting mainly lesser-known filmmakers, and is valuable for that fact. Arthur Jacobson had a busy career between 1918 and 1970 mainly as cameraman or assistant director, working with – among many others – Clara Bow, Henry Hathaway, Josef von Sternberg and George Cukor. The interviewer plies her subject with commendably brief, pertinent questions, allowing for many long unbroken answers and resulting in an interesting and comfortably 'readable' book.

As Thousands Cheer – The Life of Irving Berlin, Laurence Bergreen; Hodder & Stoughton/Coronet, £12.95

This weighty 650-page paperback may well be regarded as the definitive life of Berlin. Well researched and fully annotated, it follows his career from the early period in New York's Lower East Side with his family of immigrants from Russia, to world-wide fame and fortune – and covers his 101 years in a flowing and gripping narrative. The reference section chronologically lists his astonishing output of some 1500 songs, together with the stage and film productions to which he was the main musical contributor. So great was his musical influence over the popular entertainment of the period that his total of sixteen films seems modest. Among a host of good stories is one of his brief, unproductive telephone contact with Fritz Kreisler, one of whose songs he was anxious to buy. Kreisler refused, not because of the price offered, but because of his caller's profanity. ' "The dreadful language he used was so awful," Kreisler lamented. "My mother would not have allowed such a man into our house." '

Barbra Streisand, Peter Carrick; Robert Hale, £13.95

This is another volume in a growing and welcome series of modest-sized but competent biographies, generally well written and researched. Barbra Streisand is not everyone's favourite star (she certainly wasn't Walter Matthau's) and the author deals fairly and frankly with both the detestation and the adoration she seems to have aroused. 'She had decided to become someone special', to quote the book's jacket, and undeniably, through relentless determination and considerable courage – brought out vividly in this biography – she has succeeded.

The Best of Universal, Tony Thomas; Vestal Press, dist. Gazelle Book Services (Lancaster), £8.25

The well-known critic and historian makes his personal choice from the hundreds of films produced by the great studio. The book is divided into sections: horror, drama, Westerns etc. Not everyone will agree with the selection (Mr Thomas includes, for instance, the appalling Basil Rathbone 'updated' Sherlock Holmes travesties) but the choice *is* a personal one, and the text is both lively and informative. An enjoyable survey, embellished with a large number of often rare stills.

A Blind Bargain, Philip J. Riley; MagicImage Film Books, dist. Gazelle Book Services (Lancaster), £24.50

This finely produced book, first published in the US in 1988 and now available here, contains a detailed reconstruction of the little-known early Lon Chaney film (made in 1922). It includes a full shot-by-shot synopsis, together with all the printed subtitles, together with dozens of stills. In addition it provides a mass of related information, with production and other photographs featuring Chaney (in particular his various remarkable make-ups) and others connected with the production, together with reviews and publicity material, a complete list of related credits and an Introduction by Robert Bloch. The scope is so wide as to make it a volume to be treasured by anyone interested in either Lon Chaney himself, the horror film or the history of the early cinema. (The original title of the story was *The Octave of Claudius*.)

Celia Johnson, Kate Fleming; Weidenfeld & Nicolson, £16.99

Among the highlights of this brilliant and heartwarming biography by her own daughter are the long extracts from letters written by Celia Johnson to her husband Peter Fleming while they were separated during World War II. His own letters are witty, vivid and amusing, as expected from a renowned writer and traveller, but it is the humour and sparkle and often hilarious accounts of her own professional and personal life that remain in the memory. These, however, in no way overshadow the skill, warmth and frankness with which Kate Fleming tells her mother's story – from a comfortable, fairly conventional upbringing to a position at the very top of her profession. Celia Johnson divided her interests and activities almost equally between stage and home – a brilliant actress but a failed (and terrified) cook; a determined (though not very successful) knitter and (very successful) crossword puzzle solver; and a performer capable of touching the deepest emotions: these endearing contradictions and much else are described and delightfully counterbalanced in this book. Another highlight is Kate Fleming's concise and perceptive summary and analysis of her mother's career. An enchanting book about an enchanting actress.

The Charm of Evil – Terence Fisher, Wheeler Winston Dixon; Scarecrow Press, dist. Shelwing, £44.45

It is astonishing that a full-length study of Terence Fisher, the doyen of Hammer horror films (or, as he preferred to call them, fairy-tales for grown-ups), should have been so long in coming, but this excellent career biography makes the wait worthwhile. All the main films, the *Dracula*s and *Frankenstein*s, for instance, are examined in great detail, and even the lesser known (he made many before Hammer, and many non-horror ones both with and apart from Hammer) are given full critical treatment. Not least interesting is the long account of the making of the tense and gripping *To the Public Danger*, based on a radio play by Patrick Hamilton, whose later years were devastated by the appalling film travesties of his brilliant novels.

There is a superbly detailed filmography, together with a list of Fisher's other, earlier work in the cinema, starting off as a clapper-boy in 1933. He died in 1980, aged 76. Well illustrated and attractively produced, this is highly recommended for all horror film devotees.

Clint Eastwood, Christopher Frayling; Virgin, £6.99

An original paperback, this is a comparatively brief but solidly informative biography of one of the most famous cult figures of the seventies and eighties. It includes an eight-page interview between the author and Clint and sets the superstar's career clearly against the historical and political issues of the period. There is an outstandingly full filmography filling fifty pages and including a complete list of the *Rawhide* television series – but, regrettably, no index.

Close My Eyes, Stephen Poliakoff; Methuen, £4.99
Truly, Madly, Deeply, Anthony Minghella; Methuen, £4.99

Two very attractively and elegantly produced film scripts from the Methuen list, set out for easy reading and embellished with good stills and a note from the author in each case. Welcome additions to the growing library of such books.

The Columbia Checklist, Leo D. Martin; McFarland, dist. Shelwing Ltd, £48.75

Columbia Pictures has been one of the later studios to be documented in detail; this large, stout volume makes ample amends, recording its entire output from 1922 to 1988. A total of 2371 feature films are listed, with credits, full casts, a brief synopsis and notes where relevant. Sections on shorts and cartoons follow, together with serials – the latter including the complete chapter titles. Useful appendices group together Westerns, awards, stars and comedy series. An enormous index completes a book that (especially if taken together with Clive Hirschhorn's illustrated *Columbia Story*) puts the studio finally and firmly 'in the picture'.

The Comics Come Alive, Roy Kinnard; Scarecrow Press, dist. Shelwing, £24.40

Roy Kinnard has been lucky – or ingenious – in discovering yet another aspect of popular cinema, and he has made a good job of it. The lengthy subtitle accurately describes his book as 'A Guide to Comic-Strip Characters in Live-Action Productions'. From *Blondie* to our own *Jane*, from *Joe Palooka* to *Superman* (very fully covered), some ninety famous heroes and heroines of comic books and strips who also appeared in full-length films, serials and TV series are dealt with in several hundred separate alphabetical entries, complete with comments and historical notes, cast and credit lists. Well

illustrated and indexed, this is one more useful handbook for all those interested in the odd sidestreets of the cinema city.

The Complete Films of Edward G. Robinson, Alvin H. Marill; Virgin, £12.99

A new addition to the Virgin Film Library (previously known as the Citadel series) and one of the larger volumes, following the usual lines and well up to standard. Lists of stage, radio and television work are included. As one turns the pages it is fascinating to trace, in the many excellent illustrations, the gradual development of that unique and haunting face.

Conversations with Marlon Brando, Lawrence Grobel; Bloomsbury, £14.99

An interesting series of interviews, covering a wide range of subjects, with Brando unusually frank, and often outspoken and controversial. The book is nicely presented but, very regrettably, contains no index.

Dark City, The Film Noir, Spencer Selby; St James Press, £22.50

A concise yet very satisfactory account of a film genre that, in the words of the author, 'represented an outburst of artistic maturity, style and meaning which is still unappreciated and, in some ways, unsurpassed today'. Spencer Selby's book consists of essays on 25 of the most important productions (from *The Maltese Falcon* of 1941 to *The Killing* of 1956), followed by an annotated filmography of no fewer than 490 other titles, arranged chronologically, five useful appendices and two indexes. It forms a welcome companion to the well-known encyclopedic study by Silver and Ward (Secker & Warburg, 1980) listing, in fact, a considerably increased number of films.

Doris Day, Eric Braun; Weidenfeld & Nicolson, £14.99

After the furore preceding its publication, with talk of delays, cuts, and libel suits, the final appearance of this biography is something of an anticlimax. We may take it for granted that the facts have now been carefully checked for accuracy, and the result hardly deserves to be called 'controversial'. Its 224 pages (originally advertised as 240) contain a certain amount of padding – perhaps both this and the reduced length are the result of the cuts. The author writes with enthusiasm, but it is a pity that he cannot resist the urge to be 'amusing' at all costs, indulging in a tired facetiousness with irritating results. Jule Styne, for instance, does not play the piano, he 'tinkles the ivories'; Dennis Morgan does not sing a song, he 'got his tenor tonsils' round it; Doris Day herself 'gets her silver [!] tonsils around "Lullaby of Broadway" ', and 'carrols' (*sic*) other songs. The writer Barbara Cartland is called somewhat irrelevantly 'the pink and candyfloss *grande dame*'. If one is not at one's best on radio and stage, then it is 'hard cheese'!

Some careless errors remain uncorrected: the Wall Street Crash is dated three years too early; C. A. Lejeune ('the great English critic') appears as S. A. Lejeune (indexed correctly but on the wrong page).

According to one report Miss Day grew increasingly cool towards the book ('in view of its quality') and said she would like it to be withdrawn completely. This seems a little drastic, but on occasion one feels bound to admit she may have had a point.

Eighty Silent Film Stars, George A. Katchmer; McFarland, dist. Shelwing, £56.25
Horror Film Directors 1931–90, Dennis Fischer; McFarland, dist. Shelwing, £56.25
Epic Films, Gary A. Smith; McFarland, dist. Shelwing, £26.25
Star Trek, Susan R. Gibberman; McFarland, dist. Shelwing, £30.00
Monty Python, Douglas L. McCall; McFarland, dist. Shelwing, £22.50

An interesting and varied group of reference books from one of the leading publishers in this field.

The first two are the most considerable. *Eighty Silent Film Stars* (over 1000 pages) offers full biographical chapters and filmographies from the well-known to the obscure – many hardly warranting the description 'star' – while the most well-known of all, such as Pickford and Fairbanks, give way to make room for those less easily traced elsewhere; a welcome decision.

Horror Film Directors contains lengthy essays and filmographies on 50 major directors, together with almost the same number of those rather unkindly described as Hopeless and Hopeful. An appendix lists classics of the genre by non-horror directors. There is a useful annotated bibliography.

In *Epic Films* will be found 250 casts, credits and commentaries on a wide range of spectaculars starting with *Intolerance*, ranging from the historical to the mythical and extending to *The Three Stooges Meet Hercules*. Well illustrated.

Star Trek, An Annotated Guide covers every conceivable facet of its subject – television, films, novels, video and, of course, the characters – in 1333 paragraphs of satisfying fare for devotees.

Monty Python is a distinct oddity, a strict chronology of facts, including such side issues as 'John Cleese and Connie Booth get a divorce' and 'John Cleese gets George Burns' autograph'.

Elvis – a Tribute to his Life, 'contributing writer' Susan Doll; Omnibus Press, £29.95
James Dean – Tribute to a Rebel, Val Holley; Omnibus Press, £29.95
John Lennon – His Life and Legend; Richard Buskin, Omnibus Press, £29.95

Marilyn – Her Life and Legend; 'contributing writer' Susan Doll; Omnibus Press, £29.95

Under the general heading of 'Eternal Legends', these resplendent volumes, printed on glossy art paper, with the full set weighing all of 20 lbs, offer the ultimate in tributes to their famous subjects. The excellently reproduced illustrations, mainly in colour, may be the first attraction to catch the eye but the texts are equally impressive. As indicated by the subtitles, all four are adulatory. Though not idolatrous. None shrinks from the darker side of its subject; and the fact that all four lives ended tragically is fully brought out.

Reference material is of less concern: James Dean's few films are given a chapter each; Elvis Presley's are listed, together with his singles; Marilyn receives a brief filmography and an excellent index; John Lennon is provided with a complete list of his Beatles recordings and his films are described briefly in the text.

Marilyn presents perhaps the most satisfying and rounded portrait, but each of them is a glamorous gift book for anyone with a strong enough coffee table.

Famous Movie Detectives, Vol. 2, Michael R. Pitts; Scarecrow Press, dist. Shelwing, £35.65

This second volume adds over a dozen essays to those in the first, notably on Sherlock Holmes and Philip Marlowe, omitted because they were featured in other books published by Scarecrow around the same time. The Sherlock Holmes article, filling over seventy pages, contains probably as full a list of the films as is available anywhere, including the superb and too little known performances by Ian Richardson in *The Sign of Four* and *The Hound of the Baskervilles* (Mapleton Films, 1983). It is a pity that the TV series with David Suchet as the definitive Poirot arrived too late for inclusion (but interesting to note that he is recorded as having played Inspector Japp in *Thirteen at Dinner*, a television remake of *Lord Edgware Dies*, in 1985). Following the main essays are briefer notes on some twenty less prolific detectives, an excellent bibliography and a list of corrections and additions to the first volume.

The Films of the Eighties, Robert A. Nowlan & Gwendolyn Wright Nowlan; McFarland, dist. Shelwing, £51.40

No fewer than 3400 feature-length English-speaking films (cinema and video-only) are included in this packed 580-page book; the enormous index itself takes up about two hundred of them. Technical and other details and a reasonably full cast list are given to each, plus a brief but pithy (and when necessary acerbic) comment. The double-column pages are set out with welcome clarity. It is as difficult to realise that

such a vast amount of films were produced during the period as it is to imagine the research that has gone into their collection and presentation.

Fred Zinnemann – An Autobiography; Bloomsbury £25.00

Fred Zinnemann's memoirs apparently encountered some difficulty in finding a publisher owing to the cost of the large number of illustrations he wished to include. One can therefore be grateful to Bloomsbury for producing one of the most delightful and interesting autobiographies for many years. A chapter is devoted to each film, among them such masterpieces as *High Noon, From Here to Eternity* and *A Man for All Seasons*, the story of each one's production being described with a wealth of technical and personal details. Accounts of Zinnemann's adventurous life also fill the pages, all written with warmth and an enjoyable wry humour. The large-format pages are packed with about 400 rare and wonderful photographs. However crowded one's film-bookshelf may be, a place must be found for this.

Garbo on Garbo, Sven Broman; Bloomsbury, £16.99

The author, a well-known retired Swedish journalist, met Greta Garbo towards the end of her life and during those last years became a close friend and confidant. The result of that meeting is the publication of this unique and wholly fascinating collection of memoirs. Immeasurably enhanced by long extracts from Garbo's letters to friends (in particular Horkë, Countess Wachtmeister), illustrated with rare and wonderful photographs, written with clear-sighted affection, it carries conviction as the truest portrait of the 'real' Garbo – freed from the absurd mystique with which so many accounts have burdened her. She emerges from this book as a hard-working film personality (she herself denies that she was ever a true actress), intelligent and sharp minded, often fiercely critical of the material from which she had to work. Frequently homesick for her own country – but not pathologically so, as she is often made to appear – she was (in Broman's words) 'both shy *and* confident', capable of great friendliness and humour (she signs herself in a letter to Countess Wachtmeister as 'the Clown') – in fact a normal, if exceptionally gifted, human being, rather than some sort of cryptic, transcendental (and much less interesting) super-creation.

George Cukor, Patrick McGilligan; Faber & Faber, £16.99

This first full biography of George Cukor – significantly subtitled 'A Double Life' – is also the first to pay full attention to the homosexuality that (though concealed) wielded so major an influence on the life of the man who became known as the 'woman's director'. Perhaps the most devastating single effect on his career was being sacked from directing *Gone with the Wind*. This, however, though fully covered here, is only a brief part of a fascinatingly full account of one of the very top directors who worked with nearly all the most glamorous stars during the most glamorous periods of Hollywood history.

This is a big book, excellently indexed, generously illustrated, lively and on the whole well written.

George Sanders – An Exhausted Life, Richard VanDerBeets; Robson Books, £15.95

A sensitive, frank and understanding portrait of a film star whose film persona as an 'attractive cad' ultimately seemed almost to take over his real character – that of a deeply complex, outwardly successful but inwardly insecure man, and in many ways the most interesting of all the famous Hollywood figures. Both his public and his private lives are fully covered, with many interviews with friends and associates. The book closes with the well-publicised final tragedy when he committed suicide leaving not only a note on his 'boredom' but also another, deeply affecting and including in full the sonnet of Menander beginning 'Whom the gods love dies young . . .'. Notably well written, with good illustrations and filmography, this must rank as one of the best biographies of the year.

The Guinness Book of Movie Facts and Feats, Patrick Robertson; Guinness Publishing, £9.99

The fourth edition of this gargantuan collection continues the ever increasing mass of information on all aspects of the cinema; from the serious to the light-hearted, the weighty to the trivial, the lasting to the ephemeral. Any attempt to list the contents would be pointless – *everything* is here, arranged with commendable clarity and decorated with dozens of rare illustrations, including an attractive colour section. A masterpiece of devoted research, and at this price a glossy softback bargain.

Halliwell's Film Guide – 8th edition, ed. John Walker; HarperCollins, £30.00

The death of Leslie Halliwell was a grievous blow to cinemagoers, television viewers and film researchers alike. It is therefore cheering to know that his main work, the *Film Guide*, is to continue. In the capable hands of John Walker, and resplendently jacketed, it closely matches its predecessors in style and contains – we are assured – about 1000 new entries, including foreign films and silent classics. There are omissions, but none of them vital. The illustrations have gone; also dropped are Halliwell's very personal (and disillusioned) essay on the state of the cinema, and information on title changes. A number of films have been re-

evaluated – a reasonable step, as the *Film Guide* is an on-going production, and not an 'as they thought then' anthology. It is good to know that it is to live on and perpetuate Leslie Halliwell's memory.

Hollywood Art, Beverly Heisner; St James Press, £27.00

Art direction having received less attention than it deserves in film literature, this excellent study is very welcome. Each of the main chapters deals with a major studio during the great days of Hollywood from early times, concentrating largely on the type of production for which it was best known – MGM for musicals, Universal for horror, etc. Brief biographical details are included for many of the art directors and there are massive filmographies in an appendix. Illustrations, of which there are many, are stills chosen to show off the points raised, rather than mere photographs of bare sets. An important, detailed and very readable study.

Hollywood Gothic, David J. Skal; Andre Deutsch, £15.99

This is by far the fullest account available of the adventures of Count Dracula on stage and screen – from the German film *Nosferatu* through Hamilton Deane's original stage production to the Deane/Balderston version in America with Bela Lugosi, the Tod Browning Hollywood film, and all that developed therefrom. Many of the legal, personal and professional problems that flourished and flared in the background are related in fascinating detail. A beautifully produced glossy paperback, with a vast number of exceedingly rare illustrations and a splendid 'Dracula at a Glance' chronology from the fifteenth century to the twentieth, this is the prime prize for the Count's countless devotees.

Hollywood Rogues, Michael Munn; Robson Books, £12.95

Some years ago, a famous West End actor-manager is reputed to have said that if he had his way all his actors would be delivered to the stage door in a closed van before the performance, and similarly sent home after it, thus preventing worshipping audiences discovering any 'feet of clay'. What his reactions would have been to present-day Hollywood is beyond conjecture. In an earlier (and better) book, Michael Munn interestingly recounted a number of Hollywood murders; here he offers a veritable cornucopia (or ragbag?) of scandal and gossip for the enjoyment of feet-of-clay enthusiasts. Drugs, alcoholism, sex (straightforward and deviant), thuggery, cheating, blackmail, assorted violence and other nefarious activities fill the busy pages, bringing in names ranging from the famous to the surprisingly unexpected. Not the least of the changes from those earlier years is the fact that so many of the perpetrators seem not only to

glory in, but even to profit from, their behaviour.

A major flaw in the book is the almost total lack (except in the personal interviews) of any references to sources. These are surely essential in many cases – to take just one instance, the diatribe against Roman Polanski. However, the delight in gossip and scandal so many of us guiltily admit to will probably keep the pages turning – even if it is not possible to check the stated facts.

Horror Film Stars – 2nd edition, Michael R. Pitts; McFarland, dist. Shelwing, £18.75

This stoutly bound and well-produced paperback presents probably the fullest collection of actors in the genre. It is divided into two parts: the first, lengthy essays on seventeen stars; the second, shorter articles on 50 actors who included some horror films as part of their general output. The former are given complete film lists; in the latter category these are restricted to their 'genre appearances'. It is interesting to see Tod Slaughter given due credit among the stars – despite a misspelling of his Sweeney Tod (as 'Sweeny'). Lavishly illustrated and excellently indexed, this is an important addition to the already crowded horror bookshelf.

International Dictionary of Films and Filmmakers – Directors; St James Press, £75.00

This is the second volume of a massive five-part reference series on the cinema. (The first – on Films – was reviewed in *Film Review 1991–2*.) As in the previous book, this is a greatly expanded and generally improved edition of one which appeared some years ago. It covers the work of about 480 directors, filling over 950 pages, and includes in each case a full list of films (those on D. W. Griffith and Mack Sennett, for instance, with all their shorts, are monumental), a list of relevant publications, a still or portrait, a concise appraisal of the work, and brief personal details. As with Volume 1, this is a boon for all lovers of the cinema and essential for all libraries. To come: Volumes 3 (Actors and Actresses), 4 (Writers and Production Artists) and 5 (Title Index).

International Film Prizes, Tad Bentley Hammer; St James Press, £65.00

This huge (900-page) book lists almost all awards given to films since the earliest days in over forty countries, from Argentina to Yugoslavia. So full is the record that it is easier (and more useful) to quote the omissions rather than the contents. International film festivals such as Cannes are absent as so few productions are *invited* (Hammer's italics) to take part; other omissions are unavoidable owing to the information being unavailable in print – even in the United States. Four British awards (BAFTA, Critics' Circle, Evening Standard and the British

Film Institute) are given in full, as are eight American. The Oscar (Academy) Awards are listed in detail, including nominations where relevant. Many of the thousands of films, of course, will be little known in Britain, but part of the fascination of a browse through the well-arranged pages is discovering what familiar titles received which awards where. Brief historical introductions precede most entries, and this invaluable reference book is rounded off with two enormous indexes.

Japanese Films, Beverley Bare Buehrer; St James Press, £27.00

A useful handbook on the history of Japanese cinema, with brief essays on a large number of films from 1921 on, arranged chronologically. Many may be less than familiar, but all the best-known directors are represented, with such productions as *Rashomon*, *The Burmese Harp*, *Kwaidan*, *Godzilla* and *Tokyo Olympiad*. Surprisingly, the widely shown *Onibaba* is omitted. Appendices include a list of film and video sources, a large bibliography – and a glossary.

Jewish Film Directory; Flicks Books, £33.00

This 'guide to more than 1200 films of Jewish interest, from 32 countries over 85 years' is the first volume of a projected series from the enterprising Flicks Books which will concentrate on movies based on a particular country or culture. The main part of the book consists of a listing by title, with brief cast and credits sections and a (generally concise) note. The rest is taken up with four indexes – director, country of production, subject, and source material – of which the third is of particular interest. The range is wide, from *The Holocaust* to *Abie's Irish Rose*. An original type of reference book, well printed and clearly arranged.

Joseph Losey, Edith de Rham; Andre Deutsch, £18.99

Unfortunately an unacceptable number of errors have already been pointed out in this clearly 'unauthorised' biography. Some are straightforward examples of carelessness (such as Losey, born in 1909, reaching the age of 62 in 1967), but others are more serious and shake confidenc in the book, which also lac s any detailed of sources. All this is a pity, as it is well written, contains many facts of interest (if one can rely on them) and is well illustrated.

Kevin Costner, Todd Keith; Ikonprint, £15.99

This first ('unauthorised') biography of Kevin Costner and his meteoric rise to stardom is an acceptable account of his career and personal life to date. Each chapter ends with a 'what the critics thought' section on the films concerned, and there are several

good portraits in black-and-white and colour. The book is, however, weak on reference material – no index, no filmography and no list of sources.

Liebestraum, Mike Figgis; Faber and Faber, £5.99

One of the stranger stories (a 'stylish dark thriller') from the Faber library of film scripts, presented with the usual care and including a 30-page interview with the writer/director.

Lionheart in Hollywood, Henry Wilcoxon with Katherine Orrison; Scarecrow Press, dist. Shelwing, £31.90

The title refers to Wilcoxon's performance as King Richard I in Cecil B. DeMille's epic film *The Crusades*, but the greater part of the book is concerned with his close association with the great Director (or Dictator) himself. It is a chatty, amusing account, with many passages of recollected – or possibly invented? – dialogue, but manages nevertheless to paint a vivid picture of the God-like DeMille at work, and of the Hollywood of his time.

London's West End Cinemas, Allen Eyles & Keith Skone; Keytone Publications, £14.95 hb, £9.95 pb

Here at last, in this richly produced updated edition of a book first published in 1984, the cinemas of London's West End and Victoria are given the long overdue recognition and attention already enjoyed by its theatres. From 1907 to the present day every building is included, with a history, technical details, alternative names where relevant, and superb exterior and interior photographs. Three large clear maps are provided showing the sites of both past and present buildings, together with an index and a note on 'Theatres as Cinemas'. Apart from its contemporary interest, the book presents a feast of nostalgia to older moviegoers as they enter once again the 'palaces' where they spent so many happy hours. With this book the authors can truly claim to be the Mander and Mitchenson of the cinema.

Mario Lanza, Derek Mannering; Robert Hale, £13.95

Mario Lanza may not be well known among contemporary filmgoers, yet in his day he was regarded as a 'super-star' (a term not then over-used as it is today), and indeed hailed as the Caruso of his time – the great singer whose life he (slightly fictionally) portrayed in his best-known picture. Three great singers of today, Domingo, Pavarotti and Carreras, have indicated their appreciation of his talent – the latter providing a foreword to the book. The author has written a full and sympathetic account of Lanza's tragically short life (he died aged only 38), frankly facing the accusations of a lost or wasted gift, and providing a moving

account of the final years. There is an excellent reference section.

Marlon Brando, Paul Ryan; Plexus, £9.99

Yet *another* book on Brando? The author, however, examining the 'mythic status' of the famous star (linking him with James Dean and Montgomery Clift, 'equally mythologised', except that Brando has lived longer), views his life and career freshly and vividly. Ryan's account, for instance, of the traumatic making of *Mutiny on the Bounty* is told from a different point of view from the more usual one, and this applies to the book in general. It closes with a full and moving account of the trial and conviction for manslaughter of Brando's son and its effect on the celebrated actor.

Many good illustrations but – regrettably – no index.

Mary Pickford, Scott Eyman; Robson Books, £16.95

A definitive book on Mary Pickford has long been needed, and this fine biography assuredly fills the gap. Excellently researched, written with great sympathy, enthusiasm and frankness (the author does not shrink from recording those occasions when she appeared in a less than wholly favourable light), it paints a vivid portrait of one of the greatest and most loved of all the 'idols of silence'. On the way various myths are dispelled – such as the long-standing belief that the production of *The Taming of the Shrew* had in its opening titles: 'By William Shakespeare. With additional dialogue by Sam Taylor'. A good deal of space is given to the financial wheeling and dealing among the studios and the stars – fascinating and clearly set out. Some minor jugglings with chronology occasionally make the narrative thread a little confusing – did Mary sue Douglas Fairbanks for divorce in 1933 (p. 213) or 1934 (p. 222)? – and the sections of illustrations, very interesting in themselves, are not all that well reproduced. But these are minor points in a fine, and in its later pages a very moving, book.

If the author is to be believed, Holly..ood was up to form in composing the inscription (from *Hamlet*) on Douglas Fairbanks's tomb: 'Good Night Sweet Prince; May [*sic*] flights of angels sing thee to thy rest'!

Masters of Lens and Light, William Darby; Scarecrow Press, dist. Shelwing, £74.65
Keeping Score, James L. Limbacher & Stephen H. Wright; Scarecrow Press, dist. Shelwing, £69.40

Two massive checklists forming a useful addition to any filmbook collection. *Masters of Lens and Light* covers the films of over 700 major cinematographers, American and foreign, from 1915 to the close of 1990, together with a lengthy list of individual productions by cameramen who do not appear in the main section. Also included are awards, illustrations and an enormous index of titles. *Keeping Score* gives all the main composers of film music and their works from 1980 to 1988, plus a large supplement consisting of additions and corrections to two previous volumes, a discography, and full indexes of both names and titles.

Both books are attractively produced and set out with admirable clarity.

Me – Stories of My Life, Katharine Hepburn; Viking, £16.99

The sub-title is more accurate than the word 'autobiography' used in the *Radio Times* excerpts, as the famous star ranges – sometimes haphazardly – over the events of her life and work, her friends and associates, her films (a number grouped together in one of her most interesting chapters) and her views and comments on a vast variety of subjects connected with the profession in which she was so prestigiously prominent. Her relentlessly chatty, 'buttonholing' style is at times irritating, but there is much to enjoy in this handsomely produced and fascinatingly illustrated book.

Movie Star Memorabilia – A Collector's Guide, Brian Mills; Batsford, £15.95

The main part of this truly colossal collection of film ephemera information is devoted to popular magazines – almost complete lists of all the most famous ones since their inception, giving the names of stars featured on their covers. Other sections deal with annuals (*Film Review* prominently present), cigarette cards, souvenirs, material on 'the most popular stars', etc, together with a number of useful source addresses. Many illustrations, including a fine colour section, and everything spaciously set out. A collector's bible – no less.

The Motion Picture Guide Annual 1991; Baseline Inc, dist. Bowker Saur, £99.00

The actual review section of this massive record of the films of 1990 is fully up to the standard of the previous volume (see *Film Review* 1991–2). Unfortunately, however, one of the most valuable features – the comprehensive Obituaries – has been omitted (without comment), presumably to make way for a large and not particularly useful Master List of titles contained in other volumes. Also missing are the illustrations that lightened the pages of the previous book. Finally the print has reverted to the uncomfortably small size of the ten-volume *Guide*, from which in the 1990 volume it had happily been enlarged. To conclude, however, on a less censorious note, the Indexes – of all participants, in nineteen sections from Actors to Technical Advisers – are, as before, exhaustive and invaluable.

Movies Made for Television, Alvin H. Marill; New York Zoetrope, dist. Gazelle Book Services (Lancaster), £32.50

With the difference between television and cinema movies becoming ever less marked – the two often being interchangeable – this magnificent book, now updated and extending from 1964 to 1986, is a reference work to be treasured by any viewer – containing full cast lists, commentaries and other details together with four large indexes, of writers, producers, directors and actors. The films are arranged in alphabetical order, with a useful chronological list at the end of the book. Mini-series are also included.

Only in the matter of illustrations does the earlier 1946–79 volume (where they are considerably more numerous and somewhat better reproduced) have the edge over the present one. Anyone lucky enough to possess both editions will be reluctant to part with either.

Noel Coward, Clive Fisher; Weidenfeld & Nicolson, £17.99

This, being the first major biography of Coward since his death, is also the first in which his homosexuality can be openly discussed, requiring a sensitivity of approach which Clive Fisher has very successfully achieved. The deep effect on Noel Coward of concealing (as he felt he must) so fundamental a part of his personality is treated with both sympathy and frankness. In addition, the book is a close and perceptive study of the relationship between his published work and his private life. The creation of almost every play, and of such films as *In Which We Serve* and *Brief Encounter*, is examined in fascinating detail. An example of biography at its best – required reading for lovers of both cinema and theatre.

Nuclear Movies, Mick Broderick; McFarland, dist. Shelwing, £26.25

The book's lengthy subtitle is worth quoting in full: 'A Critical Analysis and Filmography of International Feature Length Films Dealing with Experimentation, Aliens, Terrorism, Holocaust and Other Disaster Scenarios, 1914–1989.' A 50-page general survey is followed by a filmography divided into decades. This includes not only the vast number of expected titles (and a surprising amount of rubbish) but also such marginal films as *The Best Years of Our Lives* and *The 5000 Fingers of Doctor T*. An interesting feature is a series of 'Timelines' preceding each decade, giving important dates in nuclear history from 1895 on. Illustrations are sparse, but this is a useful and well-researched study of yet another subdivision of the world of film.

Offscreen Onscreen, Peter van Gelder; Aurum, £12.95

A very entertaining and decidedly different survey of 60 famous films, British and American. Subheadings indicate what to expect: 'The Talent' – brief biographical paragraphs on players, directors etc.; 'The Business' – budgeting and other production details; 'Behind the Screen' – personal relationships and other events during the making; 'The Experience' – what happened afterwards, including reviews; and 'Can You Spot . . .' – points a casual (or sometimes even attentive) viewer might have missed, in particular unfortunate (but often hilarious) oversights and lapses. Packed with information, it is written in a lighthearted and very amusing vein – particularly in the final section, for which the author requests submissions of further similar details from other films.

Osgood and Anthony Perkins, Laura Kay Palmer; McFarland, dist. Shelwing, £33.75

It was an excellent idea to combine the Perkinses, father and son, in a single volume. Though to the filmgoers of today the son must be more familiar than the father, Osgood's reputation as actor on both stage and screen was extremely high, and it is good to have full professional records of both artistes. *Psycho*, inevitably, scores the greatest number of page references in the index, and a brilliant essay, but adequate attention is paid to even the little-known works in this exceptionally well written and interesting study. (It is probably not widely known, for instance, that in the 1950s Anthony Perkins recorded, as singer, a number of successful 45 rpm singles.) Plenty of rare stills, and thorough documentation, including a huge (even if described as merely 'selected') bibliography.

Peter Sellers – A Film History, Michael Starr; Robert Hale, £14.95

This is the first study of Peter Sellers concentrating almost wholly on his films, with only the brief biographical details necessary to an analysis of his work. The book concludes with a very frank personal interview with Blake Edwards, who directed Sellers mainly in the Pink Panther films. Very well illustrated, and of importance to all those interested in the controversial star's unique personality.

Note: It is surely going a little bit over the top to describe the courageous little Windmill Theatre ('We Never Closed') as 'infamous'?

Postmodern Auteurs, Kenneth von Gunden; McFarland, dist. Shelwing, £19.50
The New Hollywood, James Bernardoni; McFarland, dist. Shelwing, £19.50

These two books form an interesting pair, both dealing with notable rising directors of the seventies.

The first, and easier to read, concentrates on five names – Coppola, Lucas, De Palma,

Spielberg and Scorsese – offering brief but illuminating essays on their work. Despite an ominous quoted reference to 'hermeneutic controversies' in the Introduction, the writing as a whole is mercifully free from the pretentiousness of certain schools of film criticism.

The New Hollywood is sterner – and denser – stuff, weightily examining some thirteen films under such headings as The Literary Fallacy, The Hawksian Fallacy and the Hitchcockian Fallacy. At times, for instance after reading through an enormously detailed and generally destructive section on De Palma's *Carrie*, one cannot avoid a vision of a sledgehammer cracking a nut, and is reminded of Hitchcock's salutary words when his star actress became unduly worked up during filming – 'It's only a movie, Ingrid!' However, it is impossible not to agree with Bernardoni's views on the 'fallaciousness' of much of today's film output, and with the hope expressed in the final sentence of his book, for a greater appreciation and understanding of 'the enduring values of the Old Hollywood language, the language of a genuine and inestimably precious American art form'.

The Primal Screen, John Brosnan; Orbit (Longman), £16.95

Written in a light and lively style, this is at the same time a comprehensive and informative (and on occasion sharply critical) history of the ever popular science fiction film by a specialist. Covering a wide range of titles from the early silent days to the present, and including a large number of good stills (with a brief section in colour), this ranks high among the considerable number of books available in the sci-fi field. So good is it, in fact, that one readily forgives a grammatical howler in the first sentence of the text!

The book is beautifully produced; a charming touch is the little rocket that starts a journey at the top of page 2 on the left and proceeds across to finish up – bang on target – on page 389.

Prison Pictures from Hollywood, James Robert Parish; McFarland, dist. Shelwing, £37.50

The ingenuity with which Mr Parish (previously described with accuracy as 'indefatigable') finds new methods of categorising movies seems limitless. Here he deals with 293 films – theatrical and made-for-TV – from the silent days to the present, with his usual brisk efficiency. A comprehensive 57-page index and a reasonable number of stills complete yet another of his useful reference books.

Projections – A Forum for Film Makers, ed. John Boorman and Walter Donohue; Faber & Faber, £9.99

This is the first issue of a new annual publication on various aspects of the cinema, with

a number of practitioners writing on their work, ideas and speculations. It is compiled by John Boorman, who provides the major contribution, a 120-page journal for 1991 entitled 'Bright Dreams, Hard Knocks' and containing a brief personal film script. Other chapters include a lengthy interview with Jonathan Demme, director of *The Silence of the Lambs* and former associate of Roger Corman; the late Emeric Pressburger on his early life as a screenwriter; an extract from a book by cameraman Nestor Almendros on photographing beautiful women; and the script of a short film by Hal Hartley entitled *Surviving Desire*. This is an important venture, aimed primarily perhaps at the 'serious' filmgoer but mercifully free from the pretentious theorising of numerous such publications. It is very well illustrated.

Also now available from Faber & Faber in paperback at £9.99 is the story of Goldcrest films entitled *My Indecision Is Final*, covered in *Film Review 1991–2*.

Quinlan's Illustrated Directory of Film Stars, David Quinlan: Batsford, £19.99

This indispensable reference work reappears in a new and much enlarged edition, updated to the end of 1990 – with a few 1991 entries. A major attraction is the completeness of all the entries, which include features, shorts, TV movies, guest appearances and even voice-overs, plus in each case a photograph and a brief general description. Doubtless some readers will miss a favourite name (the author himself lists over twenty unavoidably omitted), but this is inevitable in any such compilation, and detracts little from the usefulness of so massive a collection.

Science Fiction, ed. Phil Hardy; Aurum Press, £30.00

The updating of this luxurious encyclopedia (highly recommended in *Film Review 1985–6*) to include 1990 is more than welcome. Every sci-fi movie (using the term in its widest sense) is covered, from 1895 on, with synopsis, commentary, cast and credit lists, and technical data, covering over 1450 titles in all. There are over 650 excellent black-and-white stills, plus a colour section. Appendices include a list of Oscar Awards and nominations. The films are arranged in chronological order by year, and a huge index refers to each title with the year in which it will be found. A most handsome production, essential for every sci-fi *aficionado*.

The award-winning volume from the same series, *The Western*, is also available in a similarly updated edition.

Science Fiction Stars and Horror Heroes, Tom Weaver; McFarland, dist. Shelwing, £26.25

This is a collection of interviews with actors, directors, producers and writers active

between 1940 and 1970, abridged from entries in specialised magazines. Its particular value is that among the 28 people interviewed are a number of less widely known workers in these fields. Much fresh and interesting information is thus made available. Filmographies are provided for actors and actresses, and there are plenty of good stills, portraits, posters and production photographs.

Screen World – 1991, John Willis; Hutchinson, £17.99

This essential annual record of the American cinema scene appears in slightly altered dress this year, but with the same excellent contents: one thousand illustrations, cast-and-credit lists of exemplary fullness, Academy Awards from the earliest days to the present, twenty crowded pages of brief biographical details of players, a comprehensive obituary, an enormous index. This year's 'dedicatee' is Frank Sinatra, with a page of chronological portraits and a full list of films.

The Screwball Comedy Films, Duane Byrge and Robert Milton Miller; St James Press, £22.00

After introductory chapters on major performers (led by Cary Grant and Carole Lombard), writers and directors, the main body of this survey is a filmography of all films in the category, from *It Happened One Night* to *The Palm Beach Story*, and including Garbo's one and only (failed) incursion, *Two-Faced Woman*. The cast lists are full and the commentaries informative. A useful handbook on an amusing if somewhat faded *genre*.

The Shoot-em-ups Ride Again, Buck Rainey; Scarecrow Press, dist. Shelwing Ltd, £46.90

This supplement to the vastly popular *Shoot-em-ups* of 1978 (reprinted by Scarecrow in 1985) covers films released between 1978 and 1990, earlier Westerns 1928–78 not included in the first volume, and additional details (generally to cast lists) to those earlier entries. Television series and full-length films made especially for television are also included, together with a massive index listing titles and dates. This large-format book is very well illustrated. For best use, as the author states, it should be combined with the earlier volume, as the additions referred to fill over one hundred pages. Together, the two books might well be referred to as 'Westerns complete' – except as regards the silents.

Sylvester Stallone, Adrian Wright; Robert Hale, £12.95

According to the filmography, apart from one undetailed 'porn movie' Stallone shot up from 'unbilled' in his first film (Woody Allen's *Bananas*) to 'top of the bill' in his second, down to nineteenth in his fourth, before achieving top billing again a few films later, in *Rocky*. This might be taken as symbolic of the varying critical reception given to his career as a whole. These extremes are well described in this nicely written and perceptive biography. The once seemingly endless *Rocky*s and the notorious *Rambo*s are fully covered – one of the latter series evoking a dubiously ambivalent comment from ex-President Ronald Reagan. Adrian Wright's book reveals a considerably more likable personality than some of the films might indicate.

Television Detective Shows of the 1970s, David Martindale; McFarland, dist. Shelwing, £41.25

This 550-page encyclopedia includes details and main casts of such famous productions as Columbo, Ironside, Mannix and Starsky & Hutch among the dozens screened between 1965 and 1984. An added attraction even to those not wholly devoted to TV movies is a vast index of over sixty pages in which it is possible to trace the appearance of very many well-known stars and feature players outside their main work on the big screen during the period covered. Fully illustrated.

Tom and Jerry – Fifty Years of Cat and Mouse, T. R. Adams; Pyramid, £14.99

Next to Mickey Mouse and family, Tom and Jerry are probably the most famous of all cartoon characters. This celebration of their half-century is an attractively produced and splendidly illustrated story of their successes – and of the drawbacks they have overcome during the period. An individual synopsis is provided of each cartoon produced during the golden years with MGM – which ran until 1967 – together with fuller accounts of the seven Oscar awards. The advent of television, the Tom and Jerry Kids' Show and other developments are included, together with much fascinating information on the technical and the creative aspects of production. Doubtless Tom and Jerry themselves, as well as their countless friends of all ages, will enjoy this lively record of their still continuing careers.

Vampyres, Christopher Frayling; Faber and Faber, £17.50

In this anthology of vampire literature from Byron to Bram Stoker the films are mentioned only briefly, but there is a great deal to interest every devotee of the *genre*. Of particular interest is the long introductory survey, with its 'mosaic of vampires in folklore, prose and poetry' in which familiar names such as Varney, Ruthven, Carmilla, Bathory and Dracula occur, together with less familiar ones such as Mary, Queen of Scots. The chapter on Stoker's Working and Research papers for Dracula is essential reading for the vampiric student; and Stoker's short story 'Dracula's Guest' is also

included. This neat, stout book is handsomely produced, and contains some fascinating contemporary illustrations. An index would have been useful, particularly for the opening survey.

Vanessa Redgrave – an Autobiography; Hutchinson, £17.99

Vanessa Redgrave, of course, is equally celebrated as actress and activist. It is with her films that we are concerned here, and these are unfortunately somewhat cursorily treated in this autobiography. There are interesting, if brief, comments on *Julia*, *The Seagull* and *The Ballad of the Sad Café*, and illuminating passages on the difference between acting on screen and stage. But one would have liked to see more on, for instance, the notorious *The Devils*, *Blow-Up* and *Agatha*, the odd attempt to solve the mystery of Agatha Christie's disappearance. The book is excellently written and there are generous sections of interesting illustrations.

Any prospective purchaser would be well advised to glance at page 42 of the first edition, where an example of careless editing or proof-reading at its most disgraceful has resulted in nonsense; a minor, less catastrophic example can be found on page 227.

Variety Movie Guide, ed. Derek Elley; Hamlyn, £12.99

To have over 5000 of the famous *Variety* film reviews gathered together in one stoutly-bound, 700-page paperback at so reasonable a price is not only a boon but a clear necessity for any cinemagoer or TV viewer. The print size is inevitably small, but is sufficiently clear for the book's purpose, and the reviews are well set out in alphabetical order. The period of coverage extends from 1914 to the present – a great benefit, as Sir Richard Attenborough points out in his Foreword, in that we can read what was written at the time each movie appeared. Partly for this reason it is a pity that so much space is given to recent and well-known films as opposed to the less famous and/or earlier ones, for which such details are more difficult to find.

Despite this, we should be thankful for so large a collection of these lively, witty, highly enjoyable reviews. Selecting about one in ten cannot have been easy!

Variety's Who's Who in Show Business, ed. Mike Kaplan; R. R. Bowker, dist. Bowker-Saur, £47.50

The third edition of this very useful reference book has been updated to November 1988 and includes 6500 show-business personalities who were still alive at the end of June 1985. Deaths occurring during the period covered are noted. The range is wide: actors, producers, directors, composers, writers, singers, editors, pop groups – British and American – and others are present. In each case a brief biographical note is

given, followed by selected film, stage and television appearances, and, in the case of pop groups, albums and recordings. The film world is very fully represented.

Obviously, in any such reference books *complete* lists are an asset, but this would have resulted in a publication several times larger and costlier, and in many cases the entries are generous. Attractively produced and clearly printed, this is a useful summary of the work of a large and varied number of people engaged in the entertainment business.

Errors are hard to find, but it is intriguing to see that John Houseman (né Jean Haussmann of Rumania in 1902) died, in large print, in 1088.

The Virgin International Encyclopedia of Film, James Monaco & the editors of Baseline; Virgin Publishing, £25.00 hb/ £14.99 pb

This huge Who's Who (rather than 'encyclopedia') covers over 3000 actors, directors, producers, writers, composers and others working in the cinema. Comparisons that have been made with Ephraim Katz's *International Film Encyclopedia* can be misleading. The latter book is almost twice the size and covers, as well as 'names', technical terms, outline country histories, institutions etc., and its coverage of the earlier years is considerably wider. (Not one of the famous Warner brothers, for instance, rates a mention here!)

The present volume, however, has taken considerable trouble to try to give *full* film credits in every case – unlike the less satisfactory 'films include . . .' lists in Katz. Above all it has the inestimable advantage of appearing some twelve years later, and (rightly) concentrates on the personalities of those years. The accompanying biographical details are often very lengthy and always useful. It is, in fact, a worthy companion to the earlier work, which it should stand beside on every film enthusiast's bookshelf.

William Desmond Taylor, Bruce Long; Scarecrow Press, dist. Shelwing, £35.65

The description of this engrossing examination of Hollywood's most notorious murder mystery in 1920 as 'A Dossier' is an accurate one. The major part of the book consists of several hundred extracts from contemporary publications, each one concerning the famous director. Despite inevitable repetitions, inconsistencies, and unreliable effusions from publicity handouts and sensation-seeking journalists the result – fully and excellently annotated by Bruce Long – presents a vivid and compelling portrait not only of W. D. Taylor himself but also of the world of the silent film in general. Reading the pages with foreknowledge of the crime to come adds strongly to their fascination. The remainder of the book is taken up with several accounts of the case, and includes a swingeing attack on the 'solution' put forward by director King Vidor and related in the book *A Cast of Killers*. No fewer than 124 'Possible Errata' are listed – the cautious 'possible' doing little to lessen the force of the onslaught. Long does not offer an alternative solution here, but undoubtedly Vidor's remains the one still most generally accepted – that the murderer was in fact a murderess. As film history, human story or murder mystery the book – no. 28 in Anthony Slide's 'Filmmakers' series – grips the attention throughout.

OTHER FILM BOOKS

Affairs to Remember – Hollywood Comedies of the Seventies, Bruce Babington & P. W. Evans; Manchester University Press, £12.95

Al Pacino – Life on a Wire, Andrew Yule; Macdonald, £14.95

All that Hollywood Allows – Rereading Gender in 1950s Melodrama; Routledge, £35.00

The Amazing Blonde Woman – Dietrich's Own Style; Patrick O'Connor, Bloomsbury, £20.00

Arab and African Film Making, Lizbeth Malkmus & Roy Armes; Zed Books, £29.95 hb/£12.95 pb

The Art of Cinema, Jean Cocteau; Marion Boyars, £16.95

Bogdanovich's Picture Shows, Thomas J. Harris; Scarecrow Press, dist. Shelwing, £31.90

Books and Plays in Films 1896–1915, Denis Gifford; Mansell, £40.00

Brando – A Life in Our Times, Richard Schickel; Pavilion, £14.99

British Film Actors' Credits 1895–1987, Scott Palmer; St James Press, £45.00 (rev. *Film Review 1989–90*)

Buff's Guide to the Movies, David Barraclough; Apple, £7.95

C. A. Lejeune Film Reader, Anthony Lejeune; Carcanet Press, £25.00

Cary Grant, Nancy Nelson; Headline, £16.95

Chambers Film Quotes, ed. Tony Crawley; Chambers, £5.99

The Cinema of Jean Genet, Jane Giles; BFI, £6.95

Cinema Sequels and Remakes, Robert A. Nowlan and Gwendolyn W. Nowlan; St James Press, £25.00 (rev. *Film Review 1989–90*)

Cinema Without Walls – Movies and Culture after Vietnam; Routledge, £9.99

Complete Films of Greta Garbo, Mark Ricci and Michael Conway; Virgin Film Library, £12.99

Complete Films of John Huston, John McCarty; Virgin Film Library, £9.99

Complete Films of Orson Welles, James Howard; Virgin Film Library, £12.99

Cronenberg on Cronenberg, ed. Chris Rodley; Faber, £12.99

Cult Movie Stars, David Peary; Simon & Schuster, £10.99

Dance While You Can, Shirley MacLaine; Bantam, £14.99

Difficulty of Difference – Psychoanalysis, Sexual Difference and Film Theory, David Rodowick; Routledge, £30.00 hb/£9.99 pb

Dilys Powell Film Reader, Christopher Cook; Carcanet Press, £25.00

Encounters with Film Makers – Eight Career Studies, John Tuska; Greenwood Press, £45.00

Femmes Fatales – Feminism, Film Studies and Psychoanalysis, Mary Ann Doane; Routledge, £40.00 hb/£10.99 pb

Films and Career of Elvis Presley, Steven and Boris Zmijewsky; Virgin Film Library, £9.99

Films of Gary Cooper, C. Homer Dickens; Virgin Film Library, £12.99

Forgotten Films to Remember, John Springer; Virgin Film Library, £12.99

Garbo – Her Story, Antoni Gronowicz; Penguin, £4.99

Hollywood at Home, Richard Schickel; Hale, £16.95

Hollywood Be Thy Name, William Bakewell; Scarecrow, dist. Shelwing, £26.25

Hollywood Eye – What Makes Movies Work, John Boorstein; HarperCollins, £16.99

Hollywood Heaven, David Barraclough; Apple Press, £7.95

Humphrey Bogart – Take It and Like It, Jonathan Coe; Bloomsbury, £16.99

Imaginary Homelands – Essays and Criticism, Salman Rushdie; Granta Books, £17.99

In a Lonely Street – Film Noir, Genre, Masculinity, Frank Krutnik; Routledge, £35.00 hb/£10.99 pb

Inside the Film Factory – New Approaches to Russian and Soviet Cinema, ed. Richard Taylor and Ian Christie; Routledge, £40.00

International Directory of Film and TV Documentation Centres, ed. Frances Thorp, St James Press, £30.00

International Film Index 1895–1990, ed. Alan Goble; Bowker Saur, £155.00

Jack Nicholson, Donald Shepherd; Robson Books, £12.95

James Dean – Behind the Scene, ed. Leith Adams and Keith Burns; Smith Gryphon, £19.99

Lovers; Virgin, £14.99

Mae West – Empress of Sex, Maurice Leonard; HarperCollins, £17.50

Marlon Brando – A Portrait, Paul Ryan; Plexus, £9.99

Martin Scorsese – a Journey, Mary Pat Kelly; Secker & Warburg, £16.99

Missing Reel, Christopher Rawlence; Fontana, £4.99

Mitchum – Film Career of Robert Mitchum, Bruce Crowther; Hale, £12.95

Montgomery Clift – Beautiful Loser; Barney Hoskins, Bloomsbury, £16.99

Movie Love, Pauline Kael; Marion Boyars, £12.95

Moving Pictures, Ali MacGraw; Bantam, £14.99

My Life with Groucho – A Son's Eye View, Arthur Marx; Pan, £6.95

Mystifying Movies – Fads and Fancies in Contemporary Film Theory, Noel Carroll; Columbia University Press, £9.95

Ned's Girl, Bryan Forbes; Mandarin, £6.99

New Poverty Row, Fred Olen Ray; McFarland, dist. Shelwing, £21.00

Notes on the Making of *Apocalypse Now*, Eleanor Coppola; Limelight Editions USA, dist. Gazelle, £12.25

On Directing Film, David Mamet; Faber, £6.99

One Lifetime Is Not Enough, Zsa Zsa Gabor; Headline, £14.99

Rebel Males – Clift, Brando and Dean, Graham McCann; Hamish Hamilton, £14.99

Red Screen, ed. Anna Lawton; Routledge, £35.00 hb/£10.95 pb

Reel Women – Pioneers of the Cinema, Ally Acker; Batsford, £22.50

Remembering Peter Sellers, Graham Stark; Robson Books, £7.99

Sex in the Movies, Sam Frank; Virgin Film Library, £9.99

So You Want to Make Movies, Sidney Pink; Pineapple Press, £11.00

Stardom – Industry of Desire, Christine Gedhill; Routledge, £35.00 hb/£10.99 pb

Stargazer: Life, World and Films of Andy Warhol, John Fowles; Marion Boyars, £9.95

Sturges on Sturges, Preston Sturges; Faber & Faber, £14.99

Talking Films – Actors, Directors and Screenwriters Talk About Films, ed. Ian Christie; Fourth Estate, £16.99

Television Horror Movie Hosts, Elena M. Watson; McFarland, dist. Shelwing, £22.50

3-D Movies, R. M. Hayes; St James Press, £32.00 (rev. *Film Review 1990–1*)

Totally Uninhibited – Life and Wild Times of Cher, Lawrence J. Quirk; Robson Books, £14.95

Trouble in Store – Norman Wisdom, Richard Dacre; T. C. Farries & Co, £14.95

The Unabridged James Dean – His Life and Legacy from A-Z, Randall Riese; Contemporary Books, dist. Gazelle Book Services, £25.95

Variety Film Reviews 1989–90; Bowker, £160.00

Vietnam Veteran Films, Mark Walker; Scarecrow Press, dist. Shelwing, £18.75

Awards and Festivals

As in previous years, we have concentrated principally on the major established festivals and award ceremonies around the world. There are of course many hundreds of others, which space does not allow us to include here; some are highly specialised events appealing principally to a small minority, while we have also – some may say unfairly – excluded many Middle and Far East festivals. Full details of most of these are published periodically in *Variety*.

Nationality is stated only where films originate from a country other than that in which the awards are given.

The 64th American Academy of Motion Picture Arts and Sciences Awards (Oscars) and Nominations for 1991, 30 March 1992

Best Film: *The Silence of the Lambs*. Nominations: *Beauty and the Beast*; *Bugsy*; *JFK*; *The Prince of Tides*.

Best Director: Jonathan Demme, for *The Silence of the Lambs*. Nominations: Barry Levinson, for *Bugsy*; Ridley Scott, for *Thelma & Louise*; John Singleton, for *Boyz N the Hood*; Oliver Stone, for *JFK*.

Best Actor: Anthony Hopkins, in *The Silence of the Lambs*. Nominations: Warren Beatty, in *Bugsy*; Robert De Niro, in *Cape Fear*; Nick Nolte, in *The Prince of Tides*; Robin Williams, in *The Fisher King*.

Best Actress: Jodie Foster, in *The Silence of the Lambs*. Nominations: Geena Davis, in *Thelma & Louise*; Laura Dern, in *Rambling Rose*; Bette Midler, in *For the Boys*; Susan Sarandon, in *Thelma & Louise*.

Best Supporting Actor: Jack Palance, in *City Slickers*. Nominations: Tommy Lee Jones, in *JFK*; Harvey Keitel, in *Bugsy*; Ben Kingsley, in *Bugsy*; Michael Lerner, in *Barton Fink*.

Best Supporting Actress: Mercedes Ruehl, in *The Fisher King*. Nominations: Diane Ladd, in *Rambling Rose*; Juliette Lewis, in *Cape Fear*; Kate Nelligan, in *The Prince of Tides*; Jessica Tandy, in *Fried Green Tomatoes at the Whistle Stop Cafe*.

Best Original Screenplay: Callie Khouri, for *Thelma & Louise*. Nominations: Lawrence Kasdan and Meg Kasdan, for *Grand Canyon*; Richard LaGravenese, for *The*

Oscar-winner Anthony Hopkins as Dr Hannibal Lecter in the award-laden The Silence of the Lambs

Fisher King; John Singleton, for *Boyz N the Hood*; James Toback, for *Bugsy*.

Best Screenplay Adaptation: Ted Tally, for *The Silence of the Lambs*. Nominations: Agnieszka Holland, for *Europa, Europa* (Germany–France); Fannie Flagg and Carol Sobieski, for *Fried Green Tomatoes at the Whistle Stop Cafe*; Oliver Stone and Zachary Sklar, for *JFK*; Pat Conroy and Becky Johnston, for *The Prince of Tides*.

Best Cinematography: Robert Richardson, for *JFK*. Nominations: Allen Daviau, for *Bugsy*; Stephen Goldblatt, for *The Prince of Tides*; Adam Greenburg, for *Terminator 2: Judgment Day*; Adrian Biddle, for *Thelma & Louise*.

Best Editing: Joe Hutshing and Pietro Scalia, for *JFK*. Nominations: Gerry Hambling, for *The Commitments*; Craig McKay, for *The Silence of the Lambs*; Conrad Buff, Mark Goldblatt and Richard A. Harris, for *Terminator 2: Judgment Day*; Thom Noble, for *Thelma & Louise*.

Best Original Score: Alan Menken, for *Beauty and the Beast*. Nominations: George Fenton, for *The Fisher King*; James Newton Howard, for *The Prince of Tides*; Ennio Morricone, for *Bugsy*; John Williams, for *JFK*.

Best Original Song: 'Beauty and the Beast', from *Beauty and the Beast*, music by Alan Menken, lyrics by Howard Ashman. Nominations: 'Belle', from *Beauty and the Beast* (Menken/Ashman); 'Be Our Guest', from *Beauty and the Beast* (Menken/Ashman); '(Everything I Do) I Do It For You', from *Robin Hood: Prince of Thieves*, music by Michael Kamen, lyrics by Bryan Adams and Robert John Lange; 'When You're Alone', from *Hook*, music by John Williams, lyrics by Leslie Bricusse.

Best Art Direction: Dennis Gassner (art direction) and Nancy Haigh (set decoration), for *Bugsy*. Nominations: Dennis Gassner (art) and Nancy Haigh (set), for *Barton Fink*; Mel Bourne (art) and Cindy Carr (set), for *The Fisher King*; Norman Garwood (art) and Garrett Lewis (set), for *Hook*; Paul Sylbert (art) and Caryl Heller (set), for *The Prince of Tides*.

Best Costume Design: Albert Wolsky, for *Bugsy*. Nominations: Ruth Myers, for *The Addams Family*; Richard Hornung, for *Barton Fink*; Anthony Powell, for *Hook*; Corrine Jory, for *Madame Bovary* (France).

Best Sound: Tom Johnson, Gary Rydstrom, Gary Summers and Lee Orloff, for *Terminator 2: Judgment Day*. Nominations: Gary Summers, Randy Thom, Gary Rydstrom and Glenn Williams, for *Backdraft*; Terry Porter, Mel Metcalfe, David J. Hudson and Doc Kane, for *Beauty and the Beast*; Michael Minkler, Greg Landaker and Tod A. Maitland, for *JFK*; Tom Fleishman and Christopher Newman, for *The Silence of the Lambs*.

Best Sound Effects Editing: Gary Rydstrom

and Gloria S. Borders, for *Terminator 2: Judgment Day*. Nominations: George Watters II and Hudson Miller, for *Star Trek VI: The Undiscovered Country*; Gary Rydstrom and Richard Hymns, for *Backdraft*.

Best Make-Up: Stan Winston and Jeff Dawn, for *Terminator 2: Judgment Day*. Nominations: Christina Smith, Montague Westmore and Greg Cannom, for *Hook*; Michael Mills, Edward French and Richard Snell, for *Star Trek VI: The Undiscovered Country*.

Best Visual Effects: Dennis Muren, Stan Winston, Gene Warren Jr and Robert Skotak, for *Terminator 2: Judgment Day*. Nominations: Mikhael Salomon, Allen Hall, Clay Pinney and Scott Farrar, for *Backdraft*; Eric Brevig, Harley Jessup, Mark Sullivan and Michael Lantieri, for *Hook*.

Best Animated Short Film: *Manipulation*. Nominations: *Backfly*; *Strings*.

Best Live Action Short Film: *Session Man*. Nominations: *Birch Street Gym*; *Last Breeze of Summer*.

Best Documentary Feature: *In the Shadow of the Stars*. Nominations: *Death on the Job*; *Doing Time: Life Inside the Big House*; *The Restless Conscience: Resistance to Hitler Within Germany 1933–1945*; *Wild By Law*.

Best Documentary Short: *Deadly Deception: General Electric, Nuclear Weapons and Our Environment*. Nominations: *Birdnesters of Thailand* (aka *Shadow Hunters*); *A Little Vicious*; *The Mark of the Maker*; *Memorial: Letters from American Soldiers*.

Best Foreign Language Film: *Mediterraneo* (Italy). Nominations: *Children of Nature* (Iceland); *The Elementary School* (Czechoslovakia); *The Ox* (Sweden); *Raise the Red Lantern* (China).

Irving G. Thalberg Memorial Award: George Lucas.

Honorary Oscar: Satyajit Ray.

Gordon E. Sawyer Award: Ray Harryhausen.

The Australian Film Critics' Circle Awards, 11 March 1992

Best Film: *Flirting*, by John Duigan.
Best Actor shared by: Noah Taylor, in *Flirting*; and Hugo Weaving, in *Proof*.
Best Actress: Genevieve Picot, in *Proof*.
Best Director: John Duigan, for *Flirting*.
Best Screenplay: Jocelyn Moorehouse, for *Proof*.
Best Cinematography: Geoff Burton, for *Flirting*.
Best Foreign Film: *Thelma & Louise*, by Ridley Scott (USA).

The Australian Film Institute Awards, October 1991

Best Film: *Proof*, by Jocelyn Moorehouse.
Best Actor: Hugo Weaving, in *Proof*.
Best Actress: Sheila Florance, in *A Woman's Tale*.

The 42nd Berlin International Film Festival, February 1992

Golden Bear for Best Film: *Grand Canyon*, by Lawrence Kasdan (USA).
Silver Bear, Special Jury Prize: *Sweet Emma, Dear Bobe*, by Istvan Szabo (Hungary).
Best Director: Jan Troell, for *Il Capitano* (Sweden–Finland–Denmark).
Best Actor: Armin Mueller-Stahl, in *Utz* (UK–Germany–Italy).
Best Actress: Maggie Cheung, in *Centre Stage* (Hong Kong).
Silver Bear, for First Film: *La Frontera*, by Ricardo Larrain (Chile–Spain).
International Critics' Award: *A Winter's Tale*, by Eric Rohmer (France).
Alfred Bauer Prize: *Infinitas*, by Marlen Chuzier (Russia).
FIPRESCI Young Cinema Award: *La Vie de Bohème*, by Aki Kaurismaki (Finland); and *Edward II*, by Derek Jarman (UK).
Jury: Annie Girardot, Sylvia Chang, Michael Verhoeven, Susannah York etc.

The 1991 British Academy of Film and Television Arts Awards, 22 March 1992

Best Film: *The Commitments*, by Alan Parker.
David Lean Award for Best Direction: Alan Parker, for *The Commitments*.
Best Original Screenplay: Anthony Minghella, for *Truly, Madly, Deeply*.
Best Adapted Screenplay: Dick Clement, Ian La Frenais and Roddy Doyle, for *The Commitments*.
Best Actor: Anthony Hopkins, in *The Silence of the Lambs* (USA).
Best Actress: Jodie Foster, in *The Silence of the Lambs* (USA).
Best Supporting Actor: Alan Rickman, in *Robin Hood: Prince of Thieves* (USA).
Best Supporting Actress: Kate Nelligan, in *Frankie & Johnny* (USA).
Best Score: Jean-Claude Petit, for *Cyrano de Bergerac* (France).
Best Foreign Film: *The Nasty Girl*, by Michael Verhoeven (Germany).
Best Short Film: *The Harmfulness of Tobacco*, by Barry Palin and Nick Hamm.
Best Animated Short: *Balloon*, by Ken Lidster.
Best TV Film: *A Question of Attribution*, directed by John Schlesinger (BBC).
Special Award: Audrey Hepburn.

The 1991 Canadian Film Awards ('Genies') November 1991

Best Film: *Black Robe* (Australia–Canada).
Best Director: Bruce Beresford, for *Black Robe*.
Best Actor: Remy Girard, in *Amoureux Fou*.
Best Actress: Pascale Montpetit, in *H*.
Best Supporting Actor: August Schellenberg, in *Black Robe*.

Best Supporting Actress: Danielle Proulx, in *Amoureux Fou*.

Best Original Screenplay: Eugene Lipinski and Paul Quarrington, for *Perfectly Normal*.

Best Adapted Screenplay: Brian Moore, for *Black Robe*.

Best Cinematography: Peter James, for *Black Robe*.

Best Art Direction: Gavin Mitchell and Herbert Pinter, for *Black Robe*.

Best Sound: Garrell Clark and Paul Sharp, for *Angel Square*.

Best Feature-Length Documentary: *The Family Within*, by Katherine Gilday.

The 45th Cannes Film Festival Awards, 18 May 1992

Palme d'Or for Best Film: *The Best Intentions*, by Bille August (Sweden).

45th Anniversary Prize: *Howards End*, by James Ivory (UK).

Grand Prix du Jury: *Il Ladro di Bambini* (*The Stolen Children*), by Gianni Amelio (Italy–France).

Best Actor: Tim Robbins, in *The Player* (USA).

Best Actress: Pernilla August, in *The Best Intentions* (Sweden).

Best Director: Robert Altman, for *The Player* (USA).

Prix du Jury shared by: *El Sol del Membrillo*, by Victor Erice (Spain); and *Samostoiatelnaia Jizn*, by Vitali Kanevski (France–Russia).

Palme d'Or for Best Short: *Omnibus*, by Sam Karmann.

Special Jury Prize, Short: *La Sensation*, by Manuel Poutte.

Camera d'Or: *Mac*, by John Turturro (USA).

Grand Prix Technique: *El Viaje*, by Fernando Solanas (Argentina–France).

The David di Donatello Awards ('Davids'), Rome, June 1992

Best Film: *The Stolen Children*, by Gianni Amelio.

Best Director: Gianni Amelio, for *The Stolen Children*.

Best Actor: Carlo Verdone, in *Curse the Day I Met You*.

Best Actress: Giuliana De Sio, in *Cattiva*.

Best Supporting Actor: Angelo Orlando, in *I Thought It Was Love, Instead It Was a Carriage*.

Best Supporting Actress: Elisabetta Pozzi, in *Curse the Day I Met You*.

Best Screenplay: Francesca Narciano and Carlo Vercone, for *Curse the Day I Met You*.

Best Cinematography: Danilo Desideri, for *Curse the Day I Met You*.

Samuel Froler and Pernilla August in Bille August's exquisite The Best Intentions, *winner of the Palme d'Or at the 1992 Cannes Film Festival*

Best Foreign Film: *Raise the Red Lantern*, by Zhang Yimou (China).

Best Actor in a Foreign Film: John Turturro, in *Barton Fink* (USA).

Best Actress in a Foreign Film: Geena Davis and Susan Sarandon in *Thelma & Louise* (USA).

Special Award: Giuseppe Ieracitano and Valentina Scalici, for *The Stolen Children*.

Best First Film: *Where the Night Begins*, by Maurizio Zaccaro.

Special Jury Prize: *Johnny Stecchino*.

The Luchino Visconti Award: Ermanno Olmi.

The 'Evening Standard' 1991 Film Awards, London, January 1992

Best Film: *Close My Eyes*, by Stephen Poliakoff.

Best Actor: Alan Rickman, in *Close My Eyes, Truly, Madly, Deeply* and *Robin Hood: Prince of Thieves* (USA).

Best Actress: Juliet Stevenson, in *Truly, Madly, Deeply*.

Best Screenplay: Neil Jordan, for *The Miracle*.

Best Technical Achievement: Sandy Powell, for *The Miracle, The Pope* and *Edward II*.

Most Promising Newcomer: Anthony Minghella, for *Truly, Madly, Deeply*.

The Peter Sellers Comedy Award: Roddy Doyle, Dick Clement and Ian La Fresnais, for *The Commitments*.

The 12th Fantafestival, Rome, June 1992

Best Film: *Sleepwalkers*, by Mick Garris, which also won the Best Director, Best Story (Stephen King) and Best Actress (Alice Krige) Awards.

Best Actor: Tim Balme, in *Braindead* (New Zealand), which also won the Best Special Effects Award.

Special Jury Prizes: *The Vagrant*, by Chris Walas (USA), *The Phantom of the Cinema*, by Mark Herrier.

The 17th French Academy (César) Awards, February 1992

Best Film: *Tous les Matins du Monde*, by Alain Corneau.

Best Director: Alain Corneau, for *Tous les Matins du Monde*.

Best Actor: Jacques Dutronc, in *Van Gogh*.

Best Actress: Jeanne Moreau, in *La Vielle Qui Marchait dans la Mer*.

Best Supporting Actor: Jean Carmet, in *Merci la Vie*.

Best Supporting Actress: Anne Brochet, in *Tous les Matins du Monde*.

Best New Actor: Manuel Blanc, in *J'Embrasse Pas*.

Best New Actress: Geraldine Pailhas, in *La Neige et le Feu*.

Best First Film: *Delicatessen*, by Jean-Pierre Jeunet and Marc Caro.

Best Screenplay: Jean-Pierre Jeunet, Marc Caro and Gilles Adrien, for *Delicatessen*.

Best Music: Jordi Savall, for *Tous les Matins du Monde*.

Best Photography: Yves Angelo, for *Tous les Matins du Monde*.

Best Editing: Herve Schneid, for *Delicatessen*.

Best Foreign Film: *Toto the Hero*, by Jaco Van Dormael (Belgium).

The German National Film Awards, June 1992

Golden Film Ribbon: *Schtonk*, by Helmut Dietl.

Silver: *Das Land hinter dem Regenbogen*, and *Leise Schatten*.

Best Director: Helmut Dietl, for *Schtonk*.

Best Actor: Gotz George, in *Schtonk*; and Mario Adorf, in *Pizza Colonia*.

Best Production Design: Nana von Hugo, for *Buster's Bedroom*.

Best Screenplay: Bernd Schroeder, for *Pizza Colonia*.

Lifetime Achievement: Special Effects specialist Karl Baumgartner and documentary filmmaker Jurgen Böttcher.

The 6th Goya Awards by the Spanish Academy of Arts and Sciences, March 1992

Best Director and Best Film: Vincente Aranda, for *Amantes*.

Best Actress: Silvia Munt, in *Alas de Mariposa*.

Best Actor: Fernando Guillen, in *Don Juan in Hell*.

Best Supporting Actor: Juan Diego, in *El Rey Pasmado*.

Best Supporting Actress: Kiti Manver, in *Solo Por la Pasta*.

Best Original Screenplay: Juanma and Eduardo Bajo Ulloa, for *Alas de Mariposa*.

Best Editing: Jose Lui Matesanz, for *Beltenebros*.

Best Cinematography: Javier Aguirresarobe, for *Beltenebros*.

The 49th Hollywood Foreign Press Association (Golden Globe) Awards, 18 January 1992

Best Film – Drama: *Bugsy*.

Best Film – Comedy or Musical: *Beauty and the Beast*.

Best Actor – Drama: Nick Nolte, in *The Prince of Tides*.

Best Actress – Drama: Jodie Foster, in *The Silence of the Lambs*.

Best Actor – Comedy or Musical: Robin Williams, in *The Fisher King*.

Best Actress – Comedy or Musical: Bette Midler, in *For the Boys*.

Best Supporting Actor: Jack Palance, in *City Slickers*.

Best Supporting Actress: Mercedes Ruehl, in *The Fisher King*.

Best Director: Oliver Stone, for *JFK*.

Best Screenplay: Callie Khouri, for *Thelma & Louise*.

Best Original Score: Alan Menken, for *Beauty and the Beast*.

Best Foreign Language Film: *Europa, Europa*, by Agnieszka Holland (Germany–France).

The 44th Locarno Film Festival Awards, August 1991

Golden Leopard for Best Film: *Johnny Suede*, by Tom DiCillo (USA).

Silver Leopard: *Cloud-Paradise*, by Nikola Dostal (Russia).

Bronze Leopards: *H*, by Darrell Wasyk (Canada); *Cheb*, by Rachid Bouchareb (France–Algeria).

Special Bronze Leopard: *Le Collier Perdu de la Colombe*, by Nacer Khemit (Tunisia–France)

FIPRESCI Prize: *Poison*, by Todd Haynes (USA).

The 13th London Film Critics' Circle Awards ('The Alfs'), 25 February 1992

Best Film: *Thelma & Louise*, by Ridley Scott (USA).

Best Actor: Gerard Depardieu, in *Cyrano de Bergerac* (France), *Green Card* (USA) and *Uranus* (France).

Best Actress: Susan Sarandon, in *White Palace* (USA) and *Thelma & Louise* (USA).

Best Director: Ridley Scott, for *Thelma & Louise* (USA).

Best Screenplay: David Mamet, for *Homicide* (USA).

Newcomer of the Year: Annette Bening.

British Film of the Year: *Life Is Sweet*, by Mike Leigh.

British Actor of the Year: Alan Rickman, in *Truly, Madly, Deeply*.

British Actress of the Year: Juliet Stevenson, in *Truly, Madly, Deeply*.

British Director of the Year: Alan Parker, for *The Commitments*.

British Producers of the Year: Lynda Myles and Roger Randall-Cutler, for *The Commitments*.

British Screenwriters of the Year: Dick Clement, Ian La Frenais and Roddy Doyle, for *The Commitments*.

Best Foreign-Language Film: *Cyrano de Bergerac* (France).

Special Awards: Kevin Brownlow, John Sayles.

Dilys Powell Award: Sir Dirk Bogarde.

The Los Angeles Film Critics' Association Awards, December 1991

Best Film: *Bugsy*.

Best Actor: Nick Nolte, in *The Prince of Tides*.

Best Actress: Mercedes Ruehl, in *The Fisher King*.

Best Supporting Actor: Michael Lerner, in *Barton Fink*.

Best Supporting Actress: Jane Horrocks, in *Life Is Sweet* (UK).

Best Director: Barry Levinson, for *Bugsy*.

Best Screenplay: James Toback, for *Bugsy*.

Best Cinematography: Roger Deakins, for *Barton Fink* and *Homicide*.

Best Music: Zbigniew Presiner, for *Europa, Europa*; *The Secret Life of Veronique*; *At Play in the Fields of the Lord*.

Best Foreign Film: *La Belle Noiseuse*, by Jacques Rivette (France).

The Madrid International Film Festival 'Imagfic' Awards, April 1992

Best European Film: No prize awarded.

Best Actor: Sam Shepard, in *Voyager* (Germany–France).

Best Executive Producer: Aki Kaurismaki, for *I Hired a Contract Killer* (Sweden–UK–Finland–France).

Fantasy/Sci-fi Films

Best Film: *Nebesa Obtovannye*, by Edgar Riazanov (Russia).

Best Special Effects: Rudolf Van Deen Berg's *The Johnsons* (Holland).

Best New European Director: Marco Bechis, for *Alambrado* (Italy).

Best Actor: Alan Rickman, in *Close My Eyes* (UK).

Best Actress: Saskia Reeves, in *December Bride* (Ireland).

The 15th Montreal World Film Festival Awards, September 1991

Grand Prize of the Americas for Best Film: *Salmonberries*, by Percy Adlon (Germany).

Jury Prize: *North*, by Xavier Beauvois (France).

Best Director: Maurizio Nichetti, for *I Want to Fly* (Italy).

Best Actress shared by: Laura Dern, in *Rambling Rose* (USA); and Lee Hyesuk, in *Silver Stallion* (South Korea).

Best Actor: Francisco Rabal, in *The Man Who Lost His Shadow* (Switzerland–Spain).

Best Screenplay: Chang Kil-Soo and Co Chehung, for *Silver Stallion* (South Korea).

Outstanding Artistic Contribution (Photography) shared between: George Dufaux, for *The Wild Girl* (Switzerland–Canada); and Ari Kristinson, for *Children of Nature* (Iceland).

Best First Film shared by: *Benjamin's Women*, by Carlos Carrera (Mexico); and *North*, by Xavier Beauvois (France).

Critics' Award: *North*, by Xavier Beauvois (France).

The National Board of Review, December 1991

Best Film: *The Silence of the Lambs*.

Best Actor: Warren Beatty, in *Bugsy*.

Best Actress: Susan Sarandon and Geena Davis, in *Thelma & Louise*.

Best Supporting Actor: Anthony Hopkins, in *The Silence of the Lambs*.

Best Supporting Actress: Kate Nelligan, in *Frankie and Johnny*.

Best Director: Jonathan Demme, for *The Silence of the Lambs*.

Best Foreign Film: *Europa, Europa* (Germany–France).

The 57th New York Film Critics' Circle Awards, December 1991

Best Film: *The Silence of the Lambs*.

Best Actor: Anthony Hopkins, in *The Silence of the Lambs*.

Best Actress: Jodie Foster, in *The Silence of the Lambs*.

Best Supporting Actor: Samuel L. Jackson, in *Jungle Fever*.

Best Supporting Actress: Judy Davis, in *Barton Fink* and *Naked Lunch*.

Best Director: Jonathan Demme, for *The Silence of the Lambs*.

Best Screenplay: David Cronenberg, for *Naked Lunch*.

Best Cinematography: Roger Deakins, for *Barton Fink*.

Best Foreign Film: *Europa, Europa* (Germany–France).

The 24th Sitges Fantasy and Science-Fiction Film Festival Awards, October 1991

Best Film: *Europa*, by Lars von Trier (Denmark–France–Germany–Sweden).

Best Director: Jean-Pierre Jeunet and Marc Caro, for *Delicatessen* (France).

Special Mention: *Poison*, by Todd Haynes (USA).

Best Actress: Juliet Stevenson, in *Truly, Madly, Deeply* (UK).

Best Screenplay: Samir and Martin Witz, for *Immer und Ewig* (Switzerland).

Best Special Effects: *The Borrower*, by John McNaughton (USA).

Best Cinematography Award: *Europa* (Denmark–France–Germany–Sweden).

Best Sound: *Delicatessen* (France).

Best Short: *Push Comes to Shove*, by Bill Plympton (USA).

The 8th Troia Film Festival Awards, Portugal, June 1992

Special Jury Prize: *Children of Nature*, by Fridrik Thor Fridriksson (Iceland), which also won the Critics' Prize and the Best Actor Award for Gisli Halldorsson.

Best Direction Prize: Imre Gyongyossi and Barna Kabay, for *Exiles* (Hungary).

Best First Film: *Tale of the Lighted Moon*, by Evgeny Tsymbal (Russia).

Golden Dolphin Award for Best Film: *Un Nos Ola Leaud – Full Moon*, Endaf Dmlyn's Welsh film, which also won the Best Script, Best Cinematography and Best Actress (Betson Llwud) Awards.

The 26th US National Society of Film Critics Awards, January 1992

Best Film: *Life Is Sweet* (UK).

Best Actor: River Phoenix, in *My Own Private Idaho*.

Best Actress: Alison Steadman, in *Life Is Sweet* (UK).

Best Supporting Actor: Harvey Keitel, in *Bugsy*.

Best Supporting Actress: Jane Horrocks, in *Life Is Sweet* (UK).

Best Director: David Cronenberg, for *Naked Lunch*.

Best Screenplay: David Cronenberg, for *Naked Lunch*.

Best Cinematography: Roger Deakins, for *Barton Fink*.

Best Foreign Film: *The Double Life of Veronique*, by Krzysztof Kieslowski (France–Poland).

Best Documentary: *Paris Is Burning*, by Jennie Livingston.

The Valladolid Film Festival Awards, October 1991

Best Film shared between: *Thelma & Louise*, by Ridley Scott (USA); and *The Adjuster*, by Atom Egoyan (USA).

Runner-Up for Best Film: *Riff-Raff*, by Kenneth Loach (UK).

Best First Feature: *Proof*, by Jocelyn Moorhouse (Australia).

Best Actress: Maria Rojo, in *Danzon*.

Best Actor: Harley Cross, in *The Boy Who Cried Bitch* (USA).

Best Cinematography: Zhao Fei, for *Raise the Red Lantern* (China).

Special Jury Prize: Viatcheslav Krichtofovitch, for his *Adam's Nest – Rebro Adana* (Russia).

The 48th Venice International Film Festival Awards, September 1991

Golden Lion for Best Film: *Urga*, by Nikita Mikhalkov (USSR–China).

Special Jury Prize: *La Divina Comedia*, by Manoel de Oliveira (Portugal).

Silver Lions: *Raise the Red Lantern*, by Zhang Yimou (China–Hong Kong); *The Fisher King*, by Terry Gilliam (USA); *I Can't Hear the Guitars Anymore*, by Philippe Garrel (France).

Best Actress: Tilda Swinton, in *Edward II* (UK).

Best Actor: River Phoenix, in *My Own Private Idaho* (USA).

Special Golden Lion: Gian Maria Volonte, for his performance in *A Simple Story*.

Osello awards: *Scream of Stone*, by Werner Herzog (Germany); *Mississippi Masala*, by Mira Nair (USA); and *Germany 9–0*, by Jean-Luc Godard (France).

Index